MAINE ANTIQUE DIGEST

THE AMERICANA CHRONICLES

MAINE ANTIQUE DIGEST

THE AMERICANA CHRONICLES

30 Years of Stories, Sales, Personalities, and Scandals

EDITED BY LITA SOLIS-COHEN

RUNNING PRESS

PHILADELPHIA · LONDON

9 8 7 6 5 4 3 2 1
Digit on the right indicates the number of this printing
Library of Congress Control Number: 2003115263

ISBN 0-7624-1896-6

Cover and interior designed by Alicia Freile
Typography: Palatino and News Gothic

All photos courtesy of *Maine Antique Digest*, except where noted.

This book may be ordered by mail from the publisher.
Please include $2.50 for postage and handling.
But try your bookstore first!

Running Press Book Publishers
125 South Twenty-second Street
Philadelphia, Pennsylvania 19103-4399

Visit us on the web!
www.runningpress.com
www.maineantiquedigest.com

CONTENTS

EDITOR'S INTRODUCTION

Since November 1973 *Maine Antique Digest* (known simply as *M.A.D.* or "*the Digest*") has pleased and piqued its readers as it chronicled the varied marketplace for Americana. *M.A.D.* is the publication of record because it reports landmark sales, record prices, watershed events, scandals, and the lives of the people who make the market.

What unfolds is the story of a 30-year bull market for American antiques with four significant downdrafts (the years 1974–76, 1981–83, 1990–93, and 2001–03). Generally, objects of superior quality offered during a booming economy brought record prices. Even when it appeared that good times were over and interest in Americana was waning, an event came along that brought new enthusiasm and new buyers to the marketplace.

It was difficult to choose the stories for each decade that best reflect the lively writing, keen insights, and comprehensive coverage that *M.A.D.* readers have enjoyed for 30 years. This volume could easily have been as hefty as a phone book if the provocative page one editorials had been included. All stories about antiques shows were cut, and most of the stories about celebrity sales were left out because they were widely reported elsewhere. An entire book has been written about the Sotheby's-Christie's price-fixing scandal, *The Art of the Steal* (Putnam, 2004) by Christopher Mason.

The best from the monthly "Letter from London" that Ian McKay has sent every month since March 1986 would make a good book of its own. Similarly, there wasn't room for the series of articles by eminent scholars and reviews of significant books and journals; they should be published. A collection of all the obituaries that marked the deaths and celebrated the lives of dealers, auctioneers, and collectors who participated in this great Americana treasure hunt would memorialize a generation.

The intent of this book is to offer a variety of articles that are entertaining and instructive for both passionate collectors and those with only a casual interest.

The book is divided into three parts by decade. There are also three larger stories that played out over time on the pages of *M.A.D.* "Tales of Hofmann" is a small selection from many articles that recorded the crimes of a brilliant forger of historical and literary documents who was also a murderer. "Mint & Boxed" traces the fate of a con man who embroiled the toy world, and a series of stories (entitled "The Dunlap Broadsides") about the Declaration of Independence translate history and patriotism into dollars and cents.

This book recounts some memorable moments in the world of Americana, such as the story of the fake Brewster chair that fooled the trade and museum curators until the maker revealed himself, the sale of Andy Warhol's collection of 155 cookie jars for $247,830, and the discovery in France of an American 18th-century desk and bookcase that sold for more than $8 million even though it had lost its feet. Without bias, *M.A.D.* reports when collectors speak their minds, and when dealers and auctioneers hype their merchandise.

At the back of the book are two lists. One documents every piece of American furniture that has sold for $1 million or more at auction; the other illustrates American folk art that has sold for more than half a million dollars.

As it enters its fourth decade, *M.A.D.* continues to mix scholarship with gossip, news with interviews, analysis with predictions, and coverage of new markets and trends. It sends its reporters out daily to dig up any good story on the Americana beat.

Lita Solis-Cohen
Senior Editor
Maine Antique Digest
Rydal, Pennsylvania

THE GENESIS OF *MAINE ANTIQUE DIGEST*

Maine Antique Digest is a fat tabloid trade paper read by everybody who has a serious interest in Americana. Regular readers first turn to the Fragments section in the front of the paper for hot news and know that the good stories are often buried in the back of Section E of the usually seven-section 250-plus-page monthly jammed with ads. Most readers study the ads before plowing through the stories, end up buying something, and may not get around to finding out what's really going on in the antiques trade until later in the month or even the next month.

M.A.D. has been published in Waldoboro, Maine, since Sam and Sally Pennington mailed the first 28-page issue in November 1973. Then it cost 50 cents on newsstands in Maine and a subscription was $5. Now it costs $3.75 in select bookstores and antiques shops throughout the U.S., and a subscription is $43 for 12 issues, $79 for two years. Some pay $85 a year to have it sent by first class mail in order to get first chance at the ads.

The masthead for the first issue lists Samuel Pennington, Editor; Sally Pennington, Advertising; and the Pennington Family, Katherine, Nellie, Sarah, Samuel, and Mary, Circulation. Next to the masthead in that first issue, Sam Pennington wrote his plans for the paper. That letter begins the First Decade section of this book.

Some things about the *Digest* have changed over 30 years, but many things have stayed the same. *M.A.D.* is still published in Waldoboro, Maine, and printed by the same printer 17 miles down the road, but it covers far more than the Maine scene. Auctions now dominate the coverage, and *M.A.D.* reports prices asked at shows. Each issue is seven, sometimes eight times bigger than the first issue, and *M.A.D.* now has an Internet component (www.maineantiquedigest.com) where news, the calendar, some stories, and a prices database are posted, and where dealers advertise and sell.

All five Pennington children worked for *M.A.D.* through high school and pursued other careers after college. Three of the children have now returned to the paper. It has been a seamless transition to the next generation. Sam is now the publisher. The editor is Samuel Clayton Pennington, called Clayton because it is confusing having two Sams in the office. Just like his father, Samuel Charles, Samuel Clayton signs his editorials "SCP." Sally is now executive editor; two daughters took over parts of her job. Kate Pennington is the managing editor, and Sarah McCleary is business manager. (When they were listed in the masthead as the circulation department, Clayton was nine years old, Kate was 14, and Sarah was 12.)

In addition to the Penningtons there are now two full-time salaried writers, three copyeditors, and an office staff of 12 to take care of production, billing, advertising, and subscriptions. A battalion of stringers cover sales and shows everywhere. Twenty years ago, typewriters were chucked for computers. Sam and Sally still read every story and ad before the paper goes to press.

Clayton decides what goes in the paper. Clayton did not train for his job and never studied journalism or art history, but neither did his father. Sam was a French major at Johns Hopkins and spent 21 years in the Air Force. Kate managed a Shakespearean theater and, like her mother, was a schoolteacher. Sarah worked in publishing and advertising.

Sam and Sally met when Sam was a 28-year-old Air Force navigator stationed at Carswell Air Force Base and Sally was teaching school in Fort Worth, Texas. Soon after they were married they visited Maine and bought a Federal house in Waldoboro, thinking that Sam would leave the Air Force. Instead, he stayed in the service until 1973. They spent weekends and summers in the Waldoboro home when Sam was stationed in Bangor, Maine, in the 1960's. For a while they were part-time antiques dealers, which Sally hated. Sally ran the shop while Sam went out looking for stock.

Sam and Sally began talking about starting a newspaper while Sam was stationed in Goose Bay, Labrador, in 1971 and 1972. After he retired from the service and the family moved to Waldoboro he decided he might like the furniture repair business. He went to the *Maine Antique Guide* in Bath to place an ad. Soon he began writing for the *Guide* and became its editor.

"They wanted to sell us the paper, but we decided to start our own," Sally recounted. "We had five subscribers when we put out the first issue on our kitchen table, and the kids helped with the mailing. We sent it to anyone we could find an address for and everyone who advertised in *Antiques* magazine."

Sam took all the pictures and wrote all the stories, sometimes under the pseudonym Lance Poulet (for chicken on a stick), which he took from the paper's logo, a wooden chicken weathervane. The stick provides the I in the word Antique, which was not given an S so it would fit neatly above the word Digest even though it is not grammatically correct.

By a stroke of luck, Maine dealer Chris Huntington sent a long article full of inside information on the antiques trade for the first issue. "It came in late and I remember staying up until three in the morning editing it," Sally recalled. "Sam said if we don't put it in the first issue there won't be a second."

Subscriptions began to fill their rural mailbox every day. When the subscription list, which Sally kept on 3 x 5 cards, reached 1,000 they took the children out to dinner. It took three years for the paper to turn a profit, and it has been successful ever since.

No other publication was doing what *M.A.D.* was doing: reporting on auctions and shows and taking pictures of them. People liked reading about and seeing what was going on at the auctions and the shows they couldn't attend. *M.A.D.* has never really changed that focus.

Sam and Sally work well together. Sam, the idea man, loves being the investigative reporter. Sally keeps him out of real trouble, oversees the books, and has always been the proofreader.

In his February 1994 editorial, Sam offered readers with computers and modems a "country road, possibly a precursor to the information super-highway" and opened up a "modest electronic bulletin board to the public." He invited readers to post letters to the editor, review the current table of contents, and check dates of shows and auctions at *M.A.D.*'s new Internet bulletin board.

Since 1995, *M.A.D.* has expanded its illustrated prices database taken from the paper's monthly auction reports. The difference between the *M.A.D.* prices database and others is that *M.A.D.* tells why the piece brought that price. If repairs or an old finish affects the price, *M.A.D.* says so.

All *M.A.D.* book reviews since 1995 are also online. Books can be searched by any word in the review, and by author, title, or subject matter. There is also an interactive bulletin board where descriptions of stolen items can be posted. Selected stories have been archived going back to 1994. The monthly computer columns by John Reid are online. Reid, a bookseller and computer whiz, gives information antiques dealers and collectors need.

Each month's show and auction calendar is posted with links to the auction houses' and show promoters' Web pages. Dealers who advertise online get a link to their Web sites. An amazing 4,000 people come to the *M.A.D.* Web site every day.

"*M.A.D.* is responsible for a lot of changes in the marketplace," says Portsmouth, New Hampshire, auctioneer and former dealer Ron Bourgeault. "*M.A.D.* was the first publication to print prices, and that made it hard for a dealer to go out and pay $5,000 for a piece and sell it for $55,000. That's why a lot of dealers have become commission agents. And what's more, as the market has become global, a little auctioneer can advertise some great piece of Americana in *M.A.D.* and know that there isn't a single Americana dealer or collector who won't read that ad, and when it is sold it will bring all it's worth."

M.A.D., a force in the antiques trade for more than three decades, continues to provide its readers with an inside, up-to-the-minute view of the Americana scene.

First Decade:
1973–1983

Editor's Note: Sam Pennington launched Maine Antique Digest *in November 1973 with this statement of purpose that has not changed in more than 30 years.*

FROM THE EDITOR

It is with some trepidation but a deep sense of pride that I launch this publication.

As many of you know, I was editor of the *Maine Antique Guide* for the October issue. I regret that I could not continue with that publication, but there were irreconcilable differences among the people putting it out as to its future and expansion and it seemed better to all concerned that I start my own publication. I will, incidentally, be using the same firm, Coastal Graphics of Bath, to produce the paper. We will be printed by the Courier-Gazette in Rockland, and published from Waldoboro. How's that for geography?

As to our purposes and aims, we shall try to be both enlightening and entertaining in covering the Maine antiques scene. Our particular fascination is with the people in the antiques business and the ebb and flow of goods in the antiques market. The people are fascinating, complex, simple, devious, open, flamboyant, learned, dense, stubborn—all of these and more—but with a rich store of stories to tell and knowledge to share.

The ebb and flow of goods in the market is our other interest. As long as antiques stay out of museums, they have lives of their own, subject to their owners' whims and the desires of prospective purchasers. Prices rise and fall in the same day on the same piece—six dealers make a profit on a piece or three lose money—that's the antiques business.

Here in Maine, we are really on the last frontier of the business. Great things are still turning up from homes. There is money around and pickers who can pay well for things, and surely there are collectors and dealers who will pay. We feel just as excited about the business of collecting today as Wallace Nutting must have felt in his day.

We are most grateful for all the support we have received from both dealers and collectors and hope we will continue to merit it.

For editorial policy, I will continue very much as I did with the *Maine Antique Guide*. We will honestly report the Maine antiques scene as we see it. We will cover auctions and print auction prices, as these are a matter of public record. We will not print shop or show prices unless requested to do so by the owner. To our mind these represent asking prices only until the goods are sold, and thus are not really news. We will try to examine some of the problem areas of the business such as fakes, thefts, lack of retail trade, and whatever else comes our way. We shall try to be forthright and call them as we see them, favoring neither collector nor dealer in this rather wonderful, fun game of antiques. GOOD COLLECTING and may you have your profit made before the devil knows you're in heaven.

—Samuel Pennington

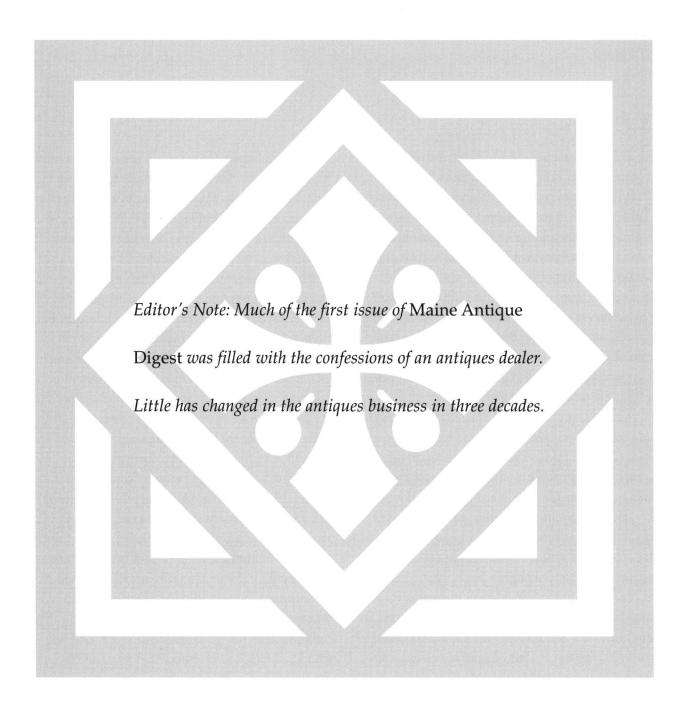

Editor's Note: Much of the first issue of Maine Antique Digest *was filled with the confessions of an antiques dealer.*

Little has changed in the antiques business in three decades.

CHRIS HUNTINGTON SPEAKS

BY CHRIS HUNTINGTON

(1973 Editor's Note [Sam Pennington]: Chris Huntington hit the Maine antiques business in 1966. It was never the same again. Freewheeling, flamboyant, wild, some called him crazy. He turned up some great things, had a lot of fun, made a lot of money, and is now retiring (so he says) from the business to go to Nova Scotia and paint. He sold his stock at auction at Bridgton and his Ezra Peters' Antiquities shop is now for sale. He never does explain the name Ezra Peters, but he covers everything else in what we consider to be a most important piece of writing about the antiques business.)

There's a new antiques shop in Mount Vernon, and, confidentially, the people running it don't know anything about antiques. Right in the center of downtown Mount Vernon in the old tinsmith's shop across from the gristmill, Toots performs impromptu concerts on the piano surrounded by old paintings hanging on the barnboard walls, a majolica umbrella stand, an alabaster birdbath, and a Bohemian vase. Out front sits a broken cupboard and a buggy that partner Carl [Tuttle] brought in from a farm in Chesterville. Then there are those damn Windsors, porch Windsors that are only about 25 years old. And how were we to know that three of the four weathervanes we bought from that dealer in York aren't even that old? 'You have to deal in everything,' we were told. Well, we had it.

Looking back I recall that Mount Vernon seemed a pretty uncertain place to sell antiques, particularly old paintings, which was what we had to start with and all we knew anything about. It began as a serious lark. I had left my job as curator of the art museum at Colby College. Luckily, my wife Ellen was teaching art in Augusta that first year. Carl was out knocking on doors, and stuff was piling up. I wondered if anyone would ever come in and buy a painting. That was the picture-buyers' heyday.

Dealers had woken up to the fact that they didn't have to kick holes in the pictures to sell the frames. Out of attics and off parlor walls, where they had been passed by for years, they came. Twenty or thirty dollars bought my choice, and there was no rush. Seventy-five dollars would acquire a battle ship by J. B. Hudson or a homestead by Wesley Webber.

We were drawn toward country things. I remember also, with a little more relish, a refinished button-foot table, bow-back Windsors, early iron, and spotty business. Dr. Martin was the high spot of those early seasons. A small wide-eyed crowd would gather as Toots played and Doc bought. Our other regular customer was one of the old-time dealers from nearby. I remember afternoons when the till was down to a few bucks and he'd roll in in his station wagon and spend a couple of hundred dollars. All of his purchases were made through Carl to whom I'd whisper the best price. Later, after Ellen and I moved our half of the business up the street, that dealer never came in. We were learning one of the many hard lessons in psychology and the antiques business, which was that he was willing to spend hundreds on our merchandise so long as he thought that Carl had picked it all out of a shed somewhere.

The second year at the tinsmith's shop was more active. We survived on four out of every five dollars coming from paintings. That began to even out as we bought better antiques. Very early we got attracted to old paint, grained decorations, and redware. Frequent journeys to Massachusetts and New Hampshire helped us to procure better, early things. I recall sitting front row center in the field across from Robert Skinner's old house in Bolton, Massachusetts, at one of his first auctions and hearing him tell the crowd that the early pine chest that I just paid $200 for was the best thing in the auction. It sat in our shop for a long time.

Looking for more business, we advertised in *DownEast*. Do you remember a picture of weather-vanes? Sam Pennington does. The wonderful primitive one of the pointing hand I bought from him for $20. Another ad pictured was a yacht race by Stubbs. Ezra Peters' Antiquities was listed in the Maine Antiques Dealers Association in 1967, and that summer you saw me in the booth at the Bristol show with a set of six Shaker chairs.

To deal in the quality that we wanted to be able to sell at the rate we needed, we took to the show circuit. That second summer we were at Boothbay, and at Bath with a big chair-table and four matching Windsors in old red, a large Prior, and a 3' Harrison Brown of North Conway. In October, we were at the Eastland in Portland with an exceptional wall box in old blue for $27.50 and a little grained bootjack chest for $32.00.

One day I walked up the street to look at the Dr. Silas Burbank house which was for sale. I was looking for a friend but instantly I saw it as a shop. After persuading Ellen's mother to buy it and after a lot of work, Ezra moved up the street in the spring of 1968. One end of the place was our art gallery and the old part housed the rest. With a bigger shop and inventory, our appetite grew. We had sat through three-day Maine shows with good early things and sometimes did less than $300. Hard to believe how times have changed! Back then, no dealers from out of Maine came to the shows, nor were there all the transported dealers who live here now, and for sure, just about nobody locally was interested in our early stuff. Once on the ladder, we wanted to climb. There was Camden; Manchester, Vermont; Framingham; Providence; Yarmouth, Mass.; Worcester; Westfield; Princeton; Hartford; Baltimore; Washington; and finally the Ellis Memorial in Boston.

Those were the days when brave dealers headed for Maine in mid-April and stopped coming after the foliage changed. Those shows exposed us to a multitude of things we never saw or took time to look at. Our style was to start out early and shop on the way to shows. We always paid all expenses that way, and we found new sources far from home. I loved to comb those cities for paintings. Some nights after the show closed down at 10 or 11 we might be swapping pictures until 2 AM at a lawyer's in Washington or a professor's in Baltimore.

A lot of contacts were made on the road and at the shows. We were the first Maine dealers with primitives to do the Concord flea markets. I heard whispers in the wind around us back in Mount Vernon: "Well, there's Huntington in Mount Vernon, but I don't think you could touch the prices. They do the big shows." Overcoming that image became the hardest task of the business.

A memorable year for hardworking antiques dealers was 1969 because we all got rich. I sold 600 paintings that year. It was the only year for which I ever took a count, but I know I never did it again. Ezra Peters' was really two businesses that were very compatible. Many customers came to see only paintings. In hunting antiques we'd find pictures where art dealers would seldom look. In that short time, the business had sort of grown up, lost its innocence. I recall that people bought because they had a preference for old things, and at a leisurely pace. It was a smart way to furnish since, if anything, antiques retained their value. Later it was obvious that art and antiques increased in value rapidly while the dollar shrank. The growing prosperity and free time spurred this concept and all of a sudden that bandwagon that some had been comfortably riding got awfully crowded and began to move faster and faster.

As a result, new patterns emerged in the Maine market. Things take a little longer to register in this part of the world, but the days when glass dealers would pick up primitives disappeared. Smaller dealers began to complain about not finding things. The numbers of dealers sprouted like buds in springtime. Dealers began moving to Maine in force. More people showed up on the roads looking for goods. Local dealer guides and flea markets finally caught on here. There was more specialization. The spring business came earlier and earlier until it started the first week in January, each person trying to be the first to the Maine bargains.

There has always been a mystique about Maine and its antiquities. I sensed this in my travels outside the state. I guess we seemed to be from so far away, not on the way to anywhere. It is a place where everyone wants to come someday. For

decades, Maine has been raped of her homespun treasures. Perhaps the people just a generation or so removed from the farms of Albion, Parsonfield, Dixmont, or Charleston were too near the humble reminders of their rural past to desire them. I think often there is a character and spirit running through the things that were made here. I like the quality of the toy whittled by a father for his son, the bucket yoke painted blue to brighten the shed where it hung, or the stuffed black-stocking doll mother made for the newborn girl. The best of all those things retain a joy and individuality as different as the faces of the folk that created them. One wants to believe there was a frontier lack of knowledge of how things were made by Boston rules, that our craftsmen followed a Down Easter instinct for workmanship and ingenuity. I like the taste exercised by our itinerant painters, our potters, or furniture decorators. Maine people made better things. Why else is there such a demand for them?

We directed ourselves toward a piece of the "new action." All those hours traveling and look-ing, buying and selling had helped us compile a mental log of values, desirability, popular styles, sources, and customers. We had learned that hardest and most imperative concept of wholesale trading, to ask ourselves not "How much can we get for that?" but "How is it going to look to the next dealer?" and "How many more people can make a profit on it?" We had long been hardened against that sense of attachment to things which says, "That's how much you must pay to get it away from me." I learned to invest $20 to make $3, $100 or $150 to make $10 or $15. Retail business was an infrequent but often pleasant surprise. (It ran 4–6 percent.) Initially our business was geared toward dealers located in richer markets, who would, according to plan, pay us 10–20 percent profit to round things up. Being off the beaten track, it seemed necessary to offer a large stock so that our customers, who had come so far, would be rewarded by a lot to see as well as a lot to choose from.

I hypothesized the Huntington Law: "When in doubt . . . BUY!" If a thing is interesting enough to ponder over, the only way to learn about it and its salability is to fork over the cash and run with it. How about an embroidery depicting General Grant lying on a slab complete with Liberty, Union soldiers, etc. framed, for $300. Oh, yes, it was 60" x 67". Seems like an unlikely item? Well, I didn't have a customer and it was too big to fit into the wagon. The owner offered to deliver it from Cape Cod free. That's when the Huntington Law went to work. I sold it two or three weeks later for $650. But it was the sort of item that usually they smash up and kick over the edge of the grave as you are lowered away. Everybody loves a spender, and buying a lot of marginal things can open the way to being shown something better that the seller has tucked away.

After two or three years on the show circuit, we felt like carnies. The routine of a long day packing, one or two days driving, a day setting up the booth, two, three, four days at the show, and the mad rush to reload and head for home exhausted us for another five days. Seeing the same faces show after show and the same tired merchandise dragged around and passed back and forth was less than inspiring. Of course, there are things to buy at every show, but ten days at a whack out of our lives got to be depressing, to say nothing of the disruption to something called "home life" and the consistency of a shop's business.

So, giving full attention to our shop, we sought to enjoy the growing wave of activity afoot in the business. Yet, Ezra Peters' as it existed was a full-time responsibility. We couldn't help but wonder if we really needed such an instrument to produce our livelihood. We questioned if it wasn't a trap, if it might not be a monster taking more from us than giving to us. I had left one field to find more time for personal pursuits. But we were on the map. Dealers called at all hours wanting to get into the shop and maybe spend the night with us. Pickers from north, east, south, and west all

had something for me to look at. We chose to invite two other dealers into an association, which began in March of 1971. A new chapter unfolded. We had a great deal of help, but then there were two more reasons for people to visit Ezra Peters'. The business functioned so well from this point that I would have to call the situation that we had arrived at ideal.

Throughout the trade today, I detect a common worry that the antiques are disappearing or becoming much harder to find. I can't say that I see less that is desirable than I did five years ago. True, I know my way around better these days, but remember that Maine was settled fairly far north at a respectably early time. It's a big state that produced a wealth of objects. Strong, Milo, Phillips, Burlington, Houlton, and Brownville are a handful of northerly villages settled in the early 1800s. Every single piece under the roofs of those old farms would be of interest to us today if they still existed—clothes, lamps, maps, skates, mixing bowls, chairs, bedpans, and even the windows, mantels, fireplace cranes and the fan over the front door. Hundreds of thousands of items have survived fires, natural wear, town dumps, and just the roofs falling in on them. Luckily the old folks valued those material things that weren't stamped out by the millions but were made with care or bought dearly. That's why there is still so much to be discovered. After we are gone, many of the old things will still be getting swapped around, sold for cash, and discovered again.

The closer the dealer can get to the original sources the fresher will be his merchandise and the better his prices. One route to this end is the picker. For all the anguish I have suffered in quest of them, I haven't the slightest reservation that it was worth it all. Let me tell you about it. In Maine there are still a fair number of men and women who make their living by driving miles each day and canvassing house to house to buy antiques. A lot of days are lean, filled with long hours, abuse, and frustration. Mostly they are looking for leftovers, things passed by others or those things that no one has been able to spring loose from the old lady who greets him at the door with her *Warman's Price Guide* in hand. Doors are closed in their faces, mean dogs bark, and farmers call them crooks. Most people don't think they have anything, but, if they do they don't want you poking around, and if they don't, you're welcome to look everywhere. When something does turn up, the picker must make an offer and then come back again after they think it over awhile. It's an independent life. A man is his own boss, and the next house in Avon or Trap Corner is full of goodies, untouched and waiting. He is "buy oriented." Often his knowledge is minimal, and once he has bought his load he needs to sell it quickly. He is fair game for dealers who prey upon his mistakes and believe the less the picker knows the better. At the same time, many of his finds are sold too cheap. He may also ask too much, $400 one day, $300 the next, finally selling to the fifth or sixth customer for $175. In an open shop, we don't have that flexibility.

The door is open to doing business with pickers if you have the patience. The antiques business as a whole attracts a lot of shifty types. After all, the essence of the business is to take things from other people at less than they are worth. The levels vary, and honor certainly exists among dealers, yet the opportunities for the swift operator are unlimited. The stories are endless of how dealers have conned things away from people or sold something for what it wasn't. Pickers are not more or less honest, but doing business with them is an exercise in judgment of character. My philosophy is that the lion's share of the potential profit should go to him who digs it out and gets things going. Generally, it works from the other end. The farther an item gets from the finder, the larger the amount of profit. Money is in large part made by being able to identify things and know where to sell them. A good dealer should be able to function well with pickers, combining their skills into a loose team. This is very difficult because an active dealer can't be waiting in a picker's yard for him to come in everyday, nor can he buy all the things the picker finds or even the best for the biggest price. There is always someone who will pay more for any given antique. Besides, the picker needs to honor the customers that live at his doorstep or soon they won't be there when he needs them. What he needs as well is a chance for a fair price for the exceptional things he finds each week or month, for it is those that allow him the chance to do better than working for wages. I attempt to impress the picker that if he will hold items for me to look at, then under those circumstances I am willing to share all I know about it and make an offer. Often I tell exactly what I think I can sell a thing for leaving him to decide what profit I shall get. I try to construct a basis of trust so that it is never necessary to haggle over prices. (I am guarded against over-paying in an effort to be too fair.) Many times I have paid people more than they have asked me for saving things. I'm talking of amounts sometimes in hundreds. I want to see pickers I can work with make more money. Many times I have been taken advantage of under the circumstances. I prefer to play the fool, being polite and chalking the experience up in a mental ledger on that person. It doesn't take long to know who is being straight and who isn't, which isn't to say that I stop doing business with the ones that aren't. I'm just less eager to go look at things and less enthusiastic about being generous.

The biggest problem for me has been reaching deep to buy a lot of stuff to keep the relationship alive. One winner pays for ten or twenty losers and, with patience, the law of averages favors me. I have done business with some pickers for a number of years where I may not have made a dime, whereas others have been rewarding. It's exciting to be seeing things right out of houses as they were found. I'm a believer that next time it will come from where I don't expect it. (It's going to be a copper kangaroo weathervane!) In essence,

I think dealers should share what they know. I'm afraid the brotherhood of man has regressed from the day your neighbor would not only lend you his wagon jack but help you use it.

I just can't think of not extending the courtesy to my customer of sending him where he can find other things. I still feel I'm owed a few hundred favors from several dealers around me to whom I have sent new business over the years and they haven't reciprocated. One in particular, who is an excellent customer himself and who has yet tossed me a customer, was surprised by someone he knew in my shop. Embarrassed for some reason to be caught there he said, "Whenever I want to pay through the nose for it I go to Ezra Peters'." Well, that's about 50 times a year baby!

Logical customers don't need to be discouraged from coming to you by your fellow dealers. They will find plenty of reasons of their own. Some dealers have come through town without looking in. If they don't like me, that is forgivable, but to be not interested enough to look!

No matter what you do, the crowd will find reason. Maybe you're too far out of the way or too knowledgeable. Maybe you're new at it or probably too expensive. Many dealers think if you buy from them, how in the world could they ever buy from you? I recall wondering why a certain Connecticut dealer I had been friendly enough to share a room with at a show once, never came to my shop. I knew he came to Maine frequently. One day another friend bumped into him on his way to Maine. "Are you going to Mount Vernon?" "Naw, I won't give him the satisfaction." What in the world did that mean?

Sure enough that customer arrived one day during a particularly lean trip with an empty truck. I sold him the bulk of a load and he became one of my best customers. Once I reminded him subtly of all the things he had missed on his Maine trips because he didn't come to me. I couldn't resist.

There is another Connecticut dealer who has bought a lot of stuff over the years from me—and

some good items. He's the kind that would rather buy out of a picker's shed. He often goes through without stopping to call. Once he said to a friend, "I was just up in Maine and bought a lot of junk from Huntington." "Oh, where is it?" "I sold it all." He bought a famous chest from me, for what I thought was a sporting price even if it wasn't just out of a shed, $175. It dated about 1720. My partner never saw it since I had just gotten it and had it in my car. Two weeks later, my partner drove in with it having brought it for $650.

That was the same week that I sold a Shaker cupboard for $125 that later changed hands twice for $1,400. Before a particular dealer from New Hampshire moved near us he made weekly trips to Maine. Everyone discouraged him from coming to see me. The philosophy being, I guess, that I had all that early stuff and it must be too expensive. This fellow was a careful buyer and he, too, finally came during a lean trip and spent over $600. I had made another customer who had avoided me for a long time. Even this August, a couple who were friendly with one of my associates and who had been prodded to come to the shop to look, seemed amazed that they could buy. Though it took them a long time to get here they said, "The best prices in Maine." Well, for the quality and quantity that is what I strove for.

As things get more expensive and harder to find, the people out to find them are more predictable. One must guard against following old patterns. New sources develop overnight; old ones fade. I re-evaluate the sources constantly, sensing where to go and how often. I move fast, look fast, make a lot of stops and a lot of quick decisions. Naturally this produces a number of poor judgments, but in the long run they are secondary to the winners.

The summer has been an excellent time for me to leave Maine to do my shopping. I see more quality merchandise and can be competitive on the prices since the crowds are here then. I think the resourceful dealer can buy anywhere. I've done well in New York City and even from some of the top dealers. Many people are intimidated by the big established dealer, thinking there is no way they could buy and make money. That just isn't true. Small dealers are apt to get a few good things a year, which they may give away or worry to death. The big dealer handles good things every day. He buys and sells in quantity. He knows what he has, and he must keep dynamic and businesslike. He has top sources and often buys things very right. He'll pass the good buys along and let you know when things are out of reach. And if you sell to him he just has to treat you well and you might like some things a lot more than he does. If you are optimistic, it will be there to buy, anywhere, even the last day of a big New York show.

One of the problems of a large inventory beyond the general care for it, is that a lot of dead weight accumulates. Much of this is due to careless purchases spurred by the constant need for stock. One should learn to realize mistakes as quickly as possible, take a loss if necessary, and dump it. You can make it up on the next item. It is not a good policy for dealers to return things. You should know what you're buying. No matter what the circumstances, returns create ill feelings all around. Among other reasons is that you are essentially insulting the other person's merchandise and showing your own lack of ability to judge. It can be painful to live with those mistakes, but they are reminders that you can get careless. I remember that I had been buying paintings in large numbers for about five years and had never made a mistake to speak of. I got over-confident and ended up with a $3,400 painting I sold for $200. Shortly thereafter I acquired an interesting portrait of Lincoln. (Mostly interesting because it turned out to be about as old as my son.)

There are more fakes on the market all the time as well as clever restorations and alterations. The high prices are the incentive and, as the prices soar, so will the number of fakes. At least they help sep-arate the men from the boys and can be a reminder

to the gentleman dealers (i.e. part-timers) that this is a full-time job. Know what you're doing or get stung! Of course, there is often a way out via the auction block, where some other sorry character gets kicked. The worst part is that all those things end up in a home where someone worked hard hours to make the money to buy it. "If they don't know and are satisfied, what's the difference?" They're going to find out sooner or later. I always believe in being honest about what I sell.

If something is Canadian, then the customer should know it. If he doesn't want it for that reason, he certainly shouldn't own it. He's apt to find out from someone else. So if he doesn't buy, you have done a small part to win his confidence.

Over the years I've learned some techniques for selling. Things set up in an orderly fashion, such as a room arranged normally, show a regard for them. This will appeal to those looking for better things. Things piled up or cluttered, with an indifferent look about them, suggest that they are going to be cheap. I put things on my porch. "How much can he care if he leaves them out?" That sort of impression hitting people as they enter says, "You can buy here." If the first one or two things a person picks up are pricey, then they are turned off. Keep as many of those items as you can away from the entrance. Prices chalked on furniture, especially at flea markets, certainly make things look for sale. While on the subject of flea markets, I was always geared to sell there, taking merchandise that would represent my shop but be as reasonable as possible. I never waited for someone to ask a price. If they picked up something to look at and it was marked $65, I said, "That's fifty-five dollars," or whatever I had to get. I let them know I was there to SELL. You'd be surprised how much can be moved by creating an atmosphere of selling. It can be done in a shop, too, but there one has to be a little more guarded because this technique requires fast pricing without referring to tags, if possible.

Pricing is most important. Two dollars can determine a $50 or $60 sale to a dealer. I've had things for months priced at $60 and, having changed to $58, it will sell in a matter of days. Re-pricing, always down, was a great sport to me. I might price it $85 on Monday and $70 on Thursday. Everything should he tagged with clean tags—prices on everything. I think the standard dealer discount is not conducive to smart business. I never know what I want for a thing until I'm asked. Who is asking, how long I've had it, how many others I can have are all factors. Perhaps it is a new customer and I bought the item right. It is marked $60. Instead of saying, "The discount is standard—ten or twelve percent," I say, "You can have that for $48." That is the sort of selling that gets them started.

A fresh look is very important. That meant hours of arranging and rearranging. At the same time, weeding out items that had been around too long and sending them to auction was a regular game for me. Once it's had its chance, let it go. I always tried to give the auctioneer some good with the chaff. It was only fair to him. Twenty percent losses on things are better than tying hundreds of dollars in tired stock that all your customers have passed. When I knew when a certain customer was arriving, I have gone so far as to drag certain pieces out of the shop and set them next to my wagon to make it look like I'd just bought them. I tried that once last spring with four things and sold them all to two dealers. Everyone likes to think they're getting first shot at something fresh and wouldn't even look at it if it was in a back room. Often I've noted that something I bought in a small disorderly shop for $6 or $8 and wondered if I should have bought it takes on a new character and value when placed next to other sympathetic things. Whereas most everyone recognizes a quality piece of furniture, it isn't easy to make much money on it. A small number of dealers by comparison are on the lookout for those unique, offbeat carvings, paintings, and folky goodies that are outside of the imagination of the average dealer. The classical folk items everyone recognizes today are among the most expensive of all antiques. It is the funky "great-in-the-eyes-of-the-beholder" where I think the sleepers are today.

Personally, I'm disturbed by the staggering prices today. I'm not talking about what I hear is happening in New York. Everybody is nuts there. But when chests and weathervanes and primitive portraits and jugs and Windsor chairs start bringing more money than a lot of people live on all year, something is out of kilter—there is a screw loose. Dealers seem to have no sense of restraint but constantly indulge by saying how great this is or that is. Fact is, it probably is not great by any standard if they think about it, it is just a case of someone else had one in their collection. We call a chalkware pair of lovebirds great. What are they really? And at $275? So the demand that we are all creating is forcing prices up, up, up. The good things are dragging up the dull everyday jugs and mass-produced pewter. Dealers are so anxious for stock that they just buy, buy, buy. The public sees the prices going up and doesn't see how they can go wrong. I've seen baskets go from no value to $1 to $10 to $25 and more. Now I ask you, what happened?

I guess we've come to a time when the antiques business has given us all the experiences it had in store. We made the big hits, the knockouts. We did the big shows. We dealt in a lot of things before the vogue hit and loved it. We built an impressive collection. We had some very large sales. We had customers charter a plane to visit us. We crawled around some attics. We built from scratch a prominent business in an area that needed it. We handled many wonderful things and met a lot of great people. We traveled from western Ohio to Cape Breton, paying our way with antiques, and we're grateful to them. We will rest assured that in the future, from attics, sheds, chambers, barn sales, estates, and auctions, things will continue on their journey. The dealer will play a vital role, for his personal measure of each object imparts a fresh image. His ability to evaluate is the essence of the dealer's or collector's role and success. True, some of his finds are relatively standardized and need only be identified within their value range. However, the majority require the personal judgment that makes the hunt really interesting. A sport? A treasure hunt? The dealer pits his taste, knowledge, energy, and luck against all comers. Rest uneasy, for out there somewhere is the finest of its kind at a bargain price. You all have a chance, and if you don't get it, the ghost of Ezra Peters will!

Editor's Note: Chris Huntington sold the contents of his shop at George Morrill's auction at the Bridgton (Maine) Town Hall on September 8, 1973. Sam Pennington covered the sale in the first issue of M.A.D. Prices were high. A tavern table base brought $300, a curly maple serving table with tapered legs and a replaced top sold for $1,900, a chalkware rooster fetched $130, and a slipware plate with a running deer on it brought $450. There were some bargains: a shoe-foot hutch table in white paint went for $250 and painted "two-holer" from an outhouse marked "Democrats" on one lid and "Republicans" on the other was a steal at $10! That sale was the prelude to the landmark sale of the Huntingtons' private collection that sold the following June 20–21, 1974, reported by Samuel Pennington in the August 1974 issue of M.A.D.

HUNTINGTON COLLECTION SOLD: AUCTION AT MOUNT VERNON, MAINE, JUNE 20 AND 21, 1974

BY SAMUEL PENNINGTON

All you need for an auction is two willing buyers and some merchandise. But what happens when you get 400 willing buyers and well over 400 pieces of first-class merchandise? Add the super-organized auctioneer team of George Morrill to Chris and Ellen Huntington's personal collection, sell it on their front lawn in Mount Vernon, Maine, and you get a $282,000 happening that set at least two auction records and certainly will be looked upon as a landmark sale for country painted furniture and folk art. Prices were far above expectations.

There was a half-page color advertisement in *The Magazine Antiques,* a lavish color catalog with descriptions of the goods and provenance ("Found in an attic in Bowdoinham, Maine") that made dealers' mouths water. The selling was rapid, and even the weather cooperated. It had rained heavily the two days before the sale so the field to be used for parking was unusable. Never mind, the sun shone most of the time throughout the sale and a shuttle was supplied to bring buyers about a mile or so up the country lane from where parking was solid. Some had to walk and surely that jaunt only increased their eagerness to buy. Less than 30 miles away there were thunderstorms

on both days of the auction, but in Mount Vernon there was barely a sprinkle.

Because the whole collection was being sold, the house was arranged in room settings for the preview day and both days of the sale. Seeing objects in a house setting made them even more desirable.

A summer estate auction held under a tent has long been one of Maine's top tourist attractions. There were license plates from Illinois, West Virginia, South Carolina, New York, Pennsylvania, and Connecticut, but there were precious few casual tourists among the first day crowd of 400. There were eager buyers for the kind of early American country furniture, folk art, and redware pottery that had made the Huntingtons Maine's most successful antiques dealers.

Admission to the sale was by catalog only and the catalogs cost $6 at the gate. Only one man balked at buying the catalog. He convinced the gatekeepers that he had driven all the way from New York City to look at an airplane weathervane and that if he liked it, he would come back and buy a catalog.

True to his word, he examined the vane, decided to stay for the auction and walked the half-mile

The truly unique vanes did very well. This copper airplane of copper flew atop the old Poland Spring Hotel before 1914. It brought $8,500 from a collector.

back to the gate for the catalog. When the vane came up in the sale, he stood at the back of the tent and, in contrast to many bidders who signaled almost surreptitiously, he raised a clenched fist for each advance in price. The crowd applauded his obvious delight when he won the vane for $8,500. The weathervane he bought so triumphantly was a famous Maine landmark. Until last fall it sat atop the old Poland Spring House. It was put up before 1914 and several in the crowd remarked that they remembered seeing it there all their lives. Now it will go to his apartment in New York City as an outstanding example of folk sculpture.

Several records were set, including $9,250 for a paint-decorated chest in the American Empire style (1830–40). A theorem painting brought $2,750, another record. Most encouraging were the purchases by the Maine State Museum. Acquisitions Director Ron Kley said the money

for the museum's purchases was made available by a private donor, partly as a result of an article he wrote in the *Maine Antique Digest* stating that the museum had no legislative appropriations for purchasing artifacts (or, in plainer words, the legislature had the museum built but did not give them any money to fill it). The museum wanted everyday artifacts and, above all, documented pieces.

The museum bought very well. The pair of 19th-century painted wooden horse legs from an early blacksmith shop were a bargain at $90. A documented and decorated country dressing stand from Readfield, Maine, was a reasonable $750. They paid a high price for a decorated yarn-winder or swift held by a female hand, carved by midshipman Colson of Franklin, Maine.

Several people ask us to play down the auction and not print the prices. We think that would not be fair to readers who were not there. These prices represent what two people were willing to pay for a specific item at a certain time and place. At another time or place, even these pieces might not have brought the same prices. An auction is a volatile dynamic mix of knowledge, ignorance, egos, money, desire, greed, profit and loss, and sometimes just pure sport. But sometimes those elements mix in such a way as to produce results that can be seriously misleading. In this case there are several points worthy of note in explaining what happened and why.

The Huntington Auction: An Analysis

First, this was an important, if fairly recent, collection. A living owner offered it in its entirety. The goods had not been picked over or offered selectively or in a group before the sale. For the most part, these were things that the Huntingtons had kept for themselves. There were many things that people had been trying to buy for years and they came to the auction prepared to buy them. I had long coveted the massive tilt-top table. I had even

copied it in cherry while stationed in Louisiana. Chris had once told me that he supposed one day someone would be foolish enough to pay him $1,000 for the table. I didn't even get a chance to open the bidding at $1,000 and it went for $4,000 to one of America's top early furniture dealers. A man sitting behind me bought a silhouette framed in the remnants of an early courting mirror that he had been trying to buy for five years.

Most auctions have a few real nuggets to draw the crowd and the money, but the rest of the lots are often poor or mediocre. Even if the big items sell cheaply, the other items generally do well enough to make the total profitable. Not so at this auction. There were no apologies for 99 percent of the goods. One chair had some added parts and a few of the paintings were of dubious quality and provenance and they went for correspondingly low prices, reflecting the judgment of the crowd. Lots of the pottery was damaged, but condition standards have been too high. To expect pottery and china to exist for a hundred years or more without signs of aging is a delusion that invites fakery and blindness to the inherent beauty of the objects. All of the lots were at least first class and some were truly exceptional.

The fish was listed as an Atlantic salmon and went for $1,050.

Moreover, Chris and Ellen Huntington owned everything in the sale. There were no consignments, no reserves, and to my knowledge very few "book" bids. (The "book" bids left with the auctioneer were so ridiculously low they really did not matter.) The principals were there with their own money, raising their own hands to do the bidding.

It is true, Chris had bought fairly heavily in the late winter and spring because some old sources had heard that he was buying and paying well. He bought only exceptional items, like a Spanish-foot banister-back chair and two chair tables. He paid incredible prices for some items. A doctor's chest painted yellow and green cost him $1,600. It brought $1,700 at the auction, giving him a loss on the piece after commission. At any sale other than this auction it would have been considered overpriced at $1,000.

One man reportedly came to the sale with a paper sack full of money—$50,000 to be precise. He handed it to the stunned bookkeepers and they nervously counted out $33,000 in change after deducting his $17,000 in purchases.

One chest, purchased for around $5,000 by a dealer on commission, will stand under a Miró painting worth several hundred thousand and facing a Picasso worth a conservative million, he said. In such company, $5,000, a price astounding to many, is not unreasonable.

There was no "ring" or pool of dealers buying together as at most auctions in Maine. Competition was the order of the day. Some of the dealers were buying for their personal collections or at prices that they knew would force them to hold the items for a few years. Several dealers have sufficient outside income so that they do not need to sell for a living. They can pay big prices, ask big prices, and not be hurt when they don't sell. There is nothing wrong with this, but it does mean that those living off the business have to be even sharper. There were lots of private collectors present or represented by agents and dealers bidding on

This Maine Empire chest made an auction record for painted furniture, $9,250.

Sold on the first day of the sale, this blanket chest brought $2,800 and gave an idea of what was to come.

Redware, $475.

Gilded pilothouse eagle, $1,700.

commission. In the past year we have seen the value of our money shrink; consequently good antiques seem to be more attractive than ever.

Don't for a minute think that there were not some good buys and money to be made at this sale. A small deer weathervane at $450 was a good buy, a Hudson Valley cupboard at $1,700 was resold the same day for $2,400, and the world record auction price for a theorem still life at $2,750 was not out of line. It sold on the phone the same evening at a profit and a third party called offering the second buyer a profit the very next morning.

Chris Huntington always generated a lot of business and few people in his wake ever lost money while he was active. He created a climate of commerce in antiques that was very healthy for the business.

What did the sale mean to Maine and the whole northeastern antiques business? It meant very little. Unlike the art market where auction prices affect prices in the galleries, the antiques business encompasses so many diverse items, one auction does not influence prices. Shop owners would be seriously mistaken to revise their prices dramatically as a result of this auction. There is a great danger that small dealers and private sellers will become paranoid about selling and try to hold on to everything or to ask comparable prices for their things.

An acquaintance with knowledge of Wall Street and the current status of the economy suggested that the sale may very well have been the equivalent of the Reifsnyder sale for country furniture and folk art. For those of you not old enough to remember, the Reifsnyder sale was held at the American Art Association in New York City, the predecessor to Parke-Bernet at the peak of the American antiques market in April 1929, just before the crash when everything looked rosy. Reifsnyder's was one of the best collections of American formal furniture to be offered for sale at auction. A highboy reached $44,000 and it was

The eagle in old paint was $1,050.

many years before any antique furniture reached comparable levels. In fact, antiques dropped in price as the Depression progressed, but the drop was not nearly so sharp as the price of stocks.

Chris Huntington had always said that the secret of his success was pricing. He realized early in the game that the only way a Maine dealer could sell was by offering items at a price that was attractive to other dealers. This is still the best guide.

We could use a happening like this about once a year.

Small things did very well. The figure was $160; the canteen he sits on, $90; the painted pine wall box, $400; the two treen canisters with sponged decoration, $550 each; the basket, $60; footstool, $100; blue baby rattle, $120; and the painted tin document box, $475.

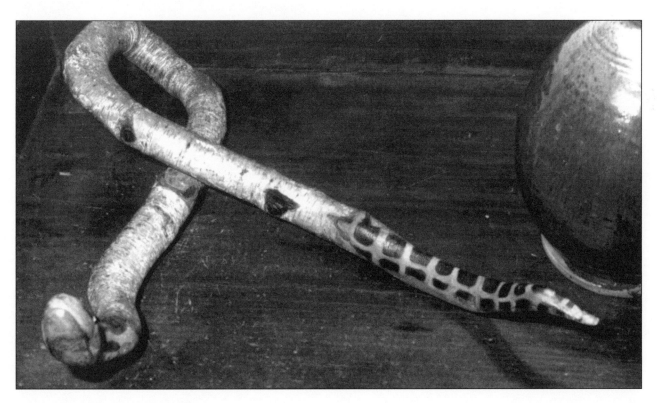

Snake from a birch root, a bargain at $175.

Editor's Note: The story of the fake Brewster chair bought

by the Ford Museum is a cautionary tale. It was the talk

of the antiques world in the fall of 1977, and when the

faker confessed, Sam Pennington interviewed all involved.

At the time, he did not reveal the identity of the seller.

MAJOR HOAX EXPOSED

BY SAMUEL PENNINGTON

The dream of every faker is to get one of his pieces into a major museum or well-known collection. But the trouble with dreams is that they sometimes come true, and that's what happened to Armond LaMontagne of North Scituate, Rhode Island, who made a great Brewster chair. He not only got it into a major museum but it is pictured on the cover of their 17th-century furniture booklet.

The existence of the fake chair, long rumored in trade and museum circles, was confirmed in an article in the Providence, Rhode Island, *Sunday Journal* on September 25, 1977, which for the first time named LaMontagne as the maker of the chair and detailed the methods by which he made it and how it entered the antiques market. The article was written by Charles Haigh who is collaborating with Mr. LaMontagne on a book tentatively titled "Good Fakers Don't Talk."

Reached at his North Scituate home, LaMontagne said he is now a successful woodcarver and sculptor who never meant for things to go as far as they did in this case. In fact, he had tried very hard to get the truth out about the chair shortly after he heard it had been sold to the Henry Ford Museum in Dearborn, Michigan.

As LaMontagne told it, he had made several pieces of 17th-century furniture for himself and had even sold a few to friends and to some antiques dealers. He noticed that they went up in price and he became convinced that many of the so-called experts were not looking at their finds closely or skeptically enough. So, in order to prove his point, he set out to make a chair that would be a real "fooler."

He says the trouble with most fakers is that they copy something already done and established. This is OK for country Queen Anne tea tables (one of the most widely faked items, he says), but they wouldn't really attract attention. A great Brewster chair on the other hand would really be a discovery! Only two are known. But it would have to be different from the accepted "great" one illustrated in Wallace Nutting's *Furniture Treasury* (plate 1799). (Brewster chairs are turned chairs made in the mid 17th-century and named for Elder William Brewster (1566/67–1644), a Pilgrim father said to have owned a chair with spindles below the seat rail as well as on the back, as distinguished from more common Carver chairs named for John Carver (1576–1621), the first governor of Plimouth Plantation, who sat in a chair without spindles below the seat rail.)

LaMontagne made his Brewster chair from oak instead of the ash used in the two other two Brewsters known, and he used an odd number of spindles. The two other Brewsters have an even number. "You have to approach a great piece of furniture the same as a piece of sculpture," LaMontagne told me when I spoke to him about it. He also said that by using oak the experts would deduce that his chair was maybe ten years older than the other recorded Brewsters.

The processes used to simulate age on the chair are better left to LaMontagne's book, which he hopes will instruct dealers and collectors on what to look out for. Suffice it to say there was a lot of torching, smoking, and chemical treatment of the chair. In addition, he removed two of the front spindles and sawed off a piece of one of the legs. These he saved as evidence to prove later that he had made the chair. "A piece of wood is like a finger-print," he said, and the sawed-off leg would match exactly. The article by Charles Haigh pictured these pieces still in LaMontagne's possession.

Removing the two front spindles gave a practical explanation of how the chair, uncomfortable at best, could have survived as a useful piece of furniture for over 300 years. With the two spindles gone, an owner could have put his feet on the rails and leaned back for some sort of rudimentary comfort.

When the chair was finished in the winter of 1969–70 (LaMontagne was hazy here; he had not kept accurate records), it was time to get it somehow into the antiques trade. Although LaMontagne admits that he had an "associate" take the chair, he firmly denies that he received any compensation for it. He did not, in fact, even sell it as a new chair—he simply gave it away. As a former member of the Rhode Island State Police he was careful not to break any laws.

It is not clear how the chair managed to spend a year or so on the back porch of a cottage on Deer Isle, Maine. From there it went to an antiques dealer in Belfast, Maine, who sold it to a Brunswick, Maine, dealer for what it was—a fake. But it was the best Brewster chair either of the dealers had seen and the Brunswick dealer decided the others were simply wrong; that it was of the period and genuine. Now convinced that the chair was old (in spite of what he had been told) the Brunswick, Maine, dealer called in a well-known dealer from New Hampshire who specialized in really early things.

It was almost too good to be true, that dealer recalls now. But there it was, the story was plausible and the chair had all the right appearances. He bought it and sold it to the Henry Ford Museum in Dearborn, Michigan. "Perhaps if we'd lived with it a little longer, we'd have seen something amiss," said his wife when I called them. But it sold quickly and was gone all too soon.

Publication of the discovery of the chair in the magazine *National Antiques Review* led LaMontagne

The Brewster Chair, circa 1969! From the collections of The Henry Ford

to realize how far his chair had gone. He started letting it be known that there was something wrong about the chair. The rumors reached John T. Kirk, expert and author of several books on American furniture, along with rumors that he had authenticated the chair. As he tells it in his *The Impecunious Collector's Guide to American Antiques* (published in 1975 by A. Knopf, and if you don't own it, you should.), "Not long ago an important museum purchased what it thought was a major early piece although it was new. Because my name had been erroneously linked to the process of authenticating the piece (I had not seen it until after the purchase), I tracked down the maker in New England. He said he had made it with the intention of getting it into a major museum and then exposing it—out of spite for people who accused him of little knowledge. If even "experts" can be fooled, how much more likely for unsuspecting collectors to be taken."

Kirk relayed his suspicions about the chair to the New Hampshire dealer who notified the Ford Museum and asked that the chair be returned for further study, According to the dealer, the museum replied that they were satisfied with the purchase.

Although Kirk used slides of the chair in some of his lectures (I attended one at Old Sturbridge Village Collector's Weekend last year) and pointed out that many of the features of the chair were a 20th-century maker's idea of what a 17th-century chair would have been, he would not publicly state where the chair was nor who had made it. He did say he had seen the cut-off piece of the leg and the sawed-off spindle.

The Ford Museum, with a lack of such evidence and only a suspicion voiced by the dealer who had sold them the chair, remained convinced, added the chair to their exhibition, and published it in its 1975 museum pamphlet. Although the past president of the Ford Museum declined comment, we were able to talk to Robert Wheeler, vice president of the collection. He told us the chair has now been x-rayed and tested in several other respects and has been determined to be a fake.

Wheeler stated that when the chair was acquired, the museum did not have a fully equipped conservation laboratory and admitted that their expertise was not perhaps then what they now feel it should be. He went on to say that every piece now proposed for acquisition by the museum, whether donation or purchase, will go through the conservation laboratory before final acceptance. Not only new acquisitions but also all past acquisitions will eventually go through the laboratory, and he feels the results will be "interesting," to say the least.

Wheeler said that the exact fate of the chair, which is not now on exhibit, is not fully decided, as it will take a full committee meeting to determine that. He added that both he and the director of the collection feel very strongly that the chair should stay at the Ford Museum, perhaps to be in a study collection. They feel that the dealer involved acted in good faith throughout and do not plan to return the chair, although the dealer has offered to take the chair back and return the money.

How could it happen? As the wife of the dealer in New Hampshire said, "Once it started, it was like dominoes failing and nothing could stop it." It is a good fake. So good that many experts believed it right to the last. It was only proved fake by the X-rays, which, as LaMontagne pointed out, proved he had drilled the spindle holes with a modern screw bit. But X-rays are not available to the average dealer and have only recently been used by the museum to test furniture.

A lot of people wanted to believe in the chair. It is a beautiful object in its own right, and if it was the third great Brewster, so much the better. Like so many reproductions and reconstructions that have been sold, the chair went through several transactions for what it was, a good reproduction, until one dealer decided that it was old. That was the turning point, just as it has been with so many other pieces.

Who are the bad guys and the good guys? There aren't any except where they've always been, on television or in the sensational press. Is there a lesson here? Well, LaMontagne says if he were doing this for a living, he never would have talked. But he says there are some guys out there who aren't talking.

Editor's Postscript: Insiders knew the dealer involved was Roger Bacon and could not believe this well-respected man could be fooled. Bacon tried to get the chair back and return the $9,000 the museum paid for it, but the curators at Henry Ford's Greenfield Village Museum in Dearborn, Michigan, decided to keep it and exhibit it. Showing how X-rays were used to reveal telltale tool marks was a good story to illustrate in their galleries. Bacon's passion for early things had blinded him for the moment—he wanted to believe.

Editor's Note: The late 1970s and early 1980s were the heyday of on-the-premises sales. Sotheby's first on-site American sale was the Marvin sale in Vermont. Two years later, Sotheby's Garbisch sale at Pokety on the Eastern Shore of Maryland was a huge garden party that went on for days. Its success brought Sotheby's the Helen Wetzel sale in Reading, a far cry from the usual Pennsylvania farm sale. In contrast, Dick Withington's dispersal of Betty Sterling's Brainstorm Farm was classic and memorable low-key New England fare. So was Ron Bourgeault's SPNEA attic sale. These five on-site sales follow in chronological order but not without a few landmark sales in between.

THE MARVIN SALE:
THE PROFESSOR'S REPORT CARD

BY LITA SOLIS-COHEN

It was the professors' turns to be graded, and they got some pretty high marks. The test was the September 30 and October 1, 1978, sale of Dr. and Mrs. James Marvin's collection of Americana in South Burlington, Vermont, where the auction scene resembled an academic conclave on a New England campus. Even the conversations about "replaced leaves" and "pieced limbs" and other repairs on antique furniture took on the scholarly tone of a discourse on botany or forestry.

That was all proper enough. Dr. James Marvin, professor of botany at the University of Vermont, was known for his basic research on the sugar maple. His wife, Alice, was director of research at nearby Shelburne Museum. After they both died earlier this year, their sons decided they could not afford to keep both the antiques and the land they had inherited. "My father was not a wealthy man, and he was as involved with conservation as he was with antiques," explained David Marvin, who is in the logging and maple sugar business in Vermont. By the time Sotheby Parke Bernet totaled the sale, the Marvin's antiques had brought a tidy $613,020, close to the high estimate despite the fact that several items failed to do as well as expected.

Collectors were disappointed in the condition of some pieces, but dealers who perceived their rarity got some good buys. Sotheby Parke Bernet

had advertised it as its most important house sale of Americana. It was also the company's first on-the-premises auction in northern New England. The weather and foliage provided an appropriate setting of spectacular New England fall scenery. The surrounding hills were ablaze with crimson, orange, and yellow and the fields were bleached by the first frost.

Dr. Marvin inherited his interest in antiques as well as some family heirlooms from his parents. After he married in 1934, he and his wife traveled all over New England seeking furniture and furnishings that might have been owned by their ancestors, who settled in Connecticut in the 1600s and who were farmers in the Norwalk-Bridgeport area for six generations. James and Alice Marvin lived in a 1730 Connecticut house, which they saved from destruction 20 years ago by moving it piece by piece from its original site in Glastonbury, Connecticut, to a meadow on a Vermont hillside. Their reconstructed house and collection was given recognition when it was published in *The Magazine Antiques* in February 1972.

Although the sale was not scheduled to begin until 10 AM on Saturday morning, bidders, like students lining up to register for popular courses, began arriving at 7 AM. By 8:15, over 100 were in line to sign up for bidding paddles and to reserve

A circa 1840 Massachusetts stenciled counterpane with circle quilting drew raves from the audience and $2,200 from an Ohio dealer. Sotheby Parke Bernet photo.

seats in the large yellow and white tent which dwarfed the small gray clapboard house and barn. The first three rows of seats were saved for the Marvin family and for what might be regarded as a faculty of venerable dealers. Ruth and Roger Bacon from New Hampshire sat next to Albert Sack from New York, and directly in front of Lillian Blankley Cogan from Connecticut. Philip Bradley from Pennsylvania sat a short distance away in the first row. Bill Samaha from Ohio and Herbert Ader from western Pennsylvania were in the third row.

John Walton from Connecticut preferred to sit in the back behind the more than 1,000 assembled collectors and small dealers, all students of Americana. Some had come from Indiana, Mississippi, California, Illinois, Michigan, Maryland, Pennsylvania, and Virginia. In addition, bids were made by mail or phone from Denmark, England, Germany and 15 different states of the United States, from Alabama to Washington.

The morning session opened with ceramics, Alice Marvin's special interest. The prices paid gave her high marks in historical subjects. An English tin-glazed polychrome plate, 8" in diameter, painted with primitive bust-length portraits of William and Mary, estimated at $300/500, sold for $2,600. A similar plate with an ermine-robed William and a nearly bare-bodiced Mary brought

Two Bristol delft plates, 1690-95, wildly exceeded the $300/500 apiece estimates and went for $2,600 (left) and $1,600 (right). Sotheby Parke Bernet photo.

Probably the piece that started the Marvin collection was this inherited cherry bonnet-top block-front chest-on-chest. One of only four known (the other three are in museums), it went to dealer John Walton for $45,000. The obviously cut ogee feet kept the price down. Sotheby Parke Bernet photo.

$1,600. Then a 20-piece Staffordshire historical blue tea set depicting Washington standing near a tomb, impressed "Wood" on the bottom (for the potters, Enoch Wood & Sons, who made these wares 1819–30) brought a hefty $4,500, even though four of the eight tea bowls were damaged. A rare historical blue egg cup with a blurry transfer print of Washington near a tomb brought $325 from a Maryland buyer because it was an unrecorded form.

Fifteen minutes before the Saturday afternoon session featuring the furniture was to begin, an Illinois collector phoned in a long list of bids, and several were successful. His $30,000 bid bought a carved cherrywood secretary bookcase attributed to Elijah Brown of Woodbury, Connecticut, believed to have been made around 1780. Collectors had known the piece, since it was sold at the George Ives estate sale in Danbury, Connecticut, in June of 1924 for $800. In 1935 it was sold again at auction at the James Coburn sale in Greenwich, Connecticut, for $750. David Marvin remembered that his father was disappointed he had arrived at the Coburn sale too late to bid on the secretary, which had been knocked down to Israel Sack. Marvin bought it later that year for $1,200 after Sack advertised it in *The Magazine Antiques*. The Illinois collector also got three Marvin family New York Chippendale side chairs for $7,000. They had been estimated at $10,000/15,000. And he bought the burled walnut William and Mary highboy for its low estimate $15,000.

The faculty of dealers preferred the Queen Anne inlaid crotched walnut and maple flat-top highboy estimated at $20,000/30,000, which went to John Walton for $19,000. Israel Sack was the underbidder. Walton got the Connecticut sunflower chest for $12,000, well below the estimated $20,000/25,000, and Sack got the flat carved lift-top Ipswich chest for $7,500, under the estimated $10,000/15,000. A rare survivor, it, like the sunflower chest, had been refinished years ago

and could not be compared with the great Ipswich chest with ball feet and polychrome carving that bought $50,000 at Sotheby Parke Bernet last spring.

Some other items did not bring what had been expected, including a Marvin family 7'5" Connecticut shell carved blockfront chest-on-chest that had been estimated at $50,000/75,000. It went to Walton for $45,000. Its feet had been cut years ago to fit it into a low-ceilinged room. It is, however, one of only four similar chest-on-chests known, and the other three are in museums.

Albert Sack, bidding for Israel Sack, Inc., got the pair of rare Federal side chairs painted with urns and flowers attributed to John and Thomas Seymour of Boston in 1795 for only $2,000, though they had been estimated at $5,000/7,000. There was some repainting.

If the sale bestowed any special honors, they were given to a curly maple carved and turned

Rare because it had three Spanish feet, this corner chair still surprised a lot of people at $7,250, over a $1,500/2,000 estimate. Sotheby Parke Bernet photo.

A curly maple Queen Anne side chair greatly exceeded its $700/900 estimate, going for $5,500 to a western Pennsylvania dealer. Sotheby Parke Bernet photo.

rush-seated side chair with big Spanish feet and strong turnings. It had been estimated at $700/900 but went to a western Pennsylvania dealer for $5,500. John Walton said he has six, every bit as fine, and the price is $2,500 apiece. Other high-priced seats included a turned maple rush-seat corner chair, circa 1750, that went to a private buyer for $7,250 and a pair of carved and turned curly maple side chairs with balloon rush seats that went to a New York private buyer for $9,000.

Dealers dominated the sale. Of the top ten lots, six went to dealers. The oak Bible box that fetched $5,500, a banister-back chair at $4,250, and a painted trestle gate-leg table that sold for $5,000 all went to dealers. It is doubtful that any of them can double the price. Buyers were careful. A painted "Guilford" chest estimated at $15,000/20,000 did not sell because the decoration of vines and flowers was largely repainted.

Editor's Note: Stewart Gregory considered weathervanes and decoys American sculpture, and found art in the naive paintings of untutored limners and in the utilitarian objects artisans transformed into something highly decorative. Mary Allis, a distinguished dealer in Connecticut, helped him choose weathervanes and paintings, and Adele Earnest of Stony Point, New York, advised him on the selection of sculptural American waterfowl decoys. The Gregory sale was a landmark, showing how far the appreciation of American folk art had come in the five years since the Huntington sale. American folk art first collected in the 1920s and 1930s was at last considered a legitimate art form.

THE STEWART GREGORY SALE: FOLK ART APPRECIATED

BY LITA SOLIS-COHEN

Landmark auctions are used as reference points. They are the result of the right combination of circumstances and property, the quality of the collection as a whole, the quality of individual works, the reputation of the collector, the reasons for selling, and the prevailing economic and political climate. According to Thomas Norton, a Sotheby Parke Bernet vice president, "It must all come together in order to produce an event that will rise above the routine activities of the auction room."

The sale of the collection of the late Stewart Gregory on January 27, 1979, at Sotheby Parke Bernet was a landmark sale. Sotheby Parke Bernet expected it to create new price levels for American folk art. Articles in the *Wall Street Journal* and *Vogue* magazine lessened any element of surprise. The preview party hosted by the Museum of American Folk Art attracted a crowd estimated at over 700.

Nevertheless, the size of the auction crowd and many of the prices were amazing. Collectors and dealers began arriving at 8 AM, and by 9:15 the lobby of the Madison Avenue gallery was full and the line of people spilled out onto the sidewalk. Among those jammed onto the sidewalk waiting for the gallery to open at 10:00 AM was Mary Allis, the white-haired grande dame of the folk art world

who had been Stewart Gregory's collecting mentor. She had helped with cataloging the sale and had written in the introduction to the catalog, "Stewart E. Gregory was a rare and distinguished gentleman, a modern version of a Renaissance man."

Educated at Princeton (class of 1936) and Harvard Law School (1939), Gregory was successful in the drug business and retired when he was 50. He was an accomplished cellist, a good golfer, a fine gardener, and he flew his own plane.

"He would never buy a plane that would not hold his cello and folk art. He would take me along and fly around the country when we heard of something he might like to own," said Allis.

"Stew didn't marry until he was sixty, and he resisted a lot of beautiful women until he met Peg (Margaret Barnard Gregory Phelps)," Allis continued. She confirmed the widely rumored story that Gregory discovered he had cancer when he went for the blood test required to apply for his marriage license. Reportedly he wanted to call off the wedding but was finally convinced that he would recover and the wedding took place. He died two years later, only weeks after he and his wife had moved into an old family house in Wilton, Connecticut, that he had spent years rebuilding. The collection was left in trust for his widow with Gregory's brother and sister as co-trustees.

This 9" x 8¾" family group watercolor by Deborah Goldsmith (1808-1836), circa 1823, estimated at $6,000/8,000 sold for $29,000 to a New York private collector. Sotheby Parke Bernet photo. (Editor's note: Ralph Esmerian was that private collector. See pages 46 and 384 of *American Radiance: The Ralph Esmerian Gift to the American Folk Art Museum,* American Folk Art Museum/Harry N. Abrams, New York, 2001.)

When Margaret Gregory remarried and moved to California last summer she sent 80 decoys to Richard Bourne's auction in Massachusetts, keeping only eight of her favorites. She wanted to take the entire collection with her but the Connecticut court decided the collection could not leave the state and must be sold at auction. "Much to everyone's horror," said Mary Allis. "It should have gone to a museum."

There was an unconfirmed story that at one point the collection was to be dispersed at a glorified private barn sale. The only problem was that the principals could not decide whom to invite.

Many pieces from the Gregory collection have been exhibited in museums in the United States and abroad. As a result, there was a well-informed public familiar with the major pieces and clamoring for them.

The temper of the sale was set early when two collectors battled over lot 7, a group of six carved and painted wood animal toys: a giraffe, an elephant, a hartebeest, a cow, a bull, and a squiggly red and black snake made in Pennsylvania circa 1850. They finally went to a persistent Pennsylvanian for $7,750. The 10 percent buyer's surcharge that Sotheby Parke Bernet instituted on January 1 apparently had no effect on the bidding. *(Editor's Note: In 1979, M.A.D. did not report prices with the buyer's premium.)*

Three lots later a small watercolor, 9" x 8¾", of Mr. and Mrs. Lyman Day and daughter Cornelia, painted in New York circa 1823 by Deborah Goldsmith, was knocked down to a New York collector for $29,000. It is a classic naive picture full of expressive distortions—and by a woman artist to boot.

Margaret Gregory Phelps came to the sale to buy back her favorite pieces. Although she didn't get every one she wanted, she did spend $92,150 for 14 lots. The oil portrait of a child wearing a gray dress and yellow slippers and carrying a basket of strawberries painted by the deaf mute John Brewster (1766–1854) and pictured on the catalog

cover went to a Connecticut collector for $67,500. A New York collector got the pair of portraits of a lady and gentleman by Ammi Phillips (1788–1865) for $62,500. But Phelps stayed in the bidding until a charming portrait of a little girl in a green dress by J. Bradley (active 1832–1847) was knocked down to her for $43,000. She paid $17,000 for a copper weathervane in the form of a leaping stag and hound. The carved and painted whirligig in the form of a Revolutionary War soldier cost her $5,000 and tied the auction record for a whirligig, a 14" high American eagle whirligig knocked down to Connecticut publisher Scudder Smith for $5,000.

Mary Allis spent a total of $102,485 for 13 lots, among them the watercolor portrait of Miss

This painting of a little girl by John Brewster, Jr. (1766-1854), brought $67,500, a record for Brewster and the highest-priced item in the sale. Sotheby Parke Bernet photo.

"Mashamoquet," a weathervane, sold for a record $25,000.

Adeline Bartlett by R.W. and S. A. Shute for $32,000. She bought her favorite weathervane, a molded copper Indian wearing a three-feathered headdress for $25,000, a record for a weathervane.

A fine grasshopper weathervane went for $23,000 to Alice Kaplan, a New York collector with a keen eye. Mike Nichols, the producer/director, got one of the best vanes, in the form of the angel Gabriel blowing a horn, for his Connecticut house. It cost him $17,000 plus the 10 percent buyer's surcharge.

Folk sculpture reached a new price level at this sale. A circa 1838 carved and painted wooden bust of Nantucket Captain Starbucks was knocked down to Massachusetts dealer Stephen Score for $30,000, a record for any folk sculpture. The life-size figure of a racetrack tout, legs astride, cigar in hand, went to a Massachusetts collector for $29,000. The new

auction record for a decoy was made when a Canada goose was knocked down to Dr. James McCleery, a Texas collector, for $12,500, topping the previous record $10,500 paid for a Hudsonian curlew carved by John Dilley from the Gregory collection sold at Bourne's in Hyannis last August.

For those who keep track of auction records there were more than a dozen. For individual artists: John Brewster, Jr. ($67,500), Ammi Phillips ($62,500 for a pair), J. Bradley ($43,000). The record $20,000 for a portrait by William Jennys was bid by a Washington, D.C., collector who couldn't get a seat in the salesroom and had to bid standing in the adjacent gallery where Sotheby Parke Bernet vice president Tom Norton, perched on a stool, took bids and relayed them to the main salesroom. The new record for an Erastus Salisbury Field is $11,000, paid by a New Jersey collector for a portrait of a little boy, Henry Allen Pease, wearing a blue dress. The pair of portraits of Captain and Mrs. Nathan Sage by Nathaniel F. Wales that Mary Allis bought for $12,000 is a record for this little-known artist. The record for William Matthew Prior is $13,000, paid for a small portrait of two children.

The new auction record for a theorem painting on velvet is $3,250, paid by Mary Allis. The record for a mourning picture, $9,500, was paid by a New York collector for a watercolor of two young ladies and a gentleman weeping at the tomb of Mrs. Mary Hebard. When a Michigan collector bid $11,000 for a wooden Civil War toy with columns of Union soldiers that marched, he scored a record for a folk art toy. The $700 paid by a New York collector for a milliner's bandbox labeled "From S.M. Hurlbert's, Boston," made circa 1820, is surely a record for a hatbox. Probably no other sternboard has sold for more than $13,000, paid for the 9'4" long carved eagle sternboard. The set of six rush-seated banister-back side chairs bought by the Hitchcock Museum in Riverton, Connecticut, for $16,000 made a record for a set of painted fancy chairs. A paint-grained corner cupboard that sold for $10,000 might be a record for paint-grained furniture, if you put the painted Guilford chest that was knocked down to a Maryland dealer for $20,000 in the category of early floral painted chests as opposed to 19th-century grain-painted furniture. It is a record for a painted corner cupboard at any rate. And the wooden park bench supported by two cast iron swans that sold for $5,000 must be a benchmark.

This hollow Canada goose decoy brought $12,500 from a Texas private collector, Dr. James McCleery. This was a record for decoys, surpassing the $10,500 set in 1973 at the Mackey sale at Bourne's and tied this summer by a Hudsonian curlew from the Gregory collection also sold at Bourne's. Sotheby Parke Bernet photo. (Editor's note: At the McCleery sale run jointly by Sotheby's and Guyette & Schmidt in January 2000 it sold for $233,500.)

Some Thoughts on the Gregory Sale
by Samuel Pennington

Seasoned auction-goers who finally managed to push their way into the Gregory sale might well have been excused for asking themselves two questions: Is this the real world? Will this sale have any real effect on the market? In spite of the sometimes incredible prices, the answer to both questions would have to be a qualified "no."

The sale was a happening—much like the Huntington folk art sale in 1974 in Maine and the Charles Gardner bottle sale at Skinner's in 1976. It was a widely published collection of a well-respected man. Collectors showed up in record members to go after a piece or two, and money was no object. One dealer, commenting on a whopping price he had paid for one object said that, after all, it had only gone for double the estimate, when many other things had brought four and five times the estimates.

There was a tremendous amount of retail buying and bidding. Add that to the $92,150 paid by Gregory's widow and the $102,485 paid by dealer Mary Allis and the figures become more understandable. Together those two buyers accounted for 14.5 percent of the sale. Sotheby Parke Bernet gave a breakdown of the $1,340,450 total (before the 10 percent buyer's commission) as 69 percent private, 29 percent dealer and 1.5 percent museum. Unfortunately, we're talking apples and oranges—the percentages are in terms of lot numbers and not dollars, but there is enough of a relationship to use the figures. This compares with a "normal" Sotheby Parke Bernet sale break-down of about 50:50 dealer versus private buying.

If ever there was a collection that had been cer-tified, signified, and approved, this was it. Museum exhibition credits dotted the provenances, which included prestigious dealer names. This certainly must have given courage to many otherwise faint-hearted bidders, and many people bidding would

A carved and painted wood lectern box brought $17,000 from a private collector. Sotheby Parke Bernet photo. (Editor's note: See *American Radiance*, page 115.)

never in the world have paid such prices without the confidence of having an underbidder.

Sotheby Parke Bernet won no plaudits for their handling of the crowd, even if it did exceed their wildest expectations. People were packed into the lobby and out on the street until 10 AM and then allowed to surge into the saleroom. There were bidders standing in the aisles and in every corner of the room. But this had a curiously exciting effect on the bidding. It was almost as if it were a privilege to spend your money there.

There were some great items in the sale, and they brought both good to incredible prices. But there was a disturbing amount of mediocre stuff in the sale that brought ridiculous prices. A barn louver at $3,750 boggles the mind. A wooden painted key trade sign at $2,600 could reasonably be expected to open Fort Knox. A badly refinished wooden ram that might have been a footstool or child's seat brought $3,400. It makes one wonder what a good carving might have fetched.

Curiously, dealers bought most of the early furniture at very reasonable prices, and a week after the sale much of it had already been resold.

As to the effect on the market, there did not seem to be any rush on the part of dealers with similar items to mark up prices, nor was there any rush on the part of collectors and dealers to rush out and buy those items. There is, however, a new perception of just how far bidders will go—$25,000 for a weathervane was more than twice the previous recorded high of $11,000.

We would have to believe that the sale will flush out on to the market many items. Big prices have a way of doing that. But we have to remember that it all happened on the 27th of January in a crowded room on the third floor of a Madison Avenue auction gallery. That place and that time and that's all.

The grained and painted blanket chest marked "N.A." brought $3,750. Sotheby Parke Bernet photo.

Editor's Note: In 1979 auctioneer Ron Bourgeault donated his services to the Society for the Preservation of New England Antiquities (SPNEA) for an old-fashioned attic sale, a kind of sale not seen anymore.

AMERICANA FUND-RAISER: RONALD BOURGEAULT'S SPNEA ATTIC SALE IN CONCORD

BY SAM PENNINGTON

The "dream" auction for antiquers used to be the country estate sale, which could be counted on to disgorge generations worth of interesting items into the willing hands of assorted dealers and collectors assembled under the hastily erected auctioneer's tent. These sales are rare now. Most such estates have long since gone under the hammer.

Today we settle for the estates and attics of early collectors and that was what we got at an August 5, 1979, auction in Concord, New Hampshire.

It came about because Mrs. Charles F. Batchelder, a former president of the Society for the Preservation of New England Antiquities (SPNEA), wanted to do something for that organization. She decided to donate some antiques to be sold at auction and called Hampton, New Hampshire, auctioneer Ronald Bourgeault, who agreed to donate his services. Batchelder literally turned him loose in her attic to pick out about 300 items, many of which had been collected in the 1920s by her late mother.

Many of the items were "in the rough," a beloved phrase for antiquers. The ads for the sale even ran a picture of the items carefully arranged in the attic, a tactic designed to entice even the stingiest of collectors.

Entice them it did. The ballroom of the New Hampshire Highway Hotel was packed with bidders, dealers, and SPNEA members. The first item up was a pair of jade green dolphin-base Sandwich glass candlesticks that opened at $100 and quickly leaped to $1,500.

"Everything is sold 'as is' and if you find it signed, don't return it," joked auctioneer Bourgeault. "Don't say you're not getting a lot for your money—of course, we're getting a lot for SPNEA, too," he added.

Top money, $16,500, was a tie between a primitive painting of a little girl and an extremely small, 30" wide lowboy. No one was sure who painted the primitive painting. Various folk art dealers attributed it to Sheldon Peck, and to W.M. Prior, and to John Bradley, but all agreed it was a wonderful picture even if it did have two fair-sized holes in it. The winning bidder was Allan Daniel, a New York dealer.

The lowboy appeared to be all original but had been scraped during the removal of the original finish many years ago. It went to a private collector for double what several dealers were willing to pay.

At least four Canadian dealers were present for just one piece, a butternut serpentine three-drawer commode in the French provincial style, probably made in the Quebec region. A Quebec dealer took it home for $8,000. "That's in U.S. dollars," reminded Bourgeault as the price went over $4,000. And with a 17 percent exchange rate now in effect, the price worked out to $9,360 in Canadian money.

There were some rather wonderful wrecks and fragments, and most brought top dollar. A

How's this for an early attic? The continuous-arm Windsors brought $1,000 apiece. SPNEA photo.

Mrs. Batchelder, right, holds a Sandwich glass candle stick to lead off the auction It was one of a pair that sold for $1,500. A young Ron Bourgeault stands at the podium to the left.

Pennsylvania trifid-foot table with only one unbroken and complete leg and missing a leaf (the whole was sold tied up in a strong rope) brought $750. A pair of tall carved bedposts brought $750, and a tavern table base brought $850. "I wanted to nail that to my wall," commented one dealer known to collect fragments, "but not for that price."

A tea table with a replaced top brought only $700, while a similar base with no top brought $750. "Tell them it's a hunk of junk and they pay more,"

shouted the happy auctioneer after that lot sold.

Earlier he had sold a small Battersea enamel box in the shape of a lemon for a very high $525. "The only lemon in the sale," he had promised. But at $4,000 for a plain country corner cupboard with a nicely cut scalloping around the shelves, someone may have gotten a lemon. The scalloping had been done well after the cupboard was made. Even in 1920, they were fooling around with furniture!

There is nothing like an old attic sale.

Editor's Note: The estate sale for Colonel Edgar William and Bernice Chrysler Garbisch at Pokety, their Maryland estate, May 23-25, 1980, was the record house sale in America, $3.9 million, and a record sale for any collection of Americana. It also scored a record for American furniture when actor Bill Cosby, bidding through auctioneer John Marion, bought a Newport kneehole bureau for $250,000.

RECORD HOUSE SALE: GARBISCH SALE AT POKETY

BY LITA SOLIS-COHEN

The party at Pokety Farms late in May 1980 was the largest ever at the Eastern Shore estate where the late Colonel Edgar William and Bernice Chrysler Garbisch summered for over 30 years. This time the occasion was Sotheby Parke Bernet's dispersal of the contents of the white-shingled house.

The auction, held under a huge tan and brown tent on the lawn overlooking LeCompte Bay, totaled $3,903,503, a record for any house sale in America and for any collection of Americana. One piece of furniture, a blockfront kneehole bureau brought $250,000, a record for American furniture. The buyer was actor Bill Cosby.

In 1930 Colonel Edgar William Garbisch, the handsome All-American football player from West Point, married the daughter of automobile magnate Walter P. Chrysler. They died on December 14, within a few hours of each other, just a few weeks before they would have celebrated their 50th wedding anniversary.

Their executors directed Sotheby Parke Bernet to sell their collections, except for their famous naive paintings, which were given to the National Gallery in Washington and to several other institutions.

At Pokety, nearly 1,400 lots of Americana were sold in seven sessions over four days. The Eastern Shore had never witnessed anything like it. More than 20,000 people came to see the 480-acre estate and walk through the boxwood and rose gardens and the buildings on the property Bernice

Three extremely rare "Jared Spencer" flasks, probably Pitkin Glass Works, East Manchester, Connecticut, 19th century, left, $22,000; center, $14,000; right, $8,500. Sotheby Parke Bernet photo.

Garbisch's father had used for a hunting retreat. The Garbisches had turned the lodge into a neo-Georgian plantation house and filled it with their collections of Americana.

More than 1,000 people came to each session of the sale, which began on the Thursday before the Memorial Day weekend. More than 400 signed up to bid each day. The rest watched the spectacle, picnicked on crab cakes and barbecued chicken, and sunned on the lawns. A flotilla of boats was anchored offshore, their decks filled with curious onlookers watching the proceedings through binoculars.

The Garbisches collected antiques the way philatelists collect stamps—by theme. They bought Delft animals, miniature furniture, historical flasks, hooked rugs. They collected

Kneehole bureau, possibly by Edmund Townsend, Newport, Rhode Island, 1760-80. It sold for a record $250,000 to a bidder on the telephone who had been the underbidder on a set of Chinese export porcelain that sold for $45,000. According to John Walton, when he first saw the piece in a dealer's shop in Philadelphia about 20 years ago it was painted white and he turned it down at $5,000. Ginsburg and Levy bought it, restored it, and sold it to Lansdell K. Christie for $45,000. In the Christie sale at Sotheby Parke Bernet in 1972, it sold for $120,000 to Garbisch, who had called John Marion from Paris the night before and said he had to have it. Reportedly the Garbisch children were allowed to choose any piece from the collection. Gwen G. Severence chose the Mifflin family highboy and matching lowboy, which would probably have brought another $200,000. It was said she urged her brother to take the kneehole bureau. "Put it in your room and put your hot plate on it," she is alleged to have said to her brother, who is an ecologist and lives in a simple style in Saint Michaels. Sotheby Parke Bernet photo. (Editor's note: Several years after the sale it was learned that Bill Cosby was the buyer of the bureau.)

Chinese export porcelain decorated with ships, and religious subjects, and scenes of cherry pickers and lotus flowers. They had five 19th-century dinner services used on special occasions. There were buyers for all of it at Pokety.

During the first day of the sale, a collector paid $25,000 for a 112-piece deep sapphire blue service decorated with a print of Lafayette's landing in New York in 1824. A 48-piece Chinese export service in the rare rose Fitzhugh pattern went to New York dealer Fred Nadler for $39,000. A Connecticut collector bidding by phone paid $45,000 for 121 pieces of Chinese export porcelain decorated with sprays of flowers. That was the highest price ever paid for a lot of Chinese export porcelain sold at auction in America.

One collector from New York bought 14 of the 30 Delft animals for $143,000. Her purchases included a pair of horses for $28,000 and a butter tub with a swan on its cover for $16,000. A dealer from Scotland came to buy a rare Lowestoft bottle decorated with views of the English town of Lowestoft, dated 1764. He paid $15,000 for it, had it wrapped, and took it with him in a taxi that had been waiting in the parking lot to take him to the Washington, D.C., airport.

"Things always bring more at a house sale than at a mixed-owner sale in New York," said Letitia Roberts, who cataloged the porcelain. Auction fever runs rampant in a garden party atmosphere.

There was applause when records were made. When Downingtown, Pennsylvania, dealer Philip H. Bradley battled Connecticut dealer John Walton for an iron candlestand with brass candle arms and won it for $23,000, the audience applauded. It was a record for the form.

The big guns went off on Saturday when groups of collectors arrived to bid on objects from their areas of interest. About a dozen flask collectors bid a total of $267,175 for 60 historical whiskey flasks. Massachusetts autograph dealer and flask collector Paul Richards paid $95,800 for 17 of them.

"That was a day's work," said Richards, mopping his brow when he had finished bidding. "Now I have about six hundred different flasks and they are all on display at the Sandwich Historical Society museum," he said.

Richards paid $27,000 for one rare green flask decorated with an eagle and concentric rings. It tied the record paid for another American flask sold last month at Robert Skinner's auction in Bolton, Massachusetts.

Four of the Garbisches' flasks brought more than $20,000 each. That is a lot of money considering they cost about a cent apiece when they were sold by the gross in the early 19th century.

This eagle inlaid spice cabinet, Chester County, late 18th century, sold to Phil Bradley for $23,000. Bradley said he bought it out of a house in the 1950's for $350 and some years late sold it to dealer David Stockwell for $2,500. Stockwell said he had sold it to the Garbisches for $6,000. Sotheby Parke Bernet photo.

Reportedly, Colonel Garbisch bought the flasks all at one time for about $10,000 from the late George McKearnin, who wrote the book on the bottles.

When the bottle collectors had removed to the boxwood garden to discuss their portion of the sale, the folk art collectors raised their bidding paddles and paid some high prices for some rare things.

An American hooked rug made in the late 19th century sold to a New York collector for $12,000, a record for a hooked rug. The most astonishing price was $7,250 paid for a small 3½" x 5½" paper box painted with a landscape on its lid and fruit and shells on its sides. The buyer was a New York collector who had left his bid with the auctioneer.

As the sun shone brighter and the temperature in the tent went above 90°, auction fever became epidemic. A painted tin apple tray sold for $3,700, a tole bread tray went for $3,200. An American

Quilt collectors hoped that one of their number would buy these two lots and reunite them. An appliquéd trapunto Baltimore friendship quilt that had been split in half by Mrs. Garbisch, with modern chintz added to make covers for twin beds. Instead, the two lots were purchased for $4,500 and $3,500 by a private phone bidder who had stayed in the room at Pokety and wanted to recreate it. He also bought much of the bedroom furniture. The first lot (left) was signed Mary White and Margaret Fusselbough 1848. The second half, at right, was signed Eliza Dembor, Baltimore. Sotheby Parke Bernet photo.

The top rug price and a record for a hooked rug at $12,000 was this 111" x 88" late-19th century example. A private collector was the buyer. Sotheby Parke Bernet photo.

eagle attributed to Kittery, Maine, carver John Bellamy in the 1860s soared to $39,000. (The last one like it to be auctioned brought $9,000 in 1970.) New York dealer Albert Sack bought the Bellamy plaque and said he hoped to sell it to the State Department for the Diplomatic Reception Rooms.

After the lunch break the bidding resumed with even more vigor as 30 pieces of miniature furniture sold for $203,360. A miniature bonnet-top highboy, which the Garbisches had bought at auction in 1972 for $18,000, went to Israel Sack, Inc. for $36,000, doubling in value but barely keeping pace with inflation. A Chester County spice box with an eagle inlaid on its door sold to dealer Philip Bradley for $23,000, three times what the Garbisches had paid for it nearly 20 years ago.

After the miniature furniture came what seemed like an endless number of pieces of decorative useful furniture, most of which had new bases, replaced tops, and other major problems, all noted in the catalog. Most of them brought prices in line with what good reproductions would cost. Only a few of these "cripples" went to the unwary for twice what they were worth. It was a knowledgeable crowd.

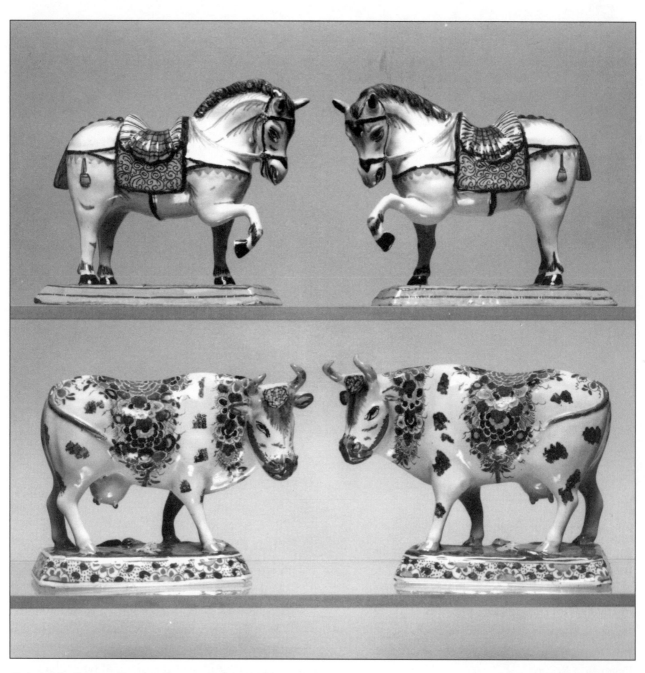

Typical of the fine ceramics were these two lots of mid-18th-century Dutch Delft. The cows were from an undetermined factory and brought $11,000. The horses had a factory mark, "P:V:M," and brought $28,000. All the pieces had been repaired. Sotheby Parke Bernet photo.

Nevertheless many in the audience had trouble understanding why a small two-drawer table with straight tapered legs that came from the Garbisches powder room brought $48,500. It was bought by dealer Harold Sack, who outbid a collector on the phone, because, he said, "I had to have it, it is unique." Sack said he bought it for stock.

Only a few moments later the block-and-shell carved Newport kneehole bureau sold to a phone bidder for $250,000. The Garbisches paid $120,000 for it at the Landsell Christie (no relation to the auction firm) sale at Sotheby Parke Bernet in 1972, and it was then the most expensive piece of American furniture ever sold at auction. The underbidder was Bernard Levy, who had sold it to the Christies in the mid-1960s for $45,000. Levy settled instead for a Philadelphia wing chair, for which he paid $62,500.

Colonel Garbisch bought a bombé chest as a Valentine present for his wife and had it delivered to Pokety with a red bow tied on it. Bernard Levy said the colonel paid him $8,500 for it. With the excitement of the Garbisch sale it went to a collector for $160,000, with Sack and Levy as underbidders.

Collectors took most of the other top lots. A large Philadelphia drop-leaf dining table with ball-and-claw feet went for $31,000, probably

A pair of mahogany side chairs attributed to Eliphalet Chapin, East Windsor, Connecticut, went for what one dealer called a "crazy" $29,000. Two weeks later a similar pair in cherry brought $25,000 at the Garvan sale in New York. Sotheby Parke Bernet photo.

a record for the form. A unique New England tea table with a scalloped top brought $56,000. A Newport tall-case clock sold for $50,000, and a shelf clock made by William Fitz in Portsmouth, New Hampshire, brought $36,000, a record for a shelf clock.

Sotheby's staff didn't disguise their pleasure that their firm now holds the records for a house sale and for a single piece of American furniture. Both previously belonged to their archrival Christie's, which in 1978 sold the contents of Ravenscliff, Charlotte Dorrance Wright's house in Radnor, Pennsylvania, for $1.7 million, and also sold a similar blockfront bureau for $140,000.

"This is part of a chain of events," said William Stahl, Sotheby's Americana specialist, trying to explain the success of the sale. In the last four months, he said, there have been a number of museum exhibitions that have influenced the market, and he mentioned the "In Praise of America" exhibition at the National Gallery and the re-opening of the American Wing at the Metropolitan Museum in New York.

"In this context, the high prices for Americana make sense," Stahl said. John Marion, who said he had been discussing the sale with the Garbisches for seven years before their deaths, felt their presence there all week. "They would have enjoyed all this. I can hear the colonel saying, 'Bernice, see what they paid for that'!"

This small bombé chest of drawers in mahogany with original brasses carried a Ginsburg and Levy provenance. It brought $160,000 from a private collector. Sotheby Parke Bernet photo. (Editor's note: It is now at Winterthur.)

Editor's Note: The four-day sale at the Wetzel farm in Reading, Pennsylvania, in the fall of 1980 followed close on the heels of the Garbisch sale. There were no $100,000 lots, but the sale totaled $3.2 million, and never before had such high prices been paid for naive watercolors by Jacob Maentel or carvings by Wilhelm Schimmel. Spatterware and Gaudy Dutch was appreciated, Pennsylvania German fraktur brought high prices, and American glass was not overlooked.

GOLD IN THE RED HILLS OF PENNSYLVANIA: THE WETZEL SALE

BY LITA SOLIS-COHEN

The $3.2-million house sale held at the Wetzel farm in Reading, Pennsylvania, September 30 through October 4, 1980, was a class act.

From the hum of the computerized billing machine that automatically added on the 10 percent buyer's premium in nanoseconds to the staccato syncopation of the auctioneer's gavel, the performance of Sotheby's was thoroughly professional and showed a keen understanding of how people who have driven out into the country to spend tens of thousands of dollars like to be treated.

As many people commented on the elegance of the spacious portable toilets—with vinyl parquet floors and vacuum flush—as on the excellent quality of the sale items. Then there was the pair of pay phones mounted on the side of the white clapboard shed near the auction tent, the trash cans full of umbrellas for borrowing when the weather suddenly turned wet and the jitney service to and from the parking lot. When it turned cold, some were provided with movers' blankets to use as lap robes.

No wonder the moneyed (and the wish-they-were-moneyed) set is seen less and less at the races and more and more at auctions. Some of those attending the Wetzel sale seemed equipped for either pastime, bringing field glasses to focus on the auction block from the back of the 125'

auction tent that was jammed to overflowing at almost every session.

To some it even felt the same. "The thrill of winning a lot is the same as seeing your horse come in," said a happy purchaser as she hugged the 17th-century portrait of a girl that she'd "won" for $850.

Some collectors complained that the late Helen Janssen Wetzel, the knitting-mill heiress, collected a lot of "stuff," and that nothing reached the pinnacle of quality of some pieces in the Garbisch collection that Sotheby's sold in Maryland just a few months earlier in May for a record $3.9 million.

True enough, no individual items brought more than $100,000, but the Wetzel sale was no ordinary farm sale either. There was enough interest to bring nearly 25,000 people to the presale exhibition and $30,000 worth of catalogs was sold at $15 each or $25 for the two-volume set.

Hundreds of absentee bids were sent in. One bidder called the Philadelphia office from Mexico City and placed $87,000 worth of bids on porcelain and English furniture. Attendance at each of the 11 sessions exceeded 1,000, and nearly 500 signed up for bidding paddles when the American folk art and furniture was sold on Saturday.

Some top-notch prices were paid. A whopping $47,000 was bid for a pair of small naive watercolor portraits of a lady and gentleman painted by the

This pair of circa 1820 portraits by Jacob Maentel, painted in bright colors in the same parlor, sold for $47,000 to a collector. Sotheby Parke Bernet photo.

Pennsylvania artist Jacob Maentel about 1820. The couple posed in their Sunday best, standing in their wallpapered parlor next to their yellow-painted chairs. The price topped the $42,500 paid for a similar pair of portraits sold at Sotheby's in the spring of 1977. Even more astounding to the uninitiated was the $40,000 paid for a 7½" high x 8½" long wooden Nittany lion carved by Wilhelm Schimmel, an itinerant whittler who worked in the Cumberland Valley toward the end of the last century.

Other small carvings by Schimmel fetched big prices. An 8" tall eagle with 13¼" wingspan went for $20,000. A much larger one brought less—$12,000 because some of its paint had been restored. Two Schimmel squirrels, each 7¼" high, sold for $7,000 each, and one squirrel, 4¼" high, sold for $2,600.

Two frakturs brought landmark prices. A Mennonite religious text went for $25,000, and what the catalog called a "labyrinth" fraktur, decorated with peacocks and doves and attributed to Pennsylvania artist G. Seiler, went for $11,000. Before the Wetzel sale, only one fraktur had ever sold for more than $10,000.

To the disappointment of many collectors, most of the furniture had a high-gloss piano finish, popular in the 1940s but detested today. Dealers said there is a way to remove it without ruining the surface, and, in any event, dealers bought the majority of the lots. A fine Philadelphia wing chair with ball-and-claw feet and shell carved knees went to New York dealer Bernard Levy for $38,000. New York dealer Harold Sack bought a similar chair with trifid feet for $37,500.

This watercolor fraktur with religious text catalogued as by M. Gottschall and as Schwenkfelder sold for $25,000. (Editor's note: It was bought by New York collector Ralph Esmerian. See *American Radiance,* pages 256 and 495.) However, the Gottschalls were Mennonites, not Schwenkfelders, though they lived among the Schwenkfelders in Montgomery County about 15 miles from Pennsburg. Martin and Samuel Gottschall, sons of Mennonite bishop Samuel Gottschall, were schoolmasters at the Franconia Mennonite School in Upper Salford Township and were both accomplished fraktur artists. Sotheby Parke Bernet photo.

Chalkware sold well. The two lovebirds over a basket of eggs brought the top chalkware price of $3,500. Other prices were: middle row, rabbit, $950; squirrel, $500; dove bank, $450. Bottom row, dove banks, $350, $425, $425. Sotheby Parke Bernet photo.

Schimmelmania seemed to grip the crowd when carvings by Wilhelm Schimmel of Cumberland County, Pennsylvania, came on the block. Top row from left, the small parrot was the first to fly at $2,600, the distelfink with yellow wings brought $4,750, the lion topped them all at $40,000 to a collector, the two remaining parrots, $2,400 and $2,000. The eagles on the middle row brought $20,000 (left, wingspan 13¾") and $16,000 (19" wingspan). Bottom row, from left, the squirrels brought $2,600 and $7,000 apiece for the next two nearly identical, 7¼" high. The roosters brought $6,000, $4,750, $2,100, $2,100 and $1,900. Sotheby Parke Bernet photo.

Philadelphia walnut wing chair, $38,000 to Bernard Levy. Sotheby Parke Bernet photo.

There was a good bit of competition for two sets of six Philadelphia side chairs with solid splats, made before 1750. One set with Chippendale yoke-shaped crest rails, scalloped skirts, and trifid feet went to New Hope, Pennsylvania, dealers Herbert and Richard Sandor for $16,000. The earlier and rarer but less graceful set, with Queen Anne reverse-arched backs, pointed feet, and flat serpentine stretchers, sold to a California dealer for $38,000.

The California dealer had asked for anonymity but could hardly be missed. Always seated in the front row, he was a major buyer in every session of the sale and ended up renting a van to drive his $250,000 worth of purchases back across the country. They included a Massachusetts blockfront secretary for $30,000, an English tall-case clock by Thomas Tompion and Edward Banger for $21,000,

and a Dutch chest dated 1630 for $19,000, as well as many smaller things.

As in any large sale, there were a number of "sleepers," that is, lots with low estimates that go for a reasonable price to someone with special knowledge. Most, but not all of the bargains came early in the week. For instance, a Chinese porcelain Kangxi period blue and white bowl, 8" in diameter, sold to a collector for $1,350, a fraction of what he might have had to pay for it in a shop. An early 19th-century book on landscape gardening, with 42 color plates and 14 overslips showing before and after designs by Humphrey Repton, the Shakespeare of landscape architects, was a bargain at $1,300. It has sold for much more. At the same time, there were several lots cataloged as reproductions that brought prices way over estimates from bidders battling for them because they were certain the pieces were indeed made in the period.

The most notable in the latter category was a cherrywood tray-top tea table with cabriole legs and pad feet estimated at $2,000/3,000, and cataloged without a date, meaning that the cataloger thought it was made of old parts or had too many repairs to list them. It brought $24,000 from Sack.

What will probably turn out to be the biggest bargain is the large serpentine mahogany side table attributed to Philadelphia cabinetmaker Thomas Affleck that was expected to bring around $50,000 and was sold to York, Pennsylvania, dealer Joseph Kindig for $27,000. It had some problems. Its legs had been extended and it was missing some brackets, but it is an extremely rare and stylish piece. Where would you fine another?

Book collectors were notable by their absence at the sales, but plenty of other collectors with special interests found their way to Reading. Roger Howlett of Childs Gallery, Boston, for instance, flew down to buy European engraved glass and went back with a number of pieces for his personal collection, including a Dutch wine goblet for which he paid $950 and a pair of 18th-century English toasting glasses that cost him $600.

These seem like paltry sums when compared with the prices of American glass. New York dealer J.G. Stradling paid $3,400 for an aquamarine lily pad bowl and $3,600 for a Pittsburgh glass pitcher engraved with an eagle. He said the pitcher would go to the Metropolitan Museum of Art, but the bowl was for his own stock.

A rare silver brazier made by the Boston silversmith John Coney in 1710 brought $20,000, and a silver coffeepot made by Philadelphia silversmith Joseph Richardson sold to New York dealer Eric Shrubsole for $18,000. Edgar Sittig, the 81-year-old dealer from Shawnee-on-Delaware, was at the sale and said he had sold the coffeepot to Mrs. Wetzel for $1,200 in the 1940s.

There was real energy in the tent when the bidding began for spatterware, Gaudy Dutch, and other Anglo-American pottery. Bidding paddles went up everywhere. Three phone lines were busy and one bidder stayed on for 140 lots. A pair of Gaudy Dutch plates sold to a phone bidder from Ohio for $3,000. Their red and blue butterfly pattern, inspired by Japanese Imari designs, had caught the fancy of the Pennsylvania Dutch in the early 19th century and is a favorite with collectors today.

A collector from Connecticut bidding by phone won a yellowware tea service consisting of a teapot, sugar bowl, and four cups and saucers for $3,700. It was considered a good buy. Six 9½" yellow spatterware plates with thistle designs in their centers sold for $3,000. Any yellow china brings a premium.

There was even more competition for Pennsylvania redware. Two 6" flowerpots decorated with birds in relief sold for $5,000 each, and one 9½" tall flowerpot sold for $5,750.

"It is great to sell folk art in Reading," said Sotheby's Nancy Druckman after the sale. "Collectors here know the fine points."

When the household goods were sold on Sunday, bidding battles continued. A wooden hayfork sold for $325, and a bundle of textiles, mostly brocades, went to a phone bidder for $2,800. Wetzel's 1962 fan-tailed Cadillac limousine brought $6,250 from a Reading car dealer.

About 40 years ago Mrs. Wetzel bought four redware flower pots decorated with birds in relief from Mrs. William E. Montague, a dealer in Norristown, Pennsylvania, and probably paid less than $100 for all four. At her estate sale, the four brought a total of $20,500. Two 6" pots sold for $5,000 each, the 9" tall one with a bird pursued by a cat brought $5,750, the other 6" one went for $4,750. Sotheby Parke Bernet photo.

Editor's Note: The sale of samplers collected by Philadelphia businessman Ted Kapnek put schoolgirl needlework on the map. Prices exceeded all expectations. Dealers John Walton, Marguerite Riordan, and Carol and Stephen Huber were major buyers, and many museums and collectors bid for themselves. In the next two decades, as a new research was published, prices soared. In 1983, Betty Ring published **Let Virtue Be a Guide to Thee,** *the catalog of an exhibit of Rhode Island needlework, which was shown in museums in Providence and Houston before going to New York City's Metropolitan Museum of Art. That out-of-print $19.95 paperback catalog has sold for as much as $1,000.*

THE KAPNEK SALE LAUNCHES SCHOOLGIRL STITCHERY ON ITS UPWARD SPIRAL

BY LITA SOLIS-COHEN

Matilda Filbert, a 12-year-old Berks County schoolgirl may have known that she'd done a pretty good job when she finished her embroidered picture in 1830. She stitched a girl wearing an Empire-style white dress offering a tumbler of wine to a spread-winged eagle. It is doubtful, however that she could have imagined that a century and a half later her work would be sold at a Sotheby auction for $38,000.

Filbert's needlework picture of a girl with a painted face was bought by Texas collector Betty Ring for a record price for schoolgirl needlework, $41,800 with buyer's premium. It was the most expensive sampler in the sale of the collection of the late Theodore H. Kapnek, but it was not the only piece of schoolgirl stitchery to fetch a fancy price.

The 172 samplers offered at Sotheby's Madison Avenue salesroom on Saturday, January 31, 1981, brought a total of $641,300, about three times what had been expected. Kapnek, a Philadelphia-area businessman who died the previous September at the age of 75, frequently said that samplers were the most reliable things to collect because most of them were signed and dated.

Four of the five Kapnek samplers that brought $20,000 or more were needlework exercises by Pennsylvania schoolgirls, and five of those that

brought between $10,000 and $20,000 were stitched in New England. Only 43 samplers sold for less than $1,000, and most of them were miniatures. The lowest price was $200 for one measuring 3" x 5" with only an alphabet, no name, place, or date.

The sale demonstrated how the best in a yet another category of folk art has taken a quantum leap in value. Within the last year a Pennsylvania German fraktur has sold for a record $29,000 and a painted wooden lion carved by Wilhelm Schimmel set a new record for folk sculpture when it brought $40,000.

This well-marketed sale of a major collection of needlework predictably pushed prices to new heights, and it will probably bring forth a number of hitherto unknown fine samplers, but there is no guarantee that these high prices will be sustained. It could take another five years of inflation for the market to catch up.

Kapnek was fond of his samplers and referred to them as his "girls." He called Matilda Filbert his "mile-high girl" because the girl in the white dress stands as tall as the pine tree towering over the red brick house. But his sentiments were combined with shrewdness. Kapnek bought Filbert's sampler about six years ago for $2,200 from West Chester, Pennsylvania, dealer Elizabeth Matlack. Then he did everything he could to assure that when the

Matilda Filbert's record-breaking sampler dated 1830 brought $38,000 (plus 10% buyer's premium). It was bought by Texas collector and writer Betty Ring. Sotheby's photo.

time came for his collection to be sold it would be under the best possible circumstances. He not only bought wisely, he invested in research and conservation so that his collection was both well documented and in fine condition.

His conservator, Doris Ashley, cleaned every sampler, backed it with cotton cloth and acid-free board, and sealed it in a dust-free frame. "She brought every piece back to a sound state. She never bleached them to make them look better," said Nancy Druckman, Sotheby's folk art specialist who cataloged the sale and acknowledged the importance of condition to the value of the collection.

Moreover the collection was well known. Kapnek generously shared his collections by inviting friends and strangers to his house, where he often lectured on samplers, and he lent his finest pieces to exhibitions. The collection was also widely published in books, magazines, newspapers, and exhibition catalogs.

"Ted would have been pleased to see the spirited bidding," said Glee Kruger, who wrote *A Gallery of American Samplers*, the book on the Kapnek collection published by Dutton in the fall of 1978 at the time that 112 of the best samplers were exhibited at the Museum of American Folk Art in New York. (Mrs. Kapnek kept a dozen samplers, including the one illustrated on the cover of the book.)

New York collector and scholar Davida Deutsch, who wrote the introduction to Sotheby's sale catalog and gave a lecture on samplers before the sale for the benefit of the Folk Art Museum, thought, "Ted must be up there chortling."

The sale was scheduled as a special event during the weeklong American heritage sale at Sotheby's and during the same week when the New York Winter Antiques Show was drawing dealers and collectors to New York. Over 450 people attended the sale and the salesroom was packed.

Bidding was strong from the start. Nancy Druckman said that when lot 3, a sampler with

Ann E. England of Delaware stitched yellow tulips in 1820 on this well-designed sampler that sold for $9,500. Sotheby's photo.

a figure of a young girl with a paper face and real hair sitting in an Athena-like pose in its central medallion sold for $13,000, she knew auction fever was rampant. That sampler, signed Barbara Baner, Harrisburg, and dated 1812, was bought by Jim and Mary Jane Edmonds of California, who are writing a book about samplers.

A number of new buyers began their collections at the Kapnek sale. A Boston man who confessed that he had never bought a sampler before asked Connecticut dealer John Walton to do his bidding. For $23,000 he got the sampler pictured on the catalog cover depicting Mount Vernon based on a print by William Birch. It is signed by Catherine Schrack of Philadelphia and dated 1815.

For $22,000, a phone bidder bought a Pennsylvania needlework sampler embroidered with a farm scene and signed with the initials KA, FA, TW and dated 1795. A phone bidder outbid Walton to pay the same price for a Philadelphia sampler inscribed "Lucy Low, her sampler, Aged

Barbara Baner's 1812 Harrisburg sampler more than doubled its top estimate of $5,000 and sold for $13,000. Sotheby's photo.

The illustration on the cover of the sale catalog was of this Philadelphia needlework by Catherine Schrack, depicting "MOUNT VERnon, the Seat of the late GENL. G. Washington." It sold for $23,000. Sotheby's photo.

This Balch School sampler from Providence, Rhode Island, is the work of Lydia Gladdings in 1796. It brought $16,000. Sotheby's photo.

This simple Quaker sampler by Ruth James was made at the Westtown School, Chester County, Pennsylvania, and is dated 1800. It sold for $1,300. Sotheby's photo.

12, 1776," showing a man and a woman in a landscape below verses and the alphabet. "I sold that sampler to Ted three years ago for around twelve hundred dollars," said Philadelphia dealer Jim Glazer after the sale. "I had bought it for six hundred fifty dollars from David Pottinger, who had gotten it from Bill Samaha for four hundred fifty dollars."

Samplers never used to bring so much at auction. A sampler in the sale with a wide floral border, signed Anne England, 1820, sold at Robert Skinner's auction in 1977 for $800. After going through a number of hands, it came to New York dealer Cora Ginsburg, who said she sold it to Kapnek for $2,500 three years ago. At the Kapnek sale it fetched $9,500. "I have only four American samplers left and I'm going back to the shop and raising the prices," said Ginsburg after the sale.

Dealers seem willing to pay big prices now. "John Walton offered me thirty-five thousand dollars for a sampler he sold me two years ago for eight thousand," said a young man from New

This needlework and watercolor by Mary B. Gove of Deering, New Hampshire, 1827, brought $9,500 from New England dealer Stephen Score. Sotheby's photo.

Jersey who was sitting next to the Connecticut dealer. "He kept upping his offers as the sale went on."

The catalog and list of prices paid will serve as a guide to values in the years ahead. Dates, design, documentation, the name of the school, color, condition, and where it was made all determine the price.

The value of having a date on a sampler was demonstrated by comparing two samplers from Miss Balch's school in Providence, Rhode Island. One, with figures and a farm scene arranged in two bands, signed "Lydia Gaddings Work Providence October 1796," brought $16,000. Another, slightly duller in color, having three bands of figures and scenes, and signed "Mary Hammons Work Providence April," without the year, sold for $8,250.

Knowing the name of the maker and the year in which the item was made somehow makes the link to the past more secure and satisfying for collectors. If Rebecca Smith could have come back for the sale, she might have wondered why her sampler, made in the same school as Matilda Filbert's only a year later, brought $9,500, only a quarter of what her schoolmate's did.

Filbert's work is undoubtedly more charming and brightly colored than Smith's, but, according to Druckman, the fact that we know so much more about Matilda Filbert from various records was also a factor in the price. "We know her grandfather came to Philadelphia in 1710 and settled in Berks County, that her father married Anna Maria Myers and moved to Womelsdorf, that she was baptized December 26th, 1818, confirmed in 1834, and married Augustus Leiss of Tulpehocken and had three daughters," Druckman said.

No one seemed to be seeking their own ancestor's needlework, but several collectors wanted those from their own hometowns. Harry Hartman, a dealer in Marietta, Pennsylvania, got Hester Cassel's sampler that was wrought "in Marietta" and dated 1828, for $1,700 (it had some stains). The only South Carolina sampler in the collection sold for $5,500 and is returning to that state and will become part of the Liberty Corporation collection of textiles in Greenville. Druckman said it has bands of alphabets, numbers, a pious verse, and is signed by a nine-year-old: "Elizabeth Hext is My Name, Carolina is My Nation, Charles Town is my Dwelling Place and Christ is my Saviour." Part of the charm of the sampler was that the little girl apparently used the word "Saviour" because she hadn't left enough space for the rhyming word "Salvation."

Editor's Note: New Hampshire auctioneer Richard Withington's sales were pure entertainment. Withington would pitch a tent wherever there was a stash of good antiques to sell. The Sterling sale was one of his best.

THE SALE IN BETTY STERLING'S FARMYARD

BY LITA SOLIS-COHEN

"Everybody raise your hand.

"OK. Now open your pocketbooks. Just wanted to know if you could do it," quipped master auctioneer Dick Withington as a crowd of about 300 bidders settled themselves in and outside the tent set up next to the asparagus patch at Brainstorm Farm in the hills near Randolph, Vermont. It was the start of the sale of over 900 lots from the collection and shop of Betty and Edward Sterling, held August 27 and 27, 1981. The Sterlings

had been in the antiques business since the summer of 1966. That October, Ed Sterling received critical injuries in a motor vehicle accident in Randolph that left him almost totally paralyzed.

"During the first few years when he couldn't even swallow, Ed's interest in the antiques business and visits from dealers and collectors kept us going," remembered Betty Sterling, before the sale. "Ed is very comfortable in our house in Hawaii now, and when I asked him if he wanted to come

Top rug price was $4,200 to Stephen Score for a yarn-sewn rug. After the sale, he learned it was ex-Mary Allis.

The "auctioneer's library," an English bookcase with fake books carved in the doors, $4,400 to a dealer.

to Vermont this summer, he said no. So, we decided to sell the farm and we had to sell the contents while the weather is good," she explained.

It was July when Richard Withington contracted the sale. The brochure read "Sale by order of Mr. Edward C. Sterling." That was because Sterling's five children had insisted that the business their father had financed be liquidated after a court-ordered accounting revealed that the business was not very active and the money tied up in real estate and antiques could be invested more profitably. (The farm is on the market for approximately $250,000.)

Withington photographed some of the furniture, paintings, iron, and rugs for a brochure, and placed ads in the *Maine Antique Digest* and *The Newtown Bee*, which drew a good crowd. There was no time for a catalog, but that didn't matter to Withington, who only prints catalogs for doll sales. He is something of a maverick. He will not accept absentee bids or reserves. Nor does he charge a buyer's premium, which he denounces as "trickery." He says what you see is what you get, and accepts no returns. He announced he's been auctioning for 32 years and this was his 1,720th sale. He keeps his audience's attention because, without a catalog, they never know what's coming next. He squeezes out every last bid with one-liners, which keeps those who haven't heard them before in stitches.

"I have a thousand and a half, eleven hundred and a half, and a half, sold. That's the way to get rid of old stale bread," he cracked, as he knocked down the first lot, an iron toaster with a man's head forged into its handle, for $1,100 to Massachusetts dealer Stephen Score.

"Bid before you think," he continued, as he quickly knocked down a watercolor profile portrait of a woman wearing an apron, by the left-handed New Hampshire painter, Joseph H. Davis, for $2,650. "You know, you were the only one bidding," he teased, as he handed it to the buyer, Gail Savage, who had sold the picture to Betty Sterling some years ago.

Trolley applique quilt, $1,450.

Before the sale, Betty Sterling and Dan Hingston, who is Withington's right-hand man, had gone through the collection and put little stickers on each piece indicating the provenance. Most of the pieces bore dealer's names. "If their names are on it, they can't knock it, but I did see a bit of tag switching," joked Hingston at the preview, which was from 8 AM to 10 AM the day of the sale.

"The more you pay for it, the more you love it," cajoled Withington as he sold a child's highchair for $2,200. "Everybody jumps in and out like a cold shower," he remarked, as half-a-dozen people bid on a settle table with old blue paint and took it up to $3,700. "One more bid and you'll beat the pool," he pleaded, but he had to knock the New England highboy down to a group of dealers standing at the back of the tent for $7,500. (They knocked it out right away for $8,500 and it had left the premises by 11 AM.)

"Here's a picture of some old dried up fruit," continued Withington with a grin, looking over an unusually bright orange and yellow theorem painting that had a Leonard Balish sticker on it. It sold for $1,150 to Steven Score.

Portrait of two children "attributed to Chandler," probably Joseph Goodhue Chandler (1813-1884), $5,600.

"Who sneezed?" asked Withington as the rain began to fall. "That's the way it starts, a little sneeze, then a sniffle, and the next thing you know the tent is in your backyard." ("That's one of his oldest jokes," commented a seasoned Withington watcher, used to his grisly humor.)

The bidding remained pretty healthy. A set of six chicken-coop Windsor chairs (maybe they are called birdcage Windsors in New England) sold for $950 each, for a total of $5,700, to a Mr. Gerdau, seated on the first chair in the first row. Dressed in a green linen blazer and a Panama hat, he sipped "apricot juice" from a thermos, consumed a picnic from a fancy hamper, and bid on anything that struck his fancy. He said he was bidding for the lady next to him, Ina L. Coleman, whose shop on Route 7 in Ridgefield, Connecticut, is called the Tontine Emporium.

Among the other high prices, a formal two-drawer stand with reeded legs and satinwood and mahogany inlay sold for a strong $3,200; a painted chest without hardware with three drawers over five, made $4,400; and a maple turned stretcher-base tavern table sold for $3,100.

A Hudson River Valley kas was a buy at $4,700 to a private collector, and so was a blunt-arrow Pennsylvania Windsor with late grained paint at $2,500 (it went to the pool of dealers). A nice country corner chair with pierced splats sold for $1,350. The Pennsylvania comb-back Windsor, however, brought only $3,200 because not everyone thought it was right. If there were more believers, it might have gone for $10,000. A straight-legged wing chair, upholstered in brown velvet, was a gift at $950.

Dealer Steve Miller bought the most expensive painting, a small head of a young girl by the naive painter John S. Blunt (1798–1835), for $6,200. It had been shown at the Museum of American Folk Art in 1977. Some of the other paintings brought disappointing prices. A larger portrait of two children with a tag that read "attributed to Chandler" sold for $5,600. It was probably by J.G. Chandler (1813–1884). A portrait of a bony middle-aged man attributed to the black artist Joshua Johnston, who worked in Baltimore 1796–1824, sold for only $1,150.

There were plenty of good prices for decorations. A delicate whalebone and baleen basket sold for $1,900, and the same price was paid for an eagle weathervane. Another fine weathervane in the form of a sailing ship, signed by its maker, Cushing & White, and dated 1869, went to collector Bernard Barenholtz for $3,500. Barenholtz also got a folk carving showing "witches" in a pillory for $2,800.

One collector really wanted a large gray-and-white-painted wooden bird (possibly an eagle) carved by a contemporary Ohio man, and he held his hand up high until he bought it for $3,450. Another bird by the same carver, similar in body form but with awkward wings and painted black and white (Withington said he was going formal), sold the following day for $350. A dealer standing on the sidelines said he sold one by the same carver for $150, a few weeks ago. No one would identify the carver nor reveal the name of the Ohio dealer who markets the carver's work.

Quilts and rugs brought active bidding. Steven Score paid $4,200 for an early yarn-sewn rug with a strong design of flowers in a vase and with sheep grazing along its border, and the firm of Stephen/Douglas of North Bennington, Vermont, paid $3,200 for another small rug with large fuschia blossoms on it.

Of all the quilts, and there must have been 30 of them, a large chintz appliquéd one with fine quilting brought competition from a dozen bidders. It finally went to Brooklyn dealer Sam Herrup for $1,400. He also got a smaller quilt appliquéd with chintz birds for $1,550. A couple from Lakeville, Connecticut, went home with seven quilts, including an apple green and tan appliquéd one with a design of four groups of flowers, for which they paid $1,525, and a green and red quilt with a repeat design of hills and cherry trees for $925.

"They don't work that hard at Sotheby's," boasted Withington as he took an 8' sawbuck table up in $100 increments from $500 to $2,900. It sold

Two scherenschnitte (cut paper work): the black paper version with trees brought $1,925, while the "J.Q. Adams' Family Record" (facing page) brought $325.

to Stephen Score, who resold it to the underbidder right after the sale.

"Here's a chest for someone with a little hope," cracked Withington, as he offered a small red-painted chest and sold it quickly for $450. "And, here's a poor but honest chest. Look at the unusual pulls," he said, as he tugged on the wire pulls of a two-drawer tall blanket chest. "Turn it around," he said to the boys who had placed it on the green felt display stand. "Something they don't do at Sotheby's," he said, as he showed off its back and continued to take bids in $50 increments until he knocked it down to Ashford, Connecticut, dealer Dominic Tailleux for $1,450.

"I want to smell your thermos bottle," said Withington to Gerdau as he handed him a heart-shaped milking stool that Gerdau had bid to $200. "Here's a milking stool for a long-legged cow," he quipped, as he offered a three-legged brown-painted weaver's stool and sold it for $275.

"I've called over 1,700 auctions and never seen one like it," Withington swore, as he examined an English Gothic Revival secretary with sham books carved and painted in the bookcase. "It's an auctioneer's reference library," quipped someone in the crowd, daring to play Jack Benny to Withington's Bob Hope.

Withington's 1,720th sale brought in around $400,000, of which $284,000 was accounted for the first day. Withington doesn't give out post-sale figures. "That's the consignor's business," he insisted.

Editor's Note: The Roger Bacon Sale gives a glimpse of the New England trade at the end of M.A.D.'s first decade and introduces Robert Skinner's new auction gallery in Bolton, Massachusetts. Roger Bacon was a legendary tastemaker and patient teacher. A generation of collectors, museum curators, dealers, and pickers beat a path to the door of his early 18th-century house, a former tavern, hidden behind a thicket in Exeter, New Hampshire.

A FITTING MEMORIAL: THE ROGER BACON SALE

BY LITA SOLIS-COHEN AND SAMUEL PENNINGTON

Roger Bacon collected with a passionate eye. He bought what he loved. "Isn't that the goddamnedest thing you ever saw? Isn't it wonderful?" he would say, with a sweeping gesture towards a Pilgrim Century chair, or a turned salt dish, or a small looking glass with a circular sunburst crest.

Thirty and 40 years ago, Roger Bacon bought wooden plates when others were buying pressed glass. He acquired straight, turned, slat-back, and spindle-back chairs while others snapped up cabriole-legged furniture, and he bought painted or scrubbed pine while others purchased polished mahogany or refinished their pine. He liked early, useful things that showed wear—baskets, boxes, old clothes, handmade toys.

Bacon was a farm lad from Gorham, Maine, who went to New York and became a Shakespearean actor in the 1920s. He will be remembered not for his brilliant Rosencrantz played opposite his twin brother Reggie's Guildenstern or as Lewisohn in the World War I drama *What Price Glory* but as a Yankee storyteller who played to small audiences in the keeping room of his old house at a crossroads near Exeter, New Hampshire. There, as an antiques dealer, he extolled the wonders of early New England artifacts.

For 30 years, Roger and his wife, Ruth, taught a generation of collectors, museum curators, and college professors to see the strong forms and rich surfaces of early New England furniture. He also taught them the art of assemblage—how to arrange a lot of things artfully in a little space, how to hang an old red plaid cape on a green-painted cupboard, and put a pair of cruddy old boots by the door. How to put an Oriental carpet on the floor under the table and a rug fragment on top of the table,

Roger Bacon in his favorite chair. This file photograph ran with a profile on Bacon by Elaine Ulman that appeared in *M.A.D.* in March 1979.

"This was the most revered lot in Roger's house," said auctioneer Bob Skinner. "I can't tell you how many times I've thought of killing for that little mirror in the bedroom." Others agreed. At the $5,000 bid level, there were still five hands up. New York dealer David Schorsch bought it for a client for $7,700.

how to build small towers of miniature wallpaper boxes next to towers of painted wooden oval boxes, how to hang painted baskets from the rafters, and brighten cupboards with collections of toys or pottery, especially English yellow-glaze slipware called combware.

Roger Bacon didn't mind if a plate was cracked, a chair repaired, a table had lost a leaf, or a basket repainted. If he saw the piece as a "great form," or if the surface had color, he bought it. Once, when New Hampshire auctioneer Richard Withington knocked down a colorful but moth-eaten hearth rug to Roger, he said to the crowd in the tent, "You just see the holes. Roger sees what is there."

A steady stream of dealers brought things to Roger, hoping it was something he would buy. He often paid high prices because he wanted them to come back with more. He paid huge prices at auction too, setting in motion the booming Americana market that began in the 1960s.

At a sale in New Hampshire two years ago, Bacon paid $4,000 for a small looking glass that had a small piece missing from its crest. It sold for $2,300 (with buyer's premium) at his estate sale at Robert Skinner's auction in Bolton, Massachusetts. He paid $7,000 for a black-painted ladder-back armchair that sold for $1,750, and the group of four primitive portraits of a family—mother, father, and twin boys—in need of restoration, for which he paid $17,000 at an auction in Maine in 1977, sold on a single bid at Skinner's for $5,200.

Bacon was 77 when he died of cancer in February 1982. His widow, Ruth, his son, and his two daughters sent Roger's collections and what remained of his stock to Robert W. Skinner to be sold in an unreserved, unestimated sale. Skinner sold almost 1,400 catalogs listing more than 1,100 lots for the three-session sale September 23 and 24, 1982. That was nearly four times the number of catalogs Skinner generally sells for a various-owners sale. Everyone who knew Roger wanted a souvenir.

The sale was not full of furniture masterpieces. In fact, too much of the furniture had been restored. It was mainly a sale of little things for huge prices that brought the total to $693,700 plus 10 percent buyer's premium. Prices ranged from $30 for an iron trammel to $14,000 for a black-painted armchair with two mismatched slats and a turned top rail that Ruth had given to Roger as a birthday present several years ago. Only two other pieces brought $10,000 or more. A collector paid $11,000 for a handkerchief table on a triangular base with one drop-leaf, and a Massachusetts collector paid $10,500 for a splayed-leg table painted black with a scrubbed top.

At Withington's sale for Marie Robbins of Wolfeboro, New Hampshire, about four years ago, Bacon paid $350 for this 2¼" high turned wood open salt painted a delicate blue-green. "I laughed then," said the underbidder at that auction, Connecticut dealer Ron Dionne, "but I'm not laughing now," he said as it sold this time for $1182.50. The buyer this time was Maine auctioneer George Morrill, who said he "needed that color" for a collection of small objects he has. "Besides, I often drop that much in a poker game. This is something I want."

Two dealers battled over a 10" x 4" looking glass with a round sunburst crest, until it sold for $7,000! George Morrill, the Maine auctioneer, had to have a tiny 4" high wooden footed salt dish painted blue-green, and he paid a staggering $1,075 for it. Roger had bought it for $350 four years ago at the sale of Marie Robbins' shop in Wolfeboro, New Hampshire. It had an old $7 price tag on it then.

A miniature towel rack with a linen napkin sold to a phone bidder for $1,200. A stuffed cloth toy pig brought $300, a hanging hourglass brought $975, a pine scouring box containing two handmade birch brushes sold for $800, a plaid cape brought $600, a lot consisting of approximately 18 tallow candles, 12 of them whole, sold to a Boston collector for $575, and four tallow candles and a wooden candle dipper went for $1,050.

It seemed that everyone wanted one of Roger's baskets, which had never been for sale, and they brought extraordinary prices. A large two-pocket wall basket painted black with a red stripe on each pocket sold for $3,200, a large melon-shaped basket painted red fetched $900, and the same price was paid for a double egg basket painted orange. A miniature polychrome splint basket sold for $750.

Bacon's collection of English combware and slip-decorated pottery provoked the most heated competition. There were 116 pieces in all that brought a total of $136,000. Connecticut dealer

Some time after Clair Franklin Luther published *The Hadley Chest* in 1935, this chest, plate 85, received a coat of flat paint, which served to put off several buyers. It went for $9,350 to a collector who said his initial was "S" and whose forebears came from Northampton, Massachusetts, the region where Hadley chests were made.

At the July 4, 1977, auction in Maine, Robert Foster had put up this set of four portraits as an unadvertised first lot because he had just bought them the night before in a garage in Waterville for $10,000. They brought $17,000 from Bacon bidding against Robert Avery Smith of New York. All were inscribed on the reverse "March, 1839, Painted by T. Wilder of Walpole, N.H.". At Skinner's they sold for $5,720 to someone who left a bid with the auctioneer.

At the July 1966 Oliver E. Williams sale held by Richard Withington in Rockport, Massachusetts, Bacon paid $600 for this late 18th-century T-base candlestand. Also attending the sale, dressed in his "resident whites" and with very little money, was a young doctor, Ed Jackson of Lynnfield. Now in private practice and a part-time dealer, he bought the candlestand this time for $1,980.

John Walton, always one of Roger's chief rivals at auction, bought most of it, spending over $100,000. He said he was bidding on behalf of some clients, but that he would keep some of it for himself.

Walton paid $6,200 for a combware charger, a large plate decorated with yellow slip that had been striped with a comb-like instrument, allowing a dark brown glaze to show through. He paid $4,250 for a plate covered with yellow slip, decorated with a trailed thistle design in brown, $4,100 for a pitcher with a similar yellow glaze decorated with brown dots, and $4,000 for a two-handled pot covered with yellow slip and a band of brown grapes.

Bacon called his dark brown pottery decorated with trailed designs in yellow slip "reverse combware," a misnomer. Whatever he called it, it brought record prices, selling for as much as $1,250 and $1,500 for round plates to $2,100 and $2,300 for oblong platters.

From her seat in the second row, octogenarian dealer Lillian Cogan, another of Bacon's chief competitors for early pieces, bid aggressively. Among her purchases were a Carver-style oak and ash spindle-back side chair for $4,400, a red-painted hanging cupboard with slatted doors for $4,200, a pine cupboard painted blue-green for $6,500, and a hanging two-armed iron candleholder for $1,050. She lost out on a Carver-style armchair that went to a collector for $7,000, and she didn't get the standing wrought-iron candlestand with an adjustable two-socket candle arm and two snuffer hooks. It went to Walton for $6,500. She did get a wooden herb drying or blanket crane for $1,900, outbidding a determined collector for it.

There were some good buys, as there are at any sale. A collector got a carved Hadley chest with modern paint on it for $8,500, and a William and Mary chest of drawers with bun feet and painted red was knocked down for $3,600 and then resold for $5,000 in a dealers' pool, and there was still room in it for a profit. An early brush-footed caned-back armchair sold for $1,200.

Birch hearth brooms were one of Bacon's real loves. These two brought $176 and $148.50.

Bacon had bought this slat-back armchair with its mushroom handholds for $7,000 about four years ago at a Robert Webber auction in Hampton, New Hampshire. That sale was for the estate of descendants of the Reverend Stephen Bachiler, who had led 60 families to Hampton and founded what was probably New Hampshire's first town in 1638. This time, New Hampshire dealer Peter Eaton bought the chair for only $1,925.

"Dealers are sad that they can't buy this stuff to sell to Roger because he's gone," said Mary Lou Kilcup, a New Hampshire dealer, attempting to explain the broad range of prices.

"The monetary levels are not important. It is the response, the outpouring of love for Roger that matters, and that Ruth and the children were here to witness it," said a pleased Robert Skinner after the sale. Collectors who had bought from the Bacons had come from all parts of the country to take home a piece or two from the sale that turned out to be a fitting memorial for Roger Bacon. He would have loved it.

Like the Old Days
by Samuel Pennington

A week before the sale, a woman from Texas called me and said she was coming East for another reason and desperately wanted to attend the Roger Bacon sale but thought it would be no use. "Won't the prices be so high and won't the pool take everything?" she asked.

I assured her the prices would, indeed, probably be high but that there would likely not be a dealers' pool. There's nothing dealers can make enough money on to justify pooling, and it's hard to pool with an auction hall full of collectors and dealers with commissions from collectors who

couldn't make it to the sale, I said. I was wrong, but only a chest of drawers and a few other items were pooled. Pooling wasn't a significant part of the auction. The woman from Texas had seven lots when I last saw her.

Other collectors came from Cleveland, from California, from Baltimore, and all over the country, and while many wanted top lots, others just came for one memento. Dealer Pam Boynton said five customers asked her "just to get something. You know," she added, "there's only about twelve hundred lots there, someone's going to be disappointed."

If there was not one staggeringly great or expensive lot, you have to remember that Roger Bacon was a dealer. "Put a year's worth of the great things he sold into one auction hall and then you'd see some headlines," said one dealer. What was at the auction was what he kept for one reason or another, the many small things he so artfully arranged, and the things he kept around him and would not sell.

The sale turned out to be a fine memorial to Bacon, but more than that, it was a shot in the arm to a business he loved so well. "This is the first sale up in the country where there has been some real excitement," said one dealer. Freed from estimates and reserves, it was almost like the old days. Only the 10 percent buyer's premium was there to remind you this was 1982.

Tales of Hofmann

Editor's Note: When it was discovered, the postcard-sized Oath of A Freeman was hailed as the earliest American printed document and said to be worth more than $1 million. Even though it passed several scientific tests and fooled several well-known experts, it turned out to be the work of master forger Mark Hofmann, known as the Utah Bomber after he murdered two Mormons while trying to cover up his crimes. Hofmann is considered one the greatest forgers of historical and literary letters and documents, many relating to the Mormon Church. Over more than a decade, the tales of Hofmann unfolded on the pages of M.A.D. and sent shudders through the autograph and manuscript trade. They inspired a book, The Poet and the Murderer *(Dutton, 2002) by Simon Worrall, which drew in part from long, much-acclaimed stories by contributing editor David Hewett, who went to Utah and covered Hofmann's trial. A decade after Hoffman told an investigator that he forged almost everything he sold, Sotheby's cataloged an Emily Dickinson poem, a Daniel Boone letter, and an award of merit signed by Nathan Hale, all three possibly the work of Mark Hofmann. Here is a collection of eight articles that ran in the pages of M.A.D. as Mark Hofmann's story unfolded.*

THE ULTIMATE EPHEMERA JUNE 1985

BY SAMUEL PENNINGTON

There is a story making the rounds in the rare book trade that the earliest American printed document has been found and is now at the Library of Congress being tested for authenticity.

The Oath of a Freeman, a postcard-sized document, was reportedly bought by a collector from a bookseller as a nice piece of ephemera. It is the oath that had to be taken by educated and landed freemen, who had the right to vote in Massachusetts in the 17th century, and is known from a mention in a 1647 book as the first piece of printing done in America. Its text is given, and that text differs from the English oaths, which is what made its owner believe that he might have something valuable.

The freeman's oath came off the press of Stephen Daye in Cambridge in 1639, a year after he sailed from London with a printing press and a two-year contract for printing from the Rev. Jesse Glover, who sailed along with him.

Daye also printed an almanac, of which no copies are known, and he printed the first book in America, the 1640 Bay Psalm Book. Twelve copies of it are known.

Raymond Wapner, who, with Justin Schiller, runs Schiller-Wapner Galleries in New York, specialists in rare children's books and illustrations, confirmed that his firm was the agent for the owner of a possible copy of the freeman's oath, but he said that it was "far from confirmation and any such claims are premature. It is being examined chemically at the Library of Congress, and if those tests turn out right, it will then be up to the scholars to authenticate it," he said in a telephone interview.

Wapner explained that among the possibilities were that the oath was printed in England. "If it were, it wouldn't be worth as much as $2,000," he said. He went on to explain that the fonts for both the oath and the Bay Psalm Book were known in England, but that it had been proved that the psalm book had been printed in America.

According to other sources, the copy of the oath now at the Library of Congress for tests, as a part of the contract work the library does for trade, is on paper without watermarks that is similar to that used in the psalm book.

Others besides Wapner exhibit healthy skepticism that the oath is a Cambridge imprint. Vermont rare book dealer Kenneth Leach said that probably only about 50 copies of the oath were printed. "If used, the copies would have been signed by the clerk of court and the logical place for an unused copy would be the archives of the state of Massachusetts, but they don't have one," said Leach.

"I'd want to see it pasted into the endpapers of a seventeenth-century book or really stuck into an early book, or at least found with something else of the period," he said.

A European reportedly found the oath in a large folio of ephemera in an American bookseller's shop.

What is the value of the oath if it can be proved that Daye printed it? The book trade seems to accept $1 million as the likely asking price. H. Ross Perot (founder of Control Data, purchaser of a copy of the Magna Carta, and more recently the man who offered to pay $70 million to move the Museum of the American Indian to Texas) and Malcolm Forbes are likely contenders for the document should it come to auction.

One appraiser we talked to said $100,000 would be more like it. "After all, it is only a printed legal form," he said.

Dealer Ken Leach, however, said if it were his, "two million would be more like it. I could get one-and-a-half-million dollars for the Bay Psalm Book, and there are twelve of them around."

Wapner and Schiller are not counting their money yet. Wapner said, "The thought is exciting, but it's like finding a lottery ticket and wondering if it's the right one."

If the oath is proved authentic—and the first tests have already proved positive, Schiller said that the owner will probably offer it first to the Library of Congress. He said, "If it is placed, there may be an announcement as early as this week."

SCOUT OR SCOUNDREL? DECEMBER 1985

BY LITA SOLIS-COHEN AND SAMUEL PENNINGTON

When a long-sought rarity turns up on the market, there are bound to be questions about its authenticity. When it turns out that the owner is a suspect in three bombings, it's hard to believe it's right.

That's the fate of the "freeman's oath," a possible example of the first piece of American printing that has been on consignment to the Schiller-Wapner Galleries in New York since last spring when Schiller-Wapner offered it to the Library of Congress for more than $1 million.

Last month, it was learned that the owner was Mark Hofmann, a 31-year-old Salt Lake City manuscript dealer, a suspect in the bombings that killed an elder of the Mormon Church and the wife of another. Hofmann had a finger blown off and suffered a knee injury when a bomb went off in his own car.

The story of Hofmann's discovery of the freeman's oath and Schiller-Wapner's attempts at having it authenticated is intriguing and sheds light on the wishful thinking and scientific testing in the field of historical manuscripts and rare books.

It appears that Hofmann, a scout with a nose for rare manuscripts, was in New York in March

THE OATH OF A FREEMAN.

I ·AB· being (by Gods providence) an Inhabitant, and Freeman, within the iurisdictiō of this Common-wealth, doe freely acknowledge my selfe to bee subject to the governement thereof; and therefore doe heere sweare, by the great & dreadfull name of the Everliving-God, that I will be true & faithfull to the same, & will accordingly yield assistance & support therunto, with my person & estate, as in equity I am bound: and will also truely indeavour to maintaine and preserve all the libertyes & privilidges thereof; submitting my selfe to the wholesome lawes, & ordres made & stablished by the same; and further, that I will not plot, nor practice any evill against it, nor consent to any that shall soe do, butt will timely discover, & reveall the same to lawefull authoritee nowe here stablished, for the speedie preventing thereof. Moreover, I doe solemnly binde my selfe, in the sight of God, that when I shalbe called, to give my voyce touching any such matter of this state, (in which freemen are to deale) I will give my vote & suffrage as I shall judge in myne owne conscience may best conduce & tend to the publick weale of the body, without respect of personnes, or favour of any man. Soe help mee God in the Lord Iesus Christ.

A slightly enlarged copy of the Oath of a Freeman on consignment at Schiller-Wapner Galleries, New York. Is this the long-sought example of the first printing done in America? Critics will be debating for sometime. A Portland, Maine, collector of early type said he was bothered by the evenness of the ink and the diacritical mark above the "o" of the word "iurisdictuio" (jurisdiction) in the second line. "That mark means a letter was left out, but it's a mark generally used on Latin texts, and it's fifty years out of period." Neither the Library of Congress nor the American Antiquarian Society, however, has found anything to worry about. Photo copyright 1985 by Justin G. Schiller Ltd.

1985 and picked up a Sotheby's catalog for a March 27 sale of American books and autographs from the Sang collection. Reading the catalog on the plane back to Utah, he noticed that lot 32 was a copy of a pamphlet, *New-England's Jonas Cast Up at London*, by Major John Child, printed in London in 1647. It illustrates the conflict over the civil and religious rites between the Puritan authorities and settlers not of the congregational fold.

The catalog noted that it also "provides the earliest reprint of 'The Freeman's Oath,' the first issue from Stephen Daye's Cambridge press, of which no copy of the original printing survives."

Hofmann reportedly got to thinking that a postcard-size broadside he had bought at the Argosy bookshop in New York for $25 during an earlier trip East was indeed the only copy of the Freeman's Oath. The "Oath of a Freeman," according to James Gilreath, American history specialist at the Library of Congress, was required of all new members of the Massachusetts Bay Company and it is considered the foundation of our country's understanding of the rights and responsibilities of citizenship.

On his next trip to New York, Hofmann took his find to Justin Schiller and Raymond Wapner, who looked it over and were sufficiently impressed to compare it with the Bay Psalm Book (which came off Stephen Daye's Cambridge press in 1640). They took it to the Boston Public Library, which has one of the 11 known copies of the Bay Psalm Book, the first book printed in English America, a book of the psalms translated in meter by Richard Mather, John Eliot, and Thomas Wilde in order to adapt them for singing during worship.

The Bay Psalm Book was, in fact, the third piece of printing from the Cambridge press. We know from Governor John Winthrop's diary entry in 1647 that "The Oath of a Freeman" was the first thing printed by Stephen Daye in Cambridge, Massachusetts, in 1638 or 1639, and that after publishing the oath, Daye printed an almanac, of which no copy survives. The following year, he published The Bay Psalm Book.

The comparison of the oath with the psalm book showed that printers' ornaments found in the psalm book also appeared around the border of the freeman's oath, and the type and paper were the same. "The chain line on some of the [psalm book] pages matched beautifully to the chain line on the oath," Wapner said.

Schiller and Wapner then agreed to market the oath for Hofmann, a commission was agreed upon, and they sent it down to the Library of Congress, a likely customer. The Library of Congress submitted it to tests. The ink, the paper, and the text passed initial scrutiny. "We would have liked to have done more tests, but questions of title, provenance, and price made us decide to return it," said Gilreath in an interview at the Library of Congress last August.

By then, the oath had been sent to the American Antiquarian Society in Worcester, Massachusetts, another likely purchaser. The American Antiquarian Society found nothing inconsistent with a mid-17th-century attribution. "It appears to have been printed in the U.S. in the mid-seventeenth century, but it is impossible to give it a precise date," said Marcus McCorison, director of that institution. He said that although he could find nothing wrong with it, he wanted further testing done. "Of course, we made those judgments before we knew of Hofmann's troubles," he added. "We first thought it was too good to be true, and then came around to maybe it is true."

According to Wapner, although they have had firm offers from both institutions and private individuals below the acceptable price, "it will have to undergo further tests, but we would like the possible purchaser to underwrite the tests."

It will be hard to convince a number of skeptics of its authenticity. They are surprised at its small size (4" x 6"), have questioned the use of a fancy border instead of a ruled one, and some had expected a horizontal format instead of a vertical one, and a place for a signature.

"How do we know it was printed before 1640?" asked Chicago map dealer Kenneth Nebanzahl. "Did Daye print up a bunch of them in 1639, or did he print them as needed? The same text was used up through 1647."

Others dismissed it as a modern forgery. "I just didn't believe it when I saw it last spring," said Westchester, New York, businessman Michael Zinman, who collects 17th-century printed Americana. (Zinman purchased the *New-England's Jonas* at Sotheby's in March 1985 for $1,650.)

"Hofmann has come up with too many remarkable documents in disparate areas," said Zinman, referring to the fact that Hofmann had recently sold the controversial "white-salamander letter" to the Mormon church, and was involved with the purchase of the McKellin collection, which purports to contain some lost papyrus and other documents relating to the early Mormon church, said to be worth millions.

"Even if you want to believe, how can you? You just don't find three Holy Grails in one year," contends Zinman, who added that even though there is very strong evidence in favor of authenticity, "it doesn't smell right."

Charles Hamilton, the outspoken New York autograph dealer, vouched for Hofmann's abilities. He said he had "authenticated the signature of a Joseph Smith letter for Hofmann. "About three years ago, he brought me a letter signed Joseph Smith, which he said he had bought from a philatelist for $15. "I said, 'upstate New York was literally alive with Joseph Smiths and the chances of yours being signed by the Mormon prophet are literally nil.'

"But he got the letter out. It was very early, 1827, and after two or three minutes, I said to him, 'I can absolutely warrant it as by Joseph Smith.' The letter was genuine beyond any question. He asked me what it was worth, and I said because of its unusual content, ten or fifteen thousand. 'But I think for incendiary purposes, the Mormon Church might want to buy it, and they would pay more.'

"The letter was about Smith wanting to buy a divining rod. He said he knew a place where treasure was buried and he wanted to go into the treasure hunting business and see if he couldn't find some gold and jewels. Now this revealed Smith in a very unusual light—it revealed his commercial side.

"Mark later told me," continued Hamilton, "that he took this letter to some Mormon elder and sold it to him for $25,000, and the guy salted the letter away. I didn't want a copy. I told Mark this is something the buyer should have an exclusive on."

Hamilton went on to say he was skeptical about the freeman's oath, and he detailed how he would go about printing one so it would pass muster under critical eyes. "First, I'd get a text, possibly from a similar document issued elsewhere. I'd get this from some book on early Massachusetts or about Stephen Daye.

"Next, I'd get some paper. This, I'd steal from a library after getting permission to use the rare book room. Preferably the paper should be the fly-leaf or any blank leaf from a book printed by Daye.

"Then, I'd get a copy of a facsimile edition of the Bay Psalm Book—very easy to get as they are worth only five or ten dollars each. I would cut the letters out, paste them together in order to make the text, and then I would add an ornamental border. This is not hard to do, and the very slight irregularity of the pasted-together letters would perfectly simulate the early type composition.

"I would photograph this, in reverse, then I'd have a slightly embossed text of the reverse made up. I would print the freeman's oath on the Stephen Daye paper so that the raised letters would slightly impinge on the verso and give the impression that the actual type was used on an early press.

"This entire job could be done in less than a week. I'd print several so that I could later produce a 'damaged' one that I could sell at a lower price.

"I'd then take the forgery to a few experts on early printing, with a really good solid story about the provenance, or where it came from, and I'd use the old method used by crooked art dealers: 'if you find this to be genuine, I'd like to pay you $10,000 for your authentication. If you find it not to be genuine, I think $100 should cover your costs, don't you?"

But others do not make light of this important discovery and believe the oath may be genuine. "It shouldn't be dismissed as a forgery. You can prove things in this field. You shouldn't speculate about things that can be proven, you should prove them," said Kenneth Rendell, the Newton, Massachusetts, autograph dealer who examined the white salamander letter for the late Steven

Christensen and could find no indication it was a forgery. Christensen bought the letter from Hofmann for $40,000 and later donated or sold it to the Mormon Church.

"Hofmann has been around for years searching for Mormon material, and there is nothing suspicious about Hofmann coming up with Mormon material and the oath. He had the best eye for it in the business; he was everywhere, the Boston Book Fair, the California Book Fair, and at the last New York Book Fair," said Rendell. Rendell said that Hofmann had bought the white salamander letter as a stampless cover for $25 from a New Hampshire dealer about a year ago.

THE OATH OF A FREEMAN   AUGUST 1986

BY DAVID HEWETT

In a surprise move in Salt Lake City, defense attorneys have won a bid to have accused bomber/killer and fake document seller Mark Hofmann's trial split into five separate trials. On June 6, 1986, Hofmann pleaded not guilty to all 32 counts and was later assigned a trial date of March 2, 1987, on the two murder charges. A separate trial on communications fraud is scheduled to follow the murder trial.

Prosecutor Robert Stott is not optimistic about chances of having the trials rejoined. "We think that all the cases should be heard together because they establish motives for the murders," he said, "but Utah law is fairly strict about conjoining trials." Mark Hofmann remains free on a $250,000 bond.

The fate of the Oath of a Freeman, purportedly the earliest piece of printing done in America, is

less secure. Hofmann claimed he had bought it at New York's Argosy Book Shop for $25. He placed it for sale with New York City's Schiller-Wapner Galleries, which offered it in 1985 to both the Library of Congress and the American Antiquarian Society for $1.5 million. The Library of Congress tested the ink, paper, and text and reported all passed scrutiny. The American Antiquarian Society said they found nothing inconsistent with its purported mid-17th-century attribution. Neither institution, however, was willing to pay the steep price. But in Salt Lake City, another oath turned up and prosecutors say it was made from a printing plate made five days before Hofmann purportedly bought his oath in New York.

On Wednesday, June 25, George Throckmorton, the forensic documents examiner with the Utah Attorney General's office, who testified at the Mark

Hofmann preliminary hearing in Salt Lake City about the forgeries made by Hofmann from newly produced printing plates, and Agent Rennet, of the U.S. Alcohol, Tax, and Firearms Division, came to New York City. They brought with them the negative used to make the fake Oath of a Freem an that was given as security to Salt Lake City investor Tom Wilding by Hofmann.

When the Utah preliminary hearing revealed the existence of a printing plate and a second copy of an oath, the validity of the Schiller-Wapner copy was seriously questioned.

Robert Stott, Salt Lake County deputy attorney and one of the Hofmann prosecution team, said he could not comment on any aspects of the tests on the Schiller-Wapner oath or results of the same, and, in fact, could not even confirm any tests had been carried out.

In carefully phrased legalese, Stott said that Schiller-Wapner had not been notified of the results of the not confirmable and supposedly nonexistent test. The county attorney's office had been dealing with the Schiller-Wapner oath through Schiller-Wapner's attorney, Steven Eckhaus. Eckhaus's office, Stott said, had been notified and they could release those results if they so chose.

Robert Stott agreed, given a hypothetical positive test result (meaning the Schiller-Wapner copy of the oath is fake), that charges could be filed against Mark Hofmann under Utah's communications fraud law, even if no money had passed hands in that state. Another possibility is that charges could be brought in federal court under the U.S. communications fraud statute. Theoretically, similar charges could be filed in New York state courts.

Since Utah already has filed 30 charges against Hofmann for theft by deception and communications fraud, it is unlikely they will press this latest charge. Steven Eckhaus was out of town at deadline time. His secretary confirmed they had the test results and consulted another lawyer in the office about releasing those results. She later told us, "We

have no comment. At this time, the firm wishes to release no information concerning the test results."

An insider who has seen those test results, however, said "It's bogus. The printing plate used to make the Wilding oath made this one too, but the ink is different."

Ray Wapner of Schiller-Wapner Galleries confirmed he hadn't seen the results of the tests yet. Wapner said, "The examination itself was done at the U.S. Postal Service building here in New York. I accompanied Throckmorton and Rennet to the building but wasn't allowed to go beyond the receptionist's desk. They took our oath in, and when I called back an hour later, I was told the tests were over. I never did find out what tests were conducted on it."

Ray Wapner added, "In return for lending our oath to them for the tests, we received permission to send the known forgery [the Wilding oath] to California for the same cyclotron testing our oath underwent."

By July 7, Ray Wapner had still not seen the Utah test report. Wapner said that an expert from England was in the U.S. the week before and microscopically examined the handwriting in ink on the reverse of his copy of the oath. That expert (whom Wapner refused to identify) said the ink had authentically aged cracking, something seen only on genuinely aged ink and not found on artificially aged examples.

In April, the Schiller-Wapner oath was cyclotron tested to compare its ink to that used on the Bay Psalm Book, a similarly dated publication made by the oath's printer, Stephen Daye. According to Wapner, the test would compare the ink on both oaths, molecule by molecule, and if the ink formulation on both is the same, or nearly identical, the conclusion would be inescapable: the Schiller-Wapner oath is a fake.

Prosecutor Robert Stott said he could not confirm any arrangements made concerning the Wilding oath. If the information we have received concerning the test results is accurate, any further testing of inks used on both oaths may be superfluous. The damning proof would be that both oaths were made from the same negative that made the printing plate allegedly ordered by Mark Hofmann. As George Throckmorton testified at the preliminary hearing, it can be conclusively shown that a specific negative made a printing plate because of flaws that often occur in the developing process. Even when an original object is photographed to make a new printing plate,

the negative will often contain flaws that don't occur on the original.

The taint of ownership, or purported ownership, of anything touched by Mark Hofmann goes on. Ray Wapner reports that the Charles Dickens manuscript *The Haunted Man*, which has never been owned or even touched by Hofmann, is meeting buyer reluctance because Hofmann used its existence in a purported scam to fleece Arizona businessman Wilfred Cardon out of $110,000.

HOFMANN PLEADS GUILTY MARCH 1987

BY DAVID HEWETT

Mark W. Hofmann, 32, the Salt Lake City documents dealer accused of making and selling fraudulent early Mormon documents, currency, and books, and of defrauding collectors and investors of a total of $1–2 million, pleaded guilty to two counts of second degree murder and two counts of theft by deception on January 23, 1987.

Hofmann, who had been free on $250,000 bail and had spent but one day in jail in his life, was immediately taken to the Utah State Prison in Draper, where he began undergoing a six-week indoctrination process prior to joining the general inmate population.

Thus the career of Mark W. Hofmann, the man whose document finds made headlines in the Rocky Mountain states, the man whose controversial Latter-day Saints-related finds had forced a wave of revisionist thought upon church historians, and the man credited with the discovery of the first piece of printing done in America (and who valued it at $1.5 million), finally comes to an end.

But does it? Do we really know what Hofmann faked? The answer is no—no but maybe. The plea bargaining arrangement worked out between Hofmann and Salt Lake County provides some of the answers. It was a most complicated arrangement. Both Hofmann and Salt Lake County received some of the things they desired, both gave up some other things in the process.

Salt Lake County wanted the murderer of two people behind bars. They got that. Hofmann admitted murdering Steven Christensen, a Salt Lake City businessman and amateur documents collector, with a pipe bomb on October 15, 1985. Christensen was to examine and authenticate a collection of documents Hofmann was to sell to the Latter-day Saints (Mormon) Church later that day. For pleading guilty to the second degree murder of Christensen (dropped from first degree), Hofmann received a sentence of five years to life imprisonment.

Hofmann admitted murdering Kathleen Sheets, wife of J. Gary Sheets, a Salt Lake City businessman associated with Christensen, with a pipe bomb on October 15, 1985. This was an "accidental" murder;

the bomb was meant for J. Gary Sheets. His planned killing was intended to divert police attention from the documents deal to the business run by Sheets and Christensen.

For pleading guilty to the second degree murder of Sheets (dropped from first degree), Hofmann received a sentence of one to five years. (As part of the plea bargain, Judge Kenneth Ringtrup agreed to sentence Hofmann to the equivalent of a manslaughter conviction sentence for the Sheets murder.)

Hofmann pled guilty to a theft by deception charge in the defrauding of Salt Lake City coin dealer Alvin Rust of approximately $132,000 in the sale of the McLellin collection, Mormon material Hofmann did not possess. Hofmann pled guilty to a theft by deception charge involving the forgery of the so-called "white salamander letter." That letter was sold to murder victim Steven Christensen and later donated to the Latter-day Saints Church.

Hofmann was sentenced to one to 15 years for both those pleas, making a total of one five-to-life sentence and three one-to-fifteen year sentences. Under Utah law, unless the sentencing judge specifically rules that sentences be served concurrently or consecutively, that decision is left to the parole board. Judge Ringtrup did not issue such a ruling in sentencing Hofmann, so the parole board will determine how many years he serves.

Salt Lake County escaped the costs it might have incurred in putting Hofmann through a long series of expensive trials. They won't have to fly witnesses in from around the country, they won't have to house jurors for months on end, and they won't have to pay for Hofmann's defense team. They have satisfied the families of both victims, and they have put Mark Hofmann behind bars.

What did Hofmann gain from the plea bargaining? He escaped the possibility of being found guilty of first degree murder and a possible death sentence. The probability of that happening was extremely unlikely. Hofmann is a Mormon, has no prior convictions, is married with three small children, and in no way could be called a hardened criminal of the Gary Gilmore type. Even the prosecutors didn't expect him to get a death sentence.

Hofmann received a guarantee from New York state that they will not prosecute him for any criminal activity in connection with the Oath of a Freeman he placed with the New York City firm of Schiller-Wapner, or for any other criminal activities relating to charges in Utah.

That's a big plus for Hofmann but leaves the fate of that document in New York in limbo. Schiller and Wapner have money invested in it, and if it does prove a fake (as it now seems), New York can't charge Hofmann with that crime. For that matter, New York can't charge Hofmann with anything concerning the Utah charges, even if it involves placing fakes on consignment with New York auction houses.

Hofmann received an agreement from federal authorities to drop all charges against him relating to the Utah charges, and also for a charge of possession of an unaltered machine gun. He received an agreement from Utah to drop all the 26 other charges against him (all relating to fraud, forgery, counterfeiting, and theft by deception) and, in addition, a guarantee that Utah would not charge him in the future for any related crimes.

There is, however, a kicker to that plea agreement. It comes in two paragraphs in section 9. Briefly, Hofmann has to answer to prosecuting attorneys, "truthfully and completely," all questions relating to the charged offenses that were dropped and "any other related offenses." The prosecuting attorneys will take Hofmann's answers into consideration in their recommendations to the parole board.

What it comes down to is that they can ask Hofmann about all those fakes, and if he does not answer them "truthfully and completely," they can tell the parole board to keep him in prison for as long as it likes. That seems to be a pretty fair incentive to come up with some answers that will satisfy the prosecution.

Mark W. Hofmann. Photo copyright Ravell Call, *Deseret Morning News*.

Some of those questions might be:

Who was the third bomb (which went off on October 16, 1985, and accidentally injured Hofmann) meant for? Why?

What had Steven Christensen learned about the McLellin collection that meant he had to be killed before seeing it?

Was Hofmann planning an ultimate scam that consisted of announcing he'd discovered the missing 116 pages of the original *Book of Mormon*?

Are other Hofmann-created fakes in circulation? What are they? How were they made?

How was the negative that made the Oath of a Freeman plate made? Does that plate, and any others, still exist? (Police have recovered the negative that made the plate and seen two pieces made from the plate but have not recovered the actual plate.)

Was Hofmann the sole creator of all the fakes associated with him?

Salt Lake County Attorney David E. Yocum has partially answered that question in a press release issued on January 23, 1987. The pertinent section reads: "The information provided by Mr. Hofmann and our investigation has revealed that Mark Hofmann was the sole perpetrator of the murders of Mr. Christensen and Mrs. Sheets. There were no co-conspirators in these murders. We are also convinced that there were no co-conspirators in the thefts he has admitted involving the 'Martin Harris to W.W. Phelps Letter' and the 'McClellan [sic] Collection'."

The prosecution has said it will make public the answers Hofmann gives it about the other crimes. However truthfully Hofmann answers those questions, there will always be someone who will insist the whole story hasn't been revealed. And that may well be true.

Since the book seems to be closed on Mark Hofmann in Utah and New York, and since the state of Utah intends to return all evidence collected to its owners, the possibility is strong that someday, somewhere, a Hofmann fake is going to re-enter the marketplace.

With the books closed on Mark Hofmann, it will be more important than ever for collectors of Mormon material to establish the provenance of an item before purchasing.

Unfortunately, despite the fact the man is known to have handled many authentic documents, the world will long remember the bad ones. Any item that includes Mark Hofmann somewhere in its provenance will have to doubly prove itself. Unless all concerned are satisfied that he has finally provided a true list of all he has faked, everything he has touched will remain under a cloud.

 ## JUSTIN SCHILLER'S LETTER APRIL 1987

Dear Mr. Pennington,

On behalf of both myself and my partner, Raymond Wapner, we would like to express our appreciation for the in-depth coverage you and David Hewett have given the bizarre and tragic circumstances surrounding Mark Hofmann and his Mormon forgeries. Geographic distances being what they are, and rumors flying from all directions, we have often relied upon your updated reporting to know current events in the case that would not otherwise reach our notice, as our involvement with Hofmann was essentially on the periphery of his more nefarious dealings.

We met him in April 1984 at the New York ABAA fair, and, often with his wife, he became a frequent visitor to our shop. During the next 18 months, we helped him put together an important collection of rare and unique children's books: first editions of *Pinocchio* (in Italian), Andersen's fairy tales (in Danish), original printings of the fables

of La Fontaine (in French), and even the only copy known of the first edition of *The Adventures of Sherlock Holmes* (1892) in its pictorial dust jacket. During this time, we developed a trusting relationship together, as we have with several of our very good clients, and it was because of this trust that he came to us to help him research his Oath of a Freeman and determine whether it was authentic.

It has now been nearly two years since we have had the oath assigned to us for research study and potential sale—somewhat longer than we all might have first expected—but from the start, we knew that it would take at least 12 to 15 months to have the proper authorities examine the document and to let scientific analyses independently support its own conclusions. It was to have been only at the time the document would have proven itself to be authentic that we would have made a public announcement about its discovery but when Hofmann's lawyers broke the story in early

November 1985, to show he was a man of substantial means, both the Library of Congress (which had studied the oath for six weeks) and our gallery were forced into making a preliminary report.

At that time, it was stated by both the Library and ourselves that preliminarily there had been no red flags, no obstacles or problems of any significance to indicate that the document under consideration was anything but genuine and consequently datable from the mid-17th century. Since that time, we have subjected the oath to cyclotron testing at the University of California (Davis), matching it against a genuine 1640 Bay Psalm Book (courtesy of The Rosenbach Foundation). The text has been computerized by experts in early American typography to see whether our image could be reconstructed from paste-ups, using all known printing of the Stephen Daye press through 1643 (after which, that typeface was abandoned and another one substituted in later publications).

The type ornament border has been carefully compared against the 16 separate fonts of the same ornament found in the Bay Psalm Book. (There are many additional fonts in the document's border that differ from any employed as the smaller of two ornaments in the 1640 publication.) And Dr. Walter McCrone has tested the oath and confirmed, in his opinion, the printing ink has been bonded together with the paper for the past 300-plus years. Likewise, paper and printing experts from Harvard, the Pierpont Morgan Library, and England have separately inspected the document at our request and have no visual problem with its genuineness.

There is one test yet to be done: testing the writing ink inscription on the reverse side of the printed document to ascertain the bonding together of that ink and the paper. (The inscription, as you may recall, says "Oathe of Ffreeman" in what would appear to be a secretarial script of the late 16th to mid-17th century.) We hope to have this test completed by a leading authority in this field within the next few weeks, about the same time we

expect to have the report back from the computerized study of all known typefaces from Daye's press, and then we will collect together these independent reports and make their findings public. But as of now, and based upon a summary that I've received from the type experts in New Mexico, the oath could not have been falsely reconstructed from already existing materials, and we do believe entirely that the iron gall ink test will likewise indicate the complete genuineness of the oath.

By that time, Mark Hofmann's testimony will have been given to the Salt Lake authorities, who (according to the New York District Attorney's office) do intend to question him extensively about the origin of the Oath of a Freeman, and we do look for some honest answers to some still unanswered questions. But these answers will be coming to us via the state prosecutor's office rather than a more neutral federal authority, and it has been the intention of Salt Lake authorities to try and blemish the reputation of everything Hofmann has ever handled. The fact that Hofmann has allegedly confessed to forging the "White Salamander" letter (Martin Harris to W.W. Phelps), despite the belief by some of its authenticity (which I have understood to believe was likewise supported as being genuine by the FBI and Kenneth Rendell), must make one ponder the possibilities. Since that which has discredited the church has reportedly now been discredited itself, the pressure to prosecute Hofmann more severely beyond his present incarceration is being relaxed.

Moreover, Hofmann apparently did forge two other freeman's oaths. One was to provide a provenance that he had made up with a Civil War poem text a week before he purchased it out of a portfolio from Argosy Book Store (thereby getting a genuine invoice from a reliable source). At that time, based upon his bringing us the document that has been in our care ever since, he considered the value to be $10,000, possibly $20,000, but certainly no more than $50,000. We were the ones who corrected his thinking that if the document proved to be genuine, it should be equated to being worth the same sort of money one could today get for a genuine Bay Psalm Book—somewhat in excess of $1,000,000. For we are not dealing with just the first piece of printing in what is now the United States, we are also dealing with the first American declaration of the rights of freedom, predating our Constitution by 150 years. And on top of that, the document is apparently unique.

That is where the second forged "oath" occurs. Several months after our oath had been securely protected, Hofmann made claims to a group of Utah investors that he actually had found two "oaths" at Argosy, not just one, and he proceeded to sell them the second "oath" for an alleged $185,000. Since this revelation was made to us— that another "oath" actually existed and it was not just a rumor—we have tried repeatedly to get the state prosecutor's office to cyclotron test the second "oath" for the sake of comparing the diagnostics, but they have rejected our request, claiming that both "oaths" are the same.

However, I understand from an authority at the Library of Congress who has visually seen this second "oath" as well as his studying our document, that the two bear no relationship whatsoever to anyone knowledgeable about paper and early printing. Moreover, where our document is closely trimmed, has undergone severe creasing and paper splits (which the Library carefully restored when it was under examination), and bears this early ink inscription on its verso, the so-called second "oath" is centered in the middle of a much larger sheet of paper that is not the same as our document, it is in fine condition, and there is no handwritten inscription on its reverse side. That being the case, we have relaxed our formal request through our attorneys to have this testing done at our expense under the auspices of the University of California laboratory and the Salt Lake authorities.

Why are we telling you all of this, and now? Let me put it this way. While we do now have a financial interest and part ownership in the document in our possession, known as the Oath of a Freeman, from the very beginning we took the approach that the document was whatever it turned out to be. While we believed from the initial studies that it was genuine, we have continued our pursuit for the truth. Not just because of our agreement with Hofmann to research the document fully, but also because if the document is genuine, then it is one of the most important discoveries of the modern age, and its reputation needs to be wholly protected amidst all the mudslinging and accusations of those who disbelieve because they either want Hofmann to be guilty of everything or because they cannot themselves afford to purchase the document if it was proven genuine.

We hope Hofmann's testimony will cover the same grounds to which we were given prior knowledge several weeks ago after the plea bargain was announced. We received a telephone call from a member of Hofmann's team telling us of the plea bargain and stating that Hofmann will identify from whom he bought the Oath. Although to avoid professional embarrassment, as the individual who sold it to him did not realize it was anything beyond an early reprint, the name and full particulars will be available confidentially to the lawyers of clients interested in considering the oath for purchase and to the actual purchaser.

At this stage, we do not know very much more except to acknowledge that after Hofmann was arrested for the bombings late in 1985, and as the case later developed early in 1986, when our own nerves were a bit shattered from current events, Hofmann had sent us $10,000 to help pay for continued testing of the document. Does that sound like something he would have done had he not looked toward the tests proving the document genuine, and where part of the money that would be realized from selling the document would go to him to help defray what can only be enormous hospital and legal expenses.

Regarding the Mormon forgeries, I suspect there is a great deal we still would like to know to understand what could make someone like the intelligent, well-disciplined collector of rare children's books we knew make him admit to murdering two people with the intent of there being a third victim. My partner and I feel very sorry for the Hofmann family as we do for those families of his reputed victims, and we pray for peace and resolution for everyone. The fact that Hofmann's forgeries have all involved manuscripts and were scientifically detected rather easily by specialists should make the job of confronting whatever the future holds somewhat more possible.

If the Martin Harris "White Salamander" letter really is a fake, then what made that so much better than all the others? And can we

protect the reputation of the genuineness of the oath (assuming the iron gall ink test will likewise follow the testing by everyone else) and let it be accepted as the important document that we believe it is in the history of America? These are serious questions to ponder as we approach the bicentennial of our Constitution later this year and the 350th anniversary of printing in America in 1988 (i.e., the printing of the Oath of a Freeman).

Justin G. Schiller
President
Schiller-Wapner Gallery
New York, N.Y.

HOFMANN CONFESSES MAY 1987

BY DAVID HEWETT

The jig is up for Mark Hofmann's "Oathe of a Ffreeman" now on consignment to Schiller-Wapner Gallery in New York. It's not the earliest piece of printing done in America. It's not worth upwards of a million dollars.

It's a fake. Perhaps one of the best ever done—but a fake.

Hofmann, the 32-year-old rare documents dealer from Salt Lake City, has been spinning a long confession as part of his plea bargain agreement for a light sentence as the confessed killer of two people in separate bombings to cover up other forged documents.

George Throckmorton, an independent forensics expert who was hired by the state of Utah to examine Hofmann's many documents, said, "We now have Mark Hofmann's confession

regarding The Oath of a Freeman. While the Salt Lake County attorney's office has decided to hold the various parts of his confession until they can release it as one document, not parcel it out piecemeal, I am authorized to confirm to you that the Schiller-Wapner Oath of a Freeman is a Hofmann-created fake and has been admitted as such by Mark Hofmann."

Throckmorton said he was honor-bound not to reveal specifics regarding how the fake was made (until Salt Lake releases the official statement), but he could tell us there were two printing flaws in the oath that condemned it.

He said, "Mark was on an airplane with the oath when he decided to get it out and examine it. He spotted the flaws and said, 'Uh-oh. I made a mistake.' He said he decided to go ahead with it and hoped no one would spot the mistake. He got his wish. No one did.

"Of course, we had some luck with the oath. We recovered the negative used to make the plate that made the Wilding oath, and we were able to put those two pieces of evidence together with the Schiller-Wapner oath.

"That gave us conclusive evidence, but let me tell you a strange thing. Over a year ago, former Salt Lake County Attorney Ted Cannon saw the oath and he spotted the two flaws within five minutes. He said, 'It's a fake.' But Ted Cannon had been a printer at one time."

The news leaves the New York firm of Schiller-Wapner holding an expensive bag. They had advanced Hofmann money on the oath and were part owners. In a long letter to *M.A.D.* last month, Justin Schiller had advanced his argument that the oath is genuine and cited a number of scientific tests the document had passed.

Justin Schiller said he was still waiting for one more scientific test from Montana and was skeptical of any confession, adding, "Because of the nature of the case, I think one must rely on scientific evidence than necessarily depend upon the statement of Hofmann in a plea bargain arrangement."

According to the evidence, however, on March 8, 1985, Jack Smith of DeBouzek Engraving in Salt Lake City made a printing plate for customer Mike Harris (an alias sometimes used by Hofmann), who had left his phone number, which just happened to be the same as that of Mark Hofmann. The negative used by DeBouzek shows that the plate was for a page of sheet music, circa 1863, with the original title removed and the words "The Oath of a Freeman" inserted in place of the title. A sheet of paper made from that printing plate was subsequently slipped into a folder at Argosy Books and then bought by Mark Hofmann.

Why? As Justin Schiller wrote in his letter to *M.A.D.*, ". . . to provide a provenance . . . thereby getting a genuine invoice from a reliable source."

On March 25, 1985, 12 days after receiving the Argosy bookstore receipt, Hofmann had another printing plate made at DeBouzek Engraving. The film negative made by DeBouzek in producing this printing plate remained there until confiscated by the police in 1986. It shows that this printing plate was again for an Oath of a Freeman, but one that was far different from the first plate.

This plate was for a small vertical oath, surrounded by a seemingly 17th-century border, and it consisted of typefaces that appear to be 17th century in origin. This printing plate was for The Oath of a Freeman as it appears in the illustration accompanying this series of articles.

Sometime after having that plate made, Hofmann went back to New York City and visited Schiller-Wapner. He showed them his find and the Argosy Books receipt. "Schiller-Wapner decided to handle the oath assigned to us for research study and potential sale," Schiller said in his letter. "Discussions of possible worth ensued. He considered the value to be $10,000, possibly $20,000, but certainly no more than $50,000. We were the ones who corrected his thinking."

On this point, all the experts agree. If the oath were authentic, its value would be in excess of $1 million. Schiller-Wapner decided to ask $1.5 million for Hofmann's oath.

What no one in the East knew at this time was that back in Salt Lake City, Mark Hofmann was making an astounding claim. He was telling people that he had found not one copy of the oath, but two. On September 17, 1985, Hofmann gave Salt Lake investor Thomas Wilding another Oath of a Freeman, for which Wilding and other investors had paid $173,870 on September 12, 1985.

As the glare of police spotlights began to shine on the many business transactions of Mark Hofmann, Thomas Wilding went to the police. An envelope in Hofmann's basement sent investigators to DeBouzek Engraving. The chain of evidence linking a negative, a printing plate, and Thomas Wilding's copy of an Oath was slowly being forged.

Schiller-Wapner found that, although its "nerves were a bit shattered from current events," the authenticity of the oath was not questioned by any of the experts they consulted. They subjected the oath, together with a Bay Psalm Book, to cyclotron testing at the University of California (Davis). That test showed the oath had been printed on authentic 17th-century paper.

Other tests proved positive.

Dr. Walter McCrone confirmed his statement to Schiller-Wapner that the printing ink on the oath appeared to have been bonded together with the paper "for the past 300-plus years."

"If this is a fake," said McCrone, "it's the best one I have ever seen."

Schiller-Wapner continued tests on their oath. One test involves a comparison study of typefaces used by Stephen Daye through the year 1643. Those tests are important, but one test has already been conducted on the oath and the results of that test have proved extremely elusive in the past.

On June 25, 1986, an investigator from the Salt Lake County Attorney's office and a Federal agent flew into New York City from Salt Lake. They brought with them the negative used by Mark Hofmann to make the copy of the oath sold to investor Thomas Wilding. Raymond Wapner met them and handed over the Schiller-Wapner oath, which the investigator and the federal agent took to the New York City Postal Service Building. There, they compared the Schiller-Wapner oath to the negative.

On March 18, prosecuting attorney David Biggs of the Salt Lake County Attorney's office, said "Last year, our expert, George Throckmorton, and a U.S. Treasury expert named Marvin Rennert took the negative that we obtained from DeBouzek printing and examined the oath brought them by Mr. Wapner. They analyzed the oath in relationship to the negative, and they both determined that the oath was produced from the plate that came from the negative."

Biggs said that Salt Lake County had planned to call both men as expert prosecution witnesses at Mark Hofmann's trial, but that Hofmann's subsequent confessions had made that action not necessary.

Testimony at last year's preliminary hearings showed that it can be conclusively proven, when a negative used by a printing house is recovered, that that negative, the resulting printing plate, and any product of the printing plate are directly linked. The reasons are that when photographing the customer's original material, minute emulsion flaws remain on the film negative.

Those minute emulsion flaws are repeated in the metal printing plate made from the negative. Any subsequent copy made from that printing plate bears those tiny flaws. The original material supplied by the customer may be long since gone (in the Hofmann case it is), but comparison of the negative and any copies suspected of having been made by the printing plate produced from the negative will remain unalterably linked and identifiable.

Attorney David Biggs's statement that two expert witnesses have determined that the Schiller-Wapner oath was made by the printing plate Mark Hofmann had made in March 1985 is very hard evidence. Add Hofmann's confession, and it appears that only way the oath will enter the Library of Congress is in a book about famous fakes.

Dear Sam Pennington:

As I was intimately connected with the Hofmann case from the start, you might be interested in some of my views.

Hofmann was the flawless, low-key con man. He was always a little astonished that what he had was worth so much, and he played the role of the modest researcher—pleasant, soft-spoken, eager to learn. Now, in his "confessions," he repeatedly lies, changes his story, makes up events, and is, in his old way, totally unreliable—a paranoid liar who always appears to be a guileless purveyor of truth.

This is the "act" that took me in when I okayed one of his first forgeries—the 1825 Joseph Smith letter. Hofmann showed up in my gallery one afternoon and extracted this now famous letter from his briefcase and put it into my hands. A one-second glance (about as long as I took with the Hitler papers) told me it was not Smith. I handed it back and said, "Sorry, Mark, you've got the wrong Smith. There were regiments of Joseph Smiths in upstate New York in the 1820s. This is one of them, all right, but it's not the prophet."

Mark explained that he'd paid $15 for the letter just for the postal marking, a very faint one and certainly not worth $15. As I trusted Mark completely at this time and never doubted that he was what he pretended to be, an easygoing guy whose life was devoted to the arcane and long-forgotten in history, I accepted this story. There was no possibility in my mind, therefore, of the letter being a forgery. It was simply the wrong man.

"How can you tell it's not Smith?" Mark asked. "You just glanced at it." I said, "Easy. This hand-writing is stiff, labored, upright, like a man walking, strutting even, with his chest out. Smith's

is bent over, like a man running and leaning forward. This script creeps; Smith's races. Further, Smith's letters are always smudged and blotted, full of ugly smears. He cared not a whit what his writing looked like and just wanted to set down his ideas. The writer of your letter was preoccupied with the appearance of his writing."

Mark said, "But you never even read it."

"Well," I said, "at my age I have to save my eyes. Why should I read boring correspondence by nobodies?"

Mark put it away in his briefcase and looked doleful. Then he said, "Would you look at it once more?"

Usually, after I've looked at and passed upon a document, I refuse to look at it again. This dogmatic characteristic of mine has often brought down upon me the scorn and wrath of my colleagues, who love to pore over old documents with microscopes and chemicals and ultraviolet and infrared rays before they reach the obvious conclusions. I am used to being criticized for my instant judgments. But, in Mark's case, I allowed myself to be seduced into taking a second look.

I looked at the date, 1825, and I said, "My gosh, Mark, Smith was only a kid, about 19, at the time this letter was written." I suddenly became aware that there was a remote possibility it might be Smith's writing. The earliest of his letters that I'd seen was about 1835, a decade later, and writing can change a lot in ten years.

Then I began to read the letter. I was instantly struck by the presence of double consonants where they didn't belong, a characteristic of Smith's. For instance, Smith always spelled the word "copy" as "coppy." This letter had a number of wrong double consonants, and I commented at once on this fact and told Mark, "There is a possibility this could be in Smith's hand."

Mark said nothing and simply waited for me to continue my reading. The script was so legible it only took a few moments. Somewhere after about five or six lines (I don't have the letter in front of me), I came to the allusion of a Spirit that was going to stop Smith from finding a treasure. At this point, I exclaimed, "Jumping Jehosephat, Mark! I think this letter was written by Smith. Listen to this. "And I read to Mark the passage about how Smith had got a magic stick (which I explained to Mark was a divining rod) and was being guided to a treasure that was guarded by the Spirit.

Eventually, I authenticated the letter for Mark. I charged him $200. He said, "What's the letter worth?"

I said, "On the open market, maybe $10,000. But the church might pay $25,000 for it, just to get rid of it and burn it. It shows Smith as a treasure hunter, not a God seeker."

When I made this last remark to Mark, I smiled, and he smiled, because it was, of course, a joke that he would ever dream of anything so

Charles Hamilton

vile as extorting blackmail from his own church. Later, I heard that he sold the letter to the Church of the Latter-day Saints for $25,000. But since the church has not favored us with any comments, we have to rely upon Mark's version, and he is totally unable to tell the truth, unless it is so watered down with lies that it's worthless.

I had met and conferred with Gerry D'Elia, the Salt Lake City assistant district attorney who was handling the Hofmann case, early in January 1986. About two months later, after I had received a contract to be the state's expert handwriting witness (I was paid $4,000 in advance, with special allowances for travel, etc., and was to receive $2,500 for my first day in court and $1,500 for each additional day.), I again met with Gerry. This time, we spent about three hours together. Gerry had brought me all the important forgeries, including the Harris salamander letter and the 1825 letter I'd authenticated. This was in March or April of 1986.

I spread all the letters out on the large dining room table in my Manhattan apartment and showed Gerry how the same person, in the same handwriting, wrote them all. This I did by judging the "feel," a method involving the size of the script, the slant of the script, size of lower and upper loops of letters, space between lines, space between words, and other factors. Then I showed Gerry how all the common words were, at least in part, written precisely the same way. These words, "of, with, from, to, for, and," etc., are the words that almost always betray a forger.

At this meeting I saw the salamander letter for the first time. Aside from the fact that the signature did not look like Harris's (a copy of which signature appears in my book, *The Signature of America.* published some years ago), the writing did not look like that of the period and was not written with a quill. It looked like modern writing. Further, the letter folds were in the wrong place, and the postmark, at least to me, looked like it had been produced from a photo of an original postmark. This, Hofmann later stated, was the way he made it, and in this he may have been telling the truth. Anyhow, a glance told me the salamander latter was bogus.

Gerry gave me a recital of all the tests to which the letter had been put. (When you hold the salamander letter up to the light, you can see the tiny holes where the "experts" had taken bits of paper and ink for scrutiny under their machines, similar to the machinery used by the police forensic experts who authenticated the Hitler diaries.) The fact remains, however, as I told Gerry, the greatest scientific instrument ever devised is the human eye attached to the human brain.

A month or so later, I again saw Gerry, this time for 12 consecutive hours. We had breakfast, lunch, and dinner together as we plotted a strategy whereby we could put Hofmann in front of a firing squad. Gerry tried to get permission from Schiller-Wapner to let me see their copy of the Oath of a Freeman. They refused on the grounds that "I did not know anything at all" and it would be a waste of time to let me see it. This so infuriated Gerry that he contacted the New York District Attorney's office and put the necessary pressure on Schiller-Wapner.

I was subsequently permitted to examine their copy, or another copy (I was not told, as I recall, precisely what copy I was looking at) of this rather obvious forgery. The most conspicuous thing about a quick look at it was that the chain lines ran the wrong way. They were horizontal instead of vertical, indicating that the Oath was probably printed from a scrap, such as might be removed from an old book, not a regular sheet of foolscap printing paper. Second, as an expert on Elizabethan literature, I observed that the type was crudely set (the leading was defective) and the hyphens were often in the wrong place, indicating that whoever set the type was not familiar with his job.

Finally, the note on the back, the "Oathe of Ffreeman," was a very crude effort to imitate the Elizabethan secretary hand. I happen to be familiar with this script because I just did a book on Shakespeare's handwriting, all in the secretary hand, and consequently I learned not only to read but also how to write this difficult script, somewhat similar to the Suetterlin German script used by Hitler and atrociously imitated by his forger, Konrad Kujau. The note on the back of the Oath was a very clumsy imitation of the secretary hand, popular until about 1675 in England. The "h" was especially awkward and did not look like any letter in any alphabet. I was also given a copy of the reports from various alleged experts on the oath, all of whom said there was no reason to believe it wasn't genuine.

Around this time, I spent a full day with George Throckmorton, and I took George to the Argosy Book Store only a few blocks from where I live. We got out the file of broadsides and I showed George precisely, down to the most minute detail, how Hofmann had contrived to get a sales receipt for the oath.

Finally, I want to add my accolades to all the others that David Hewett has received. He did a magnificent job of research in the Hofmann case, and I am full of regrets that I could not help him in many of the areas where he was unable to get the information that was being funneled to me from Salt Lake City by D'Elia as it occurred: Hofmann's diary, his alleged homosexuality, the early love affair that turned him against women. All these things would have set David off on new quests. But I had promised not to discuss the case with anyone. I had lunch with Gerry and his wife several weeks ago, and he assured me I was now free to say whatever I wished.

Right now, I'm doing a lot of court work as an expert witness. I spend most of my spare time, of which I have in each day about five minutes, in the study of law and, in particular, of cross-examination.

Charles Hamilton
New York, N.Y.

Editor's [Sam Pennington's] Note: Chain lines or laid lines are the parallel watermark lines in laid paper made by the chain wires and running with the grain. This error may have been one of two that Hofmann now admits spotting and that former Salt Lake County Attorney Ted Cannon, formerly a printer, spotted within five minutes of examining the document.

THE DICKINSON POEM OCTOBER 1997

BY DAVID HEWETT

On June 3, 1997, a manuscript poem by Amherst, Massachusetts, poet Emily Dickinson, listed as previously unpublished, sold at a Sotheby's fine books and manuscripts sale in New York City for $24,150.

The buyer was the Jones Library of Amherst, represented by Dan Lombardo, curator of special collections at the Jones Library.

On August 28, Sotheby's conceded that the author of lot 74 might not be Dickinson but a man who's been inside the Utah State Prison at Draper for the last decade, a man whose past productions have included documents purportedly written by the founding fathers of the Mormon religion as well as autographs of Betsy Ross and Jack London, and the Oath of a Freeman, the earliest printed document in this country's history.

Double murderer Mark Hofmann, the *enfant terrible* of the western document trade before his fall from grace in 1985, probably created the Emily Dickinson poem sometime before 1984.

After pleading guilty to less-than-first-degree murder charges, Hofmann went to prison, where in 1988 he listed for investigators some of his fabrications. One of the items was "an Emily Dickinson."

"I just made up a poem and signed it . . . later I saw the poem published in a magazine as a 'newly discovered poem,'" he confessed.

Cynthia Griffin Woolf, the author of *Emily Dickinson* (1986), said she was not aware of any newly discovered poem that appeared between the years 1980 to 1985.

Woolf didn't know about Hofmann's poem because it wasn't published in a literary journal. It appeared in *Collecting Historical Documents: A Guide to Owning History* by Todd Axelrod (TFH Publishing, Neptune City, New Jersey), the second edition of 1986, on page 198.

The poem begins "That God cannot/ be understood" and is the same manuscript that appeared as lot 74 of Sotheby's June 3, 1997, sale.

Provo, Utah, businessman Brent Ashworth, a historical document collector whom most believe was the intended victim of Hofmann's third pipe bomb in 1985, saw the poem in Hofmann's hands.

"I first saw it in Mark's living room in 1983," Ashworth said. "It looked fine, and I'm a collector of and deeply interested in Emily Dickinson's works. I'm the president of the Emily Dickinson Club for Utah, in fact, but the poem just didn't ring true, the content didn't seem correct. I had no reason then to think Mark was faking things. I just thought it was probably the worst poem she'd ever written. Later, Mark told me he'd sold it to Todd Axelrod of Las Vegas."

Brent Ashworth was one of Hofmann's steadiest customers before the 1985 bombings. "I think I've got the best Mark Hofmann collection in the country, outside of the Mormon Church," Ashworth admitted wryly. "I'm still buying the stuff, but now I'm buying it for what it is and who made it, not what it's purported to be.

"After everything came out about his fakes, I had a chance to reassess the Dickinson poem. I considered the pencil script, the fact that it had never been published, and that Mark had it for sale. I began to see it in a different light."

When Brent Ashworth saw the Dickinson poem in the Sotheby's catalog, he said he called Selby Kiffer, Sotheby's vice president in charge of books and manuscripts, to warn him.

"I was later told they had the poem vetted and that they found nothing wrong with it," Ashworth said.

Selby Kiffer has a different account of the call from Ashworth.

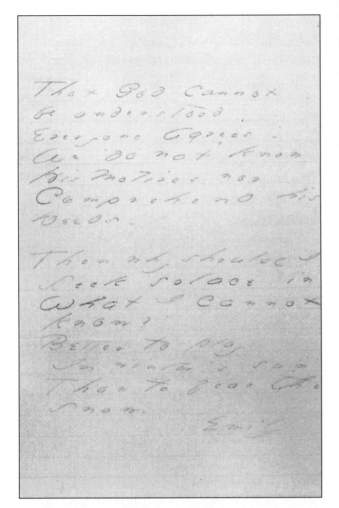

Mark Hoffman pleaded to a reduced murder charge in 1987 and has been behind bars since. He attempted suicide at least once. He tried to hire a hit man to take out a member of the parole board when he realized they weren't about to release him anytime in the immediate future. His creations are continuing to bedevil the literary and collecting communities. Hofmann fabrications are collectible as fakes. Photo copyright Ravell Call, *Desert Morning News*.

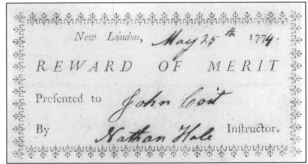

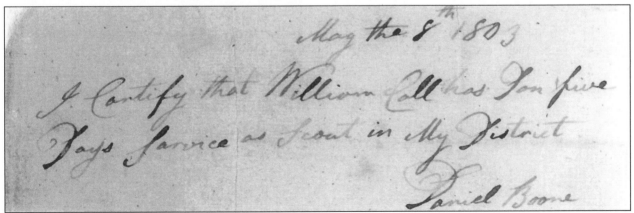

Sotheby's offered these three lots in two manuscripts, books, and printed Americana sale catalogs, on May 19 and June 3, 1997. By the time the May 19 sale was held, Sotheby's had withdrawn lot 27, the Daniel Boone-signed document, because they believed it to be a fake. Lot 76, the Reward of Merit signed by Nathan Hale remained in the sale and brought $31,050. Lot 74, the pencil manuscript poem signed Emily and attributed to Emily Dickinson, sold for $24,150. It was later returned by its purchaser, the Jones Library of Amherst, Massachusetts, as a fake. All three documents had been owned at one time by confessed faker Mark Hofmann. Sotheby's photos.

"He spoke about several pieces," Kiffer said on August 29, "but it was not indicated to me that this was a Mark Hofmann forgery."

Sotheby's went ahead with the sale, and the Jones Library bought the Dickinson poem for $24,150.

After it sold, Brent Ashworth called Ralph Franklin at Yale, the director of the Beinecke Rare Book Collection, and told him about the Hofmann connection. "He [Franklin] knew that the Jones Library had held a subscription drive to raise funds for the poem's purchase, and he informed them of my apprehensions about its authenticity," Ashworth recounted.

"We had no questions about the authenticity when we bought it," said Dan Lombardo. "We had a celebration, and I went on vacation. When I came back, Ralph Franklin called me and told me about Brent Ashworth's statement. I called Ashworth, and when I heard him say he'd seen it in Mark Hofmann's hands, it sent shivers down my spine.

"I called Marsha Malinowski at Sotheby's to see what she could tell me about its provenance. She eventually told me that the consignor had bought it from a dealer, and the dealer bought it from a collector in the Midwest who had subsequently died."

Lombardo assembled an investigative group to study the poem. "Everything seemed right: the paper was the right age, it had the correct blindstamp [embossed manufacturer's mark], and the handwriting looked authentic. Our initial thoughts were that it was an original manuscript that somehow or other had gone through Mark Hofmann's hands."

Some of the group began to doubt the style and content of the poem, but others found an explanation for that problem.

Lombardo said, "There were words Emily used, feelings she expressed in other works, just so many right pieces of the puzzle that at one time some of us examining it began to believe that perhaps Emily hadn't composed the poem, but merely paraphrased it on paper using her feelings, her words."

Lombard said a notation on the document, "Aunt Emily," provoked a search. "We went through all the cousins, then other family members, and came up with no match for her. That was disconcerting.

"I found the notation in one of the books about the Hofmann case that he had confessed to making a Dickinson poem. That led us to book dealer Jennifer Larsen, who had compiled a list of Hofmann's non-Mormon fakes. The Dickinson poem was on her list. Then I saw it in Todd Axelrod's book."

All of Lombardo's attempts to talk with Las Vegas dealer Todd Axelrod failed. He said he did talk with Shannon Flynn, a former business associate of Hofmann, who said Hofmann had told him to sell the Dickinson poem to Axelrod.

The chain of evidence finally became overwhelming. In 1988 Hofmann stated he'd faked an Emily Dickinson poem. He told Shannon Flynn to sell an Emily Dickinson poem to Todd Axelrod in 1984–85. Todd Axelrod published it in 1986 as a previously unpublished poem. It was the same poem Sotheby's offered in 1997.

The fact that Mark Hofmann had owned it meant there was a chance it was a Hofmann forgery, and that was a chance the library did not want to take. The library returned the poem to Sotheby's.

Second Decade:
1984–1993

Editor's Note: During M.A.D.'s second decade, record prices were paid in many categories of collecting. Scrimshaw, the art of the schrimshanders, the sailors who carved and engraved whalebone and whales' teeth on their long voyages, came into focus when Barbara Johnson's large collection was offered by Sotheby's in four sales held over three years. The last one took place in December 1983.

THE SAILOR'S ART: BARBARA JOHNSON'S WHALING COLLECTION

BY LITA SOLIS-COHEN

When a cane sells for $24,200, a swift for winding yarn fetches $20,900, a pie crimper brings $19,800, and a pair of hoisting blocks are gaveled down for $16,500, one expects them to be made of gold, not whalebone and whale ivory.

All were in part four of the Barbara Johnson whaling collection, a vast assemblage of more than 5,000 items that Sotheby's dispersed in four sales over the last three years. After the last sale, on December 16 and 17, 1983, fetched nearly $700,000, the grand total came to more than $2.2 million. Sotheby's and Princeton, New Jersey, collector Barbara Johnson expected the total to be higher. Although some spectacular prices were paid for rarities, some very fine items found no buyers. In some cases, high estimates may have discouraged prospective bidders.

Johnson, unwilling to sell important pieces for less than she thought them worth, made use of reserves, the system under which the consignor and the auctioneer agree on a minimum acceptable price for each object. She insisted the reserves were low, but there was no way for bidders to know that because of high estimates. Experienced auction-goers know that reserves are generally set at around two-thirds of the low estimate. The result was that 25 percent of the 645 lots offered in the December 1983 sale were returned to the seller.

One collector observed that December was not the time to sell scrimshaw. "Bones are melancholy; scrimshaw is a lonely art. At Christmastime, people buy shiny silver, highly polished wood, and Victoriana. Spring is the time of the year to sell a whaling collection, when people feel young, adventurous, and optimistic."

Even though Johnson sold three-quarters of her whaling collection, she still has a great deal left, including a large number of books about whaling, as well as whale ship journals. Moreover, she bought a number of items made of whalebone or whale ivory after 1973, and these could not be sold because of New York state's stringent endangered species laws.

Large, esoteric collections are difficult to sell, so Sotheby's marketed Johnson's whaling collection carefully, planning a number of lectures and parties for maritime museums and seafaring groups.

This undoubtedly inspired some new collectors to bid at Johnson's sale, but there are not more than half a dozen collectors or museums who will pay the price of a Mercedes for a piece of scrimshaw.

The tragedy of the sale was that journals, scrimshaw, tools, and other material that Johnson had bought directly from the heirs of whaling captains were not kept together and offered as collections within the collection. Valuable archives of Captains Edward Penniman, James Shearman, Josiah C. Long, and Henry Wilbur have now been scattered.

Two whalebone and ivory swifts made by Captain Charles H. Wilbur. The larger one sold to a collector for $4,950. The smaller one went to another collector for $3,300. "They have never been separated. It is idiotic that they went to two different collectors. They are worth more as a pair," commented Barbara Johnson after the sale. Another whalebone and ivory swift (not shown), circa 1850, with its original decorated box sold for $20,900 to a New York collector. Sotheby's photo.

"I spent twenty years gathering these things, and I had hoped to sell the entire collection to the National Maritime Museum in San Francisco for under three million dollars. It was all approved and had a presidential signature when Ronald Reagan came in and failed to appropriate the money. It would have been a good deal. The sales brought over two million dollars and I still have about four hundred journals, fifteen thousand books, and some scrimshaw worth another two million dollars," said Johnson on the phone a few days after the sale.

"It is sad now that historians won't have access to the documents in one place. I tried to set up a system whereby if a buyer got the first item in a group, the rest of the related things could be hammered down to the same buyer, even below the reserve if the buyer was interested in keeping the group together. But that didn't happen."

What will be remembered about the Johnson sales, however, are the items that made records, not the pieces that failed, or were separated, or lost (a number of items, including two engraved teeth pictured in the last catalog, disappeared).

The cane that fetched $24,200 was an unusual walking stick made in 1845 with an octagonal ivory knob inlaid with a disk of tortoiseshell and a shaft inlaid with a parade of sperm whales, dolphins, lions, elephants, hearts, and a paddlewheel steamer of tortoiseshell, abalone, and amber.

The mid-19th-century swift that sold for $20,900 has an elaborately turned shaft scribed with red and green. It came with its original cherrywood box inlaid with swags, shields, and stars of abalone, mother-of-pearl, ebony, baleen, and whale ivory.

The pair of whalebone blocks that brought $16,500, consisted of a working block and a loading block fastened with copper pins and fitted with braided rope and hand-forged iron hooks remarkable for their size (16" and 20") and condition. Johnson said she paid $6,000 for them 20 years ago and that they came from Maine.

The pie crimper, or jagging wheel, in the form of a sea unicorn that sold for $19,800 had its horn broken and replaced at Sotheby's. "If it had remained in perfect condition, it might have brought thirty thousand dollars. It is so beautiful," said Johnson after the sale. The American Heritage Society has reproduced the crimper for sale in the gift trade.

A whaling journal from the Nantucket ship *Charles Carroll* kept during a four-year voyage by her captain, Josiah Long, with more than 500 watercolor illustrations, sold for $22,000 to a new collector from Texas who was a major buyer at the sale. Johnson thought the price low for "the ultimate whaling journal."

A whale's tooth engraved by Long with an elegantly dressed woman on one side and a whaling scene on the other sold for $8,800 to a different collector. It was not the highest-priced tooth in the sale.

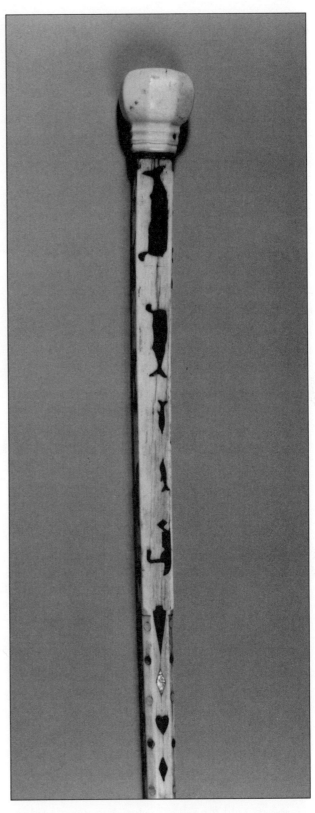

The inlaid cane or walking stick, made in Nantucket circa 1845, brought a record $24,200, surpassing the $19,800 that a captain's wooden "Going Ashore" stick brought at the last Johnson auction. Sotheby's photo.

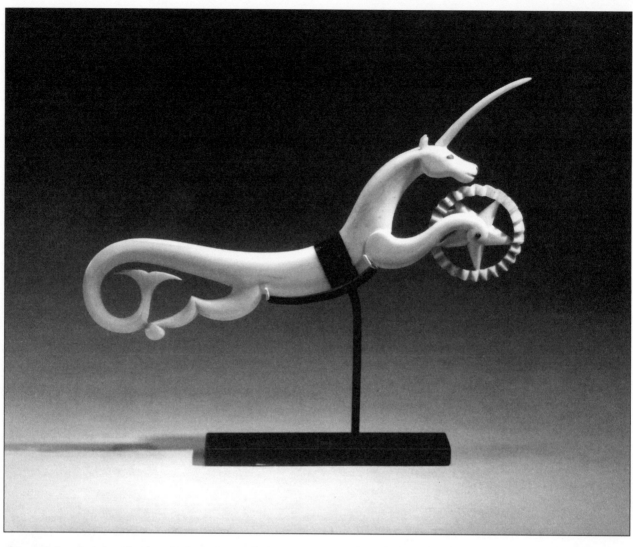

This whale ivory and ebony jagging wheel, or pie crimper, circa 1870, sold for $19,800 to a Washington, D.C., collector. It is made of two pieces of ivory joined at the center with ebony studded with silver pins. The jagging wheel is joined to the front legs with a silver pin. The unicorn's horn was broken and replaced while in Sotheby's custody (after this photograph was taken). Barbara Johnson said she bought it more than a decade ago for around $5,000. A similar crimper at the New Bedford Whaling Museum is believed to be by the same hand. Sotheby's photo.

A tooth engraved with a scene of a South Seas native in full dress standing next to a hut on one side and with a whaling scene on the other sold for $14,300.

Another tooth engraved with a seaman's chapel, a prayer book, a peacock, and two urns of flowers sold for $11,500, and a tooth engraved by Frederick Myrick with a view of "Coquimbo Harbour" sold for $10,175. Myrick is considered the Rembrandt of scrimshanders, and a tooth he engraved aboard the ship *Susan* in 1828 sold for $44,000 in the second Barbara Johnson sale.

Half a dozen other teeth in the sale, however, failed to sell, as did a whale ivory chess set estimated at $15,000/25,000. Also failing to find buyers were an elaborately carved openwork wall pocket that carried a $25,000/35,000 estimate, a mahogany and ivory birdcage with expectations of $20,000 to $35,000, and a rare group of nine Currier and Ives lithographs of whaling scenes estimated at $7,000/9,000.

A few items surpassed estimates. A set of 12 whalebone engraving tools for scrimshanders went to a collector for $4,400, double the high estimate, and an unfinished whalebone jagging wheel in the shape of a mermaid, which was found with the engraving tools, went to the same discerning collector for $3,300, five times its high estimate. It is plainly a piece of folk art.

Most items brought less than expected. A whalebone busk, a woman's corset stay, engraved with views of New Bedford harbor sold for $8,800, an openwork whalebone sewing basket fetched $9,350, and a set of four whalebone clothespins in their drawstring calico bag fetched $495.

The highest price of the sale, $71,500, was paid for an oil painting of a ship, *Huntress off the Cape of Good Hope,* signed by Frederick Stiles Jewett, and dated 1860. The dramatic whaling scene with two whaleboats in the foreground and a whaler in one boat lancing a sperm whale went to a collector from California. It may well have been Johnson's most profitable purchase. She bought the painting from Harrison Huster in 1965. He said he had bought it a few years earlier for $100 at a flea market and had had it appraised twice for $350. Barbara Johnson paid $5,000 for it.

A set of 12 whalebone scrimshaw engraving tools brought $4,400. Sotheby's photo.

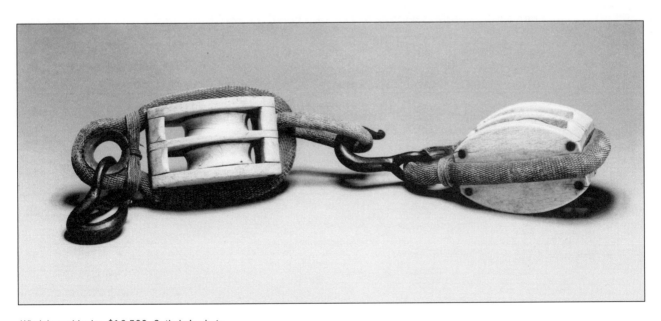

Whalebone blocks, $16,500. Sotheby's photo.

Editor's Note: When big prices are paid at small sales, M.A.D. reports them. A pewter sugar bowl found in a Pennsylvania attic sold at the Fire Hall in Farmersville, Lancaster County, Pennsylvania, for a record $42,500 and was reported by antiquarian John J. Snyder, Jr. There are only four and a half Heyne sugar bowls known. Three are in private collections, one is in a church where it was used as a ciborium, and the bottom half of another is at the Brooklyn Museum. Of the three privately owned bowls, one was auctioned for $79,500 at Northeast Auctions in Manchester, New Hampshire, on August 2, 2003, and it went from one private collection into another private collection. American pewter is a small corner of the marketplace built on two generations of scholarly research and supported by a band of passionate collectors. In the last two decades, works of the Pennsylvania German pewterer Johann Christoph Heyne have held the records. It stands at $145,500 paid for a communion flagon by Heyne sold at Sotheby's on June 16, 1998.

SWEET SUCCESS: HEYNE SUGAR BOWL SETS RECORD FOR PEWTER

BY JOHN J. SNYDER, JR.

On August 23, 1985, at the fire hall in the Lancaster County hamlet of Farmersville, Pennsylvania, auctioneer T. Glenn Horst called a world-record auction price for a piece of pewter. Within less than five minutes of bidding in the early afternoon, the bids soared from an opening of $1,000 to $42,500 for a lidded pewter sugar bowl made by 18th-century Lancaster pewterer Johann Christoph Heyne.

The winning bidder was Herb Ader, a pewter collector from Bowmansville, Pennsylvania. The underbidder was a representative from the Heritage Center of Lancaster County. The price more than doubled the previous American auction record for a piece of pewter set in 1981 when a collector in New York paid $16,500 for a flat-top quart tankard by William Bradford, Jr. of New York at Christie's, and even topped the recently set world record for any piece of pewter, $38,400, set December 1984 at Phillips in London for a decorated 17th-century charger. (This large Charles II pewter dish with an elaborately engraved border, 28³⁄₁₆" in diameter, was the fifth-largest recorded charger outside of the royal

family's collection. It bore the touch "WB" with a trotting horse, and is number 5485 in Howard Herschel Cotterell's book *Old Pewter: Its Makers and Marks in England, Scotland and Ireland*.)

The two-day auction, which concluded on August 24, included 1,094 lots, the collection and heirlooms of Clara Marie Rollman Brenner of West Earl Township, Lancaster County. The widow of Lee Brenner, owner of a local stone quarry, Mrs. Brenner had collected antiques for about 40 years, commencing about 1940. The Brenner collection was diverse, if somewhat inconsistent in both content and quality.

Items offered for sale ranged from three tall-case clocks, a curly maple Federal bedstead, 100 pieces of tea leaf pattern ironstone, and ten Victorian sofas, to dozens of milk white eggs, boxes of bisque figurines, and over 1,800 postcards, all duly cataloged by Clarence E. Spohn of Ephrata.

Although nobody could predict the price of the Heyne sugar bowl before the sale, it was advertised as the leading object in the collection. Apparently, Brenner had not displayed the piece,

Clarence Spohn, who cataloged the sale, recalled his discovery of the sugar bowl bought for a record $42,500. "There was so much to catalog that if the children hadn't taken all they wanted, the sale could have been a three-day sale instead of two.

"I put everything in categories, and when I started cataloging the metals, I put the few pieces of pewter aside on the floor. When I finally got around to the pewter and picked up the sugar bowl, took off its lid, and saw the 'ICH' touch, I said, 'It couldn't be'," Spohn related. ("I" was used for "J" until the end of the 18th century.)

Spohn said that there was one slight repair on the rim of the bowl, and a dent in the lid had been removed years ago. The sugar bowl is one of only four complete Heyne sugar bowls known. The bottom of another is in the collection of the Brooklyn Museum. The double-bellied, or pear-shaped, sugar bowl is particularly important because its design reveals the Americanization of the German craftsman. Heyne's early work is Germanic in style. The sugar bowl shows English influences and is similar to bowls by Philadelphia pewterers. Clarence Spohn photos.

for Clarence Spohn discovered it packed away. It was believed that the sugar bowl had descended in the Brenner family.

With extensive advance publicity, the sale drew several serious pewter collectors from out of state, plus several pewter specialists, including Connecticut dealer John Carl Thomas, who is the son-in-law of winning bidder Herb Ader. ("He may be my father-in-law," said Thomas, "but I often find him my underbidder, and he bought the sugar bowl on his own with no advice from me.")

Through more than 300 lots of metalware, clothing, and books in the morning, anticipation and speculation about the sugar bowl mounted. Before offering the bowl for sale, Clarence Spohn gave a brief speech, calling the piece "a Lancaster County rarity."

The only dealer who was conspicuous as a bidder was Chris Machmer of Annville, Pennsylvania; he stopped at $22,000. After $30,000 the contenders were Herb Ader and the Heritage Center of Lancaster County. When the representative for the Heritage Center cast his last bid at $42,000, an advance of $500 gave the bowl to Ader.

A quiet, amiable man, Ader is often seen in the audiences of Lancaster County sales. Probably less well known until August 23 was his stature as a serious pewter collector. His collection of pewter contains other important pieces, including a coffeepot by William Will. Ader said the sugar bowl was his only piece of Heyne pewter. He further stated that he wished to keep the bowl in private hands in Lancaster County.

On the other hand, there were very objective reasons why the Heritage Center of Lancaster County made such a strong effort to acquire this sugar bowl. A museum of Lancaster County art and decorative arts located on Lancaster's Penn Square, The Heritage Center has been collecting notable Lancaster antiques for more than a decade. In that time, it has never before had the opportunity to purchase a marked piece of pewter by Heyne.

Although Heyne has been recognized as one of America's leading pewterers for more than half a century, no public museum in Lancaster County has an example of his work. Many museums of national stature, including the Garvan collection at Yale, the Brooklyn Museum, and Winterthur, own pewter made by Heyne. Some of the majestic flagons and chalices made by Heyne remain in the ownership of Lancaster County churches.

Johann Christoph Heyne was born in Saxony in 1715; he came to America in 1742. About a decade later, he settled in Lancaster, then the most important inland town in Pennsylvania. He worked in Lancaster as both a pewterer and tinsmith until his death there on January 11, 1781. His brick house and shop on the first block of Lancaster's West King Street became the property of his stepson, John Frederick Steinman, who established a hardware store there. This store was the genesis of the multi-faceted businesses of Lancaster's noted Steinman family.

Heyne's known products include plates in three sizes, beakers, flasks, chalices, flagons, church candlesticks, and an open salt. In all, less than 100 pieces of Heyne pewter survive and 65 percent of those are in museums and churches. Undoubtedly, the $42,500 paid for this piece will spur searches for presently unknown pieces by Heyne.

At present, it may be safe and wise to regard the record price for the Heyne sugar bowl as a solitary instance. If one or two other pieces of important American pewter should sell at auction for similar prices, however, the value of 18th-century American pewter may reach some truly golden levels.

The sale of the sugar bowl marks the second time an auction record has been set at an auction called by Horst and cataloged by Spohn. In 1980, they sold a Pennsylvania German Fraktur for $29,000.

Editor's Note: The underbidder is crucial for records to be made. The underbidder, Eddy Nicholson, a private collector and a major force in the marketplace for Americana from 1985 to 1995, determined the price of Rembrandt Peale's masterpiece when it was bought by the National Gallery for a record $4.07 million on December 5, 1985.

THE RECORD PEALE

BY LITA SOLIS-COHEN AND HELEN SEGGERMAN

When the National Gallery of Art in Washington bought Rembrandt Peale's *Rubens Peale with a Geranium* for $4.07 million at Sotheby's, December 5, 1985, it paid an auction record price for American art, topping the $2.75 million paid for Frederic Church's *Icebergs* in 1979.

The winning bid was made by Larry Fleischman, president of Kennedy Galleries in New York, who was seated in the fourth row next to J. Carter Brown, director of the National Gallery. A few moments after the painting was knocked down to Kennedy, auctioneer John Marion announced that Kennedy had been acting for the National Gallery, and turning to Brown, he said, "How nice to see you here." There was a round of applause in the packed salesroom.

The underbidder was Eddy G. Nicholson, a New Hampshire collector of American paintings and furniture, one of the owners of the Congoleum Corporation, standing at the back of the room. He entered the bidding after Alexander Acevedo of Alexander Gallery dropped out at $3.4 million.

The touching and affectionate painting of the bespectacled 17-year-old naturalist with his prize geranium, painted by his 23-year-old brother in 1801, according to Brown, had been at the top of the National Gallery's want list for many years. "We felt it was of national importance and that it should come to the National Gallery," said Brown. He went on to explain that this was the first purchase from the National Gallery's Patrons' Permanent Fund.

In three years, the National Gallery raised $50 million for acquisitions. "The drive ends December thirty-first. Any contributions are welcome," added Brown. He pointed out that although the Federal government pays for upkeep and maintenance of the National Gallery, there is no federal money for art purchases. "All our art comes from the private sector," he noted.

"I think of it as the first American portrait. Its informality, emphasis on the practical, and the mixture of art and science is, in effect, an American idea," said John Wilmerding, deputy director of the National Gallery and an American painting scholar.

"It is not bombastic and royal. The plant, representing growth, is a tribute to the artist as scientist, the scientist as artist, and to American aspirations at the beginning of the New Republic. It's a most accomplished still life. A portrait and genre, that is what is unique and special," Wilmerding continued enthusiastically, adding, "It is the perfect first purchase for our great endowment fund contributed to by many people, small checks as well as big gifts."

The 28" x 24" painting belonged to Pauline E. Woolworth, the 80-year-old widow of the late Norman B. Woolworth, of the five-and-dime store family. Mrs. Woolworth watched the sale from behind the glass window of Sotheby's boardroom, which overlooks the salesroom. After the sale, she said she was "delighted with the price" and was "particularly thrilled that it would go to the National Gallery."

Rembrandt Peale, *Rubens Peale with a Geranium,* signed "Rem. Peale" and dated 1801, 28" x 24", sold for $4,070,000 to the National Gallery in Washington. The picture has been widely exhibited since it was first shown at the Pennsylvania Academy of the Fine Arts in 1923, when it was owned by a descendant of the artist. In the mid-1950's, the family sold it to Lawrence Fleischman, then a Detroit collector, who later bought Kennedy Galleries. Fleischman said that Norman Woolworth bought the painting from him in 1959 for less than $100,000. Most recently, it was one of the "Masterpieces of American Art" shown at the Boston Museum of Fine Arts in 1983 and traveled with the exhibit to the Grand Palais in Paris in the spring of 1984. Sotheby's photo.

Woolworth had reportedly refused an offer of more than $3 million for the painting last year, and a number of other museums had approached her to buy it. "Mother had been bothered constantly by collectors and institutions who wanted to purchase the painting," said Frederick Woolworth, a son of Pauline Woolworth and president of Coe Kerr Gallery in New York. "She has three children and 16 grandchildren, and this painting is everyone's favorite, so she decided to sell it now before she leaves this world and before there are any squabbles."

Woolworth said he believed that his gallery could not handle the sale because it would be a conflict of interest. "It is best sold at auction. It is the last of the [American] icons in private hands," he said before the sale.

A friend of the family said that Woolworth, realizing she would miss the painting a great deal, had a copy made of it.

Editor's Note: On January 25, 1986, Christie's won the first round in the competition between the auction houses to sell a piece of American furniture for a million dollars. M.A.D. recorded the historic moment when Eddy Nicholson's bid of $950,000 made art market history, and the 10 percent buyer's premium pushed the price he paid for a mahogany piecrust tea table to $1,045,000.

TEA TABLE BREAKS THE $1 MILLION BARRIER

BY LITA SOLIS-COHEN AND SAMUEL PENNINGTON

The auction record for American furniture was broken on Saturday, January 25, 1986, at Christie's in New York City when a Philadelphia piecrust tilt-top tea table sold for $1,045,000. It is the first piece of American furniture to sell for more than $1 million. The buyer was Eddy G. Nicholson, 47, a Hampton Falls, New Hampshire, businessman, one of the two principal owners of the Congoleum Corporation, a conglomerate that manufactures floor covering and builds ships for the navy at the Bath Iron Works in Maine.

Nicholson said he has been collecting American furniture and paintings for five years. Last December, he was the underbidder on the $4.07 million Rembrandt Peale portrait of his brother Rubens with a geranium that went to the National Gallery in Washington.

Nicholson did his own bidding standing on the stairway at the back of the auction room next to one of his advisers, New Hampshire dealer Ronald Bourgeault. Hoping to scare away competitors, he had instructed the auctioneer to open with his bid of $550,000, which was $50,000 over the high estimate.

For a few long seconds it appeared his strategy worked. Then a $575,000 bid was offered by a phone bidder, and Harold Sack, president of Israel Sack, Inc., New York City dealers in American furniture, seated in the third row, signaled a bid with a flip of his gold pencil, and the bidding moved along rapidly in $20,000 and $30,000 increments—

$620,000, $650,000, $680,000, $700,000. Sack, who said later that he was bidding for a client, shook his head when the bidding got to $950,000, and the table was knocked down to Nicholson. With buyer's premium, he paid $1,045,000. The Sack firm had owned the table in the early 1950s and had sold it to Richard M. Hanson, a Detroit collector, for $15,000.

"It started on Chestnut Street in Philadelphia," said Albert Sack, Harold's brother, before the sale. "I bought it from Joe Davidson," said Sack. Davidson, who now has a shop on Pine Street, wanted $7,000, but Sack said he had only $1,500 in the bank. "I called my brother Harold, who was in the plastics business then, and told him to send me the rest of the money or I might land in jail."

Sack said he sold the table to Hanson a few years later, and when Hanson decided to move to Florida a short time later, Jess Pavey, a now-retired Detroit antiques dealer (whose own collection was sold a few years ago by Christie's), negotiated the sale of the Hanson collection to a Bryn Mawr, Pennsylvania, collector who had to have the table and bought everything else in the Hanson collection to get it.

The collector's widow, who consigned the table to Christie's, asked for anonymity but attended the sale with her children and afterwards said she had expected to get about half as much.

Considered one of the dozen best American piecrust tea tables in existence, and made during the full flowering of the Philadelphia Chippendale

The first million-dollar piece of American furniture ever auctioned, a Philadelphia tilt-top tea table sold for $1,045,000 to be exact. Eddy G. Nicholson said he'd always wanted a first-class Philadelphia tea table and that the table would eventually go into his home. It has now been sent to Winterthur for study and in April will be shown in the loan exhibit that will mark the 25th anniversary of the University Hospital Philadelphia Antiques Show. Christie's photo.

style in 1765–75, it has a scalloped top cut from the same template as a similar table at the Metropolitan Museum of Art and it is likely it came from the same shop. It is in extraordinarily good condition, down to its original leather-covered casters. Only a small piece of molding on the top is missing, in a place long since worn smooth by dusting. Leigh Keno, a Christie's American furniture specialist, pointing out the defect at the presale exhibition, exclaimed, "Isn't that a great old break!"

Harold Sack said the table's simple elegance 0 is not embellishment but fully integrated into one of the great Philadelphia forms," he said.

Three years ago, when he bought a Newport kneehole desk for $687,000, making a new auction record, Sack predicted that a piece of American furniture would one day sell for a million dollars. "We have just reached another plateau." Sack said after the sale. "It was a bargain, bargain means value, not what the price was."

Editor's Note: As the prices of weathervanes soared,

each new record was reported on the pages of M.A.D.

RECORD INDIAN WEATHERVANE

BY SAMUEL PENNINGTON

A 36" high Indian weathervane brought a record auction price, $93,500, at Skinner's sale, May 30, 1986, in Bolton, Massachusetts. The identity of the purchaser is a closely held secret. All Skinner's staff will say is that it was a private collector and that they are forbidden to say where the collector lives.

New York dealer Steve Miller was the last bidder in the salesroom, at $65,000. From then on, the bidding was between two phone bidders, one of whom was Blanche Greenstein, a New York dealer who said she thought she had the vane at an $80,000 bid, when a last minute bid of $85,000 took it. Steve Miller said he saw R. Scudder Smith, publisher of the *Newtown Bee,* go to the pay phone as the bidding started, and gave the opinion that Smith was the buyer. "I've never known him to be the underbidder," said Miller. Called later in Connecticut, Smith denied he had been the buyer.

The Indian had a crusty untouched patina so desired by serious collectors, plus it had a good provenance. Some 45 years ago the consignor's father took it off a barn near the former town of Enfield, Massachusetts. The town was one of those inundated to create the Quabbin Reservoir. Reportedly he paid $10 for the vane.

According to Skinner's, the consignor had put the vane atop his house where it stayed for 40 years. He removed it five years ago when an insurance company refused to cover it. The consignor's entire family, down to toddlers, attended the auction and watched the rapid bidding with delight.

The previous auction record for a weathervane was $82,500 for a gilded copper Statue of Liberty by the J. L. Mott Ironworks sold at Sotheby's in 1982 and bought by New York collector Ralph Esmerian.

At $93,500 to a mystery buyer, a new auction record for an American—or any other—weathervane. Skinner photo.

Editor's Note: The furniture and household gear used and sold by the religious group called Shakers, who renounced their worldly goods, was embraced by a group of wealthy collectors who like its clear, bright colors and simple grace. They paid record prices that were duly recorded in the pages of M.A.D.

RECORD SHAKER TABLE

BY SAMUEL PENNINGTON

A 12' long Shaker trestle table with a two-board tiger maple top sold for a record $42,900 including the 10 percent buyer's premium at Wayne Mayo's August 26, 1986, auction on-site at Spruce Lodge in East Sullivan, Maine. The buyer was Greenwich, Connecticut, dealer David Schorsch, who flew to Bangor and drove the rest of the way. The next day Schorsch said the table was "the finest I've ever seen," and it was already sold to a collector. The underbidder was specialist Shaker dealer Robert Wilkins.

It was a record auction price for a piece of Shaker furniture, surpassing the $42,800 paid for a 21' community table at Robert W. Skinner, Inc. in October 1985.

At the Spruce Lodge sale a smaller 7½' long Shaker trestle-base table with a pine top sold for $23,100 to Ronald Nasser, a New York dealer who, in the past, has specialized in Oceanic art. Marshfield, Massachusetts, auctioneer Willis Henry accompanied Nasser.

According to auctioneer Wayne Mayo of Ellsworth, Maine, Spruce Lodge was originally owned by a Louise Spring, who was an avid collector of Shaker things. She sold it in the 1960s to a couple who donated the lodge to Fairleigh Dickinson University, for whom Mayo sold the contents.

The record table "was a poem," said dealer Marianne Clark of nearby Southwest Harbor. The underside of the top was in old red and was held together by tiger maple cleats. Iron rivets were also spaced evenly along the underside.

In addition to local dealers and collectors, the auction attracted a number of specialist Shaker dealers and collectors. Chichester, New Hampshire, dealer Doug Hamel commented that after the second table was sold, "We all left in a parade."

A new record auction price for a piece of Shaker furniture, $42,000.

Pine top Shaker table, $23,100.

Editor's Note: The Walters sale gives a glimpse of the maturing market for American folk art in the mid-1980s, when new standards of connoisseurship were set. After the sale due to divorce, Don Walters remarried and continued to deal actively as Walters-Benisek, headquartered in Northampton, Massachusetts. In recent years, Walters and his partner, Mary Benisek, have cut their participation in shows to just one a year in New Hampshire, but they remain active in business dealing in American folk art privately and building collections, including their own collection of Modernist paintings and decorative arts.

THE WALTERS SALE: THE MATURING MARKET FOR FOLK ART

BY LITA SOLIS-COHEN

"What to keep and what to sell" is the dealer's dilemma that plagued Faye and Don Walters for nearly a decade. "You want to keep the best, but you have to sell the best to build a reputation and stay in business," said Don on the phone.

Divorce sent their entire collection to Sotheby's, where it was sold on Saturday morning, October 25, 1986. The group of 130 objects put together by two young people of limited means who began collecting when they were in college was expected to bring close to a million dollars. It brought $1.5 million.

"We began collecting all sorts of things—Chinese and European—when we were students at the University of Michigan, but by the time we were working at Williamsburg in the early 1970s, we had zeroed in on American folk art," recalled Don, who was curator of the Abby Aldrich Rockefeller Folk Art collection from 1972 to 1978, while his wife, Faye, found craftsmen to make reproductions to be sold at the museum shop.

"When we lived on Duke of Gloucester Street, our country furniture, redware, and carvings fit well into a period setting, but in 1978, when we moved back to the Midwest and became dealers, we went back to using folk art in a more tantalizing way, set out in spaces with white walls filled with light where the juxtaposition of objects demonstrate what we think art collecting is all about," Faye added.

Since becoming dealers, the Walters kept fewer than a dozen of the objects they relentlessly pursued at flea markets, antiques shows, and auctions. They chose pieces that had clarity of design and that used pattern and color in an arresting way. They liked abstraction in portraits and in decoration.

There is nothing cute or quaint about their taste. They shared the artist's joy in materials and technique. The surfaces of their redware have wild designs in dark-colored slip, and the vinegar graining on their furniture is often bizarre, applied with the energy of a child with finger paints. "When tools were introduced that made graining look exactly like wood, it became boring," Don contends.

There is a lot of refinement in this collection that took 20 years to build. "We worked at it. We were not sentimental about what we had bought. We were willing to trade things," Don confessed.

"We never thought of our collection as an investment, though we put every nickel we had into it," Don confided. "It became a challenge, a discipline, an activity that was a large part of our lives, maybe too much."

Walters admitted that five years ago, the collection would not have been worth half as much. "The market has gone crazy," he said.

This elegant swordsman whirligig sold for $42,900, a record for a whirligig. (Dealer Steve Miller sold a fine large whirligig at the Fall Antiques Show at the Pier for what he termed before the sale, "a big price—$27,500.") Sotheby's photo.

Some pieces can be ascribed to specific makers, but most are anonymous, bought purely for aesthetic reasons after sifting through thousands of similar objects. The collection reflects a very personal taste and is full of evocative parallels to modern art.

The paintings are stark linear images, the sculpture, abstract forms. The best documented piece in the collection is a clock in a paint-decorated case made in 1801 for a Shenandoah County, Virginia, fraktur artist named Jacob Strickler by his brother-in-law, a furniture decorator named Johannes or John Spitler, who lived on the adjoining farm. On the sides of the clock, Spitler painted upside-down hearts and flowers copied from Strickler's fraktur.

It was Don who finally identified Spitler. When another decorated clock and two decorated chests were exhibited at Williamsburg in 1973, they were attributed to an artist known only as "JSP." Walters, determined to identify this hand, made many trips to the Shenandoah Valley, and finally one day, in 1975, in a library in the region, he found a typewritten genealogy of the Spitler family with an entry listing a decorated clock.

"I found the clock in a house five minutes from the library and in a Bible in the same house were seven hand-colored drawings by Jacob Strickler. This detective work was the most exciting part of my curatorial career," said Walters.

The fraktur were later bought by Williamsburg, and three years later, the five brothers and sisters who inherited the clock decided to sell it to Walters, together with one remaining drawing. "We made what seemed like an outrageously high offer at the time," Don recalled. "We did it because there had been testimony that fraktur artists and furniture artists communicated and used each other's vocabulary, and this clock is the rare proof."

Don and Faye Walters were not afraid to pay high prices. At Sotheby's in May 1980 they paid a whopping $54,906 for a carved and painted wood Dapper Dan shop figure, a gent dressed in red, white, and blue, holding a red and white barber pole, with his name "Dan" painted on his top hat.

The Walters' good taste paid off. Their painted furniture, sculpture, fraktur, decoys, stoneware, redware, painted boxes, and paintings, offered in 130 lots, attracted a standing-room-only crowd of more than 600 who spent more than a half a million dollars more than expected. Only nine lots failed to sell and the top five lots went to private collectors. Four of those five collectors bid for themselves, the fifth asked dealers Peggy and David Schorsch to do the bidding.

One collector paid $258,500 for the carved and painted wood Dapper Dan trade sign, that once stood in front of a barbershop in Philadelphia or Washington.

If decoys are counted as folk sculpture, Dapper Dan is not a record. But since decoy collectors don't consider their birds folk art, and the "folky" birds folk art collectors buy are not the very pricey ones, some will consider Dan the new record holder for folk sculpture.

The buyer of Dan also paid $203,500 for the pine tall-case clock decorated by Johannes Spitler for his brother-in-law, Jacob Strickler. Spitler copied the upside-down hearts sprouting flowers on the side of the clock from Strickler's frakturs, one of which sold immediately after the clock (to the same collector) for $6,875. The clock's price is an auction record for painted furniture but not a record for a clock. The Willard lighthouse clock that sold in January 1985 for $275,000 remains the beacon for American timepieces.

Throughout the sale, the clock and Dapper Dan remained on the stage at the front of the salesroom. Dapper Dan, set off by a frame of black molding, took on the aspect of an actor in the drama that was unfolding. When he was sold, there was a round of applause.

Half a dozen bidders in the salesroom and several on the phone were in the bidding for him, up to $100,000, but after that it was a duel between Fred Hill of Berry-Hill Gallery and Sotheby's Nancy Druckman, who cataloged the sale and took the collector's secret signals, relaying them to John Marion, the auctioneer. Dapper Dan was gaveled down to Druckman, who said the collector did not want to be identified.

After the sale, Don Walters said he was pleased with the totals but a little sad. "It was too soon to

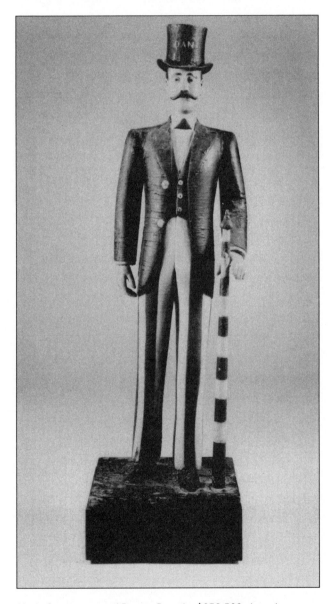

Uncle Sam move over! Dapper Dan, the $258,500 shop sign, is now the most expensive piece of American folk sculpture (a folk painting has brought a lot more). In his red and white striped trousers and blue coat and top hat, ready for any Fourth of July parade, he may become the new American icon. Sotheby's photo.

The record for American painted furniture now stands at $203,500, paid by a collector for this painted pine tall-case clock made by Johannes Spitler in the town of Massanutten in the Shenandoah Valley in 1801. He made it for his brother-in-law, Jacob Strickler, a Fraktur artist who lived on the adjoining farm. A raised panel is inscribed, "Jacob Strickler 1801, Johannes Spitler, Number 3." It is in extraordinarily fine condition. Even the clock's weights retain blue and orange paint, although the paper dial has been replaced. The details on the clock—the inverted hearts with flowers growing from their tips and the diamond-shaped patterns—closely resemble motifs on Strickler's fraktur, which is related to the German-Swiss fraktur style of Lancaster County, from where the settlers of the Shenandoah migrated. Sotheby's photo.

sell. Dapper Dan will become the million-dollar tea table in years to come," he said, as he pulled away in his van loaded with pedestals and the black molding that he had supplied to Sotheby's for the exhibition.

He said he was amazed at some of the prices and disappointed in others. He was pleased that a maple and pine cupboard painted with abstract wood graining sold for $115,500. And he was surprised at the $107,250 collectors paid for a pair of portraits of Mr. and Mrs. Moses Pike of Haverhill, New Hampshire, by Thomas Skynner.

These pictures of a fat and not-handsome husband holding a package of bank notes and his rather plain blue-eyed wife wearing an ill-fitting red dress were expected to bring $30,000/50,000, but their linear faces and the abstract design of their clothes appealed to two collectors who battled for them, pushing the price higher and higher.

Walters thought $49,500 was a bargain for the painted wood trade sign carving of a nude boy, signed "M. L. Paine, Carver." Found in Dallas, it is closely related to the well-known figure of Father Time in the collection of the Museum of American Folk Art in New York. "I like it as well as the Dapper Dan," Walters confessed.

Stoneware brought amazing prices. A jug marked "Fulper & Bros., Flemington, New Jersey," decorated in cobalt blue with a picture of acrobats, was estimated at $4,000/6,000 but sold for a stoneware record, $28,600, to a phone bidder. "Leigh and Leslie bought the jug at a sale in Garrison, New York, for $3,500 when they were only fourteen and sold it when they had to pay for college," said Ronald (Pops) Keno, father of the twins, standing at the back of the salesroom. The jug was resold at Sotheby's in November 1975 for $2,600.

Stoneware prices have fluctuated over the years, but pieces decorated with figures are in high demand right now. An ovoid two-handled crock decorated with a caricature of a running man holding an American flag, inscribed with the word

When this painted pine cupboard fetched $115,500, there was a round of applause. Sotheby's photo.

Mr. and Mrs. Moses Pike by Thomas Skynner, dated 1846, sold for $106,700, the best price for any paintings in the sale. They had sold at a 1977 Sloan's auction in Washington for $8,000. Sotheby's photo.

"Hail," known as the "politician pot," sold to the same bidder for $14,300.

Other gray stoneware pots decorated with blue figures, full face or in profile, fetched between $2,750 and $7,150.

Redware in the sale did not bring as much as stoneware. A glazed redware punch cooler, the upper portion in the form of the head of a Black man, sold for $11,000, and an unglazed head of a man, made in Ohio in the second half of the 19th century, fetched $2,530. A simple redware cylindrical jar decorated with a wild design of brown splotches went for $990.

Dated pieces in any medium often fetch a premium, and if the date is early and the design is good, they can bring double their estimates. Such was the case of a yarn-sewn hearth rug stitched in many subtle colors in a design of birds, flowers, trees, and sheep, signed "P.S. 1824." Estimated at $8,000/12,000, it sold for $25,300 to New York dealers Joel and Kate Kopp, who had pictured it in their book, *American and Sewn Hooked Rugs: Folk Art Underfoot* (Dutton, 1975).

Quilts and the dower chests they were stored in were bargains by comparison and most went to dealers. A brilliantly colored red, yellow, blue, and green Mennonite quilt in a Mariner's Compass pattern sold for $4,125, and a cotton and wool flannel Indiana Amish quilt in the Bow Tie pattern fetched the same price.

A dower chest painted yellow and decorated with an American eagle and a cat-like lionesses, by the "flat tulip artist," who was recently identified as Daniel Otto of Centre County, Pennsylvania, sold for $27,500, falling below its $30,000/50,000 estimate. Another chest from Centre County, similar to one that sold at the Jean and Howard Lipman sale in 1981 for $41,800, fetched only $19,800. One painted with birds, tulips, a heart, and a compass flower on a blue ground by Johannes Spitler, the same Shenandoah artist who decorated the clock, went within its estimate to the Kopps of America Hurrah for $14,300.

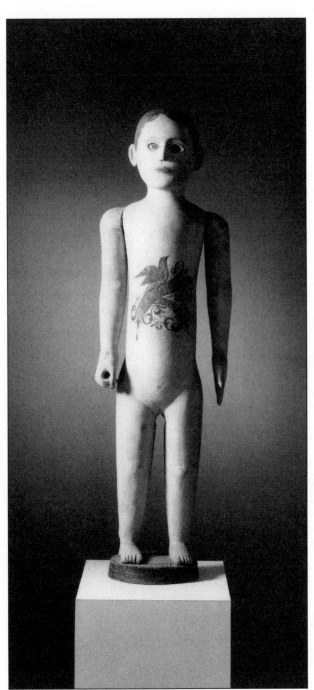

This Indian woman carved circa 1870 is similar to women painted by 20th-century French Cubist Fernand Leger. She sold for $30,800. Even though missing her feet and one arm, the abstract quality of her stylized dress decorated with red, green, and blue feathers and arrows, and her haunting stare, gives the 45" tall figure monumentality. Sotheby's photo.

Walters considered this painted wood trade sign carving, signed "M.L. Paine, Carve," one of the few buys of the sale. "I like him as much as Dapper Dan," said Walters of the 50½" high figure that sold for $49,500. Sotheby's photo.

Decorated stoneware prices were high. The Fulper Brothers "acrobats" jug (top) was a new auction record for American stoneware at $28,600. (The record lasted just a week.) It was underbid by 18-year-old Adam Weitsman, now a college student. "That one I wanted for myself," he said. He won the Macquoid "farmer" (third row, right, $7,150) for a Connecticut collector and the Cowden "man" (second row, right, $5,225) for a Washington collector. Sotheby's photo.

A yarn-sewn hearth rug signed "P.S. 1824" sold for $25,300 to New York dealers Joel and Kate Kopp. Sotheby's photo.

The smaller chests and boxes brought big prices. A miniature chest decorated with green dots made in Shenandoah County, Virginia, by Jacob Stalwart of Newmarket, sold for $9,075, more than double its estimate. At the sale of the Jean and Howard Lipman collection at Sotheby's in 1981, this chest sold for $2,420.

Not every piece that came from the Lipman sale soared in value, A painted fan-back Windsor side chair the Walters bought at the Lipman sale five years ago for $3,630 sold for $4,170 to the Kopps.

Game boards were real winners. A new record was made for a painted game board when $4,675 was paid for a checkerboard painted red and black against a yellow ground with a border of large red and black scallops. Two other game boards sold for $4,400, and an Eastlake-style one that was pictured on the back cover of Bruce and Doranna Wendel's book *Gameboards of North America* (Dutton, 1986) went for $4,070.

The Walters sale will be remembered above all for folk sculpture. Among the memorable pieces, in addition to Dapper Dan and the M. L. Paine trade sign, was an elegant swordsman whirligig that sold for $42,900, a new record for a whirligig. A fragment of a painted wood Indian woman, lacking an arm and most of her legs but retaining her Leger-like monumentality, went for $30,800.

There was soft sculpture as well. Two red and green velvet pincushions in the shape of big strawberries with little berries suspended sold in one lot for $550, and a bird on a stand made of hundreds of pieces of folded calico went for the same price.

On the other hand, paintings—mostly sober linear images—generally brought less than expected. Walters thought $66,000 paid by a collector for Amanda Power's *Portrait of an Illinois Mother and Her Baby* seated on a yellow-painted chair was disappointing. The $20,900 paid for a pair of dark portraits by I. Gilbert of a man and a woman from Cazenovia, New York, was below their $25,000/35,000 estimate. A portrait of poker-faced Maria Menfee by D.S. Packard, dated 1846 and estimated at $10,000/20,000, failed to sell, as did a portrait on bed ticking of Sally Hopkins of Woodstock, Vermont, wearing a white cap with flowers, posed next to rows of green books.

Editor's Note: Collector Eddy Nicholson dominated American furniture sales in the 1980s. Sam Pennington tells what makes this collector tick in a revealing profile that appeared in the January 1987 issue of M.A.D.

EDDY NICHOLSON, COLLECTOR

BY SAMUEL PENNINGTON

There's an aphorism in the antiques trade that to form a good collection, a collector needs either time or money. Eddy G. Nicholson of Hampton Falls, New Hampshire, has both. Only five years after he bought his first piece of American furniture, he is well on his way to amassing a superb collection of Americana.

He's paid some spectacular prices at auction, $1.045 million for a Philadelphia tea table, $1.1 million for a wing chair, $528,000 for a wainscot chair, and $660,000 for a bombé chest. His purchases have not all been public. He said he has bought a lot more from dealers.

High prices don't scare him. "It pays off in the long run," said Nicholson frankly in a recent interview about his collection and his plans. "One has to look for the best in the price range one can afford and go for it."

Nicholson enjoys collecting. "Every night I go home, I get a drink, put my jeans on, sit on the floor, and study the room. I pick out one piece and study that piece. I turn it over. I get Albert Sack's *Good, Better, Best* book or books by Nutting or Downs, and I study that piece against other pieces that are in those books. I enjoy doing that every night."

He also enjoys the company of other collectors and dealers. "In this fraternity, there is a camaraderie that I haven't seen in anything else I have ever been involved in. Collectors share with each other. Some of the great collectors, if I'm in town or if they're here, I'll ask them to come visit me or they will ask me to come visit them. We tell stories, we look at pieces, we turn them over, and we enjoy

each other's collections and pieces. The same is true with a dealer. I can go into an exhibit and four or five of us get around a piece together and everybody is sharing their information and knowledge. I've learned a great deal from them."

Nicholson paraphrases master dealer and teacher Harold Sack to explain his place in the collecting timetable. "As Harold has said so many times, collecting goes in twenty-year cycles, and generally there are various phases. In the early phase, the collector's very tentative and he is not spending very much, and then he becomes more knowledgeable and more aggressive, and then there is this period where he's finding great masterpieces and filling gaps and upgrading what he first bought. I've been collecting about six years. I'm at the aggressive stage. I guess I have gotten there faster than some people."

Aggressive indeed. Last January [1986], when he bought the Philadelphia tea table, the first piece of American furniture to break the million-dollar barrier, he instructed Christie's Dean Failey to open the bidding at $550,000—$50,000 over the high estimate. There was a long pause before Harold Sack raised his gold pencil to enter the bidding for his client.

At Sotheby's in October, when dealer Bernard Levy bid $475,000 on a bombé chest, Nicholson jumped the bidding by holding up six fingers to indicate a bid of $600,000 and won the piece. At the same sale, he spent $1.1 million for a wing chair and $528,000 for a Pilgrim Century oak wainscot chair, pushing furniture of that early period to a whole new price level. The week before, he took a platinum flute up to $187,000 at Christie's before dropping out, one of the few times he's been an underbidder.

How did Eddy Nicholson get to be the major buyer of the best American antique furniture? His is an old-fashioned American success story.

He grew up in Denison, Texas, about 50 miles north of Dallas, where his father was a foreman at a Levi Strauss plant. He went to college, did a two-year hitch as an officer in the U.S. Marine Corps, started two companies, and sold them. Then he earned advanced degrees in law and accounting and became president and CEO of Congoleum, Inc., which in 1979 was vulnerable to a takeover. With the aid of some insurance companies, he and his partner, Byron Radaker, took Congoleum private in 1980. The $445 million leveraged buyout was then the largest in American business history. That case study is taught at the Harvard Business School.

In 1985, after he and Radaker had turned Congoleum around and made it profitable, they bought out the insurance companies' interests, borrowing the money on their own to do it. In 1986, they dismantled the company, selling the four divisions separately for a reported $850 million. One of Congoleum's companies was Bath Iron Works, Maine's largest employer.

So much for the money. While he and his partner wait out an opportunity to get involved with another enterprise, he has time and he has the compelling interest that drives collectors.

Nicholson recalled his first furniture purchase at auction. "About five years ago, I bought a little New Hampshire tavern table from Christie's that had a note on the underside written by the guy who gave it to his wife on her wedding day. It's a wonderful little table, I don't think it cost more than $8,000 and I was nervous as I could be.

"I had Jean Vibert [of Christie's American, furniture department] bid on it for me. I was in California. I couldn't wait to find out whether I bought it. I was nervous because I was not

Eddy G. Nicholson at his desk.

confident in my own ability and hoped I didn't make a mistake." (According to Christie's price list, the table cost $6,600.) The under-bidder was Harold Sack.

"The auction houses have been very helpful to me, just as the dealers and the other collectors have, and the people from the museums. Even when I was collecting at the lower levels, eight-to ten-thousand-dollar pieces, they would spend as much time with me if I asked them to as they would for a million-dollar piece. I think a lot of people who start collecting don't realize how much assistance they can get at the auction houses."

Dealers have been just as helpful. "I find it often easier to deal with dealers than an auction house. I can get individual attention when I visit a dealer. I enjoy working with dealers and I have acquired some of my very best pieces in private transactions with dealers."

Part of the secret of his success is that Nicholson firmly believes in the principles of management. Good managers seek and weigh a lot of advice. Ronald Bourgeault, the Hampton, New Hampshire, dealer who has shepherded Nicholson around the trade and the auction rooms for several years, said, "You can learn something about grocery shopping from watching Eddy Nicholson buy antiques. Whatever he does, whether it's buying a company or buying antiques, or even cars, he does it the best way he can. He calls up and asks advisors which car he should buy. He's approached the antiques business that way. Everybody asks, 'What's the secret?' Well that's it, the secret is adaptability and learning."

Unlike some collectors who try to conceal their intentions in the hope of avoiding competition, Nicholson speaks frankly of his goals. "I want to have the best of each region and each form. I have country rooms. I have some good Pilgrim pieces, such as the wainscot chair I just purchased. I want our collection to span the period from 1600 to 1800, but I'm really not interested in going beyond 1800. I want the best in Pilgrim, William and Mary, Queen Anne, and Chippendale.

"The watchword is quality. I want to be sure that every piece that I have when I finally stop collecting, if I reach my twenty-year cycle or when I die, is the best that I could possibly have acquired at that time. I don't care whether it's from New Hampshire, Rhode Island, Boston, Salem, or Philadelphia. I'm not trying to be a purist as to region, but I am trying to be a purist as to form and quality.

Nicholson says the size of his collection will be limited by the size of his 1845 farmhouse in New Hampshire and the pieces he can put on loan. "I don't like to store things," he adds. The wing chair he bought at Sotheby's in 1985 for a then-record $159,500 is on loan to the Museum of Fine Arts, Boston. A number or museums have asked to exhibit his wainscot chair.

Nicholson admits he's been a major force in upping prices of American furniture but says he's not the only one and predicts the market will get stronger. "What we have to remember is that at an auction the prices don't get there on the basis of one buyer. The reason the prices are where they are is due to a number of things. Since I am a Certified Public Accountant, I always go back to economics—the law of supply and demand. We have many more Americans who are affluent, who can afford to collect at a higher level. The market has a larger demand and a diminishing supply. Great collectors often donate their collections. Museums are getting more and more of the great pieces, and then there's the natural attrition due to fires or owners not knowing what a piece is."

How many people are actually in the market is a guess right now. Garrison, New York, dealer Ronald DeSilva, who often buys important objects for collectors Richard and Gloria Manney, said there are between "fifty and one hundred collectors capable of buying a major piece today. Ten years ago, there were maybe twelve to fifteen nationwide."

Dealer Ronald Bourgeault concurs with the estimate of how many collectors are capable but said he thinks there are "only five to eight" currently buying at the top level, and on a given piece, only three may be active.

The second factor forcing prices up, says Nicholson, is more awareness of American art and antiques. "As you pointed out in *M.A.D.*, only seven pieces of furniture have sold for over a million dollars, and two of those were American. For so long, we in America, as well as people in other places in the world, have considered our art and our furniture to be second-rate," he said.

"There were the pioneer collectors who've known all along that that was not true and who've made great buys," said Nicholson. He thinks the publicity given to record prices has attracted other buyers.

"American furniture auctions could hardly get space in any major newspaper until just the last five years, and now they've been getting a lot. I've been interviewed by many of the major newspapers. I get calls from everywhere—from Denison, Texas, to Los Angeles. *Architectural Digest* wants to do a story, so does *Town & Country*. So there is a great deal of interest by those kinds of publications that are read by people who have interests other than American furniture. Those readers are saying, 'Gee, why haven't we given that some consideration? We've been buying French pieces or English pieces, maybe we should be buying some American pieces'."

Ever the businessman, Nicholson says he realizes there is a down side to the phenomenon of ever higher and higher prices. It's difficult for dealers to work in the traditional way. "I think perhaps that it has become too expensive. It takes a great deal of capital to inventory million-dollar pieces, and it takes a great deal of nerve to buy a piece to put in the shop and then have to mark it up to cover overhead. It's less risky for dealers at that level to find a client they can represent at auction and get a commission so that they don't have their money tied up in inventory."

Though Nicholson sometimes does his own bidding at auction, and sometimes has Bourgeault or auction house staffers bid for him, he isn't sure that the dealer acting solely as an agent is good for the antiques business. "The dealers who are willing to take pieces in inventory are the kinds of dealers that made the American furniture market what it is," he said.

"We need dealers badly, especially dealers with expertise such as the Sacks. We need someone to replace John Walton. We need four or five dealers at the top level."

While noting that the Sacks have recently brought to market some fine pieces from the Mitchell Taradash collection, Nicholson said he believes that if something major and fresh in the decorative arts is going to come up these days, it will generally go to auction. "I think today, with the prices that have been set, that there are few dealers who are willing to offer a price that will snap something away. The dealers are having an

opportunity to see the pieces, but they go in and offer, let's say, three hundred thousand dollars, and an auction house will come in and say, 'We can give you an estimate of two hundred fifty thousand to three hundred fifty thousand dollars, but it may go way beyond that,' and based upon what's happened in the market, people believe it."

Nicholson admitted that he had thought about getting involved in the antiques business, especially after the sale of Congoleum. "I seriously considered my involvement and I thought perhaps I should get into this marketplace because I believe there is room for someone who has the capital to come in at the present time."

But he decided against entering the trade. "I don't have a complete collection. There are a number of forms I don't have. I have gaps in my collection. To complete my collection in the serious manner that I want to, I ought to devote my time to it. If I were associated with a firm as an investor, silent investor or owner, everyone would believe that I was skimming the firm of the best pieces first. If I even had a stated policy that I would not buy from the firm at all or if I did buy from it, I would buy at the same price as it was being offered to all other customers, no one would believe that. Therefore, I would kill the firm," he admitted. "I don't think I'm at a stage in my collecting where I can be involved as a dealer."

Nicholson said he thought art dealers today are in a stronger position than decorative arts dealers. "I think the art firms are better capitalized, and I think there are more pieces on consignment with the art galleries than there are with the furniture people."

Nicholson also collects art. He was the underbidder at Sotheby's last December on the $4.07 million Rembrandt Peale portrait of his brother, Rubens Peale, but he hasn't bought a major picture publicly at auction in two years because he says there haven't been any major pictures available of the type he collects.

"I'm very much in the art market, but the kind of things I collect—major American genre paintings by Mount or Bingham, or Eastman Johnson, I haven't seen recently. I go to the dealers in New York about once every two weeks," he revealed.

What are Nicholson's plans for the collection? Will it go to a museum or be sold so others an have the fun of buying the pieces? Neither, said Nicholson.

"I hope Harold Sack's [20-year] prediction, in my case, is wrong. I hope I keep the enthusiasm as long as I'm alive. I'm having such a good time now. Actually, my wife, Linda, and my children have a tremendous interest. My daughter, Deidre, is working at a museum. She graduated from Columbia with an art history major. My son, Kevin, is 26. He buys commercial buildings and apartment buildings, renovates them, and rents them out. He's been a collector of all sorts of things ever since he was a child. He has a tremendous coin collection and he's really getting enthusiastic about it. He is now finding paintings that he likes, like a Harnett, that is too expensive for him, but at least he's got the interest. My younger son, Steve, is 22 and he is a senior at college. I would like to see my family take an active interest in the collection and for them to do whatever with the collection they would like to do, but I have no plans for it."

Nicholson has been the most visible American furniture buyer in years. Major collectors are rarely seen bidding at auction these days. They bid by phone or through agents, but Nicholson is the kind of person who likes to be involved. He's not grandstanding or celebrating conspicuous consumption by waving his paddle. He's a serious collector and he enjoys being there in the heat of battle and taking most of the best things home.

Editor's Note: In the 1980s, a broad range of collectibles gained the kind of attention in the marketplace generally accorded earlier American furniture and folk art. Noel Barrett's sale of the George Haney collection of advertising launched Barrett's new auction company, which over the next 15 years specialized in toys, trains, and games as well as advertising.

THE NEW COLLECTIBLES:
THE GEORGE HANEY SALE

BY LITA SOLIS-COHEN

It took George Haney three days to drive his collection of antique advertising material from Spencer, Oklahoma, to New Hope, Pennsylvania, where it was auctioned before a crowd of 600 at the Eagle Fire House on April 23, 1988.

"I loaded it all into a twenty-two-foot long truck. We stopped two nights on the road, padlocked the truck, and didn't worry. We had the contents insured for $400,000," said Haney, 58, a tall, graying, moustached man, dressed cowboy-style in jeans, boots, and a ten-gallon hat.

He should have worried; $400,000 was not enough. Haney's collection of tin signs and other old advertising, country store, and soda fountain items sold for a total of $822,500. It was a stellar

Buster Brown and Tige, a two-piece sign, 40" long, sold for $14,300. Haney said he paid $1,400 for it two or three years ago. Noel Barrett photo.

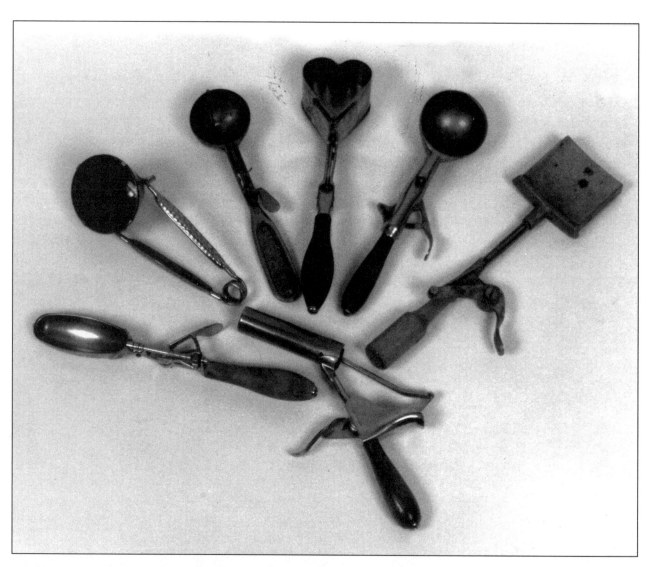

Ice cream scoops, left to right: a Gilchrist #81 banana split scoop, $605; Squeeze Action Cone scoop, $82.50; Geer Mfg. Co. A21 scoop, $330; the record heart-shaped scoop, $4,620 to a Virginia collector who said he missed the one that sold at Gaithersburg two months earlier for $3,000; a common scoop, $137.50; curved square scoop, $385; and the rare cylinder scoop at the bottom, $770. Noel Barrett photo.

performance for Carversville, Pennsylvania, dealer Noel Barrett's new auction company.

The Haney sale will be remembered as the auction where the heart-shaped ice cream scoop sold for an incredible $4,620, the salesman's sample barber's chair in its original carrying case went for $25,300, and the 5' tall cigar store Indian chief from the workshop of Detroit carver Julius Melchers brought $44,000.

The star of the Haney sale was a two-piece brightly colored lithographed tin cutout Buster Brown shoe sign showing bulldog Tige in a harness pulling Buster Brown, dressed in red and riding in a shoe-shaped cart. It went to a San Francisco collector for $14,300, and was the highest price paid at public auction for a tin sign.

"It's great graphic art, has the qualities of a good weathervane, and worth every penny," said Allan Katz, a dealer from Connecticut.

"Twenty years ago, tin signs were abandoned objects going for a song, but now they are traded for big bucks," Katz continued. "Along comes this sale and people wake up to the real worth of great advertising. That's what is going on here. It is a landmark sale. We reevaluate and go on from here."

(The market apparently agreed with Katz. A week later at the Warhol sale in New York, Jeffrey Deitch of Citibank's art advisory service paid a whopping $33,100 for an oculist's sign in the form of a pince-nez painted on both sides and with a pair of green eyes staring out. It was estimated at $1,500/2,500.)

The best Coca-Cola items brought a premium. A 1910 calendar showing the Coca-Cola girl wearing a big picture hat fetched $4,070; a 1939 salesman's sample Coca-Cola cooler with a leatherette carrying case embossed with the words "A Business Builder," together with a catalog of other coolers, sold for $3,310; and a glass electric light in the shape of a Coca-Cola bottle with a tin cap sold for $3,640.

A pot scraper is a wedge-shaped piece of tin used for cleaning pots in the days before non-stick pans or Brillo Pads. One lithographed tin pot scraper advertising Royal Granite Ware cost the buyer $247.50. Another, advertising Red Wing Milling Co., sold for $302.50.

All country stores had string holders. Favorites with collectors are those with brightly lithographed advertisements on them. Haney's advertised Dutch Boy White Lead paint, and it sold for $6,160, a record for a string holder.

Bidding paddles went up all over the salesroom when a thermometer advertising Ed. Pinaud's Hair Tonic came on the block. It was knocked down for $4,070, the most ever paid for an advertising thermometer. The buyer was Peter Sidlow, a Los Angeles collector who probably has the best and biggest collection of old advertising in the country.

A lot of collectors are sweet on antique soda fountain paraphernalia, but before the Haney sale no one had ever paid as much as $1,540 for a glass straw holder. Two glass straw holders reached that price. The first was heart-shaped in cross section for Sweetheart straws; the other advertised Green River in Bottles.

The auction record for a soda fountain syrup dispenser was $4,400 for a Cherry Fizz dispenser. At the Haney sale, two dispensers went for more than $9,000 each. A Detroit lawyer paid $9,350 for an extremely rare blue ceramic Pepsi-Cola dispenser decorated with trees, rabbits, and the slogans, "Satisfying-Invigorating-Refreshing-Strengthening" and "Cures Indigestion Relieves Exhaustion."

"I'm here on a fool's errand and they sent the right man," said David Griem, the Detroit lawyer when he'd won the Pepsi prize. "I looked at the bunnies and the trees and I couldn't resist."

Griem's Pepsi dispenser held the record for less than a minute. The very next lot, a very rare Dr. Pepper's PhosFerrates dispenser, a white ceramic square shaped tank with "Drink Dr. Pepper's" in black letters, sold for $9,900.

There was a record for gum machines—$5,720 paid for a Blinkey Eye Soda Mint Gum one-cent

Pot scrapers. Top row, left to right: by Grand Coal Burner, $175; Mt. Penn Stove Works, $27.50; Royal Granite Ware, $247.50; Fairmont Creamery, $110; Sharples Cream Separator, $121. Bottom row: Junket Powder, $154; Wards Extracts, $121; Red Wing Milling Co., $282.50; Henkel's Flour, $88. Noel Barrett photo.

machine made of cast iron and wood with a flesh-colored face and an eye that blinked. A Perfume Your Handkerchief vending machine made by Mills Novelty Company in 1927 sold for $6,070. One like it sold at Sotheby's Andy Warhol sale the following day for $4,950!

Haney also had a few toys. His cast-iron Yellow Cab Baggage Express Truck went for $9,900, a record for a cast-iron automotive toy. About ten years ago, he bought a stack of toy catalogs for $5 from an old hardware store going out of business. One was a 1927 toy catalog picturing 35 pedal vehicles made by the Gendron Company. Together with a price list, it brought a whopping $935.

Over the years, Haney had put together a nice collection of 39 occupational shaving mugs from a time when the barbershop was a kind of men's club in many communities and customers left their mugs at the barbershop, identified with their name and their occupation. A shaving mug decorated with a picture of an upright slot machine fetched $2,860. "It's an auction record for a shaving

mug, but it's not as rare as one I have with a deep sea diver on it," said the buyer, Paul Dunigan, a collector from Lowell, Massachusetts.

Slot machine collectors as well as mug buyers competed for the mug because the name on it was Thomas Watling, a manufacturer of slot machines, and it probably was the one Watling left at his barber's.

An upright black cat slot machine with a musical movement sold for $19,800. Haney said he had paid $30,000 for it and he knew he overpaid.

Noel Barrett did a fine job of organizing and advertising the Haney sale and was pleased with the premiere of his new auction company. Barrett operates a sort of boutique auction business that caters to collectors with unusual interests. He calls himself an auction promoter. He is not an auctioneer. He hires Maryland auctioneer Rick Opfer to call the sales. Barrett takes the photographs, writes the descriptions, estimates the values, lays out the catalogs, designs the ads, and handles the public relations.

Syrup dispensers. Dr. Pepper's Phos-Ferrates sold for $9,900, a new record for a syrup dispenser. The blue ceramic Pepsi dispenser with trees and rabbits sold for $9,350. Haney said he had paid $3,200 for it in Indianapolis 15 years ago. As for the Dr. Pepper's, Haney said he traded a bunch of junk for it in Texas. Noel Barrett photo.

From left, Sweetheart straw holder, $1540; flared-base straw holder, $467.50; and square-base straw holder, $440. Noel Barrett photo.

Barrett began his campaign for the sale a year ago, when an article he wrote on the Haney collection was published, with profuse illustrations, in *Collector's Showcase*, a glossy magazine widely read by collectors of toys and antiques of commerce.

He told how, over a period of two decades, George Haney bought, traded, and stashed tin signs, toys, coin-operated machines, cash registers, country store fixtures, and other items of America's commercial past.

Haney didn't find these things in Spencer, Oklahoma, a crossroads on the edge of Oklahoma City where he lives. He would spend weeks on the road going from small town to small town "junkin'," as he called it.

First, he went after gun and gunpowder advertising. Then, he moved on to signs for tobacco and liquor, almost all with girlie pictures on them. After that, he collected country store fixtures, syrup dispensers, and coin-operated

machines. In time, he was buying ice cream scoops, straw holders, pot scrapers, match holders with advertising on them, advertising clocks, salesmen's samples, and cigar store Indians.

Three years ago, Haney began constructing an old-fashioned wooden store in his backyard to house his collection, which he had kept in a storage locker in downtown Oklahoma City.

No sooner had he taken most of his stuff out of boxes then he decided that collecting wasn't fun any more. The heyday of finding the great pieces was over. He'd gone about as far as he could go.

When Haney decided to sell his collection, he asked Noel Barrett to handle the sale. He had met the Carversville dealer in Indianapolis seven years ago, and Barrett had sold him a number of items over the phone.

"It was the biggest collection of this type of material ever sold," said Barrett. "While the antique advertising market has had a small and devoted audience for fifteen or twenty years, it's finally gaining a position in the marketplace that has long been accorded earlier Americana."

Haney said he thought the time was right to sell. He said he couldn't trade up any more because he couldn't find better things to trade for.

"Of course, I can't stop collecting," he said after the sale. "I'm looking for cowboy stuff now. I'll be doing some junkin' on the way home."

Yellow Cab Express Baggage truck sold for $9,900, a record for a cast-iron automotive toy. According to Connecticut auctioneer Lloyd Ralston, who was at the Haney sale to pick up bargains (he got two), he paid the previous record, $8,600, for a cast-iron Packard at Phillips last fall. Noel Barrett photo.

Editor's Note: The Andy Warhol sale was a happening. Sotheby's placed stickers printed with Warhol's face on every object in the sale, and buyers have kept those stickers on so that when they sell, the Warhol factor will not be overlooked. Dorothy Gelatt's abbreviated story is only a fraction of the coverage this marathon ten-day sale got on the pages of M.A.D.

A HAPPENING: THE ANDY WARHOL SALE

BY DOROTHY S. GELATT

It was a spectacle. It was a happening. It was like his public life. By the time Andy Warhol died last year at 58, the Pop artist/collector, social climber/self-publicist was a household word, and his fans all over the world wanted a piece of his household. This year, thousands of them got their chance in a blast of bidding and big spending that mirrored Warhol's view of society but was the complete opposite of his own private life of daily bargain hunting and hoarding.

Warhol's executors chose Sotheby's to disgorge the 10,000-odd items the artist stuffed into his elegant East 66th Street Manhattan townhouse. And Sotheby's rose to the occasion. They staged the marathon ten-day sale, April 23 to May 3, 1988, as a major public and media event. More people than vote in the presidential election probably saw it in the press and on television. Sotheby's gave it superior hype, and the press and public responded.

Stockbrokers also responded to Sotheby's publicity and phoned customers all over to get advance orders for Sotheby's public stock offering, expected shortly. The stock sale, originally planned for last fall, was withdrawn after the Black Monday stock market crash. This time, fewer shares are being offered, and the price is said to be lower.

The ten-day Warhol sales took in a total $25,333,368 (including the 10 percent buyer's premium), more than twice Sotheby's early estimate of $10/12 million. A few prices, like those for the now famous cookie jars, were shockers, with "collectibles" collectors bidding their hearts out

for every lot before big money bidders moved in and shot them down. But, as the total shows, buyers paid only an averaged double for the celebrity or "Warhol factor."

Then there was the sales tax incentive. The New York City 8¼ percent retail sales tax was waived because all the proceeds go to the non-profit Andy Warhol Foundation for the Visual Arts, set up in the artist's will. Sotheby's, of course, charged their standard 10% buyer's commission.

A compulsive shopper throughout his life, Warhol often bought in bulk and kept everything. Sotheby's compressed the 10,000 things found in his six-story house (none of it his own art) into 3,436 lots sold in 16 sessions, over the ten days. Practically everything sold; there were only 78 buy-ins.

With unerring show business flair, Sotheby's sold the hottest items, the collectibles, at the beginning, and art at the end. They also estimated conservatively. Thousands of bidders, therefore, actually thought they could buy something and jammed the salesroom, the order books, and the phones, especially for the lower-priced collectibles.

Day 1—Saturday, April 23, the opening catalog of Art Nouveau and Art Deco displayed the prizes of Warhol's greatest shopping strength, and it brought out serious collectors, decorators, and dealers eager for superb examples fresh to the market. They set auction records for furniture by Mackintosh, Legrain, and Ruhlmann, and paid posh prices for everything else. Of the 377 lots, only two were bought in. Altogether, the two sessions of Art

Andy Warhol's elegant Georgian old-money-style Manhattan townhouse on 66th Street near Park Avenue. Sotheby's rapped it like a pinata and 10,000 objects fell out—Warhol's lifetime-hoarded possessions, from art and fine furniture to kitsch and junk.

Over 60,000 spectators and bidders jammed Sotheby's for previews and the ten-day sale. All wore a color-coded daily sticker with a preview time limit, or an "Auction" sticker if they had a bidding paddle. Matching lot number stickers were often filched from the lots as souvenirs! Crowds waited patiently outside to get in and look. Sotheby's international publicity drew worldwide bidders and lookers.

Nouveau and Deco brought $5,314,347 for the 377 lots. Sotheby's counted over 6,000 people in the salesroom that day.

Day 2—Sunday, April 24, was a day to go down in auction history—10,000 spectators and bidders packed Sotheby's for the afternoon session of the lower-priced jewelry and collectibles sale, 331 lots, including the Bakelite bracelets and cookie jars, toys, vending machines, advertising, Victorian shoes, and a 1974 Rolls Royce. Television and print reporters clogged every available inch. You had the impression there was a reporter for every 1.2 bidders.

Prospective buyers from all over the world, especially young people, started lining up early in the morning outside Sotheby's to register for

bidding paddles. By noon, the line stretched out of sight around the block and looked like kids piled up waiting for a rock concert. Sotheby's had alert crowd control and admitted people in small groups so as not to swamp the system. There was anxiety through the line, especially in people who had traveled from afar. They feared that after all their effort they might not even make it inside to bid on a scrap of their Warhol idol. Some hoped their idol was looking down and reveling in the show.

Near sale time, Sotheby's was passing out order-bid forms to the would-be bidders who probably wouldn't make it inside. They told everyone to send their order bids in and hope for the best. No one rioted, but the tension ran high.

Scott Martin, a young pharmacist who flew in from Kansas City, Missouri, for the sale, said that when he was a little boy, Andy Warhol was his idol. Some kids might have wanted to grow up and be a fireman or a policeman. Scott Martin wanted to grow up and be Andy Warhol. Asked what his parents thought, he laughed and said, "They handled it." Mr. Martin was prepared to handle the bidding too, if he ever got in. "I'm prepared to do what it takes," he announced. He was hoping to buy some cookie jars, which were estimated at $100/150 per lot of two to four jars each.

Laura Fisher, a young woman who has a shop called Antique Quilts and Americana in the Manhattan Art and Antique Center, had enjoyed selling things to Andy Warhol in recent years. "I felt very special when he came in. He bought some buggy shawls and quilts, and some toys and kitsch," she said. "I didn't see any of them in the exhibition, so I guess he used them for presents."

Just before coming to register at Sotheby's, Fisher made a quick trip to the Annex Flea Market at Sixth Avenue and 26th Street. "It was a sort of homage to Andy. He used to go there every Sunday," she said nostalgically. "He personified what he satirized."

Bidders who made it inside were hopeful and expectant as the sale began. "I want a souvenir," said a bidder from Pennsylvania who was willing to buy anything. "I'm interested in his persona, not his art. He was a charisma-type person."

For openers, there were about 200 lots of assorted jewelry and gemstones estimated mostly in the low $100s, and a few in the low $1,000s. Everything sold above estimates, mostly two to five times higher, with some ten times higher or more.

A number of Andy Warhol's old friends, groupies, and actors in his films, competed for jewelry with the adoring public. "Baby Jane" Holzer, a New York socialite and early Warhol follower, was there with streaming golden hair and an active bidding paddle. She bought at least

On Sunday, fans lined up around the block from early morning to register for bidding paddles they hoped would lead to a collectible souvenir of their idol. Sotheby's crowd control guard admitted a few at a time. Later, Sotheby's passed out order-bid forms to those who might not make it. These three finally made it inside after an early scare: Laura Fisher, New York quilt and Americana dealer who sold things to Warhol; Scott Martin, Kansas City, Missouri, pharmacist, who wanted to be Andy Warhol when he was a little boy; and Jana Starr, New York dealer in circa 1900 whites and accessories, who wanted to add to her Bakelite bracelet collection. None of them got anything.

a dozen jewelry lots for about $27,000, including two opal necklaces at $2,420 and $5,500; diamond cuff links shaped like dollar signs for $2,860; a long citrine necklace for $4,950; and a real bargain, quartz and gold cuff links plus a pendant in red enamel on gold for only $660.

Paloma Picasso was there and bought two silver and silver-gilt compacts and a lipstick case with tiny cabochon rubies by Boucheron, Paris, circa 1940, for $1,650.

Stuart Pivar, a long-time shopping companion of Andy Warhol, bought a cultured pearl necklace for $1,980, 13 unmounted opals and some tiny round rubies for $2,200, an intricate David Webb gold and hard stone pendant on a gold chain for $3,025, and other choice things throughout the sale. He told the press, who mobbed him with questions on why he bought so many jewels and crystals, that they had a very sentimental value for him.

A gold hibiscus flower brooch by Trabert & Hoeffer, Mauboussin, 1946, went for ten times the estimate at $11,000 and applause. "Let's hear it for the money," quipped auctioneer Robert Woolley.

Miscellaneous lots of Bakelite and plastic bangles, pins, jewelry, napkin rings, and salt and peppers drew souvenir hunters and collectors. They were in lots of maybe 30 to 100 items, estimated mostly at $150/200 per lot. They went from as low as $600 to as high as $2,750 and caused both joy and anguish.

Warhol's crystals, which he apparently used for health reasons, had sentimental buyers. Michael Pierce, a young artist who came up from Richmond, Virginia, bought one lot of nine quartz crystals, about 3" high, for $1,210 (est. $250/300) and was ecstatic. His friends from Venice, California, did not fare as well. Artist Frederick Fulmer and screenwriter James Berg got caught in Pierce's auction fever, but they couldn't get anything. Warhol's crystal ball, estimated at $400/500, went to an order bid for $6,600. "If only he knew," the auctioneer quipped.

Dealer Steve Weiss of Hillman-Gemini, New York City, got the two lots he wanted from the toy and old advertising groups. He paid $660 (est. $150/200) for a circa 1900 roly-poly bear with a balancing pole and thought he had a bargain. He also bought a circa 1900 American painted wood shoe shop sign for $1,430 (est. $500/700).

Advertising memorabilia collectors pronounced Warhol's American wood and cast-iron Perfume Your Handkerchief vending machine a genuine bargain at $4,950 (est. $250/350). One like it went for $6,070 the previous Sunday in New Hope, Pennsylvania, at Noel Barrett's sale of the legendary George Haney antique advertising collection.

Warhol's personalized Campbell's Kid soup bowl with "Andy" printed in the middle brought one of the sale's wilder prices. Estimated at $50/75 it sold for $3,775.

The "Andy Warhol" inscribed director's chair went even wilder for $6,050 (est. $100/150) to a man truly overwhelmed with it. Joe Di Bella, a Philadelphia dealer, bought the chair, proclaimed it "the greatest thing since the Resurrection," and said he was having a Warhol festival.

Di Bella met Warhol about ten years ago in New York City at the Armory show and found him a good friend and an interesting client. "He paid me

Warhol's 155 cookie jars drew hordes of preview spectators and over 2,000 order bids around the world. They sold for a mammoth $247,830. A duplicate collection could be put together today for about $4,000, more or less, depending on where you shop.

partly in money and partly in his own art. The first thing I sold him was an architect's rendering of the Roxy Theatre. I asked fifteen hundred dollars and we settled on twelve hundred and two of his silk screen cows." Di Bella is going to advertise the Warhol director's chair at $72,000 in New York, Philadelphia, and Washington newspapers.

Warhol's 1974 Rolls Royce four-door Silver Shadow, estimated at $15,000/20,000, went to a phone buyer for $77,000. But the lots that really rocked the crowd were Warhol's cookie jars.

"I sensed that something was going to happen with the cookie jars as soon as the catalog came out," Sotheby's collectibles expert Dana Hawkes said early in the game. "Cookie jar collectors were calling from as far away as California. Of course, everyone saw them in magazines and newspapers, too. "Then after the *20/20* television show, we had

an avalanche of inquiries, and I knew it had to be something special," Hawkes said.

A walk through any flea market in New York the Sunday before the Warhol sale brought ripples of "cookie jar, cookie jar, cookie jar" talk up and down the aisles. It sounded like the only thing people wanted to buy was cookie jars.

Dealer Bruce Block of The Antique Underground in Syracuse, New York, came down to his regular Sunday stand at the 76th and Columbus Avenue Flea Market in Manhattan with his usual American pottery, Fiesta ware, and only one cookie jar. It was a white McCoy, nothing special, and sold immediately for $20. "Everyone's asking for cookie jars," he said. "I'll bring more next week."

That was the day of the Warhol cookie jar sale. Bruce brought four cookie jars to the flea market and sold them immediately to one collector for $25

Paddle #538 bought 33 of the 38 cookie jar lots for $198,605 and filled the house with mystery as well as anguish. The cookie jars brought a total of $247,830.

to $45 each. Among them were a McCoy bear, a McCoy bananas, and a wishing well.

Meanwhile at Sotheby's, they launched into the Warhol collection of 155 cookie jars in 38 lots, estimated at prices close to Bruce Block's. There were mostly four cookie jars per lot, estimated at $150/200, and some a little higher.

The salesroom was packed as tightly with bidders, press, and television as Warhol's house had been packed with his merchandise, art, and collectibles. The impression was that thousands of people wanted cookie jars, and they all thought they could pay a hefty premium on the $100/150 estimates and get some. Little did they suspect what would happen.

The first lot of four—an American bisque yellow chick, an American bisque cats, a Shawnee sailor, and a rabbit in a basket—started innocently at $200, $300, $400, and escalated quickly to $1,980 with premium. There was applause and nervous hilarity for paddle #538 way down in front, but no one was seriously alarmed yet. They thought the first knockdown price was just a fluke and prepared to bid rationally on the next lot.

Bidding on the next lot started at $500 and ended quickly at $3,025, again to paddle #538. The third lot had people screaming in the aisles. It included a McCoy cat on basket weave, a National Silver mammy, a Shawnee Puss 'n Boots, and an elephant. The screaming started at $10,000 and ended when the lot was knocked down at $11,550 to paddle #62, Mr. Warhol's friend and shopping companion Stuart Pivar, who really had to pay up to beat the mystery buyer, paddle #538.

Paddle #538 prevailed in 33 of the 38 lots of cookie jars, and spent almost $200,000 on them, casting a dark cloud of disbelief and grief over hundreds of young bidders aghast at the power of money. Paddle #17 took the most outrageous lot away from paddle #538, spending $23,100 for two cookie jars, a mammy and a black chef, plus a pair of similar salt and peppers. Both paddles turned out to be New York businessmen.

Number 538 was Gedalio Grinberg, chairman of the North American Watch Corporation. Originally, Grinberg and his wife were going to buy one cookie jar lot for a wedding present to their son. "I decided when I saw the collection that it ought to be kept intact," Grinberg said, "and I would have gone after everything if my wife hadn't stopped me."

Television and press closed in on Grinberg, an instant media star now that he owned $200,000 worth of cookie jars. He was also a longtime Warhol friend, collector of his art, and most recently a business associate. Grinberg commissioned Andy Warhol seven years ago to design a watch for his company, and it was one of the last projects Warhol finished before he died.

The Andy Warhol watch is just coming out at $18,000 in a limited edition of 250. It consists of five oblong watches joined together as a watch bracelet. Each of the five faces is a different black and white photograph taken by Warhol of buildings in the Manhattan neighborhood of 84th and Broadway, not too far from where Grinberg lives. The watch hands are slender red, all set to the same time, the casings are dark anodized steel, and each bears a Warhol signature replica on the back. The watch comes in a wood and glass box and is meant to be either an artwork mounted on a wall, set on a table, or worn. Royalties on the watch will go to the Warhol Foundation. Time does not stand still for Andy Warhol.

Grinberg had to leave his impromptu press conference to go back and bid on a lot he wanted with three plastic Campbell's Tomato Soup can banks and a pair of giant cardboard Marlboro cigarette display boxes. They were estimated at $100/150 and he got them for only $7,150. The crowd and the auctioneer cheered, "The return of paddle 538."

Desolate cookie jar bidders at Sotheby's, as well as over 2,000 disappointed order bidders, can still have a wide open world if they want it. Dealer Laura Fisher sat next to a British couple who wanted to take cookie jars home for presents and were stunned by the prices. "You want cookie jars? I'll get you cookie jars," she told them. She left the sale instantly and made a cab dash back to the scene of her morning Warhol homage-the Annex Flea Market. "I bought all the cookie jars I'd seen there in the morning," she reported. "I got five for $115 total!"

The power of the press in the Warhol sale was felt by New York cookie jar dealers as well as by Sotheby's. The Thursday following Grinberg's triumph, Martin Dinowitz at Secondhand Rose on Hudson Street in Greenwich Village dug out his 100 dormant cookie jars and put them in the window priced from $350 to $650.

"Based on the Warhol sale, I thought those were reasonable prices," he said. In the following week, he sold about 50 cookie jars at those prices. People came down during the rest of the Warhol sale. The day after the Warhol sale was over, he did not sell any cookie jars.

Eugene Palm at Kaleidoscope Antiques, who has been selling cookie jars for 12 years, said he has not raised his prices. "I had about three hundred in stock the day of the Warhol sale, priced mostly thirty-five dollars to one hundred twenty-five dollars. A few are more. A 1960s Apollo spaceship jar goes for two hundred to three hundred dollars. A U.S.A. Aunt Jemima with cauliflower is worth maybe three hundred to five hundred dollars. Warhol's were worth forty, fifty, seventy dollars, but the auction prices went ridiculous because they were his." Palm said he would feel bad raising his prices on the Warhol basis. "If I can't keep up my stock at realistic prices, I might step out for a year," he said.

A week after the Warhol cookie jar sale, Sunday, May 1, Syracuse dealer Bruce Block brought down a dozen terrific cookie jars averaging

Gedalio Grinberg (left), paddle #538, cookie jar man of the hour, swamped by the press. Here he has the ear of the *Wall Street Journal's* Meg Cox. On the right, he has microphone and camera of BBC-TV's Michael Jackson.

$35 to $75 to the Columbus Avenue Flea Market and sold a couple. "The prices are right. Andy would have bought these cookie jars," he joked, "but people are not going wild. Actually, I never sold Andy Warhol a cookie jar. He used to buy Fiesta tumblers from me, at around thirty to forty dollars apiece."

The same day, Sunday, May 1, dealer J. M. Miller of Raccoon's Tale, Mullica Hill, New Jersey, took 12 choice cookie jars, priced $15 to $120, to a collectible show in Washington, D.C., and didn't sell one.

Scott Martin, the young Kansas City pharmacist who, when he was a little boy, wanted to grow up and be Andy Warhol, didn't get any cookie jars either, and left the sale in awe. He thought he was prepared to "do what it takes," but he never dreamed what it would take.

The Rest of the Andy Warhol Sale: Days 3–10

The days sped on, with lesser prices than the Art Deco and lesser frenzy than the cookie jars, until the big invitation-only evening art sale at the end, when everybody packed the place to the rafters again.

In the meantime, collectors bought what they always buy. They just paid a little more for it. A couple from Oconomowoc, Wisconsin, bought two assorted lots of 74 pieces of Fiesta ware china, each estimated at $500/800, for a total of $5,500. They were ecstatic and plan to display the pottery, not eat off it, as Warhol did. Syracuse dealer Bruce Block, who used to sell Fiesta to Warhol, estimated they could buy the same stuff from him for $2,200.

Buyers plowed through catalogs of 1940s jewelry and watches and spent $1,719,080. The cookie jar magnate, Gedalio Grinberg of the North American Watch Company, who originally met Warhol through the artist's interest in watches, bought about 20 watches himself. He got special examples of the brands he distributes, such as Piaget and Movado. "Some of the prices were

crazy," he said. "A watch I sell for six hundred ninety dollars went for three thousand three hundred dollars."

The salesroom was about half full for the American Indian catalog. For paintings and sculpture from Old Masters through Renoir, Degas, Dali, and contemporary artists, 89 lots sold for $3,622,602; four were unsold. For Warhol's photographs and prints, 70 of 71 lots sold for $1,231,175. Many were group lots and some were bargains. The Americana sale totaled $2,646,825, with nine of 217 lots bought in.

On Monday night, May 2, at the invitation-only contemporary art sale, the crowds, the crush, and the sizzle of money were back with a vengeance. The 21 best of Warhol's contemporary art possessions were saved until last and opened Sotheby's contemporary art evening.

Nothing Warhol owned tempted buyers to cross the one-million-dollar line, but one Cy Twombly "scribble" painting almost did. Cologne, West Germany, dealer and Twombly collector Karsten Greve bought *Untitled*, 1967, for $990,000, and said he had wanted the painting for a long time. Last year, a similar Twombly with more "scribble," from the Gilman Paper Company collection, sold for only $308,000 at Christie's.

Jasper Johns' *Screen Piece*, 1967, which some people thought would be the top lot, went for only $660,000. Roy Lichtenstein's 1961 *Laughing Cal*, the cover lot, estimated at $200,000/300,000, sold for $319,000.

The 21 paintings, including some more Lichtensteins, a Marden, David Hockney's color pencil portrait of Warhol, a Rosenquist, a Rauschenberg, and a de Kooning, went for a total $5,115,000. The next morning, Tuesday, May 3, the rest of the contemporary art Warhol owned—64 lots—wrapped up the sale at $2,762,320.

Ten days, ten thousand things, 60,000 spectators, untold thousands of bidders, 13,000 boxed sets of six catalogs, and $25,333,368 for the Andy Warhol Foundation—a marathon auction to remember.

Editor's Note: In the late 1980s, single-owner sales of

lifelong collections inspired new collectors and gave a boost

to collectors' societies and specialized shows. The Game

Preserve sale at Skinner's was followed four years later

by Noel Barrett's sale of the Siegel collection of games

and toys on June 5 and 6, 1992, where Bulls and Bears:

The Great Wall St. Game, published by McLoughlin in 1883,

sold for $31,800, a record for an antique board game.

THE SALE OF THE GAME PRESERVE

BY JANE VAN N. TURANO

Now and then come some once-in-a-life-time sales. Skinner's September 17, 1988, dispersal of The Game Preserve, Rally and Lee Dennis's private museum of antique American games dating from 1840 to 1940, was one of these, and everyone in Bolton, Massachusetts, knew it. It was exciting but a little sad too, to see the nearly 1,200 brightly colored "little boxes of history," as the Dennises called them, come to market as a collection, only to go their separate ways at day's end.

It all began when Lee Dennis bought her husband, Rally, an antique mahogany gaming table in 1953. They discovered three games in its drawers and the love affair was on. Their zeal created an archive worthy of the Smithsonian and brought them the admiration of collectors and dealers worldwide.

The Dennises have lectured on antique games all over the country and have acted as consultants to some of America's biggest game manufacturers. Lee Dennis, author of *Warman's Antique American Games 1840–1940*, has served as director of the Antique Toy Collectors of America, and Rally is the director of the American Game Collectors Association.

Many are the antique game enthusiasts who beat a path to their door in Peterborough, New Hampshire. Collectors everywhere lusted in their hearts after the chromolithographed beauties displayed in their collection, hardly daring to hope that all would be up for sale some day. No

Brilliant color and graphics made McLoughlin's Game of the Man in the Moon, 1901, (left) the favorite of Lee Dennis and everyone else. It sold for a staggering $5,060 to Bob Shepard, a persevering private collector from New York. Skinner photo.

wonder an Iowa collector drove for over 20 hours to be there.

Surely Lee and Rally Dennis would have at least kept their favorites—but no. Rally said they had made the decision to sell it all at once, while they were still together and had their health. After all those years it must have been a very hard thing to do. Rally attended the sale, but Lee couldn't bear to watch on Saturday—who could blame her.

Their grandson, who had grown up loving the old games, had walked out of the preview in tears at one point because it was all too much for him. Happily, though, the young man managed to buy a few of the less expensive lots, including a skittles game at $110 (with the 10 percent buyer's premium) that had been in "his room."

But most of the games went for sums far beyond an adolescent's pocketbook. Even the game collector from Iowa, very much a grown-up, with a wife and child in tow, couldn't afford what he had driven all that way to get. But back in the gentler days when the Dennises started buying, money was never an issue. They did their shopping at yard sales and flea markets.

Now, of course, vintage games are no longer child's play. This really hit home when Arthur Liman, one of America's great corporate lawyers, who became famous overnight as one of the sharpest of the Senate counsels at the Iran-Contra hearings walked into Skinners. Asked if he collected games of crime. "Yes," he smiled, "as a matter of fact, I want the Rival Policemen game, and now you know."

But Liman didn't get it. Estimated at $400/600, the circa 1896 game made by McLoughlin Brothers of New York, sold for $1,760 to a long-haired young rock star bidding in the audience. (The musician, who wished to be unidentified, did say he is the lead singer for the group Danger Danger and that he is about to have a record released by CBS.)

One more thing about the Rival Policemen game. Four modern-day officers of the law had

A famous attorney and numerous officers of the law wanted to play cops and robbers with Rival Policemen: A New Comic Game, but a rock star made the collar at $1,760. Skinner photo.

flown in from Los Angeles to look at it. Skinner's publicist Alicia Gordon reported having seen one of the men hold up his badge next to the game, saying, "Wouldn't this look great next to my badge?" There are as many reasons for collecting as there are collectors—that's for sure.

Lee Dennis's reason for loving the old games is their beautiful lithography. Rally Dennis particularly enjoys the play. Lee's favorite, a masterpiece of graphic art, is Game of the Man in the Moon, produced by McLoughlin about 1901. Chosen as the catalog's cover lot, it pulled everyone's heartstrings. No wonder it was bid up to $5,060 (est. $300/500). No wonder the victorious bidder, Bob Shepard, a toy and game collector from New York, was shaking during the applause as the hammer came down. He hung on through extraordinary competition and deserves an award for bravery. Lee Dennis certainly knows how to pick them.

Although private collectors were indeed a force to be reckoned with in the salesroom, some of the best games sold to people who had strong ties to Parker Brothers of Salem, Massachusetts. Back in 1884, George Parker began saving the company's games, and the archives have been maintained ever since. The company is particularly interested in games made before 1930, and its collection includes the products of its competitors as well.

Parker Brothers was able to win several games that were missing from their archives. "This may be the event that gives game collecting its legitimacy," remarked Phil Orbanes, senior vice-president for research and development and Parker Brothers spokesperson.

One of Salem's outstanding museums, the Essex Institute, also has a fine collection of antique games and toys and is especially eager to acquire early examples made there. Robert Weis, curator

The Wonderful Game of Oz by Parker Brothers, 1921, went at $1,045, entering the impressive collection of the man who supplies cardboard to the company. Skinner photo.

of exhibitions, successfully went after three early games by the Ives Company, Salem bookbinders and game makers. Fortunately for the museum, it was able to get the lot for $605. Weis also picked up three other games, by Parker Brothers and Milton Bradley of East Longmeadow, Massachusetts, for the institute.

Surely the most famous Parker Brothers game ever made is Monopoly, the unprecedented moneymaker turned down when Charles B. Darrow first offered it to them. In a story that is now an article of faith for every frustrated person with a great idea, Darrow, an unemployed heating engineer in the depths of the Depression, was told by Parker Brothers that the game was too complicated to play and too expensive to sell. Darrow then manufactured about 5,000 games privately, selling them to Wanamaker's and F.A.0. Schwartz. Parker Brothers then realized its blunder, bought the rights to Monopoly, and scarcely had the time to count the money after that.

The Game Preserve had one of these privately made Monopoly sets in the museum, and Parker Brothers bowed out again. Pitched at $300/500, the circa 1934 Monopoly set was hotly pursued by several parties, finally selling for $2,640 to a very private gentleman from western Massachusetts. Not a collector or a dealer or even a Monopoly addict, he described himself only as an "entrepreneur" and confessed that he had to have it because it is "an American classic . . . the American game."

This same buyer bid even higher for the next lot, a group of Monopoly memorabilia, including sets from other periods, a photograph of Darrow, and Darrow's unsuccessful sequel, Bulls and Bears: The Great Wall St. Game. The private entrepreneur was willing to spend thousands to get the memorabilia lot because it contained one piece that the "classic" game he had just purchased was lacking. But even he decided enough was enough and gave up.

The successful bidder, at a staggering $3,740 (est. $250/350), turned out to be Parker Brothers'

As patriotic as a Sousa march, McLoughlin's very colorful Game of Stars and Stripes or Red, White and Blue, circa 1900, brought $990. Skinner photo.

Phil Orbanes, who was buying the lot for himself. Orbanes is, I understand, the consummate Monopoly man, author of the recently published *Monopoly Companion* and judge of U.S. and world championships of the game. And in case you were wondering, "the foreigners always win," said Orbanes.

People in the games business, such as Orbanes, really do seem to love what they do. Another major buyers at Skinner's said that he is the major supplier of cardboard, that essential ingredient, to Parker Brothers and Milton Bradley. Business must be good because the gentleman from Philadelphia bought some of the nicest (and most expensive) games. Among them were the charming Game of the Visit of Santa Claus, McLoughlin, circa 1899, for $2,090 (est. $500/700); Rally Dennis's personal favorite, Game of Mail, Express, or Accommodation, McLoughlin, 1895, with a box lid scene of a snowbound locomotive worthy of Currier & Ives, for $1,100 (est. $500/700); Game of a Visit to the Old Homestead, McLoughlin, 1902,

for $1,210 (est. $350/400); The Wonderful Game of Oz, Parker Brothers, circa 1921, for $1,045 (est. $350/450); Parker Brothers' Toy Town Grocery Store, a miniature store diorama complete with groceries and furniture, for $1,980 (est. $800/1,000); and, appropriately, Milton Bradley's first effort, The Checkered Game of Life, 1866, for $1,045 (est. $200/300).

The Checkered Game of Life was actually a framed game board, the rest of the pieces probably having been lost over the last 120 years. When a game is especially important for its visual appeal or its history, it is still desirable whether complete or not. The auction included the very first American game ever made, the 1843 Mansion of Happiness by W. and W.B. Ives (est. $300/400), preserved in a frame. It sold for $990. Another framed game, the 1861–65 Running the Blockade, by lithographer Charles Magnees (est. $350/450), did extremely well, no doubt because it featured Civil War scenes. It went to a phone bidder for an impressive $2,200.

But the quintessentially American and most gloriously graphic game had to be the Game of Stars and Stripes, Red, White and Blue (est. $400/600). Made by McLoughlin about 1900, its box lid was a triumph of design. To see it was to hear a Sousa march, and the game included 44 small silver stars. It could have gone much higher than the $990 it made, in light of the rest of the day's proceedings.

This dream auction really had something for everyone and every interest. Baseball enthusiasts, for example, found plenty here. One New England collector managed to walk away with nearly all the important pinstripe-related items but had to pay dearly for the privilege. Included in his haul were McLoughlin's circa 1886 Game of Base-Ball at $2,530 (est. $800/1,000); the circa 1914 Championship Base Ball Parlor Game by the Crebnelle Novelty Company, $1,430 (estimate $700/900) and Milton Bradley's 1926–28 'Babe' Ruth's Baseball Game, $770 (est. $300/500).

Currier & Ives would have been proud of the snowbound railroad scene in this Game of Mail, Express, or Accommodation, Rally Dennis's favorite. Made by McLoughlin in 1895, it sold for $1,100 to the major supplier of cardboard to Milton Bradley and Parker Brothers. Skinner photo.

For lovers of Christmas, there were several other choice pieces besides the already mentioned Game of the Visit of Santa Claus. An 1899 McLoughlin Game of Tobogganing at Christmas exceeded expectations at $770. A group of four holiday items, including a Milton Bradley Santa Claus Puzzle Box, brought $1,320 (est. $300/400) from Pennsylvania collector/dealers.

Those interested in Black-related material also had some good choices, again at strong prices. A group of six such games, including Samuel Gabriel Sons & Co.'s Game of Black Sambo made $1,430 (est. $500/700).

There was a delightful variety of other special-interest games, including those pertaining to politics, exploration (ranging from the Arctic to Africa), transportation (including aviation and railroads), and even entire lots pertaining to the Spanish-American War. The blowing up of the Maine and Teddy Roosevelt's charge of San Juan Hill happened, very conveniently for games manufacturers, in 1898, when these parlor pastimes were at their peak of popularity.

Just what the manufacturers produced to amuse Americans in their parlors makes for fascinating study and often good humor. Auctioneer Stephen Fletcher, who has a well-developed sense of humor himself, dissolved Skinner's audience into laughter several times simply by reading aloud some of the titles that appealed to him, such as Witzi Wits the Fortune Teller and Her Box of Stunts for Parties, The Lame Duck, and Balance the Budget, the last two striking him as remarkably appropriate for this election year. And the audience kept on voting with their pocketbooks.

The Dennises and Skinner's were clearly delighted with the results. Every lot sold, usually well over the estimates, for a total of $140,629. Parker Brothers' Phil Orbanes was right. This really was the event that gave game collecting its legitimacy.

Editor's Note: On June 3, 1989, the all-time record for a piece of American furniture, $12.1 million, was paid by Israel Sack, Inc. on behalf of a client rumored to be Texas and Washington millionaire Robert Bass. The 9'4" high desk and bookcase, carved with six shells, and made in Newport, Rhode Island, in the 1760s, probably by John Goddard, has never been seen publicly again. Months after the sale it was revealed in the New Yorker *that the underbidder, a tall man who would not speak to reporters and who left immediately in a taxi, was an agent for Newport resident Doris Duke.*

THE ALL-TIME AMERICANA RECORD: THE NICHOLAS BROWN DESK AND BOOKCASE

BY LITA SOLIS-COHEN

A tall and majestic 18th-century American mahogany desk and bookcase carved with six bold shells sold for $12.1 million at Christie's in New York City on June 3, 1989, toppling a slew of records. It's the highest price ever paid at a fine arts auction for an object other than a painting. It topped the $9.87 million paid for a Bugatti Royale at Christie's in 1987, the $9.3 million paid for an 85.91 carat pear-shaped diamond at Sotheby's in April 1988, and the $11.88 million paid for an illuminated medieval manuscript at Sotheby's in 1983. Only 11 paintings by such artists as Picasso, Van Gogh, Monet, Gauguin, Renoir, Degas, Pontormo, and Jasper Johns have brought more.

It is four times the record for any piece of furniture, bettering the nearly $3 million paid for Marie Antoinette's console table in 1988, which topped the most expensive piece of American furniture, General John Cadwalader's Philadelphia wing chair that sold for $2.75 million in 1987. It is the highest price ever paid for any work of decorative arts, topping the record $3 million paid last month at Christie's in Geneva for a Faberge enameled egg.

The soaring 9'4" high shell carved blockfront desk and bookcase was made in Newport, Rhode Island, in the 1760s, probably in the shop of cabinetmaker John Goddard, for the Providence merchant Nicholas Brown. It was bought for $12.1

by the New York City firm of Israel Sack, Inc., leading dealers in American furniture.

"I bought it for a client," said Harold Sack, the 76-year-old president of the firm, who did the bidding from his seat in the second row. "I thought it was a bargain. I was prepared to go quite a bit higher."

When the Brown secretary came on the block at 11:05 am, auctioneer Christopher Burge, president of Christie's, asked for an opening bid of $2 million. New Hampshire dealer Ronald Bourgeault, standing in the back of the salesroom, signaled $5 million by raising his hand, his five fingers apart. There was a pause for a few seconds and then a man seated on the aisle toward the front audibly said "six," and Sack signaled with a flick of his gold pencil, $7 million. The man on the aisle said "eight," shaking his head and the auctioneer took a bid from the back of the room at $9 million. The mysterious man on the aisle said $10 million.

Sack flicked his pen at $11 million, there was no more bidding and the Brown secretary was sold. The bidding took less than a minute. Sack paid $12,100,000 with the 10 percent buyer's premium that goes to the auction house.

The underbidder identified himself as a private collector but declined to give his name or say where he lived. "No, I was not bidding for an institution," he said when asked. He remains a

After six months of hype, it took 60 seconds to sell the Nicholas Brown desk and bookcase in an auction room bristling with tension and expectation. The price, $12.1 million, works out to better than two million dollars a shell. Christie's photo.

mystery. No one at Christie's would identify him and he was unknown to collectors and members of the trade.

"This puts American decorative arts in the category of fine arts where it belonged a long time ago," said a beaming Harold Sack as he left the salesroom with television cameras following him. "It's a miracle the piece was available at all for any amount."

The desk was sold by the John Nicholas Brown Center for the Study of American Civilization in Providence, a private foundation set up by the three children of the late John Nicholas Brown and Anne Kinsolving Brown: Captain Nicholas Brown, USN retired, director of the Baltimore Aquarium; John Carter Brown, director of the National Gallery of Art in Washington; and their sister, Angela Brown Fischer of Massachusetts. Named for their father, the center is a memorial to the Brown family, prominent in the history of Providence.

"My father sat down at the desk and signed it over to the center because he thought the most important piece should be sold to save the most precious thing, the house," said Sylvia Brown Valenzuela, Nicholas Brown's daughter, who represented the family at the sale.

The $11 million will be spent to restore the 1792 Nightingale-Brown house on Benefit Street in Providence, the largest 18th-century frame house to survive in New England, the house where five generations of the Brown family lived. Nicholas Brown II moved the desk and bookcase into the house in 1814.

"Allen Breed, a cabinetmaker in York, Maine, is making a precise replication to go into the house. It will stand where the original stood," said Robert Emlen, the director of the center and professor of American civilization at Brown University.

The desk and bookcase is the tallest of nine similar Newport desks and bookcases with three carved shells in both the upper and lower sections. All but Nicholas Brown's are in museums.

Another with nine shells, made for Joseph, Nicholas's brother, is at the Rhode Island Historical Society.

It is believed that each of the four Brown brothers had one. John's is at the Garvan Collection at Yale; Moses's is presumed to have burned in a fire at his farm in the 19th century.

John Goddard has been suggested as the maker of the Nicholas Brown secretary on the basis of a letter he wrote to Brown in 1766 regarding a desk and bookcase for sale.

Nicholas Brown's inventory, taken shortly after his death in 1791, mentions a bookcase and books valued at 95 pounds, more than seven times as much as the value of any other item in his inventory.

There is much speculation about the identity of the new owner of this expensive piece of furniture. The names of Robert M. Bass, 41, known as the "bashful billionaire" in Washington, who in 1985 bought U.S. Grant's Georgetown town house, and New Hampshire businessman Eddy Nicholson were most often mentioned.

When asked if he bought it for Bass, whose wealth comes from Texas oil, Sack said he would neither confirm it nor deny it.

"If it is Eddy Nicholson, he is not admitting it," said Ron Bourgeault, who opened the bidding at $5 million. "I've never known Eddy to stop at one bid," he added.

Nicholson, reached by phone the following Monday, said he was not the buyer but he did bid higher. "I had an elaborate strategy," he said. "I asked Ron to open the bidding at five and then I signaled my bid to someone who has never bid for me before. I stopped at nine million.

"I am glad Harold was the buyer of record. He has made such a great contribution to American decorative arts," Nicholson added.

Sack would not reveal the buyer's name, saying only that the collector had been collecting for only three or four years.

No one was very surprised by the price, even though the estimate had been $3/5 million. Trade sources said there had been a $10 million private offer for the secretary long before it went to Christie's for auction.

Is it likely that another piece of furniture will ever sell for $12 million?

"This sale may bring out some other masterpieces," suggested Eddy Nicholson.

Sack, however, thought the Christie's sale was a collector's only chance to buy a six-shell secretary. "Have you ever heard of a museum selling a masterpiece?'" he asked.

Editor's Note: In the wake of the sale of the John Nicholas Brown desk and bookcase for $12.1 million, record prices were paid for other furniture forms as consignors decided to sell into the bull market for Americana.

CHRISTIE'S SCORES SIX MORE RECORDS

BY LITA SOLIS-COHEN

The auction market for the finest 18th-century American furniture continued its upward climb at Christie's on Saturday, January 20, 1990. New records were made for five forms of Philadelphia furniture. A pier table sold for $4,620,000, a tea table for $1,210,000, a side chair for $418,000, a mirror for $242,000, and a fire screen for $66,000. (The fire screen record lasted for less than a week. The following Friday, Sotheby's got $88,000 for another similar fire screen with hairy paw feet.)

Furniture and silver from other urban centers performed well too. A Massachusetts mahogany serpentine chest embellished with rococo carving sold for $610,000, a record for an American chest of drawers. A flat-top New York tankard by Charles Le Roux fetched $242,000 a record for American silver and a Tiffany silver punch bowl and ladle made the same record price. The sale total of $14,512,212 was the highest total for any Americana sale, bringing more than the sale in June that included the $12.1 million Nicholas Brown desk and bookcase. Some contend it was the finest group of American furniture to come to auction since the Reifsnyder sale in 1929.

The pier table is the most expensive table ever sold and the second most expensive piece of American furniture, topped only by the Brown desk and bookcase. "It is the greatest piece of its type. There is the sweetest delicacy about it," said the buyer, Harold Sack. "I had to spring for it."

Sack, president of Israel Sack, Inc., dealers in American furniture, seated in the second row, outbid New Hampshire collector Eddy Nicholson,

who was bidding from the rear of Christie's Park Avenue salesroom. In front of the podium stood one of the finest groupings of American furniture to be offered in decades, all fresh to the marketplace. There was a round of applause after Nicholson shook his head and started to leave the room saying. "I want to go somewhere and cry."

Called a pier table because it was designed to stand against a pier between two windows, the exquisitely proportioned table measures 35½" wide x 17" deep x 33½" high and is rimmed on three sides by gadrooning, a rope-like molding that prevents valuable china from falling off. The C-scrolls on its pierced apron and the spring to its cabriole legs, which end in crisply carved ball and claw feet, contribute to the table's elegance.

According to the catalog, the table was made by Philadelphia Quaker cabinetmaker Thomas Tufft at his shop on Second Street near Walnut for Burlington County, New Jersey, merchant Richard Edwards, who paid 5 pounds for it on April 19, 1776, expensive in those days but not out of reach for a successful gentleman.

The Tufft attribution is not without question. An account book noted in Christie's catalog description of the lot cannot be found, and an article in the October 1948 *Antiques* gives the date as 1779. That and other inconsistencies, as well as further research by scholars, suggest the credit for the table should go to its carver rather than Tufft.

Even without the tale spun about its manufacture, the table stands on its own as a work of art. It was consigned to auction by Samuel Harrison Gardiner, a retired Philadelphia architect who was

This tilt-top pie crust tea table consigned by Philadelphian George Gordon Meade Easby sold for $3.2 million, topping the $1,045,000 paid by Eddy Nicholson for a table of similar form in 1986, which was the first piece of American furniture to break the $1 million mark. The Easby table, attributed to Philadelphia cabinetmaker Thomas Affleck and carvers Nicholas Bernard and Martin Jugiez, is one of the only known pair of American tea tables. Its mate is in the Philadelphia Museum of Art. The table was bought by New York dealer Leigh Keno, who said he was acting for an anonymous client. Keno said there was a good chance the two tables would be reunited at the Philadelphia Museum of Art sometime soon. Christie's photo.

This carved and veneered mahogany dressing bureau made in Salem, Massachusetts, 1775-95, sold for $610,000 to New York collectors Mr. and Mrs. Irving Wolf. Related to a chest in the Garvan collection at Yale, which was made for the Derby family by Stephen Badlam, and a chest-on-chest at the Museum of Fine Arts, Boston, the bureau's sides are veneered and its handles retain their original fire gilt. Cabinetmakers John Lemon and Elijah and Jacob Sanderson are suggested as possible makers. Christie's photo.

Elaborate Philadelphia scroll-foot side chair, copied from plate 12 of the first edition of Thomas Chippendale's Director, sold for $418,000 and became the most expensive side chair. Leigh Keno was the buyer. On stylistic grounds it is thought to have been carved by Bernard and Jugiez. The chair was one of a pair from the collection formed by the discerning Alexandria, Virginia, collectors May and Howard Joynt. Its mate from the Joynt collection sold for $330,000 to a collector, and Keno sold another chair from the set at the New York Winter Antiques Show. Christie's photo.

approached by Christie's after a distant cousin of his had sold Richard Edward's highboy and lowboy at Christie's in May 1987 for $1.7 million to Sack, who was bidding on behalf of Texas billionaire Robert Bass. Bass is restoring General Ulysses S. Grant's house in Washington, D.C., and is furnishing it with fine American furniture. In June 1989, also acting for Bass, Sack paid the all-time record for a piece of furniture, $12.1 million for the Rhode Island desk—not quite as much of a bargain as the highboy and lowboy.

When asked if he bought the pier table for Bass, Sack said he bought the table in memory of his father. But when asked if he was giving it to a museum, Sack shook his head no.

The Edwards pier table was not the only piece of Philadelphia furniture to bring more than a million dollars at Christie's that Saturday. Earlier in the sale a tilt-top pie crust tea table, consigned by Philadelphian George Gordon Meade Easby, sold for $1.2 million, topping the $1.045 million paid in 1986 by Eddy Nicholson for a table of similar form. Nicholson was the first to pay more than $1 million for a piece of American furniture.

The Easby table, attributed to Philadelphia cabinetmaker Thomas Affleck and carvers Nicholas Bernard and Martin Jugiez, is one of the only known pair of American tea tables. In the 1930s, Easby's grandmother, Mrs. Cornelius Stevenson, sold its mate to Philadelphia collector Wistar Harvey, who left his collection to the Philadelphia Museum of Art. The Easby table was bought by New York City dealer Leigh Keno, who said he was acting for an anonymous client. Keno said there was a good chance the two tables would be reunited at the Philadelphia Museum of Art sometime soon.

Keno was also the buyer of the most expensive chair. He paid $418,000 for an elaborate scroll-foot side chair carved by Bernard and Jugiez and copied from plate 12 of the first edition of Thomas Chippendale's *The Gentleman and Cabinet-Maker's Director*.

This hairy paw fire screen from the Joynt collection, related to the candlestands owned by General John Cadwalader, went to dealer Keno for a reasonable $66,000 (est. $100,000/150,000). The following Friday Keno bought another similar stand at Sotheby's for $88,000. Both screens were bought against their reserves with no perceptible competition in the salesroom, even though they were part of an intensive study of Cadwalader furniture at Winterthur last summer. Both were once owned by the late Joseph Kindig, Jr., who reportedly exchanged the frames on the two screens, breaking the pole of one across his knee because he thought one was real and the other a copy. Apparently, both are period stands, possibly the ones owned by General John Cadwalader, and relate to a similar stand in the collection of Winterthur. Four other hairy paw foot stands in public and private collections are also related to the three mentioned, but they form another group. According to conservator Alan Miller, the stand at Sotheby's was in better condition and in an old finish. The break in the pole had been repaired, and it has an old frame, possibly the one that belongs on the screen sold at Christie's. The fire screen stand at Christie's had one foot broken and repaired, and showed hastier execution but by no means as hasty an execution as on the second of the two Cadwalader serpentine card tables at the Philadelphia Museum of Art. The surface was not quite as good as the one at Sotheby's. Miller considers the two screens the bargains of the week. Harold Sack said he didn't understand the screens and therefore did not bid on them. "Now that I own both fire screens, we will study them and see if we can figure out which frame belongs to which and switch the frames if we must," Keno said. Christie's photo.

A rococo mirror with John Elliott's label in both English and German affixed to its back sold for $242,000, a record for an American mirror, even though it was damaged and had been given a coat of radiator paint. It was acquired by Morrison Heckscher, curator of furniture at the Metropolitan Museum of Art, who said it would be restored and hung over the Cadwalader marble-top side table in a future exhibition on the rococo in America. Christie's photo.

The chair was one of a pair offered by Christie's from the collection formed by Alexandria, Virginia, collectors May and Howard Joynt. It matched another chair from this large set, which Keno was exhibiting at the New York Winter Antiques Show and sold before the show was over. The price Keno got was something less than the $490,000 he was asking. "It was closer to the auction prices," Keno volunteered.

With Keno out of the bidding for the second Joynt collection chair from this set, it sold at Christie's to a collector for $330,000. In 1977, a pair of these chairs found at Renninger's Antiques Market in Adamstown, Pennsylvania, and consigned to Sotheby's, sold for $26,000. Keno said, "In August 1959, David Stockwell offered the owner of the chair I sold at the show the very pair the Joynts later bought, for $12,000!"

The rococo mirror with the label of John Elliott in both English and German affixed to its back, also from the Edwards family, sold for $242,000, a record for an American mirror. It was acquired by Morrison Heckscher, curator of furniture at the Metropolitan Museum of Art. He said it would be restored and returned to its original white color and hung over the Cadwalader marble-top side table in a future exhibition at the Metropolitan Museum devoted to the rococo in America.

The hairy paw candlestand, also carved by Bernard and Jugiez and probably once owned by General John Cadwalader, went to Keno for a reasonable $66,000 (est. $100,000/150,000). The

Mahogany marble-top table, 1760-85, from the Joynt collection, $187,000. Christie's photo.

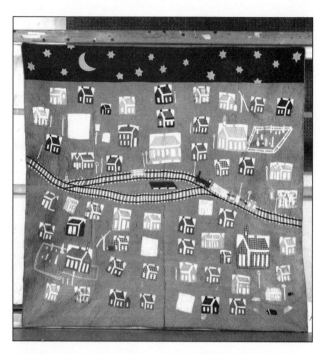

Although a dozen of the 32 quilts offered failed to sell, this pieced and appliqued cotton quilt dated '91 (1891) sold for $33,000 to Joel Kopp of America Hurrah. Christie's photo.

following Friday Keno bought the other similar stand at Sotheby's for $88,000. In January 1988, that stand was estimated to bring $150,000/ 200,000 but was passed at $80,000 with no one interested at that level.

Both fire screens on offer had been part of an intensive study at Winterthur last summer, and both were once owned by the late Joseph Kindig, Jr., a legendary York, Pennsylvania, dealer who reportedly exchanged the frames on the two because he thought one was real and the other a copy. Apparently, both are period stands, one carved more hastily than the other. "Now that I own both of them, we will see if we can figure out which frame belongs to which," Keno said.

Intensive study of Philadelphia furniture and the carvers who embellished it seems to have boosted prices for any piece made in proximity to Penn's Greene Towne. Among other pieces of Philadelphia furniture from the Joynt collection that brought strong but not record prices, were a Queen Anne easy chair that sold for $187,000 and a mahogany marble-top table of the same date that

brought the same price. A single balloon-seat Queen Anne side chair with a shell at its crest rail and one on each knee, its cabriole legs ending in trifid feet, and with a fine needlework seat depicting Adam and Eve sold for $132,000, and the same price was paid for a set of four plainer Queen Anne slipper-foot side chairs without any shells but with needlework seats. Harold Sack bought a Chippendale side chair for $121,000, well over its $90,000 high estimate.

A William and Mary plank seat armchair (est. $2,000/4,000) sold for a surprising $53,300 to Keno, who said he had to have it because he knows its mate. A classic Pennsylvania William and Mary chest of drawers of fine proportions and good color (est. $6,000/8,000) fetched a whopping $38,800, and a red-painted bedstead (est. $400/600) sold for $6,600! Another bed of roughly the same size, its turnings not as bold and the headboard not as well shaped, went for $660.

New York and New England furniture did not fare quite as well as that made in Pennsylvania. The exceptions were a sculptural carved and veneered Salem, Massachusetts, bureau sold to a collector for $610,000 and a New Hampshire bowfront chest of drawers that went to Pennsylvania dealer Clarence Prickett for $210,000. Both must be records for their forms.

There were, however, a few disappointments. Several important New York and New England pieces failed to sell. There was no interest in a rare mahogany Newport games and worktable with a demilune fold-over top made by John Goddard in Newport (est. $275,000/300,000) nor in John Brown's mahogany blockfront kneehole bureau (est. $400,000/450,000). The pair of New York Queen Anne chairs with carved shells and leaves on their crest rails that sold individually for $302,500 and $217,800 at the Benjamin and Cora Ginsburg sale in 1983 failed to find a buyer, though Keno sold another chair from the set at the Winter Antiques Show for $250,000.

The Queen Anne chairs, games table, and kneehole bureau belonged to the late Texas collector James L. Britton, who bought them for big prices at Christie's in the early eighties. Perhaps because they had sold in recent memory they had lost their freshness, or perhaps tastes have changed.

Freshness and aesthetic appeal seem to be essential ingredients for high prices. The Edwards pier table had never been out of the original owner's family, and the tilt-top tea table had not been on the market for at least three generations. The Joynt collection was put together lovingly and with great taste in the 1940s and 1950s, for the most part.

Federal chest of drawers of flame birch and mahogany veneer, made in Portsmouth, New Hampshire, 1790-1810, sold at $220,000 to Pennsylvania dealer Clarence Prickett, who battled New York dealers Harold Sack and Sam Herrup for it. A week later Prickett said he had to have it because it was the best of its kind and he had already sold it. Christie's photo.

Editor's Note: When a horse and rider weathervane made by J. Howard & Company in Bridgewater, Massachusetts, in the 1860s sold at Sotheby's in January 1990 for $770,000, it was assured a place in the firmament of folk sculpture. Other weathervanes have sold for six-figure prices, but none have topped this record.

NEW RECORD FOR A WEATHERVANE: THE BARENHOLTZ SALE

BY LITA SOLIS-COHEN

"If I had to send a piece of American sculpture to France or Japan to sum up what is American about American art, I'd send this weathervane," said Stephen Score after he bought a large horse and rider weathervane for a record $770,000 at Sotheby's on January 27, 1990. It topped the previous $203,500 paid for a locomotive weathervane at Skinner in March 1987. "It stands up as a world-class art object next to any Impressionist painting or Jasper Johns. It is the piece that says everything that can be said about American folk art, and in fact it transcends the category," Score went on.

The molded and gilded copper and zinc weathervane in the form of a straight-backed rider wearing a top hat and waistcoat, atop a smooth and well-proportioned horse with sheet copper ears and a cut and crinkled sheet copper mane, was made circa 1860 by J. Howard & Company in West Bridgewater, Massachusetts. Very little is known about Jonathan Howard's factory, which began manufacturing vanes in the mid-19th century. He employed fewer than six people and produced a limited number of vanes before he sold his business in 1868 to Horatio L. Washburn.

Regarded as the handsomest of all "factory-made" vanes, Howard vanes can be identified by their method of casting. Zinc, which provided weight was used for the front portions of the horse; the hindquarters were made of hollow copper, which responds to the wind.

The scale of the horse and rider is imposing, it measures 43" high and 41¼" long. Details, such as the braid around the rider's hat, the hammered buttons on his coat, the incised eye of the horse, its forelock of twisted and gilded sheet copper, the twisted copper wire reins and stirrup, and the star-shaped spurs, all contribute to making it a successful object. Weathered squares of parcel gilt and allover verdigris of the weathered copper give its surface a rich patina. Moreover, it is signed. "J. Howard & Co." is impressed on the rider's leg.

No one knows where the vane was used. In 1961, the late Edith and Barney Barenholtz bought the vane for $500 (after another collector passed on it) from the late Buffalo, New York, antiques dealer Haydn Parks. It was the first weathervane they bought, a beginning for their illustrious collection. After Edith's death, Barney moved the vane from his house in Princeton, New Jersey, to Shaker Brook Farm in Marlborough, New Hampshire, and installed it in the Shaker-style octagonal gallery he built to house the Barenholtz collection of toys and folk art.

"I thought the horse and rider vane would bring more," said New York folk art dealer Allan Daniel. "I thought an art collector would buy it for $1 million and think it a bargain, but the only bidders were four New England antiques dealers who know how great it is."

The underbidder was Connecticut dealer Marguerite Riordan, who remained in the bidding

This molded copper and zinc horse and rider weathervane by J. Howard & Co., West Bridgewater, Massachusetts, sold for $770,000 to Essex, Massachusetts, dealer Stephen Score. Sotheby's photo.

after Connecticut dealer Fred Giampietro and Massachusetts dealer Wayne Pratt dropped out. Score said he bought the vane for stock and has already been approached by interested art collectors, but he hasn't set a price. "Until it is sold, I will live with it," Score said. "I enjoy the remarkable sensitivity between the horse and rider. That elegant horse, its ears pricked back, is paying attention to the rider, and the rider in turn has the horse under control and is sensitive to the horse's movement."

With the record $770,000 weathervane, the Barenholtz sale of 263 lots set a record $2.6 million for an auction of American folk art. Records were also set for a whirligig, a tavern sign, a trade sign, a rocking horse, and a squeak toy.

The whirligig in the form of a painted pine sailor with paddle-shaped hands wearing a blue-painted top hat with a metal brim, a navy blue jacket with nail head buttons, and a yellowed white shirt and trousers, sold for $38,500 (est. $10,000/15,000) to New York City dealer David Schorsch bidding on the phone.

The tavern sign, picturing a stylized Indian maiden, a bow in one hand and an arrow in the other, standing above the name "N. Brown" and the date 1824, fetched $71,500 (est. $25,000/35,000) after very active bidding.

The sheet iron trade sign, a visual anagram for blacksmith and horseshoer J.B. Schlecelmilch, Jr., went for $53,900 to a New York folk art collector. Made in Pennsylvania in the mid-19th century it pictures a silhouetted figure of a blacksmith at his anvil, and behind him a horseshoe enclosing the letters "ER" with an ampersand balanced like a bareback rider on the horse above "J.B. Schlecelmilch Jr." The name fills the lower half of the sign.

The painted pine rocking horse with leather saddle and bridle stitched with stars and shields, cast-iron stirrups, and brass button eyes sold for $17,500, $10,000 above its high estimate. The squeak toy in the form of a dog wearing a straw hat went for $1,210, just $10 over its high estimate.

The painted sheet iron fire chief weathervane, one of the icons of American folk art, sold for $35,200 to New York dealer Joel Kopp. According to Sotheby's catalog, it was found in 1930 in an Alexandria, Virginia, dump by retired Boston architect Harden de V. Pratt. It had served as the weathervane of the old Friendship Engine House in Alexandria, Virginia, the volunteer company in which George Washington was an active member. The Barenholtzes bought it in 1972 at an auction in Washington, D.C., and it is pictured in Jean Lipman's 1948 book *American Folk Art in Wood, Metal, and Stone*. Lipman dated it 1850. Sotheby's photo.

Although there were some stunning high prices, dozens of items sold below their estimates, and 12 lots failed to find buyers because there was no bidding at all. Barney Barenholtz's two daughters and his widow, Betty Willis, were bidding on the items they wanted to own. Betty Willis said she had asked Sotheby's to sell every lot without reserve.

Dealers and collectors groused that the collection was uneven in quality and complained that there "was so much to look at, no one could see it all at the presale exhibition, where the Barenholtz items were mixed in with the 1,500 other lots of Americana Sotheby's offered for sale during the last week of January.

There was no question there was more than a handful of first-rate examples. For example, the gilded copper Goddess of Liberty weathervane sold for $104,500 to New York dealer Joel Kopp, outbidding two dealers, one in the salesroom and one on the phone. Betty Willis said it was the one piece she really wanted, but the price went beyond her limit.

Another Goddess of Liberty, a 20th-century wood carving of a buxom girl in a red dress waving her American flag, went to a collector for $71,000, twice its estimate. Ruth Bascom's pastel profile *Portrait of Cynthia Allen* wearing a pea green dress and a white organdy shawl appealed to half a dozen bidders and went for $66,000 to a private collector, a record for a work by this artist.

A limestone carving, a tender depiction of a mother and infant, by Kentucky sculptor William Edmondson (circa 1882–1951), the first Black artist to have a show at the Museum of Modern Art, sold for $33,000 (est. $10,000/15,000) to New York dealer Joel Kopp, who paid the same price for a painting by William Matthew Prior of a child in blue with one shoe on and one shoe off. New York dealer Stephen Weiss paid a whopping $71,500 for Joseph Stock's painting of another child in blue who has lost her shoe, playing with her cat and teething ring.

More of the Barenholtzes' folk art and the toys that they loved so well were dispersed in two auctions. One at Ron Bourgeault's in November 1989, and the toys at a grab-sale run by Alexander Acevedo and Bill Bertoia in December 1989 that brought the total for the collection to about $4 million—another landmark collection in auction history.

This $53,900 sheet iron trade sign is a visual anagram for blacksmith and horseshoer J.B. Schlecelmilch, Jr. Sotheby's photo.

Editor's Note: When Oprah Winfrey discovered Shaker furniture at Willis Henry's sale in August 1990, records tumbled.

OPRAH IN SHAKER COUNTRY

BY DAVID HEWETT

The tabloids have had their fun with Oprah Winfrey, star of both large and small screen, but those who met her at Willis Henry's annual Shaker extravaganza in New Lebanon, New York, on Sunday, August 5, 1990, know the lady is a class act.

With no bodyguards, no entourage of hundreds, and no auction agents, Oprah, along with a long-time friend from Maine, and a couple others flew into nearby Pittsfield, Massachusetts, on Sunday morning. Limos took the small group to New Lebanon where she made her own decisions and did her own bidding at Willis Henry's sale.

Bidding? Oprah Winfrey practically bought the place dry on that Sunday. She spent at least $470,580 (including buyer's premiums). She got as excited as any neophyte auction-goer (it really was her first auction), and she whooped it up when she got the cover lot, a red-painted pine work counter with three drawers, for $220,000. The estimate had been $20,000/25,000.

Consider this: Bidding on the counter started at $5,000 and actually went up by $2,500 increments until dealer David Schorsch started jumping it by $10,000 bids. It took longer to get to $60,000 than it took to fly from $100,000 to $220,000. That price is a new auction record for any Shaker piece.

The counter was as classic as they come, but many of the dealers in the back row thought a dealer had to have a customer already on the hook to even consider getting into it for that figure. Several said they'd thought the counter the best piece in the sale; none said they thought it would bring a record price.

There were four pieces of furniture here everyone wanted, and specialist dealers bought two of them. A classic Harvard slat-back side chair in red stain went to Schorsch for $5,500 and a New Lebanon spider-leg candlestand in red stain was bought by dealer Tom Queen for $38,500.

Oprah Winfrey got a New Lebanon cupboard over drawers in red wash for $55,000 and the record-setting work counter.

There were some good smalls, other decent furniture, and a very rare Inspirational Drawing.

Oprah Winfrey's presence caused a stir at New Lebanon, but strangely enough, hardly anyone even approached her for an autograph until just before she left after 4 PM. She proved she had the stamina of an auctioneer. She never left her seat for a full five hours. Her presence (and her incredible purchase total) left some looking into a cloudy crystal ball, though.

Several dealers said they thought the Shaker market had cooled down, the mid-range Shaker market was weakening. There appeared to be a smaller crowd at this sale than at sales in the last few years. Some asked what would have happened to the dollar total if Oprah hadn't been a buyer?

Hey, inquiring minds want to know!

Pine, painted red, base 29" high x 32½" wide x 18" deep, top 44" long. Painted on back, "AW" and "1830." This counter now holds the record for any Shaker item sold at auction: $220,000.

"Should I bid on it? Higher? Did I get it? Did I get it? Yeah! I got it!" Oprah's companion is Dr. David Driskell of Falmouth, Maine, and the University of Maryland. "We're old friends," Driskell said, "and I'm giving her a little advice, but she knows what she wants." Driskell told her to go for the record-breaking work counter.

Editor's Note: Ron Bourgeault's Northeast Auctions became a force in the marketplace for Americana in the 1990s. His August 1992 sale in Manchester, New Hampshire, brought a total of a little more than $2 million. His August 2003 sale totaled nearly $10 million. Northeast Auctions' sales in August anchor a series of events known as Antiques Week that brings hundreds of Americana collectors to the region for the auctions and to attend half a dozen shows the following week. Some stay in New England to attend Northeast's maritime and China trade sale, traditionally held two weeks later at the Northeast's corporate headquarters in Portsmouth, where it is on view as soon as the antiques shows are over and during the entire week before the sale.

RON BOURGEAULT'S FIRST $2 MILLION SALE

BY LITA SOLIS-COHEN

Bourgeault's midsummer auction at the Center of New Hampshire Holiday Inn in Manchester has become a rite of summer, like a Fourth of July picnic or a Labor Day clambake. A huge crowd gathered in the cavernous convention hall at 4 PM on Saturday, August 1, 1992, and, when Ron offered the first lot at 6 PM people began waving their hands, number cards, or catalogs to bid on the 410 lots of prints, lamps, ceramics, silver, and folk art. Almost everybody returned Sunday morning and were joined by an even larger crowd who came to look over the furniture and then, beginning at noon, bid on another 509 lots of furniture, paintings, and decorations.

The grand total of $2,515,441.50 (with buyer's premium) was just a tad less than the $2.6 million Sotheby's and Christie's each totaled for their June sales. It was Bourgeault's best sale to date. There is no question he's become a force in the Americana market in the last five years.

What are the secrets of Ron's success?

One is the free catalogs mailed to 5,500 collectors, dealers, and museums on his mailing list and to anyone else who requests one. But don't lose the catalog; it costs $20 at the sale.

Ron's marketing is carefully orchestrated. This time there was a special preview of Joe and Sue Keown's Federal furniture at Ron's house in Portsmouth on the Sunday before the sale, and

the rest of the items were on view for a week at his shop in Hampton, New Hampshire. There was a long line waiting to get into the two-hour Saturday preview in Manchester, which began at 4 PM. Viewing began again at 9 AM on Sunday, giving people ample time to use their bright lights and their black lights and to make up their minds about which lots to go for.

Ron was the first auctioneer to offer institutional property without a seller's commission. Now, most auction houses, anxious for museum business, have followed his lead. He charges the ubiquitous 10 percent buyer's premium, but there is no sales tax in New Hampshire.

Although he calls his business Northeast Auctions and says he is supported by a fine and loyal staff, Ron Bourgeault is the whole show. He's the expert, the PR department, the marketing department, and the auctioneer.

He has built his business on 25 years of camaraderie with colleagues and collectors. He knows everybody's name. On Saturday night after the first session, Ron traditionally takes a group of dealers out for dinner and belly dancers, and it seems to do the trick. Dealer bidding dominated the sale, and dealers won most major lots, though Ron claims there were more private buyers among the 525 registered bidders at this sale than he ever had before.

The unrestored 41" x 36" portrait of a late 18th-century Connecticut River Valley minister sailed over its estimate, selling for a whopping $181,500 to Highland Park, Illinois, and Sunapee, New Hampshire, dealers Frank and Barbara Pollack, underbid by Marguerite Riordan. Apparently the 1" x 2" hole under the minister's right arm didn't matter at all. Ron Bourgeault photo.

Reasonable estimates, a minimum of reserved lots, and high-quality antiques attracted over 1,000 people to Manchester, New Hampshire, for Bourgeault's August 1 and 2 sale, giving it the kind of excitement generally reserved for Americana sales in January in New York City. But it was different from New York.

"It's the first real auction I've been to in a long time," said English furniture dealer Chris Jussel, who went back to New York with an English globe that cost him $12,650. Jussel was referring to the fact that there is little chandelier bidding at this sale because less than 20 percent of the lots have estimates, meaning they have reserves, a secret minimum price agreed on between the seller and the auctioneer. (Chandelier bidding is a common practice with reserved lots. If there is no bidding, the auctioneer gets the bidding going by taking fictitious bids from the ceiling until the lot meets its reserve and then if someone in the audience bids over the reserve he takes bids and knocks it down to the highest bidder. If the reserve is not met then the lot is "bought in" and returned to its owner.)

In fact, some of the offerings at Ron's had already been through the New York auction houses and failed to sell. The bidders in New Hampshire knew those items were at Ron's now to be sold.

The sale was largely Americana, so it provided a good indication of the health of this market, which is alive and vigorous, although a bit leaner than a few years ago. Some very strong prices were achieved, but many lots changed hands at the prices close to those of a decade ago and well below what they might have brought at the top of the market in 1989.

A 41" x 36" life-size portrait of a late 18th-century Connecticut River Valley minister sailed over its $50,000/80,000 estimate and sold for a whopping $181,500 to dealers Frank and Barbara Pollack of Highland Park, Illinois, and Sunapee, New Hampshire. Marguerite Riordan was the "runner upper," as the late John Walton used to call the underbidder. The anonymous painter portrayed a kindly, thoughtful preacher in the manner of John Brewster, suggesting it was painted by a follower of Ralph Earl. The painting had been consigned privately and was unrestored. A 1" x 2" hole in the canvas under the minister's arm didn't matter at all.

A Federal inlaid mahogany server with white marble top, attributed to John Seymour and Thomas Seymour of Boston, was a tight, elegant design, and it brought $77,000 from Albert Sack of Israel Sack, Inc., New York City. The last time it crossed the auction block at Christie's in 1982, it fetched $60,500.

Dealer Leigh Keno bought a Pennsylvania William and Mary walnut chest of drawers with line and berry inlay used by the Welsh cabinet-makers who settled in Chester County. He paid a very strong $93,500 (est. $50,000/65,000), probably a record for this rare decorated form of chest popular with Pennsylvania collectors.

Leigh Keno paid a very strong $93,500 for a Pennsylvania William and Mary walnut chest of drawers with line and berry inlay typical of Chester County. Ron Bourgeault photo.

Set of eight Federal dining chairs (six sides and two arms) with carving attributed to Samuel McIntyre, the only set of Salem chairs known with carved bellflowers decorating their back stiles, $60,500 to New York dealer Leigh Keno. Joe Keown said he had six of them and after years of "keeping in touch" was able to buy two more from a Baltimore collector he contacted after her house was pictured in *The Magazine Antiques*. Ron Bourgeault photo.

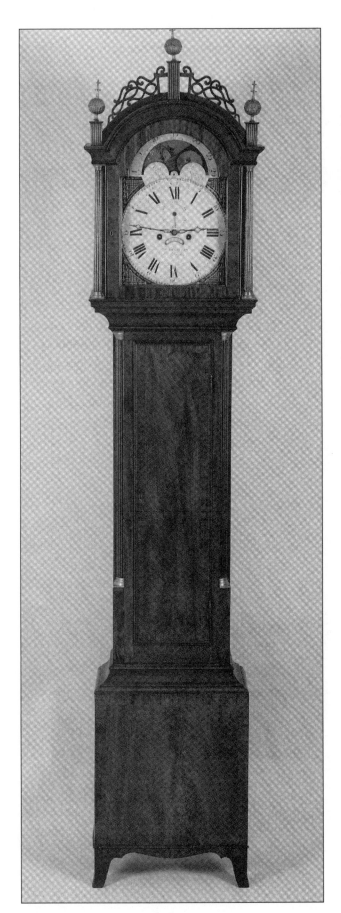

Federal mahogany tall-case clock by Elnathan Taber of Boston fetched a strong $52,800 from Exeter, New Hampshire, dealer Peter Sawyer. The dial, with its border of painted bellflowers, was probably done by ornamental painter Spencer Nolen, possibly when he was a partner of Aaron Willard, Jr. Ron Bourgeault photo.

Rare piece of historical needlework depicting the Patten family coat of arms, which impale the Wheelock and Davenport coats of arms. It is stitched by Ruth Patten, one of three sisters who kept the Misses Patten School. It sold for $22,000 to Marguerite Riordan for the Connecticut Historical Society in Hartford, underbid by Connecticut dealers Stephen and Carol Huber on the phone. The framed needlework came with a watercolor miniature portrait of Ruth Wheelock Patten and a small collection of early 19th-century leather-bound books. Ron Bourgeault photo.

Massachusetts and New Hampshire furniture from the collection of Joe and Sue Keown brought $410,300, accounting for 16.3 percent of the sale total. Their set of eight Federal dining chairs (six side chairs and two armchairs) with carving attributed to Samuel McIntyre, the only set of Salem chairs known with carved bellflowers decorating their back stiles, sold for $60,500 to Keno, who also bought a Massachusetts giltwood presentation banjo clock complete with thermometer and its original packing crate (not a Keown piece) for $26,400 (est. $10,000/15,000).

The Keowns' favorite clock was a Federal mahogany tall-case clock by Elnathan Taber of Boston, which fetched a strong $52,800 (est. $15,000/25,000). Clock collectors said it was worth every penny. Taber was Simon Willard's favorite apprentice. The dial, with its painted bellflowers, was probably done by ornamental painter Spencer Nolen, possibly when he was a partner of Aaron Willard, Jr.

Lolling chairs were not laggards in this sale. One that descended in the Sampson family of Duxbury, Massachusetts, sold for $17,600, and a similar chair fetched $16,500. Both were bought by Massachusetts dealers Elliot and Grace Snyder, who also paid $19,800, double the high estimate, for a Federal wing chair with ogival wings, serpentine seat rail, and molded tapered front legs. At Sotheby's in 1982, the last time the Keowns sold a collection of furniture, a similar wing chair fetched $6,150, and a lolling chair brought the same price.

Joe Keown, a United Airlines pilot now flying out of Denver, continued to collect after he had sold some stars from his collection at Sotheby's ten years ago to raise money for college bills for his three children. Now the children are educated and married, and Keown says he has bought a Pitts biplane for aerobatics. Living in Denver, he said he has no one to talk to about his antiques and he thought it was time to sell the rest of his collection. He and his wife, Sue, attended the sale, answered

questions during the preview, and enjoyed seeing where their pieces were headed.

"I'm thrilled the way it's been going," said Keown after his tally hit the $350,000 mark. "I think the market is strong. The Taber clock is much plainer than the one in the flame birch case I sold at Sotheby's for fifty-five thousand, and it brought almost as much. The lolling chairs did well."

But two Salem bowfront chests of drawers, each estimated at $5,000/8,000, did poorly. One with flame grained veneer went at $5,225, and another passed at $3,250. "It's supply and demand," said Bourgeault. "Salem was a prosperous port, and a lot of these chests were made."

Keown was amazed his fire bucket sold for $24,200. "I paid eighteen hundred dollars for it," he volunteered. Painted with a picture of a burning house and inscribed "John Masury - Delay Not" and the date 1820, it is related to other published examples. It went to Stonington, Connecticut, dealer Marguerite Riordan.

Riordan was the underbidder for a Boston schoolgirl needlework picture in silk embroidery that commemorated George Washington, "First in Peace, War, Fame, Virtue," and sold for $24,200 to a private buyer. But for $22,000 she got a very rare piece of historical needlework depicting the Patten family coat of arms from the estate of Arthur Metcalf Morse of Falmouth, Massachusetts. Ruth Patten, one of three sisters who kept the Misses Patten School, stitched it.

According to needlework historian Betty Ring, who came to the sale from Houston, the Pattens' arms, impaling those of the Wheelock and Davenport families, make it especially important. Eleasar Wheelock founded Moor's Indian Charity School in Lebanon, Connecticut, around 1750 and later expanded the school, moving it to Hanover, New Hampshire, where it became Dartmouth College. John Davenport, with Theophilus Eaton, led a band of Puritans to found the New Haven Colony. Lotted with the framed needlework was a watercolor miniature portrait of Ruth Wheelock

Patten and a small collection of leather-bound books from the early 1800s. Riordan said she was agent for the Connecticut Historical Society in Hartford. "That's the place for it," she added.

Several other museums did some buying. South Street Seaport in New York City paid $24,200 for a painting of the bark *Albania*. (It is not a clipper ship, as cataloged. It is a three-masted vessel with a square-rigged foremast and mainmast and a fore-and-aft-rigged mizzenmast.) It is signed F. Tudgay and dated 1869. According to the catalog, the painting was given to Thomas Fish, the ship's owner, by its captain, G. Waelelar, and the ship was named for Fish's wife. It descended in the family of Fish's daughter, Maria Fisher Morse, and came from the Arthur Metcalf Morse, Jr. estate, the source of the Patten needlework.

The Philadelphia Maritime Museum paid $3,190 for a Sheffield presentation urn with a Philadelphia connection. It had been given to U.S. Navy Commodore Charles Stewart in 1815 for capturing the British warships *Cyanne* and *Levant* with his warship, *Constitution.*

Winterthur was one of the underbidders for a Campeche mammy's rocking bench made in Boston 1830–35 that sold for $2,200. After Winterthur curator of furniture Robert Trent passed the hat, he was able to buy it from the dealer who won it, paying him a slim profit.

The New Hampshire Historical Society in Concord paid $10,450 for a Portsmouth Federal mahogany and flame birch card table that came from the Haven-White house on Pleasant Street, and Strawbery Banke in Portsmouth paid $1,825 for a Portsmouth Federal mahogany washstand attributed to Judkins and Senter with a Haven family history. A single circa 1800 Portsmouth Federal side chair by Langley Boardman and branded S. Tribe (est. $2,000/4,000) sold for $6,600 to private collectors who live in the Langley Boardman house in Portsmouth.

Among the "important" decorations saved for the Sunday sale was a 6" high stoneware crock

Boston school silk embroidery needlework picture commemorating George Washington, "First in Peace, War, Fame, Virtue," $24,200 to a private buyer. Ron Bourgeault photo.

with an incised bird and a fish going after a worm on its side. Estimated at $6,000/8,000, it sold for $14,300 to Grace and Elliot Snyder, who paid high prices for high quality throughout the sale.

Although dealers captured the top lots, often buying for collectors, some collectors who prefer to do their own bidding did not go home empty-handed. A pair of watercolor portraits attributed to Rufus Porter (est. $3,000/5,000) sold for $11,000 to a couple who said they were from New Hampshire. A southern collector on the phone paid $13,200 for Erastus Salisbury Field's *The Celebration in the Temple* from the estate of Mary Black. It had failed to sell at Sotheby's in October 1991 because of a too aggressive estimate.

For the same price, $13,200, a collector from Boston bought a 6' long Sheraton mahogany sideboard, cataloged as school of John Seymour. Another private collector paid $16,500 for a Massachusetts inlaid mahogany card table with reeded legs, bulbous tapered feet, and a fan inlaid in its figured maple front panel.

Dealer Marguerite Riordan, bought a pair of North Shore/coastal New Hampshire inlaid mahogany card tables with a rich old finish for

$27,500, and Yardley, Pennsylvania, dealer Todd Prickett bought a Massachusetts Chippendale mahogany bombé desk for $44,000. A Philadelphia Gothic-splat armchair with an Israel Sack provenance went to a phone bidder for a reasonable $17,600. The Keowns' Salem mahogany fire screen with original floral needlework panel brought a disappointing $8,800 (est. $10,000/15,000), but their one-drawer worktable fetched a strong $7,150.

A Salem, Massachusetts, Federal butler's secretary, 78" high x 40" wide sold for $13,200, but another butler's secretary with squat proportions failed to sell. "That shows how discriminating buyers are today," remarked Albert Sack, looking up from the Sunday *New York Times* crossword puzzle he was finishing in ink. "They are saving their ammunition to buy quality. It is hard to handle just average items."

Any piece with major restoration or a questionable date was left behind. A Philadelphia walnut lowboy with pad feet (est. $25,000/35,000) remained unsold at $17,500 because the boys in the back of the room said it has a replaced front skirt. A pair of Philadelphia Chippendale mahogany side chairs illustrated on plate 2216 in Wallace Nutting's *Furniture Treasury*, estimated at $120,000/180,000 the pair, but offered separately, passed at $55,000 each without a bid in the room. Their authenticity was questioned.

Editor's Note: Record prices are paid for special objects even during a recession. A small walnut marble-top table without equal, made in Philadelphia in the 1740s and with a long history of ownership in South Carolina, sold for $462,000 at Christie's in October 1992.

RECESSION-PROOF RECORD:
A SMALL WALNUT TABLE

BY LITA SOLIS-COHEN

A small marble-top table discovered by an appraiser in a house in Raleigh, North Carolina, sold at Christie's in New York City on Saturday afternoon, October 24, 1992, for $462,000 with buyer's premium.

"How can something so simple be so beautiful. It speaks of a golden age," said Allen Miller, the successful bidder, when reached by phone after the sale. Miller, a furniture restorer in Quakertown, Pennsylvania, and a student of Philadelphia furniture, said he bought the table for a client.

"It's a jewel, one of the finest things I've seen for sale," he continued. "Other things are fancier, but it is so complete and unified. Its power dwarfed everything in the sale."

It does seem bigger than it is, measuring only 36½" wide, 22¼" deep, and 29" high. Its dark crusty skin makes it appear to be made of iron instead of walnut.

Miller thinks he knows who made it. "It came from one of the preeminent Philadelphia cabinet shops active in the late 1730s through the 1740s and 1750s. What makes it hard to date is that you don't know if it is a simplified table made late or an early one. To be safe, I'd say it is from the late 1740s. The shop signatures include the shape of the trifid foot, the half-round transition between the leg and the chamfered corners, and the scalloped profile of the side rails."

During the public exhibition at Christie's last month, men smiled as they caressed its shapely walnut legs and ran their fingers along the scalloped skirt. Women envied the perfect proportions, admired the blue veins in the strongly figured marble top, and noticed the slender ankles and stylish ribbed stocking on the trifid feet.

It is a sexy little table. Michael Flanigan, one of the wits in the trade, who arrived at Christie's to find a crowd of dealers examining the table upside down, quipped, "It's just like antiques dealers. The first thing they do when they see a virgin is get her upside down with her feet in the air."

Before the sale no one wanted to venture a guess at what the table would bring, but most thought the price would exceed Christie's $150,000/250,000 estimate. Its fluted chamfered corners and high scalloped skirt give it grace. Its long cabriole legs with a stylized scallop shell carved on each front knee, thumb molding on the rectangular marble top, and gorgeous pattern of the marble's blue veining add up to make it the finest example of early Philadelphia furniture to come on the market in memory.

The table was left to three sisters who had no idea of its high value. Christie's Americana specialist John Hays said when appraiser Steve Minor phoned and described it last August, he was on the next plane to Raleigh. The appraiser, who works for a nationally known appraisal firm headed by Emyl Jenkins, told the sisters he thought it was worth a quarter of a million dollars. "I convinced them they should send the table to

Walnut mixing table with a densely veined blue-gray King of Prussia, Pennsylvania, marble top, made in Philadelphia circa 1740, $462,000, a record auction price for Queen Anne furniture. Christie's photo.

auction, where it would bring all it was worth, and they should come to New York for the sale and have a good time," said Hays.

Two of the sisters came to watch the sale and left with expressions of disbelief after the hammer fell. "I was in shock. In my ignorance I never thought that table would be worth that much," said Beverly Clark after the sale, explaining that the table was always in her family's living room with a lamp on it. "We knew it was an heirloom. It had come down in my father's family. One of my older sisters recalled our father was offered twenty-five thousand for it years ago, but he would never sell it. We knew it had some value; that's why we called Emyl Jenkins to appraise it."

When auctioneer Hays opened the bidding at $80,000, New York City dealer Harold Sack, seated in the third row, flicked his gold pencil to start the competition. New York City dealer Leigh Keno, standing at the back corner of the salesroom, raised his bidding paddle, as did Marlboro, Massachusetts, dealer Wayne Pratt, seated on the left, Washington, D.C., dealer Guy Bush, by the stairs, and Richmond, Virginia, dealer Sumpter Priddy, who was leaning against the back wall opposite the podium. In less than a minute they pushed the price to $400,000. Hays took Priddy's bid of $410,000, and then a bidder on the phone upped the ante to $420,000.

"One more?" asked Hays of all those in the salesroom. The bidders were still, and he dropped his hammer. "Sold!"

There was no applause, once usual when a benchmark has been reached, even though $462,000 is a record for what the trade calls Queen Anne furniture, which was made a generation after the queen's death and in Philadelphia not London.

There was much muttering that the price was "right" and comments that even in tough economic times a spectacular piece of American furniture can bring a big number, though many wondered aloud what it might have brought three years ago at the top of the market. "It might have brought an extra hundred thousand dollars, but the price is a healthy one, quite respectable," said Albert Sack, Harold's brother, as he left the salesroom.

Priddy said he had been bidding on behalf of Tryon Palace, a historic house-museum in New Bern, North Carolina, once the seat of the state's governors. The table had been loaned to an exhibition at the house in 1907, and a curator had asked the sisters recently if it were for sale. That inquiry prompted the appraisal, which resulted in the table's consignment to Christie's. Priddy said the table had descended in the family of John Wright Stanley, a North Carolinian who had ties to Philadelphia, and it had a history of ownership in North Carolina dating back to the 18th century.

The table was one of few bright spots in a lackluster 223-lot offering of American quilts, folk art, furniture, and decorations. Only 146 sold (65%), and 77 were returned to their owners, reflecting the nation's uncertainty about the outcome of the election and the ravages the recession has wrought on the antiques trade. The auction brought a total of $1.6 million.

Editor's Note: In November 1993 the Forbes *magazine collection got a monopoly on Monopoly games, and in the process the real story and true history of the game was told, exploding a corporate myth.*

FORBES CORNERS MONOPOLY

BY LITA SOLIS-COHEN

The *Forbes* magazine collection has a monopoly on old Monopoly games, having recently acquired three properties for $11,500 (with buyer's premium), $17,250, and $23,000, adding to the one they bought in December 1992 for $71,500.

"We thought the games were appropriate for the collection of a magazine about money," said curator Mary Ellen Sinko, who did the bidding at Sotheby's November 1, 1993, sale of printed and manuscript Americana. "We will have them on display at the *Forbes* museum during the Christmas season," she added.

As a result of the auctions, the little-known true history of Monopoly has been told in an unlikely place. Sotheby's auction catalogs explodes one of the biggest corporate myths of this century: that Charles Darrow, an unemployed heating engineer in Philadelphia, invented the game he sold to Parker Brothers in 1935. There is no question Darrow brought the game to market, and his version with the locomotive trademark is the one we all know, but he was not the inventor, as careful scrutiny of the *Forbes* games and the notes in Sotheby's catalogs reveal.

The $23,000 set has a square board, like the printed Parker Brothers' games. It came with unpainted houses and hotels cut from pine molding, old chips, scrip, and typed Chance and Community Chest cards, deeds, and a set of rules typed on the same typewriter as the rules that accompanied the set Forbes purchased in December 1992. That set has a circular oilcloth board, probably an earlier version made for use on Darrow's round dining table.

A key set in the development of Monopoly and most certainly made before Monopoly took its final form is the set that cost *Forbes* $17,250. It is laid out on a square of pale blue glazed fabric with properties marked by colored triangles at the bottom, instead of bars at the top. It came with red-roofed, gray-painted houses and hotels, Chance cards, deeds, and money. It belonged to Charles E. Todd, who taught Darrow the game.

Jay Dillon, who cataloged the sale, points out that the proof is in a spelling mistake. Todd misspelled Marven Gardens as Marvin Gardens, Darrow copied Todd's spelling, Parker Brothers copied Darrow's, and it has been Marvin Gardens ever since. The real section of Atlantic City between Margate and Ventnor is known as Marven Gardens, a combination of Margate and Ventnor.

The third set, a wooden hand-painted square game board that brought $11,500, is probably earlier than the others. It has 40 compartments like the Atlantic City sets, but the place names are for real estate in the counties surrounding Philadelphia: Kimberton, Trappe, Ambler, Valley Forge, etc. More closely related to the Landlord's Game, a game patented in 1904 by Elizabeth Magie, one corner is marked "Mother Earth" instead of "Go," and another corner square reads "Government Grant, No Rents, No Taxes, Rest in Peace and Depart" instead of "Free Parking." Consigned by the Buckwalter family of Royersford, Pennsylvania, it was made by Joseph A. Buckwalter in the 1920s, according to family tradition.

"Thank goodness the true story of the game of Monopoly is finally seeing the light of day and beginning to rightfully supersede the Charles

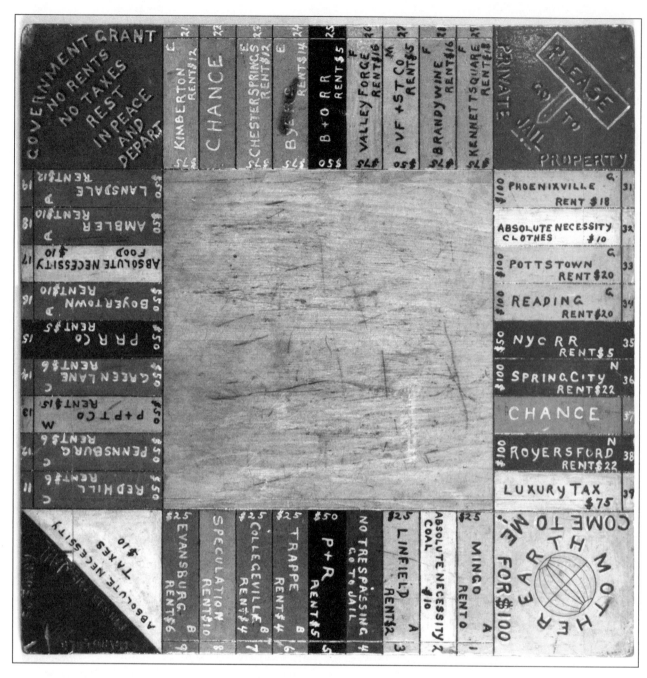

Monopoly board made circa 1920 by Joseph J. Buckwalter, with place names of towns in the counties surrounding Philadelphia, $11,500. Sotheby's photo.

Darrow myth," said Patrice E. McFarland, a graphic designer and game collector from Averill Park, New York, who is working on a biography of Elizabeth Magie Phillips as the game's true inventor. After buying an incomplete first edition of the Landlord's Game four years ago and finding the missing board a year later, McFarland was determined to restore

Lizzie Magie Phillips to her rightful place in history.

McFarland is appalled that Darrow took credit as inventor of the game. Darrow copyrighted Atlantic City Monopoly in 1933 and began making two or three sets a day by hand, drawing the boards on oilcloth and cutting the houses and hotels from strips of molding. He typed up the cards, deeds, and instructions, assembling them in his basement with the help of his wife and children, and selling them by word of mouth to family and friends.

When orders came in faster than he could supply them, Darrow enlisted the aid of a local printer who printed the black pattern and letters on oilcloth, and Darrow filled them in by hand. Within a year he was having the entire game printed and

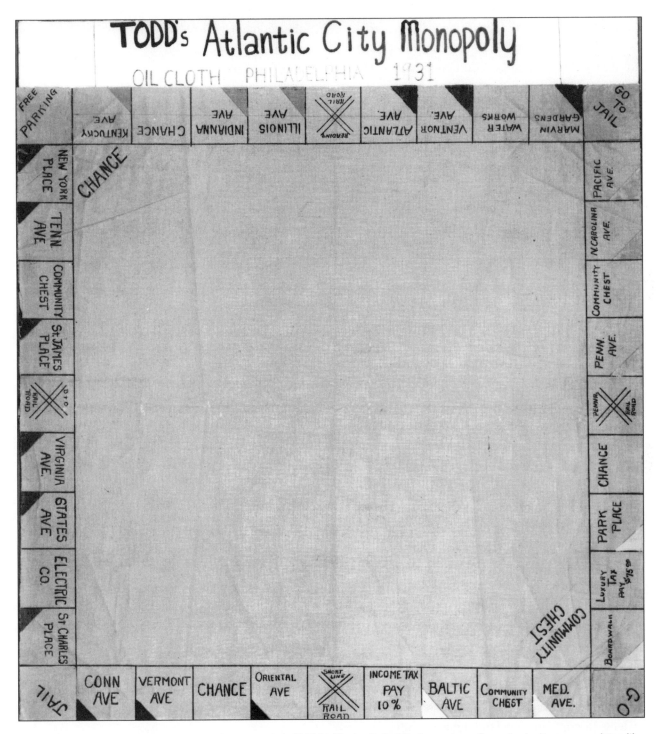

Important in the evolution of Monopoly was this set made in 1932 by Charles E. Todd in Germantown, Pennsylvania. It came complete with gray houses and hotels with red roofs, scrip, and typed cards, but the rules are missing. It sold for $17,250. Todd taught Charles Darrow how to play the game. Sotheby's photo.

boxed and sold them in quantity to Wanamaker's and F.A.O. Schwarz. In 1935 Parker Brothers, which had turned down the game the year before, reconsidered and bought Darrow's copyright.

According to McFarland, long before Darrow ever played Monopoly, Lizzie Magie's Landlord's Game had been played on college campuses coast to coast and in Europe under different names. The Landlord's Game, patented in 1904, came in two parts. "The first was like Monopoly, a game in which there is only one winner. Part two employs the same capitalistic principles but mixes them with a healthy dose of tax reform, to prevent the evils of monopolistic ownership, and then transforms all the players into enlightened winners," said McFarland, who has played the game many times. "Lizzie wanted to change the world, get us back on the right track. As a proponent of the economic ideas of Henry George, she designed her game to teach the single-tax theory as an antidote to the evils inherent in monopolistic land ownership. She saw economics as a science and an art. The game was her medium."

The patent for the Landlord's Game expired in 1921, and Elizabeth Magie, now Elizabeth Magie Phillips, took out another patent on an improved version in 1924. In order to have a monopoly on Monopoly, Parker Brothers bought that patent in 1935. "In Parker Brothers' early literature on Monopoly, Lizzie gets credit for inventing Monopoly. But after she died in 1950, Darrow was put forward as inventor, and Lizzie was dropped from Parker Brothers' company literature," McFarland complained.

Parker Brothers still sticks by the story that Charles Darrow sat down at his kitchen table and drew Monopoly. "We think there needs to be more research," said Carol Steinkraus, the company's spokesperson.

Since 1935, if anyone published a game similar to Monopoly, Parker Brothers' lawyers used their patents to prove they had the rights to both Monopoly and its predecessor, the Landlord's Game, even though the 1924 Landlord's Game they bought was not the 1904 game from which Monopoly actually evolved.

"This has been the red herring Parker Brothers has dragged across the trail in the past, so people would not know that the Landlord's Game was in public domain," said McFarland. "At this point in time, it is a moot point, but to the history of the game, it is significant."

Two of the games that have come to auction recently were used in a 1975 lawsuit, Anti-Monopoly vs. General Mills Fun Group Inc., which was tried in U.S. District Court, Northern District of California in San Francisco. Ralph Anspach, the publisher of the Anti-Monopoly game, was sued by General Mills, which then owned Parker Brothers (Parker Brothers is now owned by Hasbro). In preparing their defense, Anspach's lawyers found Charles Todd, who testified that he had taught Charles Darrow the game that Darrow sold to Parker Brothers as his own and from which Darrow's surviving children still receive royalties. Anspach initially lost the case, appealed, and won on a technicality.

When Todd died several years later, Anspach was left with Todd's Monopoly set, the one with the pale blue cloth board sold at Sotheby's. Now retired and living in France, Anspach sent the Todd set to auction.

The 1975 court testimony, cited in Sotheby's catalog, tells how the game was brought east from Indiana by a young woman named Ruth Hoskins, who came to teach at the Atlantic City Friends School. In 1929 she had learned to play a version of the Landlord's Game, called Auction Monopoly, from her brother, who learned it at college. Early in 1930 Hoskins taught it to her fellow teacher Cyril Harvey and his wife, Ruth, and the Harveys played it with their friends Jesse and Dorothea Raiford. According to McFarland, Ruth Harvey drew the first Atlantic City Monopoly board with Atlantic City streets.

The Harveys lent their games to private parties and Friends (members of the Society of Friends, a.k.a. Quakers) at Atlantic City hotels and also taught their friends. The Raifords taught their relatives Ruth and Eugene "Colonel" Raiford, who in turn taught their friends, the Todds. Charles and Olive Todd taught the game to Esther and Charles Darrow. Todd testified that Darrow asked him to type out the rules and that his secretary typed a dozen copies for Darrow.

It is no coincidence that the oilcloth boards sold at Sotheby's have all come from Quaker families in the Philadelphia area. The round board, which is probably the earliest and the first to have colored bands at the top of the properties, came down in the family of Darrow's mother-in-law, Mrs. J. Barclay Jones, who gave it to her niece. The square set came from the family of Jane Plummer

Leimbach of Swarthmore, Pennsylvania, who said her parents were friends of Barclay Jones, who gave the set to them. "I think it was a used set when my parents got it," she recalled. "It was the only set we ever had. We kept the board rolled up over a paper tube in the top desk drawer."

McFarland said she knows of a few other early handmade Monopoly sets in existence but has no reason to believe they will come to market any time soon.

On the other hand, she expects there are plenty of other homemade game boards with other than Atlantic City real estate on them, all based on the earlier, popular Landlord's Game. She wants to see all of them in order to piece Elizabeth Magie Phillips's story back together in its entirety.

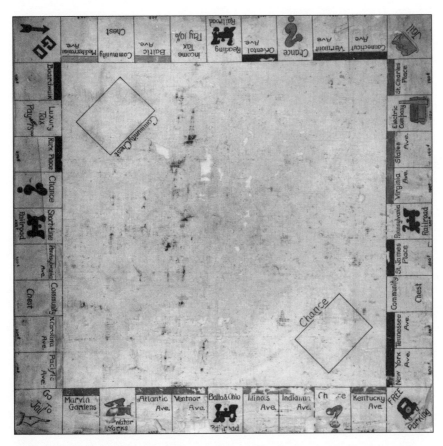

Monopoly, made and published by Charles Darrow in 1933, complete with cards, unpainted houses, hotels, chips, and money, $23,000. It is like the set Darrow copyrighted in 1933 and sold to Parker Brothers in 1935. All three sets were bought by the *Forbes* magazine collection and are on display at the Forbes museum, 62 Fifth Avenue in New York City. Sotheby's photo.

Mint & Boxed

Editor's Note: The Mint & Boxed scandal began in the 1990s and rocked the toy world. As the story unfolded over three years, it was reported in depth by M.A.D.'s New York correspondent Dorothy Gelatt. Jeffrey Levitt, a con man, tried to corner the toy market, but a resilient toy world ended up on its feet, with participants shaking their heads and wondering how they could have been taken. The stories that appeared in M.A.D. tell the whole story.

MEN AND BOYS WITH THEIR TOYS AUGUST 1990

BY LITA SOLIS-COHEN

Mergers and acquisitions and leveraged buyouts may be passé on Wall Street but not in the antique toy business. Alexander Acevedo, the multifaceted Madison Avenue art, antiques, and jewelry dealer, has sold all his toys to Jeffrey S. Levitt, the 33-year-old London toy dealer who calls his international toy business Mint & Boxed.

Mint & Boxed announced the purchase of the toy stock of Alexander Gallery as well as Acevedo's personal collection, more than 1,000 toys in all, with a retail value in excess of $15 million. Mint & Boxed said it is the single largest collection of antique toys ever acquired in one transaction.

Mint & Boxed did not release the purchase price, and Acevedo would not say what he got for the collection, but he acknowledged that it was "more than he had paid for the entire Perelman Museum collection, which he bought for $2.2 million including the toy museum building. Rumors in the trade put the figure somewhere between $4 and $10 million.

Acevedo said the deal included some restrictions. "I cannot deal in toys in my Madison Avenue gallery for three years, but I can buy and sell at shows, and I can hold tag sales."

Levitt, said to be heir to a whiskey fortune, reportedly started his toy business in England eight years ago, after his family business was sold. He said through a press agent that he will offer the toys from the Acevedo collection for sale at his gallery at 111 High Street, Edgewater, Middlesex, and at his new gallery in New York, which will open in September 1990 at 1124 Madison Avenue at 84th Street.

"It will be a three-story gallery like the one in London, with casual purchases on the first floor, toys priced from $10,000 to $100,000 on the second floor, and a third floor boardroom where luncheon will be served and items in excess of $100,000 will be offered," said Robert W. Bloch, public relations spokesman for Mint & Boxed in America.

According to Bloch, a full-color art book "will permanently showcase and enhance the value of the Alexander collection, two-thirds of which are American toys made between 1855 and 1930." The catalog will be available for sale in early autumn.

Vernon Chamberlain, 30, a well-known Canadian toy dealer, will be the director of Mint & Boxed in America. Eric Alberta, 30, who headed the collectibles department at Christie's East, will manage the new gallery, and Rick McMarrow, 26, who was assistant to Alberta at Christie's, is the administrator. At present Mint & Boxed has an office at the Roosevelt Hotel in New York.

Acevedo confirmed that Levitt bought all the toys in his gallery and all the toys he had taken home. "It was hard to believe I did it, when he came to my house and took every toy out," said Acevedo. Acevedo admitted he had already begun to collect toys again. "I bought a toy last week, and I'll be off to Brimfield next week to look for more," he said.

"You know, they said I was crazy when I paid $100,000 for the Charles [a toy hose reel made by George Brown in Forestville, Connecticut, in the 1870s], and they said the guy who bought the Charles from me for $125,000 was crazy too, but he sold it to Mint & Boxed for $250,000 and then everyone said I had given it away. Now I hear Mint & Boxed put a one-million-dollar price tag on it and sold it to a German collector. Toys are on a rampage."

Apparently the toy business is good all around. Hillman-Gemini, toy dealers at 65th and Madison, have moved out of their small shop and will be in larger premises at 927 Madison at 74th Street in the fall. "We will have twice as much space as we had in our former gallery," said Donald Hillman. "We think there will be a volatile chemistry between the two toy dealers on Madison Avenue only a few blocks away. We are delighted Mint & Boxed has come to New York. We welcome them. We know Jeffrey Levitt and Vern Chamberlain always do things first class; it should be very good for the toy business."

Expect the complexion of Madison Avenue to change this fall. Just as the Tiffany lamp shops sprouted a few years ago, toyshops will have a larger presence. Steve Balkin, who has operated Burlington Antique Toys at the lower level of 1082 Madison Avenue for the past 12 years, greets the arrival of Mint & Boxed with enthusiasm.

"It can't hurt the business," said Balkin. "I'm a toy soldier expert—both antique soldiers and current production—but I also stock die-cast autos, tinplate toys, and space toys." Balkin used to work for Peter Blum at the Soldier Shop, which has been selling soldiers, antique and new, as well as books about them for 21 years at 1222 Madison Avenue between 88th and 89th Streets.

If toys are hot, what made Acevedo sell? "It was a time for consolidation," said Acevedo on the phone. "I needed space in my new gallery [at 980 Madison Avenue, the old Sotheby's building] to open in October. " I will concentrate on paintings and furniture; the toys were all over the place and needed a lot of supervision."

TOYS R THEM SEPTEMBER 1990

BY LITA SOLIS-COHEN

It's been done before. An antiques dealer invests a lot of time, energy, and money in some neglected area and makes it much more visible so that rich collectors want it, prices climb, and a worldwide market develops.

Jeffrey Levitt is in the process of doing this for toys. Following on the heels of New York dealer Alexander Acevedo, who put that ball in motion, Levitt is bent on making antique toys, once a quiet backwater of the antiques trade,

into a category that has a place in the art world of Madison Avenue,

Levitt, a 30-year-old Londoner, bought Acevedo's toy stock and Acevedo's personal collection in June for an undisclosed amount of money with the stipulation that Acevedo not engage in the antique toy business on Madison Avenue for three years. This purchase came on the heels of Levitt's acquisition of a large Swiss collection and his purchase of the stock of a Canadian toy dealer.

Levitt is coming to New York this fall with more than 1,500 toys worth, he says, no less than $15 million, to open the American branch of his firm, Mint & Boxed. His toy store, to be housed at 1124 Madison Avenue at 84th Street, will certainly give antique toys panache.

In a recent phone interview from London, Levitt acknowledged that he went into the toy business when his family's liquor business was sold eight years ago and, over the years, has developed a worldwide clientele from this headquarters in the Edgewater section of London.

He says his most amazing feat was selling an American tin toy to a German industrialist for $1 million, which may get the toy into the *Guinness Book of Records* as the most expensive toy in the

Jeffrey S. Levitt, chairman of Mint & Boxed, with a German lithographed tinplate rear-entrance tonneau car.

world. That toy is a piece of fire-fighting equipment called the Charles, a tin hose reel painted with its name surrounded by roses, made by George Brown in Forestville, Connecticut, in the 1870s.

In the last six months, the Charles has been sold for $100,000 from the estate of New Hampshire collector Barry Barenholtz to Alexander Acevedo, who bought it privately before the auction, and for $125,000 by Acevedo again at one of his "great toy grabs," and then for $250,000 by the Pittsburgh doctor who bought it from Acevedo and sold it to Levitt. This spiraling price progression indicates how far the antique toy market may be able to go.

"If it had been marked Märklin, it would have been one-and-a-half million dollars," said Levitt of the Charles.

Levitt is mad for German toys from the golden age, 1880 to 1910. He said his favorite toy is a 36" long horse-drawn sleigh of painted brass made by Märklin in 1898, "It is sculpture in its own right," said Levitt. He said he is also really quite fond of a Carette 1906 double-decker bus made in Germany and beautifully lithographed for the French market.

He said his four-year-old daughter knows which are daddy's toys and which are hers. Apparently, his two-year-old daughter and his four-month-old son are not aware of antiques just yet.

They will be soon. Levitt said he sees toy collecting as the most popular collecting hobby in the years ahead. "It had been neglected, frowned upon, and now big art collectors are seeing what good value it is. A hundred thousand dollars will buy the greatest rarity, such as a Märklin train, one of only three produced. What people are getting excited about in Europe, where antique really means one hundred years old, is that so many of these toys are reaching their centenary. In the 1990s a lot of toys will come of age. I think this is helping the momentum."

When Levitt bought the stock of Toronto toy dealer Vernon Chamberlain, he got Chamberlain himself along with the toys, and made him vice president of Mint & Boxed, in charge of operations in North America.

"I needed him," said Levitt. "Our turnover last year was twenty-five million dollars, and we project a forty-million-dollar turnover worldwide in the next fiscal year. I know European toys, but Vern knows American."

Levitt said Chamberlain will head a staff of six who will run the New York store, and he will come over once a month and spend two or three days at a time."

Vernon Chamberlain, 30, said he started his business, called Antique Toy Attic, seven years ago but has only been dealing in "power house toys" for three years.

"European tinplate and American tin toys is the market we are gearing up for," said Chamberlain. "Jeffrey is the expert in trains and Märklin toys, my specialty is folk art and American toys. That's what the American collectors like and the Japanese and the Germans will be introduced to them. American tin has been a closet collectible. Alex [Acevedo] started the ball rolling really fast, and right now American tin has appealed to another affluent group. That's what has pushed the prices up. These collectors have realized they can have the finest toy collection for one million dollars and can get very little art in paintings for that money."

Chamberlain said Mint & Boxed will participate in toy shows and antique shows worldwide. "I showed at the Fall Antiques Show at the Pier last year, and Mint & Boxed will show there this year," he said. "But entering our store on Madison Avenue will be like turning the clock back to the turn of this century. It's basically boys' toys, no dolls or Teddy bears, but there will be several automatons."

The marketing scheme of Mint & Boxed has also helped the momentum of the antique toy business. Catalogs issued quarterly generally cost $20, but for the opening in America, Mint & Boxed will publish a 350-page scholarly art book with illustrations in color that will be for sale for $100. "It will be the definitive guide to great toys," said Levitt. "It will cover a broad range of toy collecting from cast iron to tinplate and include automatons. A price booklet will be available, which will be updated in the future."

MINT & BOXED COLLAPSES JULY 1991

by Dorothy S. Gelatt

All the king's horses and all the king's men can't put bankrupt Mint & Boxed together again.

London and New York antique toy dealer, Mint & Boxed, went into administrative receivership in London late Thursday, May 23, 1991, only eight months after their flashy million-dollar Madison Avenue opening, starring owner Jeffrey S. Levitt, 34.

The 169 secured creditors in London (banks and others) appointed the international accounting firm of Arthur Andersen & Co. as administrative receivers of Jeffrey S. Levitt Ltd. Trading as Mint & Boxed. This is a British procedure similar to bankruptcy in the United States, according to Anthony Briereley, joint administrative-receiver with John Talbot.

Among the Mint & Boxed creditors are banks and the 1982 Lord Mayor of London, Sir Anthony Jolliffe, who wrote the epilogue to the elegant Mint & Boxed toy catalog.

Within a week of the receivership, acting for the creditors, Andersen personnel took over the Mint & Boxed premises in North London; on Madison Avenue in New York; and in Allentown, Pennsylvania, where Levitt had bought out the business of America's leading toy repair service, Joe Freeman's Toy Works.

It is not a pretty situation on either side of the Atlantic. American toy dealers and collectors greeted the news with everything from explosive shock to nervous dismay. Suspicion abounds, and everybody is telling everybody else it will be a long time before the true facts are really known.

Within days the question of possible hanky-panky came up on all sides—industrial strength hanky-panky. Dealers began receiving from Arthur Andersen faxed copies of Mint & Boxed invoices for toys the Americans claim they never heard of, never ordered, and were never billed for. The invoices are dated variously from August 1990, with 180-day terms. A polite Andersen cover letter requests payment for the invoice, or clarification of how it was already paid.

Such invoices request amounts from roughly $50,000 to $100,000. The general impression in the New York trade is that Levitt might have been using the alleged invoice accounts receivable as collateral for bank loans. It's a move American accountants call jokingly "getting cash flow from the bank." In a sort of black humor game, American toy dealers began checking their fax machines, to see if they were among the elite who got six-figure invoices for toys they didn't buy.

Dealer Alexander Acevedo said he was invoiced for a Bing horse-drawn omnibus, circa

1901, finely hand-painted, complete with original composition figures (No. 9689). Terms: 180 days.

"I never bought that," said Acevedo.

A Pennsylvania toy dealer who asked not to be identified said he received an invoice for a Märklin train station, price $45,000. "It's a toy I never saw," he said.

Opinion is divided on what happened. Some suggest that Levitt was just a swinger in collectible toys who wanted to make a big splash, fell in over his head, and put invoices for non-existent purchases on the books as receivables in the hope of ultimately working things out. Others suggest darker motives. There are a number of investigations going on in London and New York.

Levitt was rumored to be heir to a $40 million (or pounds, the rumor wasn't too specific) British beer fortune that sold out to the Japanese, and that he did not need to make money. When asked about the family fortune, he declined to identify the company. Everyone assumed he had endless wealth.

The Levitt plan was to elevate antique toys to the status of art and sell them to wealthy men. He talked in terms of million-dollar toys and billionaire buyers in Japan, Saudi Arabia, Europe, everywhere. Americans feared a two-tier toy market would develop, in which billionaires would buy for investment and toy-lovers would get left in the lurch.

Levitt bought out everyone and everything he wanted to set himself up in antique American toys. The acknowledgements in his coffee-table-size catalog include the cream of the American toy market. It looked as if he bought everything that was not nailed down.

When Levitt bought out Joe Freeman's toy repair business in Allentown, Pennsylvania, he caused an unexpected upheaval. He raised the price of repairs so high that dealers stopped buying toys in need of restoration or repair because they could not sell them for enough to recoup expenses.

Big money was the name of the Mint & Boxed game even before they opened in New York. They spent heavily at the Ainslie Hewett toy sale held at Christie's East March 28, 1990. Dealers reported nervously that Mint & Boxed planned to open in New York and wipe up the American market. They thought he had the financial muscle to do it. American dealers do not have that kind of money for toys and were concerned about being priced out of business.

In a phone interview from London, before he opened in America, Levitt had said, "We've been in business for eight years, and we're the largest antique toy dealers in the world. Our major clients are in Japan, the Middle East, the Far East, Europe, and America. We've put discipline into the toy market."

He said that four months ago he sold his most expensive toy, a $250,000 1906 Märklin London bus to a German collector. But he claimed that they bought and sold collections for much more. For instance, he said they sold a collection to a Japanese investment company for £10 million, or $16 million. No American dealer had ever reached remotely comparable prices, and there was real foreboding in the market.

Shortly before he opened Mint & Boxed in New York, Levitt threw fireworks into the American market when he announced the sale of a legendary American toy the Charles hose reel, circa 1870, to a German collector for $1 million. People were surprised to see it on view at the Madison Avenue opening in September, but Mint & Boxed said it was held over for everyone to enjoy, and would be shipped immediately. Perhaps it was never sold. Perhaps it was never shipped.

After their New York extravaganza opening, Mint & Box continued to report huge exotic sales all over the world, but the American toy world, which usually knows everything about everybody, didn't see it happening.

Little by little the tide appeared to turn. Toys did not seem to be moving out of Mint & Boxed the way they did the first couple of weeks. Mint & Boxed began to search out deals.

Mr. Acevedo was offered his toy trains back, he said, for about 40 cents on the dollar. He bought them, and did not think it was too odd at the time," because you have to realize that people value things differently, he said. "I knew that Jeffrey sold a lot of my rare American tin toys for very high prices, but he considered the trains small change. He's not like me. I love toys. Jeffrey loves high prices. So I figured Jeffrey got a lot of money for the tin toys and didn't care what he got for the trains."

Other dealers were suddenly offered toys at steep discounts too, although when Mint & Boxed originally opened in New York, they did not offer any dealer discounts. It did not occur to most people that Mint & Boxed might need money because what they saw was Levitt's lavish spending on his New York shop and his extravagant lifestyle .The elegant New York three-story glass-box shop with Waterford crystal chandelier and custom interior reportedly cost over $1 million. Levitt traveled between London and New York on the Concorde with his family and staff at $8,350 per round trip ticket. He told dealer friends that in Paris he stayed in suites at The Ritz at $5,000 a night. In London he drove the proper car, a Bentley. Those who visited the Levitt home in England now decline to discuss it for publication, in deference to the family, but it was in Hertfordshire and apparently more than just nice.

Nothing seemed too much or too expensive for Jeffrey Levitt. At his star-studded opening and benefit auction, he gave $250,000 to actress Brooke Shields for her favorite charity, helping children suffering from AIDS. To the end, most people thought Mr. Levitt had big money.

Hints that the Levitt antique toy empire might be in financial trouble surfaced a few months ago when Mint & Boxed arranged a hefty six-figure sale to an American dealer at a very substantial discount. The terms were instant cash, in the form of federal funds deposited to their bank account by 3 PM, bank closing time. Otherwise the deal was off. At that time Mint & Boxed contended they were just revamping their inventory and making way for new things.

Some dealers now feel the public tip-off of the Mint & Boxed money problems could be seen at the Atlantic City show in March. Vern Chamberlain, manager of the New York shop, was selling off toys at roughly 30 cents on the dollar. But most people still thought money was no object with Mint & Boxed, and they must just be selling off their leftovers.

Now that the ax has fallen, everyone is asking everyone: Was there a family liquor fortune? Did he inherit anything? Did he maybe inherit less than people thought? Did he run through it all? Was there anything to run through? Or was it altogether something else? Nobody knows.

The big losers appear to be banks and private backers. This is a big surprise to everyone who thought Levitt was independently and endlessly wealthy. American dealers who helped Levitt prepare for his New York opening said they were paid by Mint & Boxed for services rendered or for toys.

Sources familiar with the current scene said that Levitt recently sold a one-third interest in the Madison Avenue shop to a group of outside investors, who are now apparently among the creditors.

Some publications where Mint & Boxed advertised heavily report not being paid for advertising space, but the full range of creditors is not yet known. Under English law the receiver must file a statement of affairs listing assets and debts, but those familiar with the process say it will take some time.

Sotheby's has been retained by Arthur Andersen as appraisers of the Levitt stock and properties in England and America. The full extent of Levitt's toy and other operations is not now publicly known. His phone has been disconnected. His lawyer has not returned calls.

A press statement from Arthur Andersen said "reported" Mint & Boxed turnover in the fiscal year ended June 1990 was $12.9 million. Levitt had predicted his turnover for this year would be $40 million.

Toy insiders feel the main impact of the failure will fall on the international market for high-priced European antique toys, where Mint & Boxed souped up prices to unrealistic levels and lured new wealthy buyers with forecasts of big art-market prices.

Final Royal Irony: Just before Mint & Boxed went under, they won The Queen's Award for Export Achievement.

BANKRUPTCY OF THE HIGHEST CLASS NOVEMBER 1991

BY DOROTHY S. GELATT

Mint & Boxed, the classiest bankruptcy ever to hit the antique toy world, owes money in all the best circles, from Her Majesty's government in London to the magazine *Art & Antiques* in New York City.

Jeffrey S. Levitt Ltd. Trading as Mint & Boxed in London, and its New York affiliate, Mint & Boxed Inc., which Levitt opened with regal splendor on Madison Avenue only last year on September 13, have stiffed London's finest for about $20 million, plus another partly questionable $20 million in New York. (All figures quoted in U.S. dollars.)

The Mint & Boxed strategy was to raise prices and sell million-dollar toys to billion-dollar people. "We have put discipline into the antique toy market," Levitt declared in London a few months before his flashy New York opening and about a year before his transatlantic collapse. At the time, nobody dreamed what an odd turn "discipline" might take. And nobody knows for sure even now. The "tale of two cities" bankruptcy is still wending its way slowly through the bureaucratic procedures on both sides of the Atlantic.

In London, the administrative receivers have not yet filed a "Statement of Affairs" listing the exact creditors, however a source familiar with the case said that Jeffrey S. Levitt personally lists combined assets of about $1.7 million, which includes his home and the Mint & Boxed shop and building in Edgewater, London. Against this is secured lending of about $1.02 to $1.19 million. He also personally owes creditors about $6.8 million, mainly on guarantees by the National Westminster Bank.

Separately, the Mint & Boxed business owes about $20 million. The major chunk is about $13.6 million of export credit debt guaranteed by the British Government Export Department. The $13.6 million apparently covered false invoices issued by Mint & Boxed for toys not sold, billed, or shipped.

What is ironic to some and a hoot to others is that Mint & Boxed, apparently on the strength of the fake export invoices, won "The Queen's Award For Export Achievement" just before they went broke. They announced the award in jubilant magazine ads, which apparently have not been paid for either.

American antique toy dealers, such as Alexander Acevedo and Tom Sage, said that they received copies of such apparently false invoices from the administrative receiver after the bankruptcy. The full extent of such invoices around the world is not currently known. Private collectors in America are not talking.

Mint & Boxed London also owes another $5.1 million in overdrafts from banks, plus about $3.4 million to trade creditors. Sir Anthony Joliffe, a former Lord Mayor of London, who wrote the epilog to Jeffrey Levitt's $100 catalog, figures in here someplace among the creditors. Exactly where will not be publicly known until the London Statement of Affairs is filed.

Altogether, the Mint & Boxed London debt seems to be a little over $20 million, plus Levitt's personal debt of about $6.8 million. And plus, of course the $20 million New York debt, which has progressed a little faster on the paperwork than in London.

New pennants are flying over the chic glass box building at 84th and Madison Avenue that for eight brief months housed antique toys with the highest price tags ever seen in the business.

"Mint & Boxed" banners are now replaced by "Searle," a New York Seventh Avenue fashion name known by shoppers from Bloomingdale's to Neiman Marcus as designers, makers, and purveyors of upscale made-in-America women's clothes.

Gone is the sumptuous Mint & Boxed Waterford chandelier, the elegant made-to-order carpeting with the Mint & Boxed red and blue logo woven into a gray ground, the rich dark wood custom paneling and handsome display cases—all of it costing a reputed $1 million or more, according to the antique toy intelligence network. Many people assumed Mint & Boxed had bought the building, otherwise why would anybody spend that much money on a rental. Levitt said he owned it, but it turns out he rented it, and the Arthur Andersen people in New York were glad to get rid of the lease.

Searle, which got the space for its fourth New York retail shop, gutted the place except for the floating staircase. They installed plain display fixtures for women's clothes and painted everything white—the richly dark-paneled walls, the ceilings, and even the hardwood floors.

In New York, Mint & Boxed has filed a Voluntary Petition of Bankruptcy, Chapter 7, with the United States Bankruptcy Court, Southern District of New York. The estimated assets are between $1,000 and $9,999. The estimated liabilities are between $10,000 and $99,000. According to the petition, "Debtor estimates that after any exempt property is excluded and administrative expenses paid, there will be no funds available for distribution to unsecured creditors." But that's not the end of it by any means.

"Location of Principal Assets" is listed as c/o Sotheby's Inc., 1334 York Avenue, New York, New York 10021. And of course it is common knowledge in the trade that Dana Hawkes, Sotheby's New York toy and collectibles specialist, did the inventory of the New York shop for Arthur Andersen after the bankruptcy.

So how come the listed assets are under $10,000 and the New York creditors claim $20 million? Well here's how it stacks up in the New York bankruptcy court records.

The biggest creditor of New York Mint & Boxed is listed as—hold on to your toy hats—Jeffrey Levitt Ltd., who claims it owes him $16,037,916.90. At press time the actual meaning of that figure was not available. It is not yet known what Levitt gave Mint & Boxed in New York that was worth $16 million.

The second-largest New York creditor is apparently some poor university professors' pension plan in Liverpool, England. The Universities Superannuation Scheme Ltd. claims Mint & Boxed Inc., New York, owes it $4,305,107.50. At this time it is not known what it got for its $4.3 million. Stock? Bonds? Toys? Who knows?

Arthur Andersen & Co. in New York claims $150,789.14; Kroll Associates wants $112,453.89; Devries Public Relations, $38,659.81; ACE

Productions, $22,500; Hilde Basch, $19,583.34; and Robert W. Bloch International, the Mint & Boxed Wall Street liaison PR firm, $14,466.99. From the sidelines it looks as if Mint & Boxed got its fancy public relations campaign on the arm.

Art & Antiques claims $14,941.80, *The Antique Trader,* $1,090.83, and *The Inside Collector* magazine, $3,068, for what may turn out to be free advertising. Chemical Bank MasterCard is up for $10,570; Federal Express, $6,314.27; Blue Cross & Blue Shield, $5,536.96; Christie, Manson & Woods, $4,235; AT&T Consumer Products Division in Lisle, Illinois, $3,682.04; Nynex Mobile Communications, $1,380.37; New York Telephone, $642.87; and AT&T Retail Processing, $308.52.

Mint & Boxed New York apparently owes everybody, from Xerox and Pitney-Bowes to the local stationer, Con Edison, and the garbage pick-up company. In New York it's bad luck to owe anything to your garbage man.

With one exception, the antique toy trade is conspicuous by its absence in the New York creditors list. Apparently, Mint & Boxed paid up-front and early for all the toys and services it bought from American toy collectors, experts, and dealers. The only one on the list is The Robert Lesser Company, in for $9,262.41. Levitt apparently also paid $250,000 in cash at his grand opening to actress Brooke Shields for her favorite charity, The American Foundation for AIDS Research. Neither Shields nor the foundation appear as creditors in New York.

Joe Freeman, who sold his Allentown, Pennsylvania, toy repair outfit to Mint & Boxed, is not back in business as of our press date and it is not known when or if he will be.

Vern Chamberlain, who reputedly sold his Toronto antique toy business to Mint & Boxed and moved to New York to run the shop for Levitt, opened Chamberlain Galleries, Inc. in Place des Antiquaires on 57th Street last month. Earlier this year, when it looked as if Mint & Boxed was trying to sell off stock in a hurry to raise funds,

Chamberlain said nothing could be further from the fact. "Mr. Levitt is very, very wealthy," Chamberlain said.

The question of Levitt's wealth has been on the tip of everybody's tongue ever since last year when we first heard it rumored that he was going to open in New York and wipe up the American trade. Everyone we know professed to think Levitt had inherited millions from the sale of a family booze business to the Japanese. Some said it was beer, Levitt said it was a distillery. A source close to the situation has suggested to us that there never was a distillery or a family fortune.

As for the toy inventories, Sotheby's London told us it will hold a special Mint & Boxed catalog sale on January 23, 1992. Sotheby's thinks the toys will hold more appeal together than scattered through other catalogs, and the publicity of the collapse will do the sale good. The idea apparently is that people will want a piece of the corpse.

Sotheby's New York says the London sale has about $600,000 worth of toys and it will not include the famed Charles hose reel toy. It is currently not a matter of record where the Charles was at the time of the bankruptcy, although presumably that would be of interest to creditors in both London and New York,

The Charles, made by George W. Brown in Forrestville, Connecticut, circa 1870, is probably the most expensive and revered antique American tin toy today. Part of the Levitt legend that crossed the Atlantic before his New York opening was that he had sold the Charles to a German collector for $1 million, an incredible price. People were there-fore a mite surprised to see it on a prominent pedestal at the Mint & Boxed Madison Avenue opening. But we were all assured it was here just for people to enjoy and would be shipped immedi-ately thereafter. Later on, Chamberlain revealed that Levitt loved the toy so much, he bought it back from the German collector. The current toy grapevine says it's at Sotheby's in New York. The auction house has not exactly denied it.

So far Jeffrey Levitt and Mint & Boxed are in hock to everyone from Her Majesty the Queen and a Lord Mayor of London to the New York phone company and a garbage pick-up service. But hang in there, ladies and gentlemen. As the saying goes, "It ain't over till it's over."

A SECOND COMING JANUARY 1992

BY DOROTHY GELATT

Is Jeffrey S. Levitt about to rise from the ashes of his May 1991 Mint & Boxed antique toy bankruptcy and loft a new transatlantic toy business hot-air balloon?

Reports of a possible Levittation are drifting in to *M.A.D.* from points as far apart as London and California. Levitt sightings have replaced Elvis in the antique toy collecting world.

From England we heard that Levitt appeared boyish, friendly, and full of good spirits at the November Sandown Park toy show in London. He was greeting old friends, shaking hands, and spreading the word that he would shortly open a toyshop in London somewhere off Baker Street, a good old Sherlock Holmes neighborhood.

From New York we heard that Levitt was negotiating to sell the collection of a Hamburg, Germany businessman and just charge him a commission.

From the West Coast we heard that a Levitt representative, called Hal Ballon, was phoning local dealers in California to say he is a London toy dealer visiting his son in California and would sell the Jeffrey Levitt private toy collection at the big Glendale, California, toy show in January. He told one dealer the business would be called Jeffrey Levitt Antique Toys. He told *M.A.D.* he would be dealing under his own name.

A delightful man with an enchanting London cockney accent, Mr. Ballon sketched a career from steward on the *Queen Elizabeth* to a traveling man of women's fashions for 12 years. He said he met Mr. Levitt in London a few weeks before, he lived in America for 30 years, and he has been an American citizen for five years. He thought Mr. Levitt might come to the Glendale show.

California dealers said Mr. Ballon did not have a list of toys or prices to send them, but expected to get back to them. When *M.A.D.* asked Mr. Ballon what he's selling, he said he'd make a phone call and would get us a nice story line. Later he asked us to call him back in two weeks.

MINT & BOXED SALE FEBRUARY 1992

BY DOROTHY S. GELATT

The leftover American stock of London toy dealer Jeffrey S. Levitt's bankrupt Mint & Boxed Inc., which elevated antique toys on Madison Avenue to an unmatched level of alleged high-toned fraud and deception, was unloaded for $1.5 million in a fancy unreserved garage sale at Christie's Park Avenue on December 16, 1991, by order of the New York Bankruptcy Trustee.

Bankruptcy records in New York show claims of over $46 million against Levitt and Mint & Boxed in New York and London. Nevertheless, Christie's toy specialist Joshua Arfer said that both the trustee in bankruptcy and Christie's were pleased with the $1.5 million sale.

New York bankruptcy records also reveal that Levitt ran Mint & Boxed primarily on loans from banks and pension funds secured by faked invoices for faked orders. He went from borrowed riches to rags on Madison Avenue in eight short months, from September 1990 to May 1991.

The pinnacle of last year's Mint & Boxed price fraud was also the top lot at Christie's December sale. Christie's sold the treasured circa 1870 American Charles hose reel. Estimated at $200,000/300,000, it went to an anonymous phone bidder for a toy auction record, $231,000 (with buyer's premium).

This was only one-fifth as much as the faked $1 million sale of the Charles that Levitt reported worldwide in 1990, before he opened in New York City. He even bamboozled the *Guinness Book of Records* into running this trumped-up $1 million Charles as the world's most expensive toy.

Levitt's fake $1 million price for the Charles quickly migrated into toy fire engine literature as well. It appears on the dust jacket of a new book, *The History of American Firefighting Toys* by Charles V. Hansen (Greenberg Pub. Co., 1991), in a caption that says it recently sold for the highest recorded price ever paid for a toy, $1,000,000.

Despite Levitt's faked $1 million price for the Charles, the hose reel was still on view at the Mint & Boxed New York opening in September 1990. It was apparently never actually sold to anybody until the bankruptcy sale at Christie's. Compared to Levitt's claim of $1 million for the Charles alone, Christie's total of $1.5 million for the complete sale of 361 lots was a lesson not lost on toy collectors.

Christie's declined to name the anonymous buyer of the Charles, but trade insiders quickly insisted it was Pittsburgh physician and antique toy collector Dr. Anthony Haradin, a previous owner of the the Charles. He first bought it for $125,000 in 1989 at the December 17 Acevedo-Bertoia grab-bag sale, and sold it in 1990 to Levitt before his New York opening. Levitt claimed he paid Haradin $250,000, but the doctor said it was less.

When he heard Levitt sold the Charles for $1 million, Dr. Haradin said he felt terrible and wanted to buy it back. At Christie's sale, he had a second chance at the Charles and got it quietly on the phone for only double what it cost him in 1989.

Underbidders for the Charles in the salesroom included Marlboro, Massachusetts, dealer Wayne Pratt and New Jersey dealer Bill Bertoia, both of whom acted as if $200,000 was their cutoff price. Kansas City collector G. Randall Smith dropped out earlier. Dr. Haradin's son, Ray, a toy collector and dealer, was also at the sale but said he did not bid for his father. "I didn't get to raise my paddle," he remarked, hinting obliquely that he was only prepared to pay less.

Dealers and collectors thought Christie's had the biggest turnout they had ever seen for a toy sale. Christie's does not release numbers, but people were estimating 300, 400, or 500, take your choice. There were buyers from Europe, England, and all over America, and lots of phone and order bidding.

It was rumored that Jeffrey Levitt was in town for the sale. It was said that the New York Trustee in Bankruptcy told Christie's not to let him in. No one admits seeing him.

Alison Kurke, from Sotheby's London collector's department, sat through the whole sale, and handed out circulars for Sotheby's London January 22–23, 1992, sale of the Mint & Boxed London shop leftovers. David Redden, Sotheby's New York books and manuscripts specialist, dropped in, saw a camera aimed at him, smiled, and left.

Dealer Wayne Pratt thought the unreserved feature of the sale encouraged the bidding considerably. People don't like bidding against a reserve, he suggested. They feel it pushes them artificially.

New York dealer Steve Weiss of Hillman-Gemini agreed. "In a recession especially, people want to know what is the true value. They want to know what someone will actually pay, not what the reserve buy-in price is."

Levitt's plan to hoist toy prices to major art market levels and sell million-dollar toys to billion-dollar people came after the peak of the 1980s credit binge, and it never really got off the ground. His Mint & Boxed toy catalog prices were pegged far above the prices Christie's estimated and buyers actually paid.

The second-highest lot at Christie's sale was a circa 1919 Märklin tin fire set, including a firehouse and three fire engines. Mint & Boxed priced it at $575,000, and nobody bought it. Christie's estimated it at $75,000/95,000 and sold it to phone bidder Paul Chambers for $79,200. The underbidder was Tampa, Florida, collector Max Zalkin, a former Mint & Boxed customer and admirer.

Third-highest lot was a circa 1880 tramcar with two horses. It was the cover lot of the summer 1989 London Mint & Boxed catalog, which called it

Märklin/Lutz (German) made for the French market, priced at £55,000 ($93,500). Nobody bought it. Christie's auction catalog called it "magnificent early French tinplate" (est. $60,000/80,000), and it went at $71,500 to Washington collector Max Berry, who bid in person and was accompanied by his wife, Heidi Berry, who covers collectibles for the *Washington Post*.

The price level then dropped into the $20,000s. A carved wood model of the passenger liner *Empress of France* brought $28,600 from London collector/dealer/veterinary surgeon David Pressland, author of *The Art of the Tin Toy*. Pressland, whose wife, Hilary Kay, heads Sotheby's London collectors' division, bid in person with his publisher and toy colleague, Allen Levy, head of New Cavendish Books. Together or separately they bought a considerable portion of the sale. Toy collectors were happy to see Pressland recovered from a mysterious and near-fatal London attack last summer.

Underbidder on the *Empress of France* was Koji Ichida, a Japanese gentleman living in New York, who attended the sale with his wife, Seiko, his Harvard undergrad son, Atsumi, and his Barnard graduate daughter, Mas. Mr. Ichida, who writes for the Japanese antiques magazine *Mé no Mé* said he and his wife both write books about America for

Top lot at Christie's, The Charles hose reel, made circa 1870 in Connecticut by George W. Brown, sold to an "anonymous" phone buyer for $231,000 (est. $200,000/300,000). In 1990 Jeffrey Levitt faked a $1 million sale for The Charles, which unfortunately made the Guinness Book of Records.

the Japanese, she on American literature, he on American furniture and collectibles. He is also in the export-import business and wants to introduce American antique toys, especially boats, to the Japanese market. Ichida was surprised to learn that Levitt had the same idea before he went bankrupt.

Ichida was also the underbidder on the next highest lot, a painted wood model of the passenger liner *United States*. It, too, went to the Pressland-Levy team for $24,200, within estimate.

Both the *Empress of France* and the *United States* came from Christie's February 12, 1985, sale of property from the Seaman's Institute of New York, where they brought $25,300 and $17,600. The *Empress of France* was a 1958 gift to the institute from the Canadian Pacific Railway; the *United States* was a gift from H.R.H. King Frederick I of Denmark.

Other toys at the same level included a circa 1902 Bing tin key-wind open phaeton at $24,200 to an American dealer, and a circa 1895 Märklin hand-drawn fire pumper at $24,200 (est. $15,000/20,000) to a German private collector. A circa 1896 Märklin horse-drawn live-steam fire pumper, offered by Mint & Boxed for $145,000, was estimated at $8,000/12,000 by Christie's and sold to a German collector for $24,200.

One thing that concerned a lot of people about Mint & Boxed toys, both before and after the bank-ruptcy, was condition. Astute dealers and collectors felt many of the toys had considerable restoration or actual replacements that were never mentioned or, in some cases, were complete fabrications.

An extreme example of this was lot 1, which was cataloged as "a Märklin tinplate 'Aeropal' hand or steam operated lighthouse, circa 1909," (est. $6,000/8,000). At the opening of the sale, Christie's auctioneer Kathleen Guzman announced the toy was an undated German reproduction. Despite the fact that the toy was not Märklin, but a fabrication, it brought $22,000 from a German phone bidder. It is not clear if the phone buyer heard the announcement made in New York.

Tampa, Florida, collector Max Zalkin (left), underbidder on the 1919 Märklin fire set, with Vern Chamberlain, formerly manager of the now bankrupt New York Mint & Boxed, who currently runs Chamberlain Galleries Inc., in Place des Antiquaires, New York City.

After the sale Joshua Arfer, Christie's toy specialist, said he was not aware of the announcement and that the toy was part Märklin.

Prices at Christie's ranged from the record $231,000 down to $66. The majority of the toys sold in the low thousands or hundreds of dollars, reflecting the reality of today's antique toy market when compared to the hopped-up prices Levitt hoped to achieve.

Every available scrap was sold. The large oval rug with the Mint & Boxed red, white, and blue logo, made to order for the Madison Avenue shop, was lotted with two of the blue and white company banners that hung outside (est. $150/250). They brought an astounding $2,640 from a European private buyer in the salesroom.

Patient buyers who waited to the end got some actual pin-money bargains. A group of five Corgi toys with original boxes (est. $100/200) went to a lucky bidder for $66. It included several James Bond Aston Martins with missing passengers, Kojak's Buick Regal, and a Charlie's Angels van.

Two Dinky Toy No. 106 Thunderbirds with original boxes (est. $75/100) brought $77. Sixteen Corgi Juniors with original boxes (est. $100/150) went for $99. They included a Pink Panther motorcycle, The Saint's Jaguar, a Starsky and Hutch Ford Gran Torino, Popeye's tugboat, and a Bugs Bunny buggy. What a find!

The sale wound up with a super lot of Matchbox toys (est. $400/600) that sold for a rousing $825. The bonanza included 28 earlier models, featuring some coveted London buses and fire engines, plus 19 later models, featuring the 40th anniversary gift set and four Tomica No. F 26 Morgans, all with original boxes.

In Mint & Boxed's headiest days, their catalogs carried Matchbox toys—with box—at prices from roughly $50 to over $100 apiece, a shock to this reviewer who bought them in the U.S. as they came out in the 1950s for 25 cents and later 50 cents apiece at a country drugstore. In 1990 Mint & Boxed offered Matchbox No. 1, the Aveling Barford steamroller, for $93.50; No. 2, the little red and green dump truck with yellow driver, for $75; No. 3, the blue cement mixer with orange wheels, or the model with gray wheels, for $75; and No. 4, the red tractor with yellow driver, for $93.50. They priced early cars, such as the No. 22 Vauxhall Cresta or the No. 10 Foden Tate & Lyle sugar truck, at $110 each.

Some *M.A.D.* readers have written complaining that Mint & Boxed hyped the die-cast toy market prices forever out of reach of the average collector. In the end that is unlikely. Prices tend to find their natural level over time, following both binge and bust, be it for toys, stocks, bread, or oil wells.

 # ENGLISH BANKRUPTCY FEBRUARY 1992

The $46 million bankruptcy proceedings against Jeffrey S. Levitt and Mint & Boxed have recently been upstaged by the $4.4 billion bankruptcy of the late Robert Maxwell's publishing and business empire. Both bankruptcies are being handled in London by the same receiver, appointed by the creditors. It is possible that a little $46 million bankruptcy like Mint & Boxed could get lost in the shadow of a massive $4.4 billion deal like the Maxwell affair. Levitt told an English acquaintance recently that the Mint & Boxed bankruptcy was unimportant. That remains to be seen.

In any case, bankrupt individuals in England get financial help from the government totally unlike anything available in America. The British government pays a bankrupt's living expenses, medical expenses, and even his psychiatrists. So far as was known at press time, Levitt and his family were still living in their stately English country home, allegedly at the government's expense. No charges had been filed against him, but knowledgeable people say they ultimately will be.

It is hard to guess how the Mint & Boxed scenario will wind up. Maybe all the jolly bankrupts will end up living happily ever after on the Maxwell yacht at the British government's expense.

LONDON SALE MARCH 1992

BY DOROTHY S. GELATT

Sotheby's London coded the sale "unboxed" and took in $1.045 million on January 22 and 23, 1992, for what may or may not be the remaining stock of Jeffrey S. Levitt's antique toy empire. Mint & Boxed, declared bankruptcy last May 23 in New York and London. Christie's unloaded the high-flyer's New York stock for $1.5 million last December. Currently, Mint & Boxed/Levitt owe over $46 million, much of it to banks that paid them for allegedly fake export invoices.

Toy pros think there are still a lot of Mint & Boxed/Levitt toys unaccounted for, but nobody is yet prepared to go on record as to where they might be. The first to surface so far are 25 antique toys, apparently with a Levitt/Mint & Boxed connection, that turned up in a car stopped by police on November 30, 1991, for speeding on the M-25 highway in England. The men in the car claimed they were on the way to Cornwall to have the toys appraised.

At about that time an effervescent man in California with a cockney accent, who said his name was Hal Ballon, approached West Coast dealers and said he would sell antique toys for Jeffrey Levitt at the Glendale, California, show in January. He was not able to tell dealers or M.A.D. what he'd be selling, or prices, and he was not seen at Glendale.

Hal Ballon, who told M.A.D. he was Levitt's man in California, could not be reached after the show. A gentleman who said he was Hal Ballon's son, Larry Balloonie, told M.A.D. his father went back to England and he did not know his phone number. He calls me, I don't call him, Mr. Balloonie said jovially. Larry Balloonie told M.A.D. that his father did not come to the Glendale show because

there was "some problem" about the toys.

A question has now arisen as to whether there is any connection between the toys found in the speeding car on the M-25 and the toys Mr. Ballon was expecting to sell for Mr. Levitt in California. The London bankruptcy administrator, Arthur Andersen, has put in a claim for the toys. Levitt's former New York manager, Vern Chamberlain, told M.A.D. the week of the bankruptcy he was surprised to learn that Jeffrey Levitt had a fabulous private collection of priceless toys at home.

Bankrupt Mr. Levitt and his family are still living in their stately English country home in Hertfordshire. His wife has a nice new car. Inquiring minds are waiting breathlessly for the next installment in "The Further Adventures of Jeffrey S. Levitt" expected soon, now that the fraud squad at Scotland Yard is on the case.

Sotheby's catalog, "An Important Sale of Tinplate and Die-cast Toys," did not mention Mint & Boxed on the cover, and it took careful reading to realize that 66 outsider lots were dropped into the middle of the sale, swelling the catalog total to 518 lots. There was also another complication. Twenty of the Mint & Boxed lots in the catalog were withdrawn from the sale in a dispute over ownership. Sotheby's is regretfully returning to the bankruptcy receiver a charming selection of mostly Märklin toy sleighs, prams, kitchenware, cars, and trains estimated at $77,000/115,000. Levitt claimed most of them were gifts to his wife and small children. Others are claimed to be property of other people connected to Mint & Boxed.

The Mint & Boxed lots, which at first appeared to be 518, were whittled down to 431. Unlike Christie's unreserved New York Mint & Boxed sellout in December, Sotheby's London sale did not fly out the window. Seventeen lots failed to reach their reserves and were bought in; 19 lots had no bids and were passed. Sotheby's Alison Kurke reported that the 36 leftover lots were being disposed of post-sale, but the transactions are not made public.

The toys at Sotheby's were primarily German and British with a sprinkling of French, Italian, and Japanese. They drew a big European audience. American toys were sold at Christie's sale in New York, and nothing in London came near the $231,000 reached for the famed Charles tin fire hose reel made circa 1870 by George Brown in Connecticut.

Twenty-five percent of Sotheby's $1,045,343 take came from the five top lots: four made by Märklin and one by Bing. Almost nothing reached the stratospheric prices Mint & Boxed was asking when it went bankrupt.

The two top lots each brought $85,100 each. A rare Märklin circa 1902 set of five tinplate horse-drawn fire toys (est. $54,000/72,000) went to a German collector. Last year the price was $575,000 in Levitt's fancy toy catalog, but there were no takers. And a Märklin circa 1910 tin carousel (est. $45,000/63,000) sold to an American collector. The German underbidder on the phone hung up, but he later tried for the top-lot fire toys, which he also gave up on.

A Märklin circa 1905 Gauge III steam engine with tender and two cars (est. $32,000/45,000)

limped in at $27,720 from a British dealer. The Mint & Boxed pre-bankruptcy catalog listed it "price on request," indicating Levitt thought he could get a zillion for it. Levitt also claimed the toy was presented in 1905 to Tsar Nicholas on a visit to Paris, where it was left at the Hotel Crillon because the royals had too much luggage. It came with a family picture of the Tsar showing a toy train in the background.

A Märklin Commodore Vanderbilt locomotive, tender, and two cars (est. $1,800/2,700) brought a whopping $19,800 from a Swiss buyer who already has one of the locomotives. He bought the lot at close to Levitt's pre-bankruptcy asking price because he needed the tender, which is in good but not original paint.

A Märklin circa 1930 Leipzig two-story station for Gauge I (est. $16,200/21,600) went to a German collector for $17,820. Mint & Boxed bought it in the 1989 Coluzzi sale at Christie's South Kensington for roughly $8,000.

A Bing circa 1906 rear-entry tonneau went to an anonymous buyer for a mid-estimate $16,830.

If you stayed the course through the two-day sale, you could pick and choose in the die-cast toys that Mint & Boxed originally started out with nine years ago. About 39 assorted Tootsie Toys in a lot brought a low estimate $495. For $770, well under the estimate, you could have bagged a large lot with about 80 boxed Matchbox toys and another 95, neither mint nor boxed, cataloged as "unboxed."

TRIAL JANUARY 1993

BY DOROTHY S. GELATT

Now, after another year and a half of tortuous worldwide investigation by the British government, Jeffrey S. Levitt is finally committed to actual trial in a London Crown Court, on charges of "fraud and forgery." He allegedly borrowed millions from banks, institutions, and others, using faked international orders for antique toys as collateral.

In December 1992, a London Magistrate's Court ruled that the government prosecutor's charges merit a Crown Court trial. Levitt did not contest the ruling and reportedly verified the charges. Trial date and court will be arranged some time in 1993.

Levitt had the Magistrate's Court practically to himself the day of the ruling. A van full of explosives had been discovered around the corner the night before and nobody showed up in court the next day unless they absolutely had to.

Mr. Levitt was his usual jaunty self, chatting around as if he had not a care in the world.

Although his Mint & Boxed and personal bankruptcy involves debts of over $40 million, Mr. Levitt's lifestyle does not appear to be cramped. Under the current British system, the government pays the bankrupt's legal expenses plus some sort of living stipend, but many people have questioned whether that is all he lives on.

After the 1991 bankruptcy, it was said that a bank would take over Levitt's lovely country estate on which he owes several million. But Levitt, his wife, who is expecting their fourth child in January, and the family are still living there. Those familiar with the case have suggested that since British real estate is on the rocks, the bank may feel it is better to have the Levitts live there than to risk having an empty house vandalized.

THE GUILTY PLEA SEPTEMBER 1993

BY DOROTHY S. GELATT

Bankrupt toy dealer Jeffrey S. Levitt pleaded guilty to a major charge of fraudulent trading and to associated charges of forgery and tax evasion on July 26 in Wood Green Crown Court, London. Fraudulent trading is considered a very serious offense in England.

Released on bail and awaiting sentencing in the autumn, the former high-flying owner of the

Mint & Boxed antique toyshops in New York City and London has been removed from his elegant country home in Hertfordshire. It was immediately taken over by squatters.

Levitt, along with his wife and four young children, moved to a smaller rental house nearby. Terms of his bail require him to stay there nightly, and not leave England.

After two years of diligent search around the world by the British authorities, Levitt's Mint & Boxed forged documents and faked invoices were presented in evidence in London by the government to the British courts.

Following a number of preliminary legal skirmishes, Mr. Levitt pleaded guilty on July 26 to the major charge of fraudulent trading. He also pleaded guilty to an attempt to defraud an Arab bank and various charges of tax evasion, including evading customs duties and the British Value Added Tax.

A letter Levitt forged in the name of Harold K. Skramstad, Jr., president of the Henry Ford Museum & Greenfield Village in Dearborn, Michigan, was presented in evidence by the British government. In Levitt's faked letter, dated March 14, 1991, Skramstad appeared to order $10,550,000 of antique toys from Mint & Boxed.

"The letter is specious. I did not write it," said Mr. Skramstad after it surfaced in 1991. "I can't understand anybody having the chutzpa to do anything like that," Skramstad said in wonderment.

THE SENTENCE DECEMBER 1993

BY DOROTHY S. GELATT

A London court crowded with reporters called him a Peter Pan personality and a Walter Mitty type and he seemed to enjoy it.

Looking fit and well tailored, Jeffrey S. Levitt, 36, did not bat an eyelash on October 22, 1993, when Southwark Crown Court Judge Christopher Hardy sentenced the Mint & Boxed antique toy dealer to four years in jail for fraudulent trading amounting to about $24 million. Another chunk of alleged fraudulent millions in New York was not included in the London action.

Levitt had already pleaded guilty in London on July 26 to eight charges of fraudulent trading and associated charges of forgery and customs and tax evasion. He told friends he expected to get a two-year sentence and do one year.

Sources in London suggest he's more likely to do one-and-a-half to two years of the four-year sentence. He will probably be held in an "open" (light-security) prison, since he was not convicted of a violent crime.

Stephen Solley, Levitt's lawyer, introduced psychiatric reports into the court, evidence indicating Levitt had psychiatric treatment as far back as 1981, at age 24, when the doctor stated he was more like an adolescent.

A psychiatric examination released in court said there was "something worrying, even crazy, about his thoughts." He was deemed to have a severe personality disorder, and was described as "a Walter Mitty."

Mr. Solley maintained in court that Levitt's primary motive was not financial gain. It was to be at the center of the toy antique market. "It gave him great respectability and persona."

If it had been established that Levitt had an "extreme psychiatric illness," he would not have served a prison term. The court concluded he had only a "personality disorder" that did not prevent him from serving time.

Nor did the court disqualify Levitt from starting out again and being a business director at some future date. It did, however, keep some of the charges against him "on file," meaning that if he were to come afoul of the law again, these charges would be on his record and count against him.

The Queen's Award for Export, which Levitt received by virtue of his fraudulent trading, was a bone of contention. Levitt's lawyer, Mr. Solley, wanted it excluded from the charges, but the judge left it "on file."

Since Levitt has no visible means of support, he does not have to pay his legal costs. Hoping to minimize the sentence, his lawyer pleaded on his behalf that his four children (another child was born earlier this year) would now be left in a one-parent family and on "benefits," which in London means welfare.

The judge was apparently unmoved. A source familiar with the situation has indicated that the three older children go to good private schools, and that's not cheap. There is no public information on who pays for the children's private schooling. British government "benefits" do not cover it.

Life in antique toyland has survived the momentary Levitt explosion. People here are buying, selling, and collecting very much as they always did. A few "amateurs" who bought at Levitt's inflated "art market" prices are trying to sell.

A circa 1870 American tin Tally-Ho coach of uncertain manufacture that Levitt sold for a remarkable $195,000 at his splashy New York 1990 Mint & Boxed opening, showed up last month at the Atlantique City show. The unfortunate buyer would like to unload it, preferably for what he paid. Most people don't think he has a chance.

A Levitt German Bing brake car , circa 1902, was put up for sale in September at Christie's South Kensington by the London Levitt/Mint & Boxed receivers (est. $12,000/16,000). Although it looked good, it had clockwork and paint repairs and did not sell.

LEVITT CHARGED WITH THEFT NOVEMBER 1996

Jeffrey Levitt, whose Mint & Boxed antique toys business collapsed with debts of 12 million pounds in 1991, is due to appear at North Oxfordshire Magistrates Court, Banbury, on October 29, charged with handling $34,000 of stolen antiques, the property of Richard Atkins of Steeple Aston, Oxfordshire, according to an article in London's *Antiques Trade Gazette*.

The Dunlap Broadsides of the Declaration of Independence

Editor's Note: The Declaration of Independence was debated by the Continental Congress on July 2 and 3, and approved on July 4, 1776. A handwritten copy was sent at once to the shop of Philadelphia printer John Dunlap on Market Street, where it was set in type during the night of July 4 and 5. It was corrected on the morning of July 5 and copies were printed that day. No one recorded how many copies Dunlap delivered to Congress, which had directed the declarations be sent at once to the state assemblies, conventions, and committees or councils of safety, and to the commanding officers of the Continental troops, and be proclaimed in each of the states and by the head of the Army. In Philadelphia, the Declaration was read publicly from one of the broadsides in the State House yard at noon on July 8 in the presence of a large gathering of citizens. Readings were repeated throughout the colonies. Some of the broadsides may have been posted, others were saved by the signers or officers. The sales of copies of the Dunlap broadside have been reported in M.A.D. since 1983, when there were 21 copies known. Over the years a number of other copies have been found, and the discoveries and sales made very good stories.

PUTTING A PRICE ON HISTORY JUNE 1983

BY JERRY E. PATTERSON

Putting a price on documents that have changed the history of the world is difficult. What, for example, is a copy of the first printing of the American Declaration of Independence worth? It is unquestionably one of the most influential items ever printed. The answer, at the moment, is $412,500 (including the 10 percent buyer's premium), which Christie's got at auction on the 22nd of April, 1983, for the copy that descended in the Johnston family of Hayes Plantation, Edenton, North Carolina. It was the centerpiece in a sale of books and manuscripts from various sources held as part of the "Britain Salutes New York" festivities. The sale totaled $742,687 knockdown, with only $12,390 of buy-ins.

The Declaration of Independence is not a particularly rare item, as rarities go. The very detailed catalog that Christie's issued for the sale located 21 other copies. All but two are in public institutions, however, and it is unlikely that they will come on the market. The Hayes Plantation copy, which was consigned by John Gilliam Wood, had not been sold before. It was part of a large group of documents relating to the American Revolution and the early republic found in the plantation house. The considerable remainder of these documents will probably be given to the University of North Carolina.

The history of copies of the Declaration of Independence at auction (it is not known that any have changed hands privately) in the last 30 years is this: none at all were sold between 1950 and 1969. Those sold after that date were:

In May 1969, the Leary copy, named after the bookstore in Philadelphia where it was found during a closing-out sale, was sold at Freeman's, Philadelphia, for $404,000 after one of the most dramatic saleroom battles of the century between H.P. Kraus, the New York bookseller, and Ira Corn, a private collector from Texas. At that time, only 17 copies of the Declaration were known. The Corn copy was on the market at a markup a few years after the sale but was unsold and is now in the Dallas Public Library.

In October 1970, the John Stewart copy was offered at Sotheby's New York but failed to find a buyer, or even much interest, and was bought-in at $130,000.

In CONGRESS, July 4, 1776.

A DECLARATION
By the REPRESENTATIVES of the
UNITED STATES OF AMERICA,
In GENERAL CONGRESS ASSEMBLED.

WHEN in the Course of human Events, it becomes necessary for one People to dissolve the Political Bands which have connected them with another, and to assume among the Powers of the Earth, the separate and equal Station to which the Laws of Nature and of Nature's God entitle them, a decent Respect to the Opinions of Mankind requires that they should declare the causes which impel them to the Separation.

We hold these Truths to be self-evident, that all Men are created equal, that they are endowed by their Creator with certain unalienable Rights, that among these are Life, Liberty, and the Pursuit of Happiness——That to secure these Rights, Governments are instituted among Men, deriving their just Powers from the Consent of the Governed, that whenever any Form of Government becomes destructive of these Ends, it is the Right of the People to alter or to abolish it, and to institute new Government, laying its Foundation on such Principles, and organizing its Powers in such Form, as to them shall seem most likely to effect their Safety and Happiness. Prudence, indeed, will dictate that Governments long established should not be changed for light and transient Causes; and accordingly all Experience hath shewn, that Mankind are more disposed to suffer, while Evils are sufferable, than to right themselves by abolishing the Forms to which they are accustomed. But when a long Train of Abuses and Usurpations, pursuing invariably the same Object, evinces a Design to reduce them under absolute Despotism, it is their Right, it is their Duty, to throw off such Government, and to provide new Guards for their future Security. Such has been the patient Sufferance of these Colonies; and such is now the Necessity which constrains them to alter their former Systems of Government. The History of the present King of Great-Britain is a History of repeated Injuries and Usurpations, all having in direct Object the Establishment of an absolute Tyranny over these States. To prove this, let Facts be submitted to a candid World.

He has refused his Assent to Laws, the most wholesome and necessary for the public Good.

He has forbidden his Governors to pass Laws of immediate and pressing Importance, unless suspended in their Operation till his Assent should be obtained; and when so suspended, he has utterly neglected to attend to them.

He has refused to pass other Laws for the Accommodation of large Districts of People, unless those People would relinquish the Right of Representation in the Legislature, a Right inestimable to them, and formidable to Tyrants only.

He has called together Legislative Bodies at Places unusual, uncomfortable, and distant from the Depository of their public Records, for the sole Purpose of fatiguing them into Compliance with his Measures.

He has dissolved Representative Houses repeatedly, for opposing with manly Firmness his Invasions on the Rights of the People.

He has refused for a long Time, after such Dissolutions, to cause others to be elected; whereby the Legislative Powers, incapable of Annihilation, have returned to the People at large for their exercise; the State remaining in the mean time exposed to all the Dangers of Invasion from without, and Convulsions within.

He has endeavoured to prevent the Population of these States; for that Purpose obstructing the Laws for Naturalization of Foreigners; refusing to pass others to encourage their Migrations hither, and raising the Conditions of new Appropriations of Lands.

He has obstructed the Administration of Justice, by refusing his Assent to Laws for establishing Judiciary Powers.

He has made Judges dependent on his Will alone, for the Tenure of their Offices, and the Amount and Payment of their Salaries.

He has erected a Multitude of new Offices, and sent hither Swarms of Officers to harrass our People, and eat out their Substance.

He has kept among us, in Times of Peace, Standing Armies, without the consent of our Legislatures.

He has affected to render the Military independent of and superior to the Civil Power.

He has combined with others to subject us to a Jurisdiction foreign to our Constitution, and unacknowledged by our Laws; giving his Assent to their Acts of pretended Legislation:

For quartering large Bodies of Armed Troops among us:

For protecting them, by a mock Trial, from Punishment for any Murders which they should commit on the Inhabitants of these States:

For cutting off our Trade with all Parts of the World:

For imposing Taxes on us without our Consent:

For depriving us, in many Cases, of the Benefits of Trial by Jury:

For transporting us beyond Seas to be tried for pretended Offences:

For abolishing the free System of English Laws in a neighbouring Province, establishing therein an arbitrary Government, and enlarging its Boundaries, so as to render it at once an Example and fit Instrument for introducing the same absolute Rule into these Colonies:

For taking away our Charters, abolishing our most valuable Laws, and altering fundamentally the Forms of our Governments:

For suspending our own Legislatures, and declaring themselves invested with Power to legislate for us in all Cases whatsoever.

He has abdicated Government here, by declaring us out of his Protection and waging War against us.

He has plundered our Seas, ravaged our Coasts, burnt our Towns, and destroyed the Lives of our People.

He is, at this Time, transporting large Armies of foreign Mercenaries to compleat the Works of Death, Desolation, and Tyranny, already begun with circumstances of Cruelty and Perfidy, scarcely paralleled in the most barbarous Ages, and totally unworthy the Head of a civilized Nation.

He has constrained our fellow Citizens taken Captive on the high Seas to bear Arms against their Country, to become the Executioners of their Friends and Brethren, or to fall themselves by their Hands.

He has excited domestic Insurrections amongst us, and has endeavoured to bring on the Inhabitants of our Frontiers, the merciless Indian Savages, whose known Rule of Warfare, is an undistinguished Destruction, of all Ages, Sexes and Conditions.

In every stage of these Oppressions we have Petitioned for Redress in the most humble Terms: Our repeated Petitions have been answered only by repeated Injury. A Prince, whose Character is thus marked by every act which may define a Tyrant, is unfit to be the Ruler of a free People.

Nor have we been wanting in Attentions to our British Brethren. We have warned them from Time to Time of Attempts by their Legislature to extend an unwarrantable Jurisdiction over us. We have reminded them of the Circumstances of our Emigration and Settlement here. We have appealed to their native Justice and Magnanimity, and we have conjured them by the Ties of our common Kindred to disavow these Usurpations, which, would inevitably interrupt our Connections and Correspondence. They too have been deaf to the Voice of Justice and of Consanguinity. We must, therefore, acquiesce in the Necessity, which denounces our Separation, and hold them, as we hold the rest of Mankind, Enemies in War, in Peace, Friends.

We, therefore, the Representatives of the UNITED STATES OF AMERICA, in GENERAL CONGRESS, Assembled, appealing to the Supreme Judge of the World for the Rectitude of our Intentions, do, in the Name, and by Authority of the good People of these Colonies, solemnly Publish and Declare, That these United Colonies are, and of Right ought to be, FREE AND INDEPENDENT STATES; that they are absolved from all Allegiance to the British Crown, and that all political Connection between them and the State of Great-Britain, is and ought to be totally dissolved; and that as FREE AND INDEPENDENT STATES, they have full Power to levy War, conclude Peace, contract Alliances, establish Commerce, and to do all other Acts and Things which INDEPENDENT STATES may of right do. And for the support of this Declaration, with a firm Reliance on the Protection of divine Providence, we mutually pledge to each other our Lives, our Fortunes, and our sacred Honor.

Signed by ORDER and in BEHALF of the CONGRESS,

JOHN HANCOCK, PRESIDENT.

ATTEST.
CHARLES THOMSON, SECRETARY.

PHILADELPHIA: PRINTED BY JOHN DUNLAP.

The Declaration of Independence was first printed by John Dunlap in Philadelphia on the night of July 4 and 5, 1776, as a broadside, measuring about 18" x 15". Of the 22 copies that are known to have survived, the copy sold by Christie's for $412,500, which can be traced back to Joseph Hewes, signer from North Carolina, is one of the finest as it is completely unrestored. Most of the others, all but two of which are in public institutions, have been re-backed or restored. Dunlap used a mixture of papers, all of Dutch origin, to print the Declaration. A beta radiograph in the catalog showed the watermarks of the Hewes copy, reading "D&C Blauw" and showing a crown and post horn within a shield. On the verso is shown endorsement "Declaration of Independence" in the handwriting of Joseph Hewes, making this the only copy clearly associated with one of the signers. Christie's photo.

In July 1975, the same copy was sold at Christie's London for $92,000.

In April 1982, the Chew family copy from Philadelphia was sold at Christie's New York for $313,500 and bought by New York dealer John Fleming for the Pierpont Morgan Library.

The Hayes Plantation copy of the Declaration has many distinctions. It is the first state of the first printing, it is a previously unrecorded copy, and it is in remarkably fresh physical condition. The greatest distinction, however, and the one that obviously counted the most with the bidders, is that it is the only copy that is clearly associated with one of the signers. It is endorsed "Declaration of Independence" on the verso in the hand of Joseph Hewes, the signer from North Carolina.

The Chapin Library at Williams College is now the owner of this Declaration, and the purchase had an element of saleroom drama. Williams was very anxious to have a copy of the first printing of the Declaration, according to Robert Volz, custodian of the Chapin Library. "When I heard that the Hayes Plantation copy was coming up for sale," he said, "I began trying to raise money to buy it. We approached various alumni. Some gave five thousand dollars toward the purchase, some ten thousand dollars. In all, more than twenty persons contributed. When we left Williamstown the night before the sale, however, we had raised only three hundred thousand dollars and we were not certain that would buy it."

The bidding was to be done by Laurence Witten, a Connecticut bookseller and Williams alumnus. During the first part of the sale, Volz was on the telephone in Christie's corridor talking to donors, with a runner to Witten in the saleroom keeping him informed as to the progress of the

fund-raising. "At lot seventy-four we knew we had enough," said Volz.

Stephen Massey, Christie's senior vice president in charge of books and manuscripts, after remarking that he was honored to be selling this great document, his second Declaration of Independence in a year, opened the bidding at $100,000 and called it in increments of $10,000. The saleroom was surprised to see Witten bidding, as he is noted for dealing in illuminated manuscripts and early printed books, not Americana. At $370,000, he asked that increments be changed to $5,000. Massey agreed, and the lot was knocked down to Witten at $375,000, costing him $412,500 with the 10 percent buyer's premium.

After the sale, Volz revealed why Williams was so anxious to have the Declaration. "We are now the only library in the world able to display the first printings of the four great foundation documents of the U.S.: the Articles of Confederation, the Declaration of Independence, the Constitution (we have George Mason's copy), and the Bill of Rights." The documents are to go on display at the college, which is about the same age as the documents, in a case specially prepared for them. For Larry Witten, it was a happy celebration of his 35th anniversary of graduating from Williams.

Stephen Massey expressed himself as satisfied with the price, especially since the Hayes Plantation copy was a considerable advance on the Chew copy of last season. "I was hoping a little that we might get to four hundred five thousand dollars," he said, "and so have the world record here for a Declaration, but still I am pleased." By the way M.A.D. reckons record prices, though, which includes the 10 percent premium, it is a record price at $412,500. Later, a spokesperson for Christie's said they would claim it as a record.

THE MOST IMPORTANT PIECE OF PAPER EVER PRINTED MARCH 1990

BY LITA SOLIS-COHEN

As freedom was breaking out all over the world, the most important piece of paper ever printed in America, the first printing of our Declaration of Independence, sold for a record $1,595,000. The buyer of the record broadside sold at Sotheby's on January 31, 1990, was Chicago rare book dealer Ralph Geoffrey Newman, who said he was bidding for a client.

The broadside, set in type by John Dunlap in Philadelphia on the evening of July 4, 1776, just hours after the Declaration had been approved, to convey the great news to the people as quickly as possible, is one of 23 copies that have survived. The size of Dunlap's edition, which was distributed to the members of the Continental Congress and sent to provincial assemblies and committees of safety, is not known.

The Declaration of Independence broadside was one of the most important items of Americana in the library of the late H. Bradley Martin, heir to the Phipps steel fortune and one of the great book collectors of this century. Martin died last year at the age of 82, and his books are being sold at Sotheby's in a series of sales expected to total more than $30 million.

"I figured one-and-a-half million was enough to get the Declaration, but I should have gone higher," said underbidder Tom Lingenfelter, an autograph dealer from Doylestown, Pennsylvania, who calls his business Heritage Collector's Society. Lingenfelter said he was bidding for a client.

"Compared to the prices people are paying for paintings and furniture," Lingenfelter went on, "it is an embarrassment to see the Declaration go for as little as it did. How could I go wrong buying the most famous document in the world? I'll be there bidding when the next copy turns up. There's hope. After all, in 1969 there were only sixteen copies, and now there are twenty-three."

The 16th copy was discovered during the liquidation of the old Leary's Bookstore in Philadelphia and was the first copy ever auctioned. It sold on May 7, 1969, for the then astounding sum of $404,000 at Samuel T. Freeman's and Sons in Philadelphia. Freeman's had estimated the Declaration at $30,000/35,000, based on a copy at Independence Hall appraised at $27,000 in 1951. The buyer was Ira G. Corn, Jr., a Texas businessman who gave it to the city of Dallas. That price remained a world record for any printed item until Christie's sold a Gutenberg Bible in 1978 for $2.2 million.

According to David Kirschenbaum, the 95-year-old New York book dealer with whom Bradley Martin lunched every Thursday at Gino's Restaurant on Lexington Avenue, Martin bought his copy privately more than 40 years ago. Sotheby's estimated it would bring $400,000/600,000.

One dealer said he had a bid for $800,000 and never got his paddle up. The bidding opened at $250,000 and moved quickly past $600,000, with Newman, a dapper silver-haired man wearing a red, white and blue striped shirt and a red handkerchief in the pocket of his gray suit discreetly nodding his bids from his seat on the aisle near the back. Lingenfelter, casually dressed in a sweater and jacket and standing in the rear of the salesroom, answered with positive nods. "My last bid was one million four hundred twenty-five thousand dollars, and with the ten percent buyer's premium that took me past my one-and-a-half-million limit," Lingenfelter acknowledged.

Newman said he had been bidding on behalf of a client who was not yet ready to make his purchase public. "This is one of the finest copies in existence, and it was the last copy that could be bought at private sale. The other copy owned privately belongs to John Scheide, a Princeton collector, and I understand it has been pledged to Princeton," said Newman, who last year paid the highest price ever paid for a manuscript when he paid $440,000 at Christie's for the letter Caesar Rodney, a signer of the Declaration of Independence, wrote to his brother on July 4, 1776.

$4 FIND WORTH $2.42 MILLION AUGUST 1991

BY LITA SOLIS-COHEN

It was like winning the lottery for the Pennsylvania man who owned the broadside of the Declaration of Independence printed in Philadelphia during the night of July 4, 1776 that sold for $2.42 million at Sotheby's on June 13, 1991. There are only 24 known copies; three are in private hands, the rest in institutions.

The consignor told Sotheby's he had found it behind an old torn painting he bought for $4 at an Adamstown flea market two years ago because he thought he could salvage the frame. It's a great story that some believe and others say can't be true.

No one in Adamstown admitted to selling it. The locals say it was sold at Barr's Auction, not at one of the markets, but Colonel Barr, who runs the auction on the Reading Road, said it just isn't true. Who knows?

Sotheby's declared the price the record for any printed historical Americana. "An Audubon elephant folio has brought more, but for a single printed sheet this is clearly a record," said David Redden, a senior vice-president of Sotheby's who heads its book department in New York.

Redden wielded the gavel as the price toppled the previous high, $1,595,000, paid 18 months ago for another copy. That one came from the library of well-known collector H. Bradley Martin and was in a leather slipcase. Chicago dealer Ralph Newman bought it for Albert Small, a Washington, D.C., collector who has the finest private collection of historical manuscripts and documents relating to the Declaration and the Constitution.

The buyer on June 13 came out of the blue. No one in the trade knew Donald J. Scheer of Atlanta, who was seated toward the back on the left side of the salesroom and, without hesitation, kept raising his green plastic paddle with number 198 on it. The underbidder, Kaller Associates, Asbury Park, New Jersey, had an elaborate bidding strategy.

Myron Kaller and his son, Seth, and daughter, Robin, let it be known they thought a first printing of the Declaration would be the cornerstone of the collection of historical manuscripts they have been putting together for two wealthy collectors. For the past two years the Kallers have been good customers of the autograph trade and a strong presence in the salesroom when American books and manuscripts crossed the block. Robin Kaller did the bidding up to $1.4 million, and then her brother, Seth, took over. He stopped at $2.1 million. "Changing bidders sometimes works. It scares the competition," explained Myron Kaller after the sale.

It didn't scare Scheer. After the sale Scheer, pressed against a wall by 11 TV cameras and a dozen reporters, said he was prepared to go higher. Finally, he moved onto the stage and stood next to the broadside displayed in a glass case behind the auctioneer's rostrum for a photo opportunity.

In response to questions, Scheer said he was president of Visual Equities Inc., an art investment firm, and this was the first historical document the company had added to its art portfolio. He said the company's holdings numbered less than 100 items and included Japanese, primitive, European, and American art. He noted his company was publicly traded on NASDAQ.

The stock opened at $3⅝ the morning of the sale and is now quoted as $4½ bid, $4¾ asked. The symbol is VZEQ.

Donald J. Scheer of Atlanta, after buying the Declaration of Independence broadside for $2.42 million. He told reporters he expected to pay more. He is president of Visual Equities Inc., a publicly held art investment company traded on NASDAQ. Reached by phone a few days after the sale, he said he might not have made the purchase if he had not gone to Romania a little more than a year ago. Though he bought no art while there, as he walked around the cities and towns he saw graffiti and placards on the walls with quotations from the Declaration of Independence.

"There in Romania were Thomas Jefferson's own words in English," he marveled. "I realized then the Declaration is one helluva document."

What does Visual Equities plan to do with the Declaration? "We expect to hold it until 1992 and sell it during the celebration of the 500th anniversary of the discovery of America," Scheer disclosed. Will the Declaration be sold again at auction? "Possibly," said Scheer, "but we have already had some interesting offers that have not yet fully hatched."

Selby Kiffer of Sotheby's, who cataloged the Declaration and came down to Philadelphia with David Redden to accept its consignment, said he hopes to find another. Shortly after the sale, another Declaration did turn up, but it's not for sale. The Maine Historical Society in Portland announced that a copy that had been left to them in 1893 by autograph collector John Fogg of Eliot had recently been authenticated as the 25th known copy of a Dunlap printing.

Scheer said he had bought the Declaration for more than just investment. "It is a living document," he said. "The words are every bit as alive today as when Thomas Jefferson penned them in 1776. These are the words that knocked down the Berlin Wall, freed Poland, put Havel in office in Czechoslovakia, and elected Boris Yeltsin yesterday in Russia," he went on.

The fellow who found the broadside and struck it rich watched the sale from a glass-enclosed box overlooking the salesroom, but he had no comment for the press. "He was mighty pleased, but he wants his anonymity," said John Van Horn, librarian of the Library Company of Philadelphia, a research library where the broadside was first examined and declared authentic. Horn had come to bid on another lot.

Copies of this proclamation, printed by John Dunlap at his shop at 48 High Street just hours after the Continental Congress dissolved political bonds with England and declared "that these United Colonies are, and of Right ought to be Free and Independent States," were given to the signers and sent to the governors of the colonies to be read to the people and to the officers of the militia

to inform the troops. Scholars believe between 200 and 500 were printed. In 1969, when a copy sold at Samuel T. Freeman's in Philadelphia for the then staggering sum of $404,000, just 16 copies were known. There is always a chance that another copy will turn up folded between historical papers.

According to Sotheby's catalog, the $2.4 million copy is one of the top four in condition. It is marred by only one brown stain, some creases from being folded once vertically and three times horizontally, and a small hole at the "n" of John Hancock.

Dealers were jubilant after the sale. "It's great for the industry. We have another new player," said Doylestown, Pennsylvania, dealer Tom Lingenfelter. He had pushed the price over $1 million for the Bradley Martin copy of the Declaration broadside in January 1990, but this time he didn't even get his paddle up before the bidding topped his limit.

Just a week before the sale, on June 6 at Freeman/Fine Arts in Philadelphia, Lingenfelter had paid $36,300 for a Stone copy of the Declaration. This 1822 engraved copy of the original handwritten Declaration signed by the 56 signers, now in the National Archives, came from a New Jersey estate. Stored in a cardboard tube, it was nearly thrown away with old Christmas wrappings, according to the consignor.

It is one of the 200 copies printed on vellum that were ordered in 1822 from the Washington engraver William I. Stone by John Quincy Adams when he was secretary of state. Copies were given to members of Congress, surviving signers, the families of deceased signers, and visiting dignitaries. The one presented to the Marquis de Lafayette was sold at Christie's in 1985 for $45,200, and the one that descended in the family of Roger Sherman, a signer from Connecticut, fetched $60,500 at Sotheby's in 1989.

The copy sold at Freeman/Fine Arts has good margins but no provenance. "We don't know who the original recipient was," said David Bloom, who heads Freeman/Fine Arts' book department, while pointing out the impression of the copper plate and the names of Stone and John Quincy Adams at the top of the engraving.

Lingenfelter said he is in no hurry to sell it. "Now I have copies of five nineteenth-century engravings of the Declaration, three printed in Philadelphia between 1816 and 1819 by William Woodruff, John Binns, and Owen Tyler, and one printed in New York in 1845 by Humphrey Phelps. I like the idea of having a collection."

INTERNET AUCTION RECORD AUGUST 2000

BY DOROTHY S. GELATT

Sold twice and bought in once at Sotheby's over the last ten years, fought over in a sticky court suit, and of uncertain provenance, a Philadelphia Dunlap July 4, 1776, broadside first printing of the Declaration of Independence rocketed past its $4/6 million estimate and sold via Sothebys.com for an Internet document auction record $8.14 million. The price includes Sothebys.com's 10% buyer's premium.

Pioneer television producer Norman Lear partnered with Silicon Valley corporate whiz David Hayden to make the purchase. Sothebys.com offered the one-page single-side Dunlap broadside on line June 29, 2000, from 9 AM to 5 PM EDT, preceded by months of presale publicity.

Lear and Hayden envision their Declaration as the centerpiece of a traveling theatrical show with music that will bring Americans, especially children, a new awareness of our country's history and national roots. The plan is yet to be fleshed out, since the partners only heard about the auction a few days before it happened. Lear had the initial idea and then invited Hayden to join him.

Norman Lear created TV landmarks, including Archie Bunker in *All in the Family, Maude, The Jeffersons,* and *Mary Hartman, Mary Hartman.* David Hayden's corporate coups include Critical Path (NASDAQ: CPTH) and the McKinley Group, creators of Magellan, the Internet search engine sold to Excite. Lear and Hayden, a duo steeped in show business and corporate savvy, both live in southern California.

Serious on-line bidding began half an hour before the 5 PM deadline, when both Hayden and Lear were not available to do their own on-line bidding. Hayden was in an airplane flying to California, and Lear was at his farm in Vermont, so they had tapped Lara Bergthold, executive director of the Lear Family Foundation, to man a computer at Sotheby's and enter their bids, which they relayed to her by phone.

We learned after the sale that Lear/Hayden bid with paddle No. 29630. They were opposed by one other bidder: No. 29644, identity not disclosed. Paddle number, bid price, date, and time appeared cumulatively on the computer screen with each bid, so in the end viewers had a record of the complete bidding. Viewers just didn't know who the bidders were, and unlike at the humongous eBay site, there were no catchy e-mail names to give the bidding flavor.

The minimum advance was $100,000, and Sotheby's extended the bidding past 5 PM in ten-minute blocks until bids stopped totally for ten minutes, similar to a regular telephone auction.

Lear/Hayden opened the bidding on June 29 with $4 million at 9:02:21 AM. Their opposition, No. 29644, logged in at 11:29:06 AM at $4,100,000. Nothing more happened until half an hour before the 5 PM close, when Lear/Hayden upped their bid to $4.2 million at 4:32:06 PM. Bidding proceeded gingerly in $100,000 jumps until 5:17:47, when Lear/Hayden raised the ante $200,000 to $6.3 million. Four seconds later an opposing bid showed at $6.4 million. Lear/Hayden jumped $200,000 again, to $6.6 million, but that did not shake out the opponent, who came right back with another $100,000. It is possible that the opposition bids were automatic up to a maximum registered from the beginning.

From then on the two paddles slugged it out with eight more $100,000 raises, ending with Lear/Hayden's $7,400,000 hammer price at 5:37:59 PM. Paddle No. 29644 retired, gallantly or otherwise, we'll probably never know. Including Sotheby's 10% on-line buyer's premium, Lear/Hayden invested $8.14 million in one of the four Dunlap first printing copies of the Declaration still in private hands. The other 21 known copies are all in institutions.

At a Sotheby's press conference, where the new owners showed up as if by magic the next morning in Manhattan, Norman Lear said the series of ten-minute time extensions after Sotheby's 5 PM deadline enabled them to confer and rethink their bidding strategy. "With time to think, I spent more money on line than I would have at a live auction, where you have to make up your mind instantly," he said.

While no one has ever questioned the authenticity of this particular Dunlap Declaration broadside, there have been private, unpublished experts' questions about its provenance and original ownership ever since it surfaced in

Philadelphia in 1989. Questions were raised publicly when it was offered at auction for the first time by Sotheby's in New York in 1991.

Anonymity cloaks the original scene in 1989 when a man (publicly anonymous to this day) brought the broadside to the Library Company in Philadelphia, where it was examined and declared authentic, according to librarian John Van Horn, who spoke on June 13, 1991. That was the day Sotheby's first sold the Declaration, for $2.42 million. It was bought by Atlanta businessman Donald J. Scheer, president of Visual Equities, as an investment. The company planned to sell the Declaration in 1992, in what was the 500th anniversary of Columbus's discovery of America.

Neither Sotheby's nor the Library Company has ever publicly identified the mystery consignor except to say that he was a Philadelphia stock analyst. Recently a member of the Library Company staff who asked to remain anonymous said that the man has left Philadelphia, whereabouts unknown.

Originally the consignor claimed he found the Declaration folded behind a $4 painting he bought from some dealer at Renninger's in Adamstown because he thought he could salvage the beat-up frame.

From the beginning not everyone believed him. Doubters felt the condition was too good for a Declaration allegedly stashed inside a beat-up picture frame for a couple of centuries. Now, however, following the June 2000 Sotheby's $8.14 million auction, a distinguished New York expert and dealer in rare printed works has given his frank opinion to *M.A.D.* for publication.

Graham Arader said: "I've been selling prints for thirty years. I open at least fifty frames a week, and anything inside a frame for a couple of centuries is always horribly stained or browned or faded. There's no way this broadside came out of the back of a frame! The condition is too good. I think it probably came from one of the many little Pennsylvania historical societies, and they don't know it's gone. The whole thing stinks! Some day it will all come out! Some day somebody will blab. They'll tell their wife, their girlfriend. They'll tell somebody. Or somebody will remember something, and it will all come out," Arader boomed. "And you can quote me!"

According to a member of the Library Company staff, when the man brought it to the Library Company, he had it folded up in his breast pocket.

The Dunlap Declaration seems to attract continuing drama. On May 21, 1993, Sotheby's again offered the broadside at auction, this time for its then owner Donald J. Scheer and his Visual Equities company. It failed to sell and was bought in at $1.7 million, considerably less than the $2.4 million Scheer paid for it. Later in the sale, however, auctioneer David Redden announced from the podium that the Declaration was sold privately for an undisclosed sum, later reported to be $1.5 million to Kaller Historical Documents, Inc. for private clients.

After that things grew sticky. Visual Equities' New York lawyer Lawrence Levine obtained a court order in Manhattan temporarily blocking Sotheby's from selling the Declaration, claiming Sotheby's misled the firm and tried to defraud it. It seems Visual Equities found out Sotheby's was holding the New-York Historical Society's copy of the Declaration as collateral for a loan, thus, according to Visual Equities' complaint, undermining the value of its copy.

Sotheby's press contact Diana Phillips said Sotheby's was enraged at the court order, claiming the auction house told Visual Equities it was too soon to put the Declaration back on the market and tried to discourage Visual Equities from selling. Scheer claimed otherwise. The dispute was ultimately settled at court in December 1993 in a confidential arrangement, in which Kaller Historical Documents did not retain ownership and the Declaration was returned to Visual Equities. Terms of the settlement were not revealed. Scheer said at the time that he planned to let it rest for a while.

Now the curtain goes up on a brand-new act starring the most familiar, the most celebrated, and the most expensive of the 25 known Dunlap Declarations. Everyone is looking forward to an exciting Lear/Hayden Declaration of Independence show.

But wait! Several months before the Lear/Hayden purchase, out of the blue an old-time Renninger's dealer named Hugh Thomas, well known to the market's regulars for over 30 years, claimed to be the dealer who sold the famous beat-up picture frame that allegedly housed the now famous Declaration.

How did he know the Declaration was in the frame?

"There was a hole in the back of the cardboard, and I could see 1776 clear as day," Thomas explained.

So why hadn't he done anything before? Thomas said he really didn't know, and all he wants is whatever anyone wants to give him for his pain and suffering.

Third Decade:
1994–2003

Editor's Note: The recession in the early 1990s caused the market to change in a number of ways. The deaths of Bertram K. Little and Nina Fletcher Little in 1993 resulted in the dispersal of their vast collection, which refueled the folk art market. The Little sales—there were two of them, one in January 1994 and another in October 1994—ushered in a decade of growth, new high-price levels, and an expanding market. A Little provenance is magic in the marketplace. Collectors beat a path to the door of Cogswell's Grant, the Littles' 1740 red clapboard house in Essex, Massachusetts, which SPNEA (the Society for the Preservation of New England Antiquities) has opened as an historic house museum, reflecting the taste of the premier 20th-century New England collectors and tastemakers.

THE LANDMARK LITTLE SALE

BY LITA SOLIS-COHEN

PART ONE

The Little sale was a big one. The sale on January 29, 1994, brought total of $7,391,292, twice expectations, for 423 of the 457 lots offered, a record for any private collection of Americana. And it was only the first half of the collection. In October Sotheby's will sell the rest of this pioneer collection of folk art amassed by the legendary Massachusetts antiquarians Bertram K. and Nina Fletcher Little.

Nina—everyone speaks of her as Nina (pronounced nigh-na, with the accent on the first syllable)—was the collector, researcher, and writer. Bert, who served as the director of the Society for the Preservation of New England Antiquities (SPNEA) from 1947 to 1970, was her support, not financially but in every other way. They filled every room, including bathrooms, closets, and attics, of two houses—a pumpkin-colored Federal house in Brookline and a 1740 red clapboard farmhouse in Essex—with naive portraits, historical blue Staffordshire, painted fireboards, needlework pictures and other schoolgirl art, boxes of every size, shape, color, and material, 18th-century furniture, and an assortment of other New England antiquities.

In 1966 they promised their farmhouse, Cogswell's Grant, to the Society for the Preservation of New England Antiquities, and it will be open by appointment in June as a case study in collecting.

The Littles had refined their collection of folk art over a period of 60 years. Every item had a special relationship to the collection. Nina Fletcher Little defined the current taste for folk painting in her books and articles that began appearing in *The Magazine Antiques* in 1938. The collection was publicized in a way no other Americana sale has ever been. There was such a fine line between scholarship and marketing, it was imperceptible.

Portraiture and painted fireboards were Nina's long suits. She was one of the first historians in the field, and her collection was widely exhibited.

The masterpieces of the collection were a pair of life-size portraits of Mr. and Mrs. James Reynolds of West Haven, Connecticut, painted by Ruben Moulthrop in the 1790s, that sold for $745,000 with buyer's premium, a record for a pair of naive portraits. The splendid pictures of a stern young lady elegantly dressed in a transparent lace bonnet, gold and blue damask dress with lace apron, and shawl, seated at a table with a potted flowering rose, and a serious young gentleman wearing a silver-buttoned blue coat over a pale gray waistcoat, standing next to a table with a tobacco box on it, his tricorn hat hung on the wall, were illustrated on the front and back covers of the catalog.

The portraits of Mr. and Mrs. James Reynolds of West Haven, Connecticut, by Ruben Moulthrop sold for $745,000 to a then-anonymous buyer. They are part of the Ralph Esmerian gift to the American Folk Art Museum. Little sale, part one. Sotheby's photo.

The anonymous buyer will give them to the Museum of American Folk Art in New York City. "I think they were a good value when a Hicks *Peaceable Kingdom* brings one million," said Stonington, Connecticut, dealer Marguerite Riordan, the underbidder. "Where have you seen anything as charming?"

Riordan, bidding for a client, bought a painted overmantel by Winthrop Chandler, a landscape with gray, red, and yellow houses nestled in the countryside for $596,500, a record for a painted overmantel. It was one of Nina's favorite possessions and hung over her desk. She loaned it only once.

The buyer of the overmantel also got Nina's cherry and birch slant-front desk made in Connecticut in the late 18th century, paying $54,625, more than double its $25,000 high estimate. Nina's desk chair, a turned birch and ash high weaver's chair with a splint seat estimated at $400/500, sold for $2,587 to another bidder.

In a recent article in the magazine *Worth*, former Fidelity money manager Peter Lynch was bullish on Sotheby's, and he did his part at the Little sale to make his predictions come true. He bought a 6' long oil on masonite picture of the troops marching from Marblehead to Boston, signed "J.O.J. Frost" and inscribed "1861, April 16th at 7 o'clock these men left town for Boston . . . the first to reach Faneuil Hall in the State." It cost him $486,500, a record for a work by a 20th-century self-taught artist and over six times the $80,000 high estimate. Painted about 1925, it was found reversed and used as a wallboard in Frost's house at 11 Pond Street, Marblehead in 1952 when the house had changed hands and was undergoing renovation. The underbidder was Essex, Massachusetts, dealer Stephen Score, bidding for a client. Score did not compete for the next lot, a small whaling scene by Frost, knocked down to Lynch for $11,500.

Lynch did his own bidding for the Frost, holding his green pencil high in the air, but earlier in the sale, he had asked New Hampshire auctioneer Ron Bourgeault to bid for him on the well-known Esther Lyman chest. The carved oak and pine lift-top blanket chest, made in Northampton, Massachusetts, 1712–22, a relatively late date for a so-called Hadley chest, has its owner's full name carved on the top rail. The flat scroll and leaf carving is characteristic of the Connecticut River Valley, and it is in remarkably fine condition, with its top and feet intact and remains of old black and red paint. Several bidders pushed the price way past the $100,000/150,000 estimate until it was knocked down to Bourgeault for $354,500, a record for any blanket chest.

There is no question money is around again, and it is no longer unfashionable to spend it. "The eighties are here again for a day," quipped one dealer. "On Monday we will be back to 1994."

Collectors labeled the sale "a first-time, last-time, once-in-a-lifetime opportunity" and began lining up at 8 AM to sign up for bidding paddles and to claim one of the 800 seats in the salesroom.

It was good theater. There were plenty of exciting moments and hard-to-follow bidding signals—an index finger raised, a flick of a pen, glasses off, pencil in the mouth, barely perceptible nod—all in competition with 19 phone lines. Some bidding styles were not so subtle—paddle pushed up and down, paddle flicked forward and back, paddle raised high and kept there, a jumped bid called out. Peter Lynch jumped from $60,000 to $100,000 when bidding on the Frost painting.

The overmantel painted by Winthrop Chandler sold for $596,500 to dealer Marguerite Riordan bidding for a client. This landscape hung over Nina's desk where she typed out her jelly labels, books, and articles on her manual typewriter. Little sale, part one. Sotheby's photo.

Esther Lyman's carved oak and pine Hadley chest sold for $354,500, a record for a blanket chest, to New Hampshire auctioneer Ronald Bourgeault, acting as agent for financial writer Peter Lynch. Little sale, part one. Sotheby's photo.

Auctioneer Bill Stahl didn't miss a beat in his marathon performance.

There were crazy prices and some good buys. A group of six late 19th-century nesting Nantucket lightship baskets with swing handles in fine condition, labeled Davis Hall, and estimated at $12,000/15,000, sold for an outrageous $118,000 to Harold Sack, president of Israel Sack, Inc., apparently bidding for a customer. "I bought them to keep my money in," quipped octogenarian Sack about the ash and maple baskets woven tight enough to hold flour.

A miniature leather fire bucket sold for $24,150 (est. $10,000/15,000), underbid by Stephen Score, who had paid $16,500 for it at the sale of the estate of George Considine in North Dartmouth, Massachusetts, in June 1986.

Inside a tiny oval cardboard box covered with green patterned wallpaper was a miniature watercolor portrait of a young girl wearing a white lace bonnet and sheer organdy gown with one blue slipper in her hand and the other on her foot, said to be Mary H. Huntington, the daughter of Reverend Daniel Huntington, painted circa 1825. It sold for $37,950, nearly eight times its $5,000 high estimate, to a New York collector.

In Durham, New Hampshire, in 1837, Joseph H. Davis painted a watercolor and pen and ink double-portrait of Minister Thomas Thompson and his wife Betsey Thompson sitting at a table with a mourning picture hung on the wall behind them and with their black cat nearby. It sold for $90,500 (est. $10,000/20,000) to an absentee bidder even though it had turned brown. It is a good example of Davis's work and the only one with a memorial in it.

An appealing naive picture of a little girl in a white dress, holding a red rosebud and sitting on a red flowered stool placed on a red flowered rug, the composition anchored by a little red bird in the tree outside the window, signed S.J. Hamblen, fetched an astounding $189,500, six times its $25,000/35,000 estimate, from Marguerite Riordan

bidding for a client. A paper label gives the child's name as Ellen. "There are just not any outstanding paintings of this quality on the market," said Riordan, explaining the competition.

Riordan also bought for $78,500 a portrait of a little girl named Ann Elizabeth Crehore (1834–1917) of Milton, Massachusetts, by John Ritto Penniman, a Boston portrait and ornamental painter and lithographer. In the background is a view toward Boston from Milton Hill with the State House and the Park Street Church in the distance. It is both a historical document and a charming painting.

There were several bidders for a portrait of a young girl in a dark green dress sitting at a piano, attributed to William Matthew Prior (1806–1873), although it may be by S.J. Hamblen or W.W. Kennedy—both worked in a similar style. It sold to dealer David Schorsch on the phone for $90,500, six times its high estimate.

Portrait of Ellen by Sturtevant Hamblen, $189,500 to dealer Marguerite Riordan bidding for a client, underbid by Essex, Massachusetts, dealer Stephen Score. Little sale, part one. Sotheby's photo.

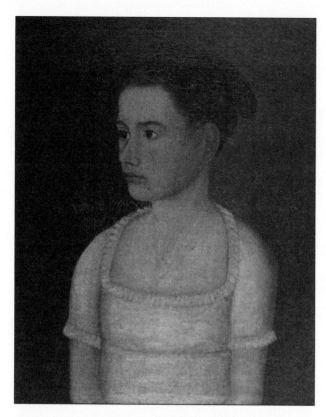

This portrait of a dark-haired young girl wearing a white Empire gown, inscribed on the back "Henry Folsom pinxit," sold for $68,500 (est. $10,000/15,000) to a New York collector. It was painted circa 1812 and Nina identified the sitter as the artist's sister, Anna Gilman Foster. Little sale, part one. Sotheby's photo.

A watercolor said to depict Lafayette at John Leavitt's tavern in Chichester, New Hampshire, in 1825, in its original inlaid maple frame made by Moses Morse, a local joiner, sold for a whopping $101,500 (est. $25,000/35,000) to a New York collector.

In *Little by Little* (Dutton, 1984), the book Nina wrote about the collection, she describes how she acquired it in 1940 directly from the Morse family with a label telling about the cabinetmaker Moses Morse, who made the desk and bookcase depicted as well as the frame for the picture, and identifying the artist as Joseph Warner Leavitt and the gentleman in the foreground as Lafayette, who came to New Hampshire in June 1825 but did not pass through Loudon.

Collectors and dealers paid a premium to buy their local history. New Hampshire dealer Peter

Sawyer spent $211,500 for the luminous painting of the schooner *Charles Carroll* of Portsmouth, New Hampshire, painted by Thomas P. Moses (est. $80,000/120,000). It is pictured on the dust jacket of *Little by Little,* making it an icon. Carl Crossman, a Danvers, Massachusetts, dealer and author, said he found it at the Salisbury (Connecticut) flea market 30 years ago and sold it to Nina for $15,000.

Among the good buys, but selling way over estimates, was a pair of still life oil paintings, 17½" x 22¼", one with a pitcher, a glass of cider, a basket of nuts on a vine-patterned tablecloth, and a winter scene out the window, the other with a platter of fruit, a glass of milk, and a summer landscape, that sold for $43,125 and $19,550, both to Riordan for a client. "They were among my favorites in the sale," she said.

Others said their favorite was a portrait of a dark-haired young girl wearing a white Empire gown, inscribed on the back "Henry Folsom pinxit," that sold for $68,500 (est. $10,000/15,000) to a New York collector. It was painted circa 1812 and Nina identified the sitter as the artist's sister, Anna Gilman Foster. Its quiet beauty transcends folk art, suggesting northern Renaissance painting.

Several museums were successful bidders. The Abby Aldrich Rockefeller Folk Art Center in Williamsburg, Virginia, bought a watercolor of a young girl in an Indian costume, a portrait of Denny Soccabeson, inscribed on the back "Denn . . . daughter of Francis Joseph, Governor of the Passamaquoddy Tribe, Eastport, Sept. 18, 1817." On a jelly label on the back of the picture, Nina wrote that it was painted in the garrison house when Eastport (Maine) was occupied by the British, 1814–18. It is believed to have been painted by Lieutenant Villars, a young British officer stationed in Eastport during the occupation. Baltimore dealer Milly McGehee did the bidding for AARFAC , winning it for $25,300, well over its $5,000/7,000 estimate.

SPNEA got two of the three late 19th-century views of interiors. Nina's jelly labels on the backs identified them as the parlor and bedroom of the Matthew Cushing House on East Street in Hingham, Massachusetts, painted by Ella Emory in 1878, bought by Bertram K. Little in Boston in 1942. The view of the parlor cost $40,250, that of the bedroom $52,900, and then SPNEA ran out of money and had to let the view of the east parlor go to a collector for $18,400. These interiors are considered significant documents attesting to the conservative and cumulative aspect of many New England homes.

In 1750 an unidentified girl of the Cushing family stitched the coat of arms used by Matthew Cushing of Hingham, Massachusetts, in 1638, the same Matthew Cushing whose house was documented in Ella Emory's 19th-century paintings. The Henry Francis du Pont Winterthur Museum in Delaware purchased it for $57,500, considered a low price for what needlework historian Betty Ring called the finest and most sophisticated example of schoolgirl embroidery in American art. In its original diamond-shaped frame, it measures 22" x 22".

According to Ring, the girl who stitched it was probably a classmate of Hannah Quincy (1736–1796), who worked the closely related Quincy/Sturgis arms at a Boston school in 1750. Both girls used the newly popular pattern supplied

"A board to hide ye fireplace painted with a fierce lion in the forest," together with an engraving by Thomas Kensett published in 1825, the printed source the artist used, sold for $96,000 to the phone. Nina typed on two jelly labels attached to the back, "Fireboard from the Dresser House on Dresser Hill, Charleston, Mass., used in the main room when the house was a coaching inn owned by Harvey Dresser. He died in 1806." Rennie Little, one of Bertram and Nina Little's sons, said, "We always called him Harvey the Lion and especially liked his wonderful set of false teeth." Little sale, part one. Sotheby's photo.

by heraldic artist John Gore (1718–1796). Ring made a point of saying it is not a hatchment, the name given to painted coats of arms used in funerals and on houses of the deceased and, after a period of time, removed to a church. These needlework accomplishments were decorations treasured by proud parents and displayed in colonial parlors.

The Milwaukee Art Museum bought an important 19th-century needlework document, the watercolor and chenille embroidery on silk view of St. Joseph's Academy near Emmitsburg, Maryland by Anna May Motter, dated 1825, showing her school, founded by Saint Elizabeth Ann Seton. In the foreground is depicted the arrival of students by horse-drawn coach. It sold for $42,500 to Connecticut dealers Stephen and Carol Huber, who also did the bidding for Winterthur on the Cushing coat of arms.

Some marine items brought strong prices, and others seemed like good values. An American eagle figurehead attributed to John Haley Bellamy (1836–1914), which the Littles called the "Snooty Eagle" because it had its nose in the air, sold for $90,500 to a phone bidder even though the beak was repaired. A pair of billetheads of vigorously carved anthemia within a scroll, carved in New York City by Simeon Skillin III (1789–1839) sold for $8,625. They descended in the Skillin family, possibly intended as models for full-size carvings.

Some astonishing prices were paid for small boxes. A circa 1825 pine and watercolor bank box with "Mary F. Kelley Savings Bank" inscribed on the front of the top and watercolor pictures on the sides depicting a young girl in a red dress with a tortoiseshell comb in her hair and a young man wearing a blue coat sold for $57,500 to a New York collector, even though the glass panels were cracked.

Furniture generally brought strong prices. The finest of a set of six white-painted bentwood patented fancy chairs made by Samuel Gragg of Boston, circa 1810, and decorated with peacock feathers sold for $50,600 (est. $3,000/4,000) to New York dealer Stuart Feld on the phone. The other chairs from the set are all in museums.

Harold Sack, bidding from his seat in the first row, bought the bonnet-top Massachusetts highboy and matching lowboy that had belonged to John Chandler, a loyalist in the American Revolution in Petersham, Massachusetts, paying $145,500 for the highboy and $57,500 for the lowboy. A pair of English looking glasses from the same family sold for $57,500 to Ohio dealer Bill Samaha. The portrait of Nathaniel Chandler, an owner of the highboy and lowboy and the mirrors, painted by his cousin, Winthrop Chandler, sold to an absentee bidder for $17,250.

Historic Deerfield was the underbidder for a painted pine and maple lowboy owned by Susan Hawkes of Deerfield that went to a private collector for $42,550. The same strong price was paid by a phone bidder for a painted maple and pine oval-top tavern table with single drawer, turned legs, and stretchers that was estimated at $15,000/25,000.

Among the 25 lots that remained unsold because no one would meet the reserve (the minimum price acceptable to the consignor) was a life-size portrait of the Reverend Jonas Coe by Ammi Phillips. The imposing and penetrating character study of a preacher with a kindly expression but a heavy five o'clock shadow and outstretched hands failed to make its $50,000 low estimate, and as the sale progressed, it became clear that any lot that did not make its low estimate would not sell.

PART TWO

Massachusetts and Ohio dealer G.W. Samaha remembers the day in 1969 when he got a call from a picker named Skip Carpenter saying he had just gotten an oak chest-on-chest with a funny flat top and wooden knobs. A "flat-top" without its original hardware didn't sound like much, so Samaha said he put off going to look at it for a few days. When he got there, he learned that collectors Nina and

Bert Little had been there the day before and bought it for $1,600. Samaha always referred to the paint-grained maple chest-on-chest-on-frame attributed to the Dunlap family's shop in Bedford, New Hampshire, 1777–92, as the "one that got away."

Samaha was not one of the half-dozen bidders who battled for it at Sotheby's sale of the Little collection, part two on Saturday, October 22, 1994, in New York City. When the bidding was over, the Dunlap painted chest-on-chest-on-frame had sold for $310,500 with buyer's premium to a New England collector. A note in the catalog said, "The original brass bail handles will be made available to the purchaser." Since the yellow and orange paint graining and wooden knobs were added sometime in the 19th century and enhance its folkiness, it is likely those brasses will remain in a drawer. But this documentary piece of New Hampshire furniture, over which dealers Wayne Pratt, Leigh Keno, Ron Bourgeault, and several phone bidders fought, was not the top lot in the sale.

The most expensive piece was a rare carved oak 17th-century great chair made in Essex County, Massachusetts, that sold for $332,500. The successful bidder was David Warren, director of Bayou Bend, administered by the Museum of Fine Arts, Houston. "We are going for the top items on our priority list," said Warren, clearly pleased with his purchase. The underbidder was a New York collector who will have another chance at a similar chair when Eddy Nicholson's Pilgrim Century chair is offered at Christie's in January 1995. Nicholson paid $528,000 for his chair at Sotheby's in October 1986.

Several other museums were successful bidders at part two of the sale of the collection of legendary Massachusetts collectors the late Bertram and Nina Fletcher Little, who over their 60 years of collecting had often loaned objects from their collections to exhibitions.

The Philadelphia Museum of Art bought several watercolors by Joseph Shoemaker Russell (1795–1860) of Philadelphia houses, both exterior views and interiors, paying $37,375 for *The Russell*

Grain-painted maple chest-on-chest-on-frame attributed to the Dunlap family workshop in Bedford, New Hampshire, 1777-92, with Victorian graining and wooden knobs, $310,500 to a New England collector on the phone. Underbidder Leigh Keno said he thought the painted surface was added in the last quarter of the 19th century, not the early 19th century, as stated in the catalog. Little sale, part two. Sotheby's photo.

Residence at Mrs. Smith's, Broad and Spruce Streets, Philadelphia, showing a drugstore on the ground floor.

Jack Lindsey, the PMA's curator of American decorative arts, did the bidding, and he had to pay $16,100 for a view of the *N.E. Corner of Chestnut & Strawberry Streets, 1818, Philadelphia,* $14,950 for the interior view of *Mrs. A.W. Smith's Parlor,* and $25,300 for the watercolor inscribed *Sarah &*

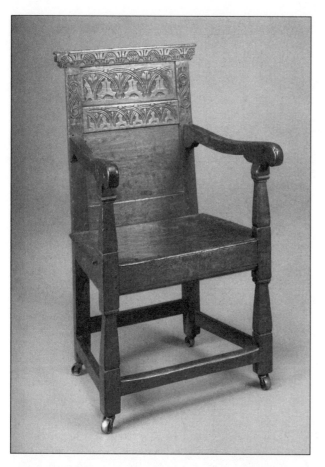

The Pilgrim-Century oak great chair, Essex County, Massachusetts, 1640-55, one of six known by Essex County joiners, sold for $332,500 to the Museum of Fine Arts, Houston. A paper label attached to the front seat frame reads: "Oak arm chair from Essex County bought by Uncle James Little from James Moulton, Lynn in 1875 for $26.50. Bought from Laura Little in 1946" signed "N.F. Little." A catalog note says the Littles paid $500 for the chair in 1944. A documentary photograph reproduced in the catalog shows the chair in James Lowell Little's house in Brookline in 1896. Little sale, part two. Sotheby's photo.

Elizabeth Russell's Room . . . , 1854. Lindsey lost out to a phone bidder willing to pay $28,750 for the watercolor of J.S. Russell's bedroom, and he dropped out of the bidding long before Russell's *View of Union or Main Street New Bedford* sold for $123,500 to another bidder. This view, taken from the second story of the Russell house at the head of the street, was illustrated on the catalog's cover. The Philadelphia house on Spruce Street was illustrated on the back cover.

Another museum curator, Philip Zea, bidding for Historic Deerfield, paid $7,187.50 for a mahogany and cherrywood bowfront Connecticut River Valley chest of drawers, signed "Eliphalet Briggs, Keene, New Hampshire, January 9, 1810," and $4,025 for an artist's box filled with stencils that, according to notes on a jelly label in Nina Fletcher Little's hand pasted on the back of the box, belonged to a Mr. Bailey of Worthington, Massachusetts, circa 1797.

Zea was outbid by Gerard Wertkin, director of the Museum of American Folk Art, for a grained, paint-decorated artist's stenciling box that had belonged to Henry Coolidge of Orange County, Massachusetts, in the early 19th century. It contained 115 stencils for walls and chairs as well as stenciling powders, tools, and an account book, and cost $12,650. The Museum of American Folk Art, which has a large collection of decorated tin and furniture, also bought another group of watercolors, drawings, and stencils belonging to a schoolgirl named Mary Nettleton, circa 1830, paying $1,840 for it.

New Hampshire auctioneer Ron Bourgeault said he was bidding for the Brookline, Massachusetts, historical society when he bought a watercolor on paper *A View of Boston* by Susan Heath for $20,700. According to Bourgeault, it will be hung in memory of Bertram and Nina Fletcher Little, who were active members of the society.

While museums were competitors, most of the successful bidders were collectors or dealers representing collectors. There was a large crowd of nearly 600 in the salesroom, and a dozen phones were available for absentee bidders. One determined phone bidder paid $228,000 for J.O.J. Frost's *View of Marblehead, Massachusetts.* There was speculation that the buyer was Boston-based money manager and Frost collector Peter Lynch, who paid a record $486,500 for Frost's *Troops Marching from Marblehead to Boston in the Civil War* at part one of the Little sale last January. According to one member of the Little family, Lynch was expected to be bidding by phone from California.

There was a bidding battle between a phone bidder and Sotheby's folk art specialist Nancy Druckman when a painted overmantel depicting the southwest view of Boston lighthouse and harbor, signed "Jona W. Edes," crossed the block. Druckman prevailed, and it sold for $151,000.

New York dealer David Schorsch, bidding by phone, said he bought for a client a Winthrop Chandler overmantel panel from the Ebenezer Waters house in Sutton, Massachusetts, paying $195,000 for the view of the river with trees and figures painted prior to 1790. According to a catalog note, Chandler's portraits of Mr. and Mrs. Samuel Waters and the overmantel from the southwest chamber of the Waters' house are in the collection of Cogswell's Grant, the Littles' country house, which they gave to the Society for the Preservation of New England Antiquities and is now a museum.

Determined bidders ignored estimates. Even though the catalog photograph made a blue-green-painted apothecary chest look white, those who came to the preview noted that the paint was original and in remarkably good condition. Two

Joseph Shoemaker Russell (1795-1860), watercolor *View of Union or Main Street New Bedford taken from the 2 Story Window of Abm Russell's house at the head of the Street 1812*, 8¼" x 11¼". One of a group of watercolors by the artist, it sold for $123,500 to an absentee bidder. Others in the group ranged from $6,325 for *A View of the Dining Room at Mrs. Smith's in Philadelphia* to $37,375 for *The Russell Residence at Mrs. Smith's, Broad and Spruce Streets, Philadelphia*, showing a drugstore on the ground floor. The latter was one of four bought by curator of American decorative arts Jack Lindsey for the Philadelphia Museum of Art. The Littles had loaned them to the PMA for the 1976 exhibition *Philadelphia: Three Centuries of American Art*. Little sale, part two. Sotheby's photo.

Portrait of a blonde-haired boy wearing a red coat, identified by a jelly label on the back as "Samuel Tracey Coit b. May 8 1790." Painted circa 1790 by the Denison Limner (Joseph Seward), it sold for $63,000 to a Pennsylvania collector. Little sale, part two. Sotheby's photo.

collectors wanted this tall, shallow storage unit. Nancy Druckman of Sotheby's appeared to be getting secret signals from a bidder in the salesroom, and the other bidder was on the phone. The 42-drawer chest with two shelves in the upper section went to the phone bidder for $151,000, five times its $30,000 high estimate.

Dr. John Ribic, a collector from Dayton, Ohio, was the determined buyer of the rare Shaker dwarf clock. He was in the salesroom and did his own bidding, standing in the back and raising his bidding paddle high, battling a phone bidder until he bought it for $109,750. He was not intimidated when the phone bidder, David Schorsch, jumped his bid of $72,500 to $80,000 and his bid of $82,500 to $90,000. He had to have this little clock by Benjamin Youngs—he is not likely to find another. It will go to Ohio, not to a Shaker collection in Pennsylvania.

Two women fought over a full-length portrait of a young boy in a gold-buttoned blue suit with a ruf-

fled collar, holding his book and his hat. The winner, who held a portable phone to her ear throughout the bidding, competed with Massachusetts dealer Pam Boynton and paid $85,000. One of Nina Fletcher Little's now famous jelly labels on the back of the picture identified the boy as "George Richardson circa 1820, artist unknown." The portrait of his brother, Charles Richardson, Jr., sold to Rhode Island collectors for $36,800, double its high estimate, and the portrait of his little sister, Louisa, standing near a cradle with her dog fetched $23,250. The portraits of Mr. and Mrs. Richardson (est. $20,000/30,000) failed to sell. Some said they were sorry to see a group of family pictures, which had been kept together since 1820, dispersed.

There were plenty of lots in this second Little sale that went under high estimates and were considered good buys. A fair price was paid for Rufus Hathaway's portrait of a red-haired gentleman wearing a brown coat and a waistcoat with silver buttons and holding a pair of calipers, said to be Ezra Weston (1743–1822) of Duxbury, Massachusetts. It sold to a collector for $59,700. "I'm sorry I did not go higher," said underbidder Stephen Score. "Here is a man in full control of his facilities, and in full control of his goods with a smile on his face." Score said he also wished he had been the buyer of the portrait of a blonde-haired boy wearing a red coat, identified on a jelly label on the back as "Samuel Tracey Coit b. May 8 1790." Painted circa 1790 by the Denison Limner (Joseph Seward), it sold for $63,000 to a Pennsylvania collector.

A large (18" long) whalebone birdcage seemed like a good buy at $8,050. The pair of Ruth Henshaw Bascom profile portraits of Mary Burr and Perley Gates of Ashby, Massachusetts, went to Connecticut dealer Marguerite Riordan for $23,000. A single-profile portrait by Bascom of a little girl, Elizabeth Cummings Low of Boston, sold for $46,000 in the afternoon.

A number of lots far exceeded their estimates when bidders found their charm irresistible.

Joseph H. Davis's full-length profile portrait watercolor of schoolmaster John F. Demeritt seated in a fancy chair at his paint-grained table sold for $65,750 (est. $10,000/15,000). It is the earliest dated example of Davis's work.

A 13" long pine document box painted by Rufus Porter with stylized trees on the sides and a border of leaves and flowers on its top surrounding the name "P. Porter," possibly Pauline Porter, the artist's sister-in-law, sold for $69,000 (est. $12,000/18,000) to Essex, Massachusetts, dealer Stephen Score for a client.

A tiny watercolor of a young boy wearing a blue waistcoat and a red- and yellow-striped vest and holding a sprig of roses, which sold for $19,550 (est. $1,200/1,800), was related to the watercolor portraits under glass on the Mary Kelley Savings Bank sold in part one of the Little sale for $57,500. A miniature watercolor portrait of a man wearing a black coat, a red waistcoat, and a tall black hat and with a telescope under his arm, only 3½" x 5½" and in a red and black painted frame, sold for $39,100. The estimate was $4,000/6,000. A watercolor by Eunice Pinney (1770–1849), depicting a young lady in a pink Empire dress picking grapes and accompanied by her dog, sold for $17,250 (est. $1,200/1,500). Pinney, who delighted in copying prints, was one of the earliest female folk artists and her work was championed by Jean Lipman and Alice Winchester a generation ago.

There were, however, some disappointments. In all, 74 of the 614 lots offered failed to sell, though several found buyers immediately after the sale. Virginia dealer Sumpter Priddy said he bought the overmantel painted with a hunting scene that was bought in at $26,000 (est.

$40,000/60,000). There was no interest in the honest portraits of Mr. and Mrs. Jacob Farrar by Asahel Powers. That of Mrs. Farrar was estimated at $30,000/40,000, and that of Mr. Farrar at $15,000/25,000. No one wanted the pair of portraits by William Matthew Prior of the artist's brother-in-law and his wife, Captain Eli and Marie Louis Hannaford Hamblen, painted in Prior's better style (est. $20,000/30,000). If they had been in his cheaper, flat style, they might have sold. A sun-bleached walnut blockfront bureau made in Boston, 1750–70, also failed to sell (est. $50,000/70,000).

There was not as much electricity in the salesroom for part two of the Little sale. Nevertheless, it brought a total of $4,908,236 for 540 lots, which when added to the $7.3 million total from part one, brought the grand total for the Little collection to $12.3 million, a record for a single-owner sale of Americana and certainly a record for any sale of folk art.

"These sales have been the greatest thing that has ever happened in the world of Americana," said Nancy Druckman, Sotheby's senior vice-president in charge of folk art. Clearly, she was sorry to see the sale end. "The Littles had scholars' minds and eyes of connoisseurs," she noted. "Bert and Nina loved the material, and they wanted others to love it too. That was behind all the books and articles they wrote and all of the notes on the jelly labels too."

Sotheby's two Little collection sale catalogs, which reprint all Nina Fletcher Little's jelly-label notes, are also a contribution to folk art literature. The excerpts from Nina Fletcher Little's writings at the back of Volume II are well worth reading.

Editor's Note: Sotheby's was basking in the success of the $12 million Little sale when rival Christie's announced it would sell the collection of Eddy Nicholson. Nicholson said he was raising cash for a new business venture when he sold his collections for more than $13 million in January 1995. Nicholson seemed to have more passion for the deal than the object. He loved the power of being the million-dollar man, and when the stakes became higher after the sale of the $12 million Nicholas Brown desk and bookcase, he was through.

EDDY NICHOLSON SELLS

BY LITA SOLIS-COHEN

"Y ou made the market, and you brought it back," Christie's American painting specialist Jay Cantor told Eddy Nicholson after Nicholson's collection of Americana brought a tidy $13,586,678, more than a million over its high estimate, at a landmark sale on January 27 and 28, 1995.

"My sale proved you don't buy for investment, you buy quality and workmanship. Some prices were up, and others were down, but overall I did just fine," said Nicholson on the phone from California after the sale.

Asked if he really came out even, taking into account expensive restoration costs, Nicholson said he did very well. "Add to this sale total the private sale of some furniture to the Chipstone Foundation and the paintings I sold to Marguerite Riordan, which included a million-dollar Edward Hicks, plus the three million dollars worth of silver and furniture I sold earlier at Christie's, I figure I got about twenty million for my antiques," he volunteered.

Nicholson probably had spent close to $20 million on paintings, furniture, and decorations in the last 15 years. He was a zealous hunter of Americana who went after the big ones. In January 1986 at Christie's, he was the first to pay more than a million dollars for a piece of American furniture—$1,045,000 to be precise, for a Philadelphia tea table.

At his sale the tea table made history again when it sold for more than twice as much,

$2,422,500, with buyer's premium, to New York City dealer Leigh Keno bidding for clients sitting in front of him. Keno outbid Harold Sack, president of Israel Sack, Inc., who said he was bidding for stock.

Keno was also the buyer of the Willing-Francis-Fisher-Cadwalader family easy chair made in Philadelphia circa 1770, paying $618,500 for the chair that had cost Nicholson $1.1 million at Sotheby's in 1987. When pressed, Keno said, "Yes, it is likely the table and chair will stay together."

Keno was the biggest buyer at the sale. His bill for furniture totaled just over $4 million. Some said this sale marked the passing of the mantle to the

Mr. and Mrs. Eddy Nicholson's name was on the glass doors at Christie's during the weeklong exhibition. At the door is Gil Perez, the nicest doorman in New York and one of Christie's great assets.

Dealer Leigh Keno inspecting the $2,422,500 Philadelphia tea table for which Eddy Nicholson paid $1,045,000 nine years ago.

younger generation. For the first time in 50 years, the Israel Sack name did not appear among the buyers of the top ten lots. If not for the Sacks' underbidding, however, the tea table might not have sold for $2.4 million.

The Sack firm is still active and purchased the Salem, Massachusetts, matching high chest and dressing table for $167,500, within estimates. The firm had owned them twice before. Nicholson bought the two pieces at Sotheby's in 1990 for

$165,500. The price increase reflects the increased buyer's premium; the hammer price was $150,000 at both sales. Sack outbid Keno to buy a classical girandole mirror carved with a spread-winged eagle flanked by delicate acanthus leaves, made in Salem 1800–1810, paying $118,000, topping its $100,000 estimate. Sack had also owned it twice before.

The more expensive furniture was bought by Keno and by Pennsylvania dealer Clarence Prickett

The bombé chest sold for $605,000 in 1987 when Nicholson jumped a bid. This time it sold for $574,500 to Yardley, Pennsylvania, dealer Clarence Prickett. Christie's photo.

and Connecticut dealer Wayne Pratt. Keno was bidding on behalf of a member of the decorative arts committee of the Philadelphia Museum of Art for the marble slab table made for Pennsylvania Governor John Penn, 1765–75, and he got it for $376,500. Nicholson had paid $605,000 for it at Christie's in January 1987 when Keno was underbidder. At the same Sotheby's sale, Nicholson paid the same price, $605,000, for a serpentine bombé chest of drawers made in Boston circa 1770. Here it sold for $574,500 to Yardley, Pennsylvania, dealer Clarence Prickett, who also bought a block-and-shell kneehole dressing table attributed to Edmund Townsend and Daniel Goddard for $443,500. Nicholson had bought the kneehole privately and reportedly paid more for it.

Woodbury, Connecticut, dealer Wayne Pratt, the underbidder on both the bombé chest and the kneehole dressing table, bought a Boston tray-top mahogany tea table with candle slides for $552,500, an auction record for the form. It was one of the pieces Nicholson had bought from Israel Sack, Inc., and Pratt said he thought Nicholson had made a profit.

Nicholson took a big loss, though, on a carved oak wainscot armchair for which he paid $528,000 at Sotheby's in October 1986. It sold for $218,500 to Keno, who said he hoped it would go to a museum.

Nicholson made sizable profits on several paintings and took losses on others. In May 1985 he paid $297,000 for Grant Wood's large pencil cartoon for his famous painting *Parson Weems' Fable,* depicting George Washington and the cherry tree. It sold for $508,500 to Debra Force, director of Beacon Hill Fine Arts, the new gallery at 980 Madison Avenue owned by Detroit collector Richard Manoogian. Force said she was buying for a client.

The First Fish of the Season, a luminist painting of a man and his dog in a boat by William Tylee Ranney (est. $150,000/200,000), sold for $431,500 to a collector.

Dealer Clarence Prickett bought the block-and-shell kneehole dressing table attributed to Edmund Townsend and Daniel Goddard for $443,500. Nicholson had bought the kneehole privately and reportedly paid more for it. Christie's photo.

Nicholson's American furniture attracted the biggest crowd and the keenest competition. There was something for everyone. Sack outbid Keno for a Federal satinwood and mahogany Pembroke table attributed to William Whitehead, New York, circa 1795, paying $85,000, topping its $40,000/60,000 estimate. Nicholson had paid $49,500 at Sotheby's in February 1985.

Marguerite Riordan outbid Keno to buy a Federal card table inlaid with an American eagle for $132,500. The table had sold at Sotheby's in February 1985 for $115,000 to Sack, who sold it to Nicholson immediately after the sale, no doubt for a profit. Riordan outbid Pratt and Connecticut dealer Arthur Liverant for a fine maple side chair with a Chinese vase-shaped splat, a yoke back, a scalloped skirt, pad feet, and an old surface, paying $79,500 for it, more than double its high estimate. In October 1989 it sold to Nicholson at Christie's for $44,000.

Grant Wood's cartoon for his painting *Parson Weems' Fable* sold for $508,500. Nicholson had paid $297,000 for it in 1985. Christie's photo.

Wayne Pratt paid more than double the estimate, $134,500, for a small Salem sofa attributed to Samuel McIntire, 1800–11, and Keno paid the same price for a bird's-eye maple veneered Federal sofa of the same date, made in Portsmouth, New Hampshire, that had cost Nicholson $49,500 in 1984.

Not every lot brought six figures. Southern dealer Sumpter Priddy bought a pair of Portsmouth, New Hampshire, chairs for $8,626 because of their history as venture cargo to Virginia.

A few private collectors did their own bidding the way Eddy Nicholson used to do. A private

collector from California standing at the back of the salesroom kept his paddle in the air until he won for $209,000 a Federal dwarf clock made by Reuben Tower, Hingham, Massachusetts. Nicholson bought it at Christie's in 1988 for $93,500.

Another aggressive private collector, accompanied by his decorator, bid well over estimates for early 18th-century furniture, outbidding Keno to win a maple turned gate-leg dining table for $89,100, more than double its high estimate, and a diminutive New England drop-leaf table with pad feet for $74,000 (est. $50,000/80,000). A Pennsylvania stretcher table with scalloped skirt was his for $21,850, and he paid $16,100 for a small

New Hampshire turned-leg stretcher table with an oval top, estimated to bring at most $8,000. A Massachusetts veneered chest of drawers with bun feet, early brasses, and a Sack provenance cost him $40,250. The same buyer also liked delft. He bought an Adam and Eve English delft charger for $29,900, a tad under its $30,000/40,000 estimate, and paid $12,650 for another blue dash charger painted with tulips and lilies estimated at $10,000/15,000. Both were probably good buys.

Phil Steer, a young Kansas City collector, was the successful bidder for a Boston or Salem, Massachusetts, card table that cost him $48,300, just under its $50,000 high estimate. In October 1984 at Christie's, the table sold for $41,800. According to tradition, it descended in the family of John Adams. In 1984 Nicholson paid $44,000 at Christie's for a paint-grained cupboard that once belonged to the late Yale professor and Winterthur

director Charles Montgomery. That same cupboard sold for only $11,500 because careful examination showed the cornice was replaced.

Among the accessories, some brass fire tools attributed to Daniel King, the Philadelphia brass founder who billed General John Cadwalader for andirons, fire tools, and fenders, evoked spirited bidding. Keno, bidding for a Philadelphian, bought a shovel and tongs for $23,000. Nicholson had paid $7,700 for the tools in January 1991 when they were consigned by Anna Cadwalader Ingersoll. They may be the very ones John Cadwalader ordered.

Nicholson also bought the finest 18th-century Philadelphia needlework to come to market in the last decade, and he made a profit when he sold it. One piece sold for less than he paid, but the other brought considerably more. The silk-on-silk needlework picture of a hunting scene stitched by

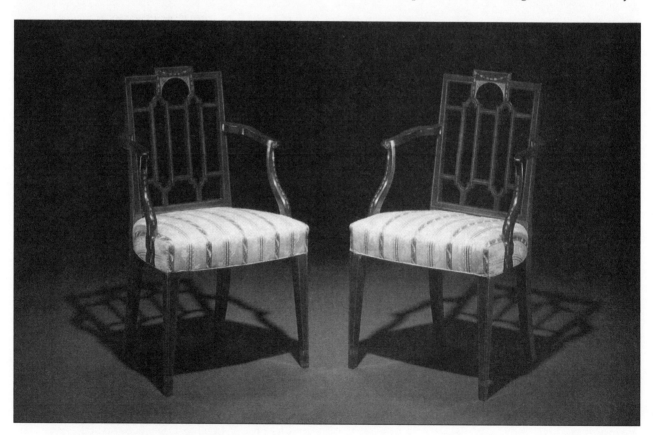

A set of eight Federal side chairs branded Anderson, New York, 1790-1810, sold for $99,500 to dealer Clarence Prickett with competition from New York dealer Tom Schwenke and a phone bidder. Christie's photo.

A bright spot in the silver sale was this tankard by Simeon Soumain that sold for $195,000. It had cost Nicholson $148,500. Christie's photo.

Mary Flower in 1768 sold for $145,500 to Connecticut dealers Stephen and Carol Huber. Nicholson paid $187,000 for it in January 1987. The following spring, when another needlework picture by Mary Flower of a shepherd and shepherdess came up for sale at Christie's, Nicholson bought it for $66,000. It sold to the Hubers for $123,500, so taken together Nicholson gained $25,000 on the two.

In the same way, some pieces of silver netted Nicholson a profit, and on others he suffered a loss. A fine tankard by Simeon Soumain sold for $195,000 to Boston dealer David Firestone, who had a client in tow. Nicholson paid $148,500 for it at Sotheby's in 1989. Firestone also paid $145,500 for a large Boston salver with a rococo cartouche by John Coburn, for which Nicholson paid $82,500 in June 1986. The silver teapot by John Brevoort went to dealer Jonathan Trace for $145,500. It had cost Nicholson $181,000.

The biggest disappointment of the sale was the failure of two pieces of American silver with engravings signed by Joseph Leddel, Senior. The cup and its Jacobite engraving was explained in detail in Jeanne Sloan's notes in the hardcover catalog, and the engraving was used for the design of the catalog's end papers.

Nevertheless, the trade questioned the authenticity of the engraving, in part because they remembered another engraved cup that came on the market six months after Nicholson paid $250,000 for this cup. The second engraved cup, signed Leddel, was withdrawn from the sale when the trade became suspicious of two rare cups appearing out of the blue. Several members of the trade said that the entire group of objects signed by Leddel require fresh study. They made their point again when the next lot, a copper sundial engraved with a charming poem by Leddel, also failed to get a single bid.

Nicholson made the market for Dedham pottery in the 1980s, and it did not come back quite as strong in the 1990s, although some high prices were paid for the crackled wares with blue borders depicting animals, and flowers.

The Nicholson sale gave the Americana market a shot in the arm when it needed it. New collectors appeared and old ones came back with enthusiasm. "Good times are here again," said Harold Sack as he left the salesroom.

Editor's Note: In the world of schoolgirl needlework, the sale of the Hannah Otis's chimney piece at Sotheby's in 1996 was the equivalent of the sale of the Brown desk and bookcase in 1989 for the American furniture market. The record million-dollar-plus price paid for an incomparable object of historical importance likely will not be reached again soon.

HANNAH OTIS'S CHIMNEY PIECE

BY LITA SOLIS-COHEN

Hannah Otis came from an illustrious family of patriots, poets, legislators, and business leaders, but she may be remembered longer than any of her forebears. She stitched the most expensive needlework picture ever sold.

She was 21 years old in 1753 when she recorded in stitches a hilly view of Boston, showing every detail of the gambrel-roofed Thomas Hancock house, complete with stone quoins and window lintels, the livestock, and the pets. In the foreground is young John Hancock, astride his horse, a Black groom in attendance. To the right is Beacon Hill with its tar-pot beacon; the church spire is probably the West Church, destroyed in 1776. The neighbors' houses in the distance were later owned by John Singleton Copley around 1769. The fort-like structure flying the British flag has been identified as the only extant rendering of the Block House, destroyed by fire in 1761.

This charming and historically important piece of needlework, estimated at $300,000/500,000, was bought at Sotheby's on Saturday, January 20, 1996, by the Museum of Fine Arts, Boston, which had taken care of it since 1954 when it was put on loan there by the Otis family. It cost the museum $1,157,500 with buyer's premium.

When it goes on view at the MFA, this most expensive needlework will likely attract crowds. The Museum of Fine Arts, Boston was determined to buy the needlework, which was consigned to Sotheby's by Martha Gray Otis (b. 1943) and her brother, Samuel Allyne Otis (b. 1940), who felt they could not afford to give it to the museum. "We are happy to have the museum have it. We hated to take it away from them," said Martha Otis after the sale. "My greatest joy, besides being out of debt, is that the Boston museum has it."

It was estate planning that drove the Otises to sell the needlework. "We are not wealthy enough to own it and pay inheritance taxes, and now by the time we pay the capital gains tax, we are not talking about a fortune divided between the eight of us," Martha Otis continued. "I think Hannah Otis, who struggled to support herself, taking in boarders and running a shop, would be pleased to know that the monies from the sale of her needlework will give my children and my brother Sam's children a boost when they need it."

Auctioneer William Stahl opened the bidding for the needlework at $170,000. Connecticut dealer Stephen Huber, bidding for a collector, took it to $300,000, bidding against the reserve. Then Jonathan Fairbanks, curator of American decorative arts at the MFA, standing on the far left side of the salesroom, raised his paddle, bidding $310,000. He battled Huber to $840,000, when Huber shook his head.

Nancy Druckman, head of Sotheby's folk art department, on the phone with a client, then entered the competition, raising Fairbanks's bids. Druckman asked her bidder for $1 million and got it. Fairbanks, taking his signals from his major benefactor at the back of the salesroom, raised his

Hannah Otis canvas work bought by the Museum of Fine Arts, Boston, sold for a record $1.15 million.

paddle at $1,050,000, and that was enough. The audience gasped and then applauded as Stahl knocked down the lot to Fairbanks. The bill came to $1,157,500.

Martha Otis ran over and embraced Fairbanks. Amid congratulations, Fairbanks said, "A lot of people helped us."

The primary donor is said to be Edward C. (Ned) Johnson, chairman of Fidelity Investments, Boston. The underbidder on the phone was the New York collector Ralph Esmerian, who had paid the previous record price for a needlework, $198,500 for a folk art sampler by Ruthy Rogers, a Marblehead, Massachusetts, girl, at Robert W.

Skinner Inc. in June 1987. Esmerian had also paid a record $374,000 for schoolgirl art when he bought a watercolor of Aurora on silk at Christie's in 1989. Both records are now shattered. This new record, surpassing the needlework record by nearly $1 million, is not likely to be broken.

Needlework historian Betty Ring acknowledged that the Hannah Otis chimney piece is the most important colonial schoolgirl embroidery that we know because it is so historically significant. "We don't know of anything like it," she said. "But who knows. With a price like this, in sixty or ninety days another might pop right out of the woodwork."

Editor's Note: The Meyer sale at Sotheby's was a landmark that pushed the market for American furniture to a peak in 1996. The furniture offered met the criteria collectors demand: classic forms, old surfaces, and traceable provenance.

A MARKET PEAK: THE MEYER SALE

BY LITA SOLIS-COHEN

Did the Meyer sale set a new level in the market for Americana, or did it set a new level in marketing Americana? It did both.

The Americana collectors who pushed the total to $11.1 million for just 221 lots of American furniture and decorations collected by the late Michigan machine tool manufacturer Adolph (Bob) Meyer and his wife, Ginger, offered at Sotheby's on Saturday afternoon, January 20, 1996, were not a new cast of characters. They had been buying American furniture for three, ten, 20 or more years. But they did spend at a new level for some of the finest American furniture to come on the market in the last decade, paying record prices for several forms.

A whopping $3,632,500 (including buyer's premium) was paid for the Samuel Whitehorne family Newport, Rhode Island, block and shell carved mahogany kneehole bureau with an old worn surface reflecting years of use. The previous record for a kneehole was the $687,500 paid in January 1983 for one made for George Gibbs, Jr. Samuel Whitehorne, for whom the Meyer kneehole was made, married Ruth Gibbs, George Gibbs's sister, on December 19, 1771.

The $1,432,500 paid for a 1738–48 Boston mahogany desk and bookcase with gilded carving, made for Harvard-educated Boston merchant and manufacturer Edward Jackson, was a record for Massachusetts furniture.

Six-figure prices were plentiful. Two pieces made in colonial Philadelphia sold for more than half-a-million dollars each. An open armchair with an upholstered back, seat, and arm rests, acanthus-carved handholds, molded front legs, and raking back legs brought $585,500. A mahogany tea table with a thick piecrust top, acanthus-carved legs, and a ribbon-and-flower-carved ring at the base of its shaft sold for $530,500. A circa 1770 block and shell carved cherrywood chest of drawers from the Colchester-Norwich area of Connecticut, clearly influenced by Newport designs, sold for $398,500, as did a 1770 Newport bonnet-top high chest with a single carved concave shell and angular cabriole legs ending in slipper feet. A Boston blockfront chest of drawers with a pendant fan on its skirt and a rich patina, circa 1750, its thumb-molded top with a generous overhang, fetched $321,500.

Did Sotheby's hardcover book with glorious photographs, the scholarly seminars, the careful cataloging with researched histories, and the series of boardroom lunches play an important role in getting the collectors to ante up these big sums for furniture? The hype didn't hurt, and it brought out a large audience to watch the seasoned collectors and their advisors compete.

The hype may have been responsible for a few crazy prices for minor items, but it was the quality and condition of the furniture selected in the 1940s and 1950s by Michigan antiques dealer Jess Pavey for his closest friends, Bob and Ginger Meyer, that made the most passionate and well-heeled collectors stretch for what they wanted.

Pavey, reached by phone after the sale, said he was not surprised at the results. "I told Bob

The Samuel Whitehorne blockfront kneehole bureau attributed to Edmund Townsend, Newport, Rhode Island, circa 1780, with a reddish brown surface and original brasses sold for $3,632,500, a record for the form and the third most expensive piece of American furniture. Its untouched condition made the difference. The buyer was Leigh Keno for a client. Sotheby's photo.

[Meyer] he'd never get another chance in his lifetime to buy a better blockfront when it came up at Parke-Bernet in the Norvin Green sale in 1950," Pavey recalled. "We went for it and paid a record sixteen thousand dollars. The one at Bayou Bend had sold for twelve thousand, and it had busted feet. This one was pristine, not a break, and with that untouched surface."

Pavey thought the Boston secretary might have brought more. "It is so rare," he said. He was disappointed he could not buy one thing for himself. "I chased a few lots," he said. "I went to sixty-five hundred for the William and Mary looking glass with the warped crest. Where will you find another?" It sold for $13,800 to a collector.

He underbid the Schimmel eagle, which sold for $39,100 to a Michigan collector who said she was thrilled to get it. Pavey left a bid of $1,000 on the pair of damaged dolphin Sandwich glass candlesticks, and it wasn't half enough. They sold for $3162.50 to a phone bidder. "They had belonged to my late mother-in-law," he said, "and I wanted to leave them to her granddaughter."

Pavey contends the success of the Meyer sale could never have been achieved if money were the driving force. "It was a pure love affair," he said. "I never made much money in the antiques business, but it has been a rich experience. My wife, Grace, and I were in love with the business, and we worked as hard as terriers to secure the pieces. Take the piecrust table for example. I bought it for eighty-three hundred and I sold it for ten thousand and took another dish-top tea table worth fifteen hundred in trade."

Pavey was clearly pleased he had lived to see the success of the Meyer sale. "It was always a dream I never thought I would live to realize," he confessed.

Pavey is nearly 90 and, because of his wife's poor health, was not able to attend the sale and witness the dynamics of the salesroom. He missed the secret bidding signals and the aggressive paddle waving and the bank of phones manned by young

Mahogany blockfront chest of drawers, Boston, circa 1750, $321,500, a record for the form. The ample overhang of the top and rich, untouched surface made the difference. Sotheby's photo.

A collector competing against Sack and the phone bought this circa 1770 Philadelphia piecrust tilt-top tea table for $530,500, slightly more than the $508,500 paid for the fancier Logan tea table at Christie's the following week. The thick top and rich color helped the price. Sotheby's photo.

men and women from Sotheby's bids department talking to dozens of bidders who chose not to be in the salesroom. He had to hear secondhand that Jonathan Boos was the underbidder at $3.2 million for the Newport kneehole bureau. According to the trade, Boos was acting for Richard Manoogian. Massachusetts dealer Bill Samaha had taken the bidding to $3.1 million and then stepped back into the standing crowd. Auctioneer Bill Stahl knocked the lot down to Roberta Louckx of Sotheby's bids department for $3,632,500.

Pavey missed the hushed silence when the Boston secretary was selling, and when it was broken when the bidding reached $1.3 million. Bill Samaha put down his paddle in answer to Stahl's call at $1.3 million and said, "Sell it!" So Stahl knocked it down to Roberta Louckx, making it hard to sort out the buyer(s) of the top lots.

During the bidding, however, Leigh Keno was observed holding a white ballpoint pen to his cheek. Would that he had bid openly like Samaha, who stood in the crowd in the back, brandishing his paddle number 817. According to the trade, Samaha was bidding for Boston collector Fidelity Investments chairman Ned Johnson, who was seen in the salesroom. Leigh Keno was probably signaling Roberta Louckx on behalf of New York collectors Tony and Lulu Wang, who were sitting next to him. No buyers for the top two lots have been confirmed, and when asked, Keno would neither confirm nor deny that he was the buyer of record of the two top lots.

Keno, however, bid openly for the $585,500 Wharton open armchair, beating out Baltimore dealer Milly McGehee and New York dealer Albert Sack. Albert Sack, seated in the first row, flipped his paddle number 144 often. He was successful on half a dozen lots, buying for clients and for stock. He got the Newport high chest for $398,500 and the other slightly later (1750–75) blockfront Boston secretary for $255,000. The William and Mary flat-top highboy was his for $167,500. The three-part New England dining table, circa 1800, cost him $74,000. He paid $51,750 for the set of ten New York Federal dining chairs attributed to Elbert Anderson. Deanne Levison, bidding for the Sack firm, bought the Newport serpentine card table with stop-fluted legs for $41,400.

Samaha was successful a number of times. In addition to the $321,000 Boston blockfront, he bought the adjustable drawing table attributed to Samuel McIntire for $189,500 and an inlaid satinwood and burled wood sewing table attributed to Thomas Seymour for the same price. He was also the buyer of the Mandarin palette Chinese export punch bowl at $60,250.

Connecticut dealer Marguerite Riordan, bidding from her seat in the second row, with barely

Green and yellow painted Windsor sack-back child's highchair, $51,750 to Stonington, Connecticut, dealer Marguerite Riordan, underbid by Wayne Pratt and Arthur Liverant. Sotheby's photo.

The adjustable drawing table, Salem, Massachusetts, attributed to Samuel McIntire, circa 1800, sold to Massachusetts dealer Bill Samaha for $189,500, a record for the form. Sotheby's photo.

Edward Jackson's parcel-gilt, inlaid figured mahogany desk and bookcase, 1738-48, sold for $1,432,500 to Leigh Keno for a client, setting a record for Massachusetts furniture. Sotheby's photo.

a nod, bought the block-and-shell Norwich-Colchester, Connecticut, cherry chest of drawers for $398,500. "Of course," said Pavey on the phone after the sale, "it is the finest piece of Connecticut furniture. It belonged to the richest family in Norwich, the Carews."

Riordan also bought a green-painted New York Windsor highchair for $51,750 and a rush-seated New Hampshire side chair with Spanish feet and a vase-shaped splat for $7,475.

Other dealers had to settle for just a couple of lots. Washington, D.C., dealer Guy Bush waved his paddle high and was twice successful for clients, buying the whalebone-inlaid pipe box with the initials "EH" for $21,850 and a circa 1760 Massachusetts card table for $134,500. Clarence Prickett got two lots: a Massachusetts firescreen with a needlepoint panel at $79,500 and a New Hampshire bowfront chest of drawers at $189,500. (He had paid more for a similar one at Christie's last year, which he said was just a tad better.)

Connecticut dealer Wayne Pratt also won two lots. He said he bought for stock the $129,000 Philadelphia armchair with three shells, a strap-work splat, a dark patina, and an old leather seat. *Major John Berrien*, painted by Charles Willson Peale, could have sat in such a chair,

and Pratt bought his portrait for $101,500, outbidding a collector.

Several private collectors in the salesroom did their own bidding successfully. A couple from St. Louis bought the Queen Anne side chair for $85,000. Another collector paid $255,000 for the Boston kneehole dressing table.

Soon after the sale was underway, auctioneer Bill Stahl announced from the podium that "interested parties would be bidding," meaning that the Meyer family would be bidding for some things they wanted. The collection was consigned by the Meyer Foundation Trust, and the Meyers' grandson, Jonathan Thomas, was bidding by phone from a box above the salesroom on behalf of his mother, Barbara Livy, his sister, Kate, and for his own account.

Among the lots he nabbed was a circa 1800 mahogany marble top table for $35,650, a Philadelphia ladder-back side chair for $4,887.50, three American glass fluid lamps for $1,610, and three Continental brass candlesticks for $3,162.50. Thomas also managed to outbid a half dozen competitors to pay $17,250 for the charming Auguste Edouart silhouette of the Josiah Quincy family with a freehand background wash drawing depicting their parlor in 1842.

Editor's Note: More and more collectors and specialist dealers have embraced schoolgirl needlework over the last three decades, and prices have climbed significantly. The sale of the collection of the late Joan Stephens in January 1997 was the second landmark single-owner sale of needlework, and it provided a measure of how far the market had come, due in large part to the scholarly research by needlework historian Betty Ring, whose book Girlhood Embroidery, *published by Knopf in 1993, is the bible for the field. The Stephens sale took American needlework to a new plateau. American needlework in fine condition seems immune to recession.*

STEPHENS SALE, A BAROMETER FOR SCHOOLGIRL NEEDLEWORK, PREDICTS CLEAR SAILING AHEAD

BY LITA SOLIS-COHEN

Sotheby's January 19, 1997, sale of the late Joan Stephens's collection of samplers and needlework pictures was another landmark. Not since the January 1981 sale of the collection of the late Theodore H. Kapnek has there been a single-owner sale of American needlework with a separate catalog.

"The Stephens sale was more important than the Kapnek sale in many ways," said Stephen Huber, who was the major buyer at the Stephens sale. "The research published in the catalog and the quality of the material surpassed Kapnek. We have learned a lot in the intervening sixteen years."

The Hubers, Stephen and his wife, Carol, had sold Joan Stephens more than half of her collection, and they had tried to buy it all after she died. When they learned the collection was going to auction at Sotheby's, they did all they could to promote it. "Last summer we started talking about it to our clients," said Carol Huber. "When the catalogs were late, we bought a hundred and sent them out Federal Express."

It paid off. The Hubers were the successful bidders on 46 of the 143 lots offered (eight of which passed) and were the underbidders on 20 other lots. They spent $780,000 in all, nearly half the sale's $1,771,397 total. Five of the top ten lots went to the Hubers for clients.

Two of the top lots, including the highest-priced sampler at $145,500 with buyer's premium, were knocked down to American furniture dealer Todd Prickett, partner with his father, Clarence,

This Chester County, Pennsylvania, sampler by Eliza Dutton was used for the catalog cover partly because it was never before published. Many of the samplers in the sale had been pictured in the Hubers' sampler engagement calendars. This sampler descended in the family of the maker until 1990, when it was bought by Philadelphia dealer Amy Finkel, who sold it to Stephens. It sold for $26,450 (est. $10,000/15,000) to New York City dealer Leigh Keno for a client. Sotheby's photo.

and brother, Craig, in C.L. Prickett Antiques, Yardley, Pennsylvania. Prickett said he got seven of the 12 samplers he bid on, spending $311,000 for his client, who has a fine collection of furniture and now is collecting comparable needlework. "Where else could he find a better selection?" he asked.

The other major competitor was phone bidder #573, a collector not a dealer, according to Sotheby's. The absentee bidder was successful eight times, generally getting lots within their estimates. The remainder of the needlework and needlework tools went to a variety of private collectors and dealers, a few of them English, who had spent

Needlework sampler signed Anna Braddock, Burlington County, New Jersey, 1826, executed in blue, green, yellow, brown, and white silk in a variety of stitches on a linen ground. The verse within the floral wreath is titled "Friendship." The building is the Westtown School, flanked by birds on willow trees, and there are farm animals on the lawn and flowers in the border. The 22⅛" x 26" sampler is inscribed, "Anna Braddock, the daughter of William Braddock & Anna his wife, AB work wrought in the 14th year of her age 1826." (In 1828 Anna's sister, Jemima, also worked a sampler picturing Westtown School when she was 12. It is in the collection of the Philadelphia Museum of Art.) This sampler was bought by Stephen and Carol Huber at Skinner's in October 1987 for $41,800. Sotheby's sold it for $145,500 (est. $40,000/50,000) to Yardley, Pennsylvania, dealer Todd Prickett. The Hubers were the underbidders but said they went way over their client's bid, so had they bought it, their client wouldn't have been under any obligation to take it. Sotheby's photo.

hours examining the collection during the week-long presale exhibition on Sotheby's third floor.

Sotheby's did a masterful job of marketing the collection. Seminars on needlework were held in Washington, D.C., at the D.A.R. museum on Friday, January 10 and in New York City on Sunday, January 12. Thirty needlework enthusiasts in Washington heard American needlework historian Betty Ring, octogenarian Margaret Swain, Britain's foremost needlework historian, and Nancy Druckman, who heads Sotheby's American folk art department. In New York City 60 potential bidders listened to the same speakers plus textile conservator Dorothy McCoach, historian Gloria Allen, and Elisabeth Garrett, who heads Sotheby's educational projects.

Betty Ring wrote an introduction to the catalog, telling how she first met Joan Stephens at a summer session of the American Institute of Textile Arts at Pine Manor College in Boston in 1981 and how they became best friends. Ring wrote: "Joan Stephens was one of the smartest, most energetic, and generous women I have ever known. She had a vast knowledge of weaves, threads, printed textiles, every imaginable stitch that could be performed with a needle, and the function of all the needlework tools of the last three centuries!"

Joan Stephens had helped Betty Ring gather material for her book *Girlhood Embroidery*. The two women traveled together and encouraged each other. Many of Joan Stephens's samplers were illustrated in Betty Ring's book, and that did not hurt their value at auction.

The sale showed that, in general, prices for the finest American samplers have more than doubled in the last decade, while prices for needlework pictures have not gone quite as high. For example, the 1826 Anna Braddock sampler picturing Westtown School was bought by Stephen and Carol Huber at Skinner's in Bolton, Massachusetts, in October 1987 for $41,800.

This time around, estimated at $40,000/50,000, it sold for $145,500, the highest-priced lot in the

Mary Butz's 1842 sampler showing St. John's Church and Franklin Academy in Kutztown, Pennsylvania, was once owned by the late Ted and Ruth Kapnek. Ruth Kapnek sold it at Sotheby's in January 1987 for $14,300. Estimated at $20,000/25,000, it sold for $34,500 to the Hubers. Sotheby's photo.

sale, to Todd Prickett, underbid by the Hubers. A needlework sampler signed Mary Butz, Kutztown, Pennsylvania, and dated 1842 sold at Sotheby's in 1987 for $14,300 and was bought by the Hubers at the Stephens sale for $34,500.

Not every sampler in the Stephens collection increased in value, but one had to look hard to find one that didn't. A needlework sampler by Hannah Thayer, Randolph, Massachusetts, dated 1818, that sold for $6,900 at the Stephens sale had brought $9,075 at Sotheby's in 1987. A similar undated sampler, however, sold for $12,650. Such is the quirkiness of auctions.

"The borderline between great things and the merely very good keeps widening," suggested Stephen Huber after the sale, adding, "a smaller portion remains in the 'great' category as knowledge increases."

There is no question that Betty Ring's careful scholarship has been the catalyst for the thriving needlework market. Her books and articles have moved samplers from being merely decorative needlework to historically important documents of women's education in the 18th and 19th centuries. Moreover, in her writings Ring has pointed out good design and quality in the stitchery taught by the

This 18¼" x 16¼" needlework sampler, signed Prisce Gill and dated 1782, attributed to the Sarah Stivours School in Salem, Massachusetts, is one of the most important in the sale. Stivours was the first American schoolmistress to have her name on a group of samplers. Her name is not on this one, but it clearly belongs to the group. Estimated at $35,000/50,000, it sold at $79,500 to the Hubers, who bought it at Skinner's in June 1987 for $47,300 when the new owner was the underbidder. Prisce Gill stitched, "...Wrought 1782 in the 11 year of Her Age...Prisce Gill is my Name, New England is my Nation, Salam [sic] is my Dwelling Place and Christ is my Salvation." According to Betty Ring, this is the first sampler to name Salem, even though Gill spelled it incorrectly. Sotheby's photo.

This 16⅞" x 25¼" English canvaswork picture, initialed EP and dated 1746, sold for $101,500 (est. $30,000/50,000) to a New York private collector who said she was a new collector and that she bought most of Joan Stephens' library. There was plenty of bidding in the salesroom and on the phones. The Hubers were the underbidders. It was sold to Stephens by Jackie and Leonard Balish, who in 1984 sent a picture of it to a curator at the Victoria & Albert Museum in London and learned that another canvaswork picture by the same hand depicting the same family in 1738 shows nine adults and one dead child. This one shows three adults and four dead children, including twins. It is rare to find domestic embroideries that are family histories. Most canvaswork pictures copied prints. Sotheby's photo.

schoolmistresses. The accident of an example surviving in good bright condition plays a major role in determining the value of antique needlework.

Dealers who have championed needlework over the years have played an important role in driving the market to higher levels. The landmark sales, Kapnek in 1981 and Stephens in 1997, established new plateaus.

The fact that every one of the ten top lots at the Stephens auction brought more than the record $41,800 paid at the 1981 Theodore H. Kapnek sale for Matilda Filbert's 1830 sampler is a measure of the market's growth.

The top Stephens lot reached $145,500. In the years between the Kapnek sale and the Stephens sale, half a dozen samplers have sold for $100,000 or more and in January 1996 Hannah Otis's needlework picture went over $1 million.

Five samplers in the Kapnek collection sold for $20,000 or more, while 27 of Joan Stephens's topped the $20,000 mark. The 172 samplers in the Kapnek sale brought a total of $641,000; the 143 lots in the Stephens sale, which included some needlework tools, realized $1,771,397.

Editor's Note: Outsider art is a relatively new segment of the Americana market. Sotheby's single-owner sale of a collection of the work of Bill Traylor in 1997 was Sotheby's first Outsider art sale with a separate catalog. Sotheby's continues to sell Outsider art in general Americana sales with mixed results. Not until 2003 did Christie's put together a sale of works by self-taught artists with a separate catalog. M.A.D. continues to cover this segment of the Americana market at shows and auctions in various parts of the country.

BILL TRAYLOR, FOLK ART HERO

BY DOROTHY S. GELATT

A cadre of devoted Bill Traylor fans sat patiently through Sotheby's complete December 3, 1997, American paintings sale, just waiting for their pot of gold at the end of the rainbow. The holy grail was a separate catalog of 21 inspired drawings by a dirt-poor former Alabama slave, whose life spanned the years 1854 to 1947, and who at age 85 suddenly began to draw prodigiously in Montgomery, Alabama.

At the end of the Great Depression and the beginning of the Second World War, during three short years, 1939 to 1942, Bill Traylor created approximately 1,200 drawings. Maybe he made 1,600. Nobody knows for sure. At first he drew with pencil on any scrap of paper or cardboard he could find. And he might have gone on that way if a successful White Montgomery, Alabama, artist with a conscience had failed to notice him

Blue Man, Black Mule featured on the catalog cover (est. $30,000/40,000), went for $178,500 to a private American phone bidder, beating out an anxious young couple in the house. Sotheby's photo.

Man With Stick, black on gray postmarked cardboard (est. $16,000/20,000), sold to a private buyer in a tough phone battle for $107,000. Sotheby's photo.

drawing behind the funeral home, also Traylor's sleeping quarters. Charles Shannon recognized Traylor's talent and gave him paper, colors, and moral support for a kind of genius that might not otherwise have seen the light of day.

At 85, Bill Traylor began to transform the memories of his life into acute drawings of people, animals, activities, and actions, all revealed with riveting clarity, simplicity, and an insight he did not pick up at art school. Except for Charles Shannon, nobody else ever appreciated Traylor's work seriously during his lifetime. Only one more link, Joe Wilkinson, kept him from total obscurity and brought him finally to national museum notice, a national audience, and ultimately to Sotheby's.

Joe Wilkinson and his wife, Pat, now of Evanston, Illinois, took on Shannon's crusade, bought Shannon's Traylors, and finally in 1982 got Traylor exhibited at the Corcoran Gallery in Washington, D.C. Then it was on to American folk art fame. Hirschl & Adler Modern in Manhattan did a show in 1985, and there have been shows at the Dallas Museum of Fine Art, The Milwaukee Art Museum, and others, to say nothing of important catalogs, articles, and books. New York City folk art dealers Ricco and Maresca's book, *Bill Traylor: His Art—His Life,* was published in 1991 by Alfred A. Knopf.

So, 40 years after Bill Traylor's concentrated three years of unique creativity, a folk art hero was born and has flourished ever since. He's no doubt out there in eternity somewhere setting it all down on ethereal paper, even as we speak. What could he be thinking now?

The man lived on welfare through the Depression. It is known that he did sell an occasional drawing. It is also known that he once said, "Sometimes they buy them when they don't even need them." But what might he think of $178,500 (including the buyer's premium) for the top lot, pictured on the catalog cover, *Blue Man, Black Mule?* Or the sellout total of $777,700?

Now retired and thinking of moving to France, the Wilkinsons, as Shannon before them, were never able to find a museum or institution to house the Traylors, so they too decided to sell, knowing that by now there is an appreciative national audience for Traylor's rare accomplishments.

Sotheby's Nancy Druckman did them proud with exhibits and symposia in four cities, Washington, Los Angeles, Chicago, and Brooklyn, all of which were documented in the catalog, along with a fine reference bibliography. Sotheby's estimated the sale at $400,000/600,000, which skeptics pooh-poohed, but the true believers were out there with checkbooks waving, and the Wilkinsons' 21 Bill Traylor drawings, some on scraps of old gray cardboard, thundered out at $777,700.

Collectors appreciated the chance to share Traylor's heritage and rare vision and did not hesitate to reach for it. It was a short, thrilling, and very moving sale. Buyers were ecstatic. They felt they knew something nobody else knows. Private collectors, including phone bidders, got all the top lots, but a few dealers, acting more like collectors than vendors, managed to scoop up a few here and there.

New York City antiques dealer John Torson, who bought *Geometric Shape with Tree* for $11,500, spoke for everyone when he said, "I first saw Traylors about twelve years ago and I regret with all my heart that I didn't buy every one of them then. Today's auction is insane!"

Geometric Shape With Tree in gray, black, and red pencil on cardboard, with red base, black and red grid was the only actual bargain in the sale. It went to New York dealer John Torson for $11,500 (est. $12,000/16,000). Sotheby's photo.

Editor's Note: This is a story about a record price paid for a children's book, a record price, in fact, for any book printed after Shakespeare. It takes the reader to the auction room and inside the book world. Moreover, Justin Schiller, who figures prominently here, appears in stories elsewhere in this book.

ALICE IN WONDERLAND

BY DOROTHY S. GELATT

American collectors love England's *Alice's Adventures in Wonderland* at almost any price. They own 17 of the precious 23 copies known to survive from the original 1865 London first edition of Lewis Carroll's classic book, which was withdrawn before it hit the market because its powerful illustrator, *Punch* magazine's John Tenniel, didn't like the printing.

Ultimately, when Christie's landed the unique 1865 withdrawn first-edition *Alice*, the only known copy with annotations in purple ink, untrimmed pages, and ten original Tenniel drawings bound in, it was offered in New York City, *not* London. It changed hands between Americans on December 9, 1998, and went to an anonymous phone bidder. The price, $1,542,500 with buyer's premium, was a stunning auction record for a children's book or, indeed, any printed book dating after Shakespeare.

Alice still has market competition from the Declaration of Independence, a copy of which sold for $2.42 million at Sotheby's June 1991 printed Americana sale. But she is right up there now in the literary seven-figure realm, and who knows what another copy might bring should one spring to market any time soon. Most are now locked up in libraries and institutions. Only five remain in personal collections, four of them American, and one of those copies brought $800,000 in a private sale last year.

Christie's rare book specialist Francis Wahlgren credits the legendary Americana and rare book dealer A.S.W. Rosenbach of Philadelphia with introducing Lewis Carroll first editions to

American collectors in the 1920s. "The British did not have much money to spend on such things between the two world wars, and Rosenbach recognized the value of Carroll for Americans," Wahlgren said.

In 1928 Rosenbach sold the current $1.54 million copy of *Alice* for the widow of its original British owner, Louis Samuel Montagu, to American Eldridge R. Johnson, president of the Victor Talking Machine Company, for $40,000. When the Johnson estate was sold in 1946, Rosenbach bought the volume again at Parke-Bernet Galleries, paying $23,000 for its next owner, Francis Kettaneh, another American businessman. The Rosenbach Museum & Library in Philadelphia still owns the book's companion copy of *Through the Looking-Glass, and what Alice found there* in a matching binding, bought in the 1928 transaction.

In 1998, to mark the 100th anniversary of the death of Lewis Carroll, the pen name of Charles Lutwidge Dodgson (1832–1898), a mathematics lecturer at Oxford University, Wahlgren nabbed one of America's unique personal Carroll hoards for Christie's. He also designed its exquisite catalog, dubbing the 38 select lots *Lewis Carroll and Alice: The Private Collection of Justin G. Schiller.*

Book people know New Yorker Justin Schiller as a leading dealer in rare children's literature. So it was a real bonanza when his Carroll collection came up following the printed books and manuscripts sale at Christie's Park Avenue rooms. In person and by phone and order book bids, newcomers did battle with seasoned collectors,

Auction record for a post-Shakespeare literary work. Charles Lutwidge Dodgson's (a.k.a. Lewis Carroll) personal copy of *Alice's Adventures in Wonderland* (1865), first edition, withdrawn before publication because illustrator John Tenniel did not like the printing quality. It has untrimmed pages, purple ink notations, and ten original Tenniel drawings bound in by the volume's first private owner, London banker Louis Samuel Montagu, who in 1899 commissioned the original full brown levant morocco binding from Riviere & Son. Estimated at $1.5/2 million, the volume, from the Justin G. Schiller collection, sold to an anonymous American phone bidder for $1,542,500. Christie's photo.

including members of the Lewis Carroll Society of North America, which Schiller helped found in 1974. It was a rousing sale with plenty of live action even though seven of the ten top lots, including the star *Alice*, went to phone or order bids.

Thirty-three of the 38 lots (est. $1.7/2.3 million) sold for $1,914,827. Three additional lots sold after the auction, so joy radiated over everyone, including Justin Schiller, who sat impassively in the back of the room watching the dollars pile up. He did not bat an eyelash when the climactic lot 38, his 1865 untrimmed first-edition copy of *Alice's Adventures in Wonderland* with unique purple ink notations, was gaveled down at the low end of its $1.5/2 million estimate.

An extra half-million would have been nice, but it is clear from Schiller's writings and anecdotes that he still made a mint. The book originally cost him about $45,000 at a 1980 Paris auction he did not attend. So aside from expenses, taxes, and maybe a bottle of champagne, the record $1.54 million *Alice* was mostly profit. It's an unusual story.

Schiller's catalog notes, plus his privately published 1990 monograph on *Alice's Adventures in Wonderland*, reveal that as an absentee bidder on May 20, 1980, he bought the final lot, No. 125, at the auction of American businessman Francis Kettaneh's library, sold in Paris via Claude Guerin, at the Hotel Drouot. The lot contained two copies of the withdrawn 1865 first-edition *Alice* (including

Christie's rare book specialist Francis Wahlgren showing the title page and frontispiece of Lewis Carroll's annotated copy of *Alice's Adventures in Wonderland.*

Two Lewis Carroll book-collecting friends: North Carolina collector Charles Lovett (left), who bought four treasures at the auction, and New York City rare children's book dealer Justin G. Schiller (right), who sold his personal cache of Lewis Carroll material at Christie's for $1,914,827.

the only one known having untrimmed pages, purple ink notations, and ten original John Tenniel drawings bound in), a little Lewis Carroll poem, and some other small items thrown in. With Rosenbach's successor, John Fleming, bidding for him, Schiller said he paid a total of $65,000 for the lot.

The Carroll lot came at the end of an intense sale at the Hotel Drouot with many high-priced works doubling or tripling their estimates, including an auction record for a Shakespeare First Folio. Apparently, the auctioneer was tired and anxious to end the sale. He gaveled the Carroll lot instantly to Fleming, the first bidder, and left the room immediately before anybody could complain. Luckily for Schiller he was never tested at his top bid, which he said was $200,000.

Schiller kept for himself the unique *Alice* with the untrimmed pages, purple ink notations, and ten original Tenniel drawings, valuing it at $45,000, and sold the second copy, which ultimately ended up in Princeton University's Firestone Library. Wahlgren suggests that at current prices the Princeton copy with standard trim and no purple notations or original art is worth $1.2 million.

Over years of consideration and research, Schiller came to the conclusion that what he owned was the withdrawn first-edition file copy owned by Carroll's publisher, Macmillan, who made the marginal notations: purple ink lines next to type and purple circles next to Tenniel's printed illustrations. Their meaning was not clear to Schiller, but they made the volume unique. It was also known that the ten original drawings were bought later from Tenniel and bound with the pages in 1899 by the volume's first private owner, London banker Louis Samuel Montagu, second Baron Waythling.

Ultimately in 1990 Schiller set down his "file copy" conclusions in the privately published, elegant scholarly monograph *Alice's Adventures in Wonderland: An 1865 printing re-described and newly identified as the Publisher's "File Copy."* It's a beautiful illustrated book bound in a handsome facsimile of the "file copy" Montagu-commissioned binding. But as things developed recently, the "file copy" hypothesis apparently does not apply.

Somehow, the Macmillan "file copy" idea did not sit well with Christie's Francis Wahlgren. Just before his auction catalog went to press, Wahlgren suddenly sensed a clue to the real meaning of the purple notations in Schiller's own documentation. Schiller's 1990 bibliography cited a footnote to a 1956 article by William H. Bond in the *Harvard Library Bulletin*. It suggests that ". . . the purple markings by Dodgson could be in preparation for *The Nursery Alice*."

That clicked with Wahlgren, who checked it out at The Morgan Library in Manhattan and discovered that the text and pictures marked with purple ink coincide exactly with the material ultimately used by Carroll in his 1880 *The Nursery Alice*, a simplified version for very young children. In Christie's auction catalog Schiller charmingly concurs.

History also tied the purple ink not to Macmillan but to Carroll, who started using it in 1870 when Oxford made it the official ink for grading student papers. As Carroll's, not

Lewis Carroll, *The Beggar-Maid*, circa 1858, an albumen photograph of Alice Liddell in costume at age 6, originally given to Miss Mary Prickett, governess to the Liddell children. This is Carroll's best-known portrait of the original Alice, for whom *Alice's Adventures in Wonderland* was written and named. A few other copies exist, mostly in institutions. Estimated at $30,000/40,000, the print went at $63,000 to an American dealer bidding on the phone. Christie's photo.

"The Wonderland Quadrilles," Composed for the Piano-Forte, by C.H.R. Marriott (London, 1872) with illustrations after Tenniel drawings, the first *Alice* art in color; dedicated to Alice, at Carroll's suggestion when queried in 1871. Estimated at $800/1200, the sheet music sold to North Carolina collector Charles Lovett for $977.50. Christie's photo.

Macmillan's, copy, the purple ink volume now assumes a greater status and value than ever before. Such are the mysteries and joys of collecting.

The auction room's action was another kind of joy to North Carolina collector Charles Lovett. Since he started collecting Carroll in 1984, Lovett had never come to a sale in person. He used phone or order bids or had Schiller bid for him. "This time I thought I'd better come because it was a landmark sale, and there were things that might never come up again," Lovett said. "I didn't realize how important it is to be there and get the feel of the room and the live action. You just don't get that on the phone. Prices went so high in the beginning that I thought I wouldn't get anything. But later on, the bidding slowed down for the copy I wanted of *The Hunting of the Snark,* and I thought, 'I can get this,' and I did. It was personally very exciting, and I was glad to be in the room."

Schiller's copy of *The Hunting of the Snark, an Agony, in Eight Fits* was Carroll's own copy, and it cost Lovett $20,700 (est. $20,000/30,000). Although he didn't get everything he wanted, Lovett took home four rarities. Five proof copies of *Eight or Nine Wise Words about Letter-Writing* cost him $21,850 (est. $15,000/20,000). A copy of the 1872 piano sheet music "The Wonderland Quadrilles" by C.H.R. Marriott cost him $977.50. Five Tenniel drawings decorate the "Quadrilles" cover, the first *Alice* art to appear in color. It was a great find for Lovett, who already owned "The Looking-Glass Quadrilles" and "The Jabberwocky Quadrilles."

For $4,600, Lovett also bought a facsimile copy of Carroll's original handwritten manuscript of *Alice's Adventures Under Ground* (est. $5,000/7,000),

later expanded into *Alice's Adventures in Wonderland.* Lovett did not need Schiller's 1865 withdrawn first-edition copy of *Alice* because he's one of the four private Americans who already owns one.

The same anonymous phone bidder/paddle number who bought the $1.54 million *Alice* also bought three other top lots. The 1866 first-edition second-issue *Alice* (est. $15,000/20,000) cost him or her $43,700. The first-edition first-state copy of *Through the Looking-Glass,* inscribed by Carroll/Dodgson on the half-title page, cost $36,800 (est. $20,000/30,000). A first-edition copy of *The Hunting of the Snark* in its original dust jacket went at $17,250 (est. $10,000/15,000).

Besides books, reference works, catalogs, photographs, and letters, Schiller had a beguiling assortment of *Alice* souvenirs that ranged from sheet music, wallpaper, a boot scraper, and garden statuary to a circa 1950 child's *Alice in Wonderland* illustrated tin paint box. The latter, estimated at $100/200, sold in hilarious bidding for $517.50 and was proclaimed a tin paint box record by Francis Wahlgren, who was also the auctioneer.

As a final note in his Christie's auction catalog preface, Justin Schiller discussed the size of his personal 20-year collection: "I would not compete against our private clients or institutions that sought my guidance. This explains why mine is a relatively small collection, but I hope you will still find each item special or (at the least) interesting and unusual. Everything in it reminds me of Dodgson's magic and how he transforms our simple dreams into fantasy." Happily for Mr. Schiller, his $1.9 million sale was not a fantasy.

Editor's Note: The Appleton desk and bookcase is the second most expensive piece of American furniture, topped only by the Nicholas Brown desk and bookcase. No one knows who paid $8,252,500 for it. For months after its sale, it was on view at the Philadelphia Museum of Art without the ball feet Sotheby's added for its New York exhibition. Conservators and furniture scholars reportedly were trying to decide what kind of feet were missing.

WHO OWNS THE APPLETON DESK AND BOOKCASE?

BY LITA SOLIS-COHEN

The Americana discovery of the year—maybe even of the century—was Nathaniel Appleton's Newport, Rhode Island, plum pudding mahogany dome-top desk and bookcase, 1730–50, signed twice in pencil by Christopher Townsend. It has silver hardware made circa 1755 signed by Newport silversmith Samuel Casey.

Found in Paris and consigned to Sotheby's in the fall of 1998 by French descendants of the Appleton family of Boston, Massachusetts, it arrived at Sotheby's via air freight 48 hours before it was put on presale view, just a little more than a week before it was sold.

When it was upended, holes were discovered in its brackets to accommodate lost feet. New ball feet were hurriedly turned at Sotheby's restoration shop and attached by noon on Saturday, January 9, the first day of public viewing, in an effort to give it some lift and improve its proportions.

Estimated at $500,000/800,000, it brought $8,252,500 on January 17, 1999, and became the most expensive piece of furniture ever sold at Sotheby's worldwide and the second-highest price ever paid for American furniture, topped only by the John Brown Newport desk and bookcase that brought $12.1 million at Christie's in June 1989. (Christie's London sold the so-called Badminton House cabinet, a Florentine pietra dura, ebony, and ormolu cabinet for $15,178,020 in London on July 5,1990, for the all-time furniture record.)

Christopher Townsend (1701–1773) was a patriarch of the Townsend dynasty. His son, John, signed many pieces, but only one other signed piece by Christopher Townsend is known. The interior tiered drawers capped with distinctive articulated carved shells, the bird's beak profile of the partitions, the concave drawers behind the prospect drawer, and a storage space, called a well, incorporated into the writing surface are found on other Newport desks. The silver hardware, including silver ornaments in the form of birds at the ends of the pull-out supports for the lid, are unique to this piece.

According to the catalog, the desk was made for Nathaniel and Margaret Gibbs Appleton. Nathaniel was minister of the First Church in Cambridge, Massachusetts, from 1717 until his death in 1784. He graduated from Harvard in 1712, received his A.M. in 1715, was made a Doctor of Divinity in 1771, and was a member of the Harvard Corporation for over 60 years. The desk descended from Nathaniel Appleton (1693–1784) and his wife, Margaret (1699–1771); to their son Nathaniel Appleton (1731–1798); to his son John Appleton (1758–1829), American consul to Calais, France; to his son John-James Appleton (1792–1864), American diplomatic envoy to Sweden, who later settled in France; to his son Charles-Louis Appleton (1846–1935) of Lyon, France, a law professor who was born in Rennes; to his son Henri Appleton; and then by descent to the present owners. No one knows why a Boston

The Appleton desk and bookcase made in Newport, Rhode Island, 1730-50, sold for $8,252,500 to an anonymous buyer. The interior has bird-beak profiles to the plum pudding mahogany separators typical of early Newport bookcases. There is an unusual tempietto in the center, flanked by Doric columns, and the use of mahogany for the secondary wood is unusual. Sotheby's photo.

clergyman would order a secretary from Newport, Rhode Island, and there is some speculation that it may have been a gift. It certainly was a special order, and it did come down in the Appleton family.

This monumental early work by a member of the first generation of Newport cabinetmakers appealed to two very rich collectors. Bidding opened at $500,000, the low estimate. Roberta Louckx of Sotheby's bids department, in the front of the salesroom, and Bill Samaha, hiding on the very last row, competed as bidding quickly reached $6.25 million, $6.5 million, and on up to $7.25 million, Samaha's last bid. Auctioneer Bill Stahl dropped his hammer at $7.5 million saying, "It is with Roberta." The buyer's bill came to $8,252,500 with the buyer's premium (15 percent on the first $50,000

and 10 percent on any amount in excess of $50,000).

Who was the buyer? Everyone wanted to know. Was it Tony Wang sitting on the front row with Leigh Keno, who had signaled bids to Louckx at the Meyer sale? Keno denied his clients bought it and "anonymous" was the word Sotheby's used when announcing the sale.

The Appleton secretary was not the only good story of the week. The other was the rediscovery in a San Francisco consignment shop of a figured mahogany serpentine front marble-top table made in Boston, Massachusetts, 1755–75. It is the very one that sold at the Joynt sale at Christie's in January 1990 for $187,000. It was sent to a thrift shop by a decorator who was making a clean sweep for a client whose taste had changed and it was bought

for a few thousand dollars by an astute dealer who recognized its quality, even though it had a crack in its marble top. Estimated at $150,000/250,000, it sold for an astonishing $882,500 to Albert Sack of Israel Sack, Inc., bidding from the first row, underbid in the salesroom by collector Peter Brant of Brant Publications, owner of *The Magazine Antiques* sitting behind him.

Sotheby's various-owners furniture session on Sunday afternoon accounted for $16,053,750 of Sotheby's $20,929,970 total. The bull market for fine Americana raged on.

The Chipstone Museum in Milwaukee bought this 1740-60 Philadelphia bonnet-top chest-on-chest of figured mahogany with original openwork cast brass hardware, 7'10" tall x 41½" wide, with a shell- and leaf-carved drawer in the upper section and urn- and leaf-carved finals. It had been purchased about 1972 in Bronxville, New York, by New York dealer George Subkoff and sold to the consignor. It sold for $266,500 (est. $50,000/80,000) on the phone to Alan Miller bidding for the museum. "It has real feet, real brass, and real tobacco leaf finials and was not made for a Quaker," said Miller. The cores of the drawers are not the same wood as the veneer, and Quakers had a religious need to have the core and veneer of the same species. It was considered false vanity if they did not. This piece has mahogany veneer on white cedar. Miller said Chipstone has Philadelphia case furniture from the 1750's, 1760's, and 1770's. Now they have a piece from the 1740's and can show the whole progression. Moreover, last year Chipstone acquired a Charleston, South Carolina, chest-on-chest at an English furniture sale at Sotheby's New York that has the same brasses. "This piece gives the museum a lot of traction from a storytelling point of view," Miller added. Sotheby's photo.

The brown- and green-painted Philadelphia Windsor table, third quarter 18th century, illustrated in Charles Santore's *The Windsor Style in America, 1730-1830,* had sold at the Moore sale at Sotheby Parke Bernet in 1977 for $4,250 to George Samaha. According to the catalog, it has since been owned by David Pottinger and Marguerite Riordan. Estimated at $25,000/50,000, it fetched $101,500 in a battle between two private collectors. It holds the record for a Windsor table, and it held the record before in this record-sensitive market. Sotheby's photo.

Editor's Note: In hindsight, January 1999 was another market peak. While record prices were paid and there was no shortage of consignments, careful scrutiny shows there was some hesitancy among bidders; momentum seemed to be slowing down. The buy-in rate—that is, the number of lots that did not meet reserves, the confidential minimum price agreed upon by the seller and the auctioneer to consummate a sale—was significantly higher than in the previous season. The market was becoming more selective, even though new records continued to be made for exceptional objects as the economy faltered; the middle market stalled, and then moved lower.

PEACEABLE KINGDOM, CHRISTIE'S 1999

BY LITA SOLIS-COHEN

The record $4,732,500 (including buyer's premium) paid for an Edward Hicks *Peaceable Kingdom*, the $1,432,500 spent for Hicks's nostalgic painting of the *Residence of David Twining, 1785*, plus the $1,212,500 bid for a Newport, Rhode Island, three-shell chest of drawers pushed Christie's total for its various-owners sale, held January 15 and 16, 1999, to a hefty $11,668,148.

Add to that the $6,880,815 spent for the collection of the late Mr. and Mrs. James Britton of Houston, swelled by $1,542,500 for the Eyre family Philadelphia piecrust tea table, and $2,779,088 for the collection of New York folk art dealer and collector John Gordon, and the total for Christie's 1999 January Americana Week sales came to $21,327,051, a record for any series of Americana sales.

That same week, Sotheby's sold $20,929,970 worth of silver, prints, china, folk art, and furniture, and strong sales of American furniture and folk art were reported by dealers at the New York Winter Antiques Show. It made the market for Americana seem as healthy as it was a year ago when the total sales were just slightly lower.

The new benchmark for the January sales, $41 million, does not include the China trade sales, or sales at Christie's East, and Sotheby's Arcade, all of which were held in January.

Close scrutiny of the sales, however, shows that the market is definitely two-tiered. The top tier is driven by works of high aesthetic merit in good condition, while pieces with flaws in design or with considerable restoration lag well behind. "The middle market was soft today," said New York City dealer Albert Sack, doyen of American furniture dealers, as he left Christie's salesroom on Saturday afternoon, January 16, having bid successfully on major lots. "Good things were strong because we have educated buyers today."

The Hicks paintings, which sold on Friday, established new records for the artist and for folk painting. *The Residence of David Twining, 1785,* one of four versions of a farm scene recalling the artist's childhood spent on that farm, sold on the phone and broke the previous record for a Hicks painting, $1.21 million paid at Sotheby's in 1991 for one of Hicks's 63 versions of his favorite subject, the *Peaceable Kingdom*, inspired by the book of Isaiah.

Then the record for any folk painting was broken again when the hammer dropped on the next lot, Hicks's 1837 *Peaceable Kingdom*. New York City American paintings dealer Richard York, seated on the right side of the salesroom, paid $4,732,500, twice the estimate, for the so-called middle-period *Peaceable Kingdom* filled with a panoply of animals. Scholars believe Hicks used the *Peaceable Kingdom* theme to comment on the schism between Orthodox Quakers and the Hicksites, followers of Quaker preacher Elias Hicks, Edward Hicks's cousin.

Mahogany block-and-shell carved chest of drawers, signed, probably by Job Townsend II (1726-1778), Newport, Rhode Island, 32" high x 35¼" wide. A faint chalk signature on the bottom appears to read Job Townsend, who, according to the catalog, may have made it in collaboration with another member of the Townsend-Goddard group of cabinetmakers. The chest was made for the Bartlett family and purchased in 1921 for $550 by Alfred Barmore Maclay, a collector, horse breeder, and horticulturist. It stood in Maclay's 84th Street New York City townhouse and had remained in his family ever since. It sold for $1,212,500 to a phone bidder, underbid by Baltimore dealer Milly McGehee. Christie's photo.

Edward Hicks, *Peaceable Kingdom*, a so-called middle-period Kingdom painted between 1835 and 1837, oil on canvas, 29½" x 35¾" inches. It is full of optimism. The lion and the ox share their straw. The leopard and the kid, the wolf and the lamb, and the cow and the bear lie down together. The child with an olive branch stands by the lioness to lead them. Hicks's message of peace appears in the figure of Liberty in the lower left and in Penn's making a treaty with the Indians in the background. "Drawing from the gamut of biblical, historical, and contemporary themes and engraved sources...Hicks was at a zenith of his powers..." when he painted this *Peaceable Kingdom*, suggests Susan Kleckner, who wrote the catalog entry. It surpassed its $1.5/2 million estimate to sell for $4,732,500 to New York City American paintings dealer Richard York, underbid by Massachusetts and Ohio dealer Bill Samaha. When this same work sold at a Samuel T. Freeman auction on April 22, 1980, for $210,000 to art collector Robert S. Lee, Sr., it was the most expensive painting ever auctioned in Philadelphia. The oil painting was consigned to Christie's by the Lee estate. Christie's photo.

The painting came from the estate of Philadelphia car dealer and art collector Robert Lee, who bought it for $210,000 at a Samuel T. Freeman auction in April 1980, when it was the most expensive painting ever sold in Philadelphia. According to Caroline Weekley, whose book on Hicks will be published in February in conjunction with the opening of an Edward Hicks exhibition at the Abby Aldrich Rockefeller Folk Art Museum in Williamsburg, Virginia, Mrs. Rockefeller paid $325 for her similar *Peaceable Kingdom* back in 1932.

At the beginning of Friday's session a restless audience in the salesroom waited while auctioneer Barbara Strongin sold 90 lots of silver and Christie's chairman Christopher Burge plodded through 20 lots of prints before reaching Plate

CCCCXXXI, *The American Flamingo.* This fine copy of Havell's aquatint after John James Audubon's watercolor for *Birds of America* sold on the phone for an impressive $151,000, more than twice its high estimate. People began to take notice.

By then, auction watchers, collectors, and dealers had filled the room, and the Hicks farm scene came on the block. Bidding opened at $300,000 for *The Residence of David Twining, 1785,* with the major competitors on two phones. It was knocked down to a phone bidder said to be a Pennsylvania collector who paid $1.43 million.

There was even more bidding in the salesroom for the *Peaceable Kingdom.* The major competitors were Richard York in the front and Massachusetts and Ohio dealer Bill Samaha, the underbidder, in the back. Asked if he had bought the picture for a museum or a collector, York said he could not say. He has been paying record prices of late for masterpieces of American painting, and word on the street is that he is putting together an important collection for a private client.

All else in this Friday morning sale paled before these major lots. Connecticut dealers Stephen and Carol Huber, bidding against a phone bidder, were able to buy an American needlework coat of arms for $12,650, which they thought a very fair price. It had been cataloged as an English hatchment, which it is not, and estimated at $6,000/8,000.

Most of a large collection of miniature portraits on ivory sold below estimates with only a few lots eliciting real competition. One tiny 18th-century miniature by Joseph Dunkerly (active 1784–87) sold to a New Hampshire dealer for $8,625. A portrait of a baby, the reverse engraved J.M. Hardy, was cataloged as by Joseph Whiting Stock, but according to two dealers in the salesroom, it was the work of Mrs. Moses P. Russell. Nevertheless, it surpassed its $6,000 high estimate to bring $7,475. A collector in the salesroom paid $7,475 for a hairwork bracelet with a miniature of a woman cataloged as by Matthew Pratt and signed MP.

The work of John Wood Dodge was embraced. A sweet postmortem portrait of young Mary Eliza Washington with a paper inscription, "Painted by John W. Dodge (after death) Nashville Ten. april 25th 1842," fetched $3,220 (est. $4,000/6,000). Bidding for a client, New York City dealer Elle Shushan paid $4,370 for a pair of portraits of a U.S. officer and his wife by Nathaniel Rodgers (1788–1844), probably painted in New York City. A phone bidder bought the self-portrait of Aramenta Dianthe Vail, sold together with a portrait of her son, signed "A.D. Vail artist, 4 49 Broadway," for $10,350.

After John James Audubon, *The American Flamingo,* Plate CCC-CXXXI, engraving and aquatint with hand coloring on J. Whatman paper dated 1838, small tear along top edge, but in otherwise good condition, framed, $151,000 (est. $50,000/70,000). Christie's photo.

The Cabot-Perkins family blockfront chest-on-chest, 1780-1800, attributed to Benjamin Frothingham, Jr. (1724-1809), Charlestown, Massachusetts, 86½" high x 43½" wide, sold to Israel Sack, Inc. for $244,500 and seemed to be a good buy. The underbidder was Washington, D.C., dealer Guy Bush. This high-style Boston chest-on-chest with its elaborate carved shell and pilasters and blocked lower section embodies the restrained elegance of late 18th-century Boston. The shell appears to be identical to one on a labeled Frothingham chest-on-chest and like the shells on other pieces of Boston furniture. Christie's photo.

There was bidding on three phones and in the salesroom for this silver quart cann by Paul Revere with an acanthus grip and the Phillips family crest. It brought $51,750. The Phillips crest is that generally used by Samuel and John Phillips, founders of the academies at Exeter, New Hampshire, and Andover, Massachusetts. At Christie's Eddy Nicholson sale in June 1992, it sold for $40,700. A similar cann sold for $38,500 at Christie's Joynt auction in January 1990, indicating that the work of Paul Revere continues to hold its value. Christie's photo.

The collection, identified in the catalog as the Chieffo collection, reportedly came from a Maryland collector who had been collecting for a long time and had been working with the legendary dealer E. Grosvenor Paine on his book on miniatures, not yet published. It was surprising to hear dealers complain about misattributions in the auction catalog, saying that none of the Peale family attributions were correct and that the Malbone was an English miniature. Novice collectors apparently need guidance by the few dealers in the field.

The January 16 afternoon session of the various-owners sale was far more spirited. Christie's had opened the salesroom to its full capacity for the Britton collection in the morning, and nearly every seat was taken in the afternoon as well.

It was business as usual for the first 25 lots. Only a few regional pieces sparked much interest, including an early Long Island, New York, slant-top maple desk with bun feet, 1710–30, that soared to $19,550 (est. $5,000/8,000).

The sale climaxed when the three-shell Newport, Rhode Island, chest came on the block. It was probably made by Job Townsend II, as his signature could be seen in raking light on the bottom drawer. A phone bidder battled Baltimore dealer Milly McGehee. Sack was out at $950,000, McGehee at $1,050,000, and auctioneer John Hays knocked it down to a phone bidder for $1,100,000, which came to $1,212,500 with buyer's premium.

Not every piece of Newport furniture brings a very big price. An adjustable walnut kettle stand (est. $50,000/80,000) failed to sell—there was no interest at all—and a single carved mahogany side chair, identical to four others labeled by John Townsend, brought $7,475.

The same is true of furniture from other cabinetmaking centers. Major case pieces and chairs with good proportions and fine carving continue to fetch far more than they did a decade ago, while plain-Janes and those with repairs or repainting sell at a different level. A Philadelphia mahogany chest-on-chest was similar to the grand Loockerman chest-on-chest in the Britton collection that brought $882,500, but this one had some minor losses to the feet and to the brilliantly carved finial. It sold for $662,500 to Sack, underbid by the buyer of the Loockerman chest-on-chest.

A graceful Boston hairy paw foot side chair, 1760-80, similar to one at the Museum of Fine Arts, Boston, and very much like English examples, went at $244,500 (est. $30,000/50,000) to Washington, D.C., dealer Guy Bush, underbid by Baltimore dealer Milly McGehee. It had an old dark finish that made it look like cast bronze. Christie's photo. Detail, Pennington photo.

Editor's Note: In the 1990s, major on-site sales became rare occurrences. Pook & Pook, Downingtown, Pennsylvania, auctioneers, produced the farm sale of all time for the family of the late collector Bill Koch. On a gorgeous June day in 1999, the right people with money in their jeans found their way to Turbotville, a crossroads near Danville in rural Pennsylvania, and proved again that good material can bring all it's worth anywhere when the word gets out. The Koch sale brought nearly $4.3 million for 386 lots, scored some records, and is remembered as a landmark in auction history.

THE FARM SALE OF ALL TIME: THE KOCH SALE

BY Lita Solis-Cohen

A record for an American folk art watercolor, a record for a Pennsylvania German fraktur, and a record for a farm sale was made June 5, 1999, at Long Square Farm in Turbotville, Pennsylvania, when the collection of the late H. William Koch was sold by Pook & Pook, Downingtown, Pennsylvania, auctioneers, on a picture-perfect day in a picture-perfect setting.

The folk art watercolor record now stands at $687,500 (includes buyer's premium), paid by a Pennsylvania collector for a Jacob Maentel family portrait of a husband, his wife, and their child, identified on the back as "Mr. and Mrs. Samuel Ensminger taken at Manheim 1831."

Samuel Ensminger is depicted standing at his desk, and his wife is seated in a bow-back Windsor chair under a tree surveying their farm, their baby on her lap. Maentel mounted them together on gray painted paper, 17" x 21", that served as a mat within the original frame. There was plenty of competition in the salesroom up to $150,000, and then the bidding was between the buyer and a phone bidder until the hammer fell at $625,000, and the crowd in the tent applauded.

Sue Koch, Bill's widow, said her husband bought the Maentel privately years ago on a visit to a friend of hers in Manheim, Lancaster County, her hometown. "I had told him Sylvia had a lot of old things, so we went down to see her and bought the Maentel," she said after watching the sale from her front porch.

The record watercolor was nearly five times the previous record paid for a pair of portraits by the German-born Maentel who painted in York, Lancaster, and Lebanon Counties before moving west in 1841 to New Harmony, Indiana, where he died in 1863.

At Sotheby's in January 1987, a record $143,000 was paid for two circa 1830 Maentel portraits, each one framed, of Louisa and John Hamm in their parlor in Lititz.

The previous record for a folk art watercolor was $374,000, paid at Christie's, June 3, 1989, for a schoolgirl watercolor on silk depicting Aurora, the goddess, in a chariot hovering over a New England town.

The record for fraktur was broken twice at this sale. First when the 1814 homespun-covered copybook of Johannes Whisler, Mifflin Township, Cumberland County, sold for $198,000. It has seven full-page frakturs, two full-page folk art drawings, 14 smaller drawings, and 164 illuminated page headings,

Bill Koch had bought the copybook just two years before he died when Horst Auctions sold it at its 1988 Memorial Day sale at the Farmersville Fire Hall in Lancaster County. He paid $67,600 for it, outbidding the Winterthur Museum. "He kept the big book in the bottom drawer of the schrank

Jacob Maentel's watercolor of Mr. and Mrs. Samuel Ensminger and their baby, painted at Manheim in 1831, sold for a record $687,500 (est. $100,000/150,000) to a Pennsylvania collector at the sale. The price was nearly five times the previous record for a Maentel at auction or retail. The previous record for a folk art watercolor was $374,000, paid at Christie's on June 3, 1989, for *Aurora*, a schoolgirl watercolor on silk. Pook & Pook photo.

in our bedroom and rarely took it out to show someone," said Sue Koch.

The buyer of the copybook, on the phone, was number 68. Kellie Seltzer, administrator at Pook & Pook, said the buyer was a private collector, not a museum.

Because there were many frakturs in the copybook, the record for a single fraktur is $181,500 paid for a birth certificate by Haines Township, Centre County, artist Daniel Otto (active 1792–1822). Decorated with a big heart, tulips, two parrots, and a dog-faced alligator, it

was made for the birth of Georg Weber and dated October 22, 1794. There was plenty of competition for it, and it was knocked down to Baltimore dealer Milly McGehee, underbid on the phone.

The price topped the previous record for a fraktur, $145,000, paid by a collector on May 11, 1991, at Horst's auction in Ephrata for a birth certificate by Karl E. Munch, dated September 8, 1805, and decorated with four vignettes depicting the four seasons.

It is hard to predict what these high prices will mean. Collectors bid until they got what they wanted. A few dealers bought for stock, paying a premium. Other dealers bought little unless they had strong bids from clients in their pockets.

Bill Koch would have loved it. His younger son Fred, who orchestrated the sale as he had done for two other sales of his father's collection held at Horst Auctions in Ephrata in the nine years since his father's death, said he wanted to sell the core of the collection at a farm sale like the sales

his father used to attend every weekend.

Bill Koch would have been astounded and pleased to learn that the 386 lots brought a total of $4,299,289, certainly a record for a farm sale, and a record for any single-owner sale in Pennsylvania. Because it was an estate sale, no Pennsylvania state taxes were charged.

Swelling the total were three paintings by Charles C. Hofman, the German-born Berks

Fraktur by Daniel Otto (active 1792–1822), Haines Township, Centre County, Pennsylvania, made for Georg Weber, dated October 1794, and decorated with a heart, two tulips, two birds, and a dog-faced alligator. It sold for a record $181,500 (est. $50,000/70,000) to Baltimore dealer Milly McGehee. That record stood until April 24, 2004, when Westborough, Massachusetts, dealer David Wheatcroft paid $366,750 at Freeman's, Philadelphia, for a verse from a *Hymn to the Nightingale*, an ink and watercolor Pennsylvania-German fraktur signed and dated "Gr. Geistweit, 5 June 1801." The Reverend George Geistweite (1761–1831), who painted it, lived in Centre County, Pennsylvania, from 1792 to 1804.

County almshouse painter. They brought a total of $715,000. In 1879 Hofman painted the three pictures on tin for John B. Knorr, an undertaker, cabinetmaker, and clerk of the Berks County Almshouse. One shows Knorr's house, one shows his church, and one shows the whole town of Wernersville. The picture of the house, where these pictures were found in the attic, sold for $253,000 to Clarence Prickett, the Yardley, Pennsylvania, dealer who was bidding at the side of the tent.

The picture labeled Hain's Church depicts Hofman as a hobo smoking a pipe on the left near the crossroads sign. It was knocked down to Prickett for the same price.

The largest picture of the town, labeled Wernersville, sold for $209,000 to Westborough,

The pair of Mahantongo Valley painted and stenciled chests of drawers that Bill Koch bought at Sotheby's in New York City in 1970 for $4000 will not stay together. A local collector, underbid by Patrick Bell of Olde Hope Antiques, bought the one (shown) made for Julien Drion, dated 1829, for $220,000. Pat Bell won the chest made for Pali Drion for $192,500. Both were estimated at $100,000/150,000. Pook & Pook photo.

Massachusetts, dealer David Wheatcroft on his cell phone with a client. Wheatcroft was the underbidder on the other two, and thought he got a bargain on his favorite one.

A 30-day clock by Solomon Gorgas in a folk art case decorated with a tin appliqued tulip and shell in relief sold for $121,000 to the collector in the salesroom who was the biggest buyer at the sale. He said he had grown up in Lancaster County and bought only at auction. He asked that his name not be printed.

The same collector paid $143,000 for a circa 1770 Philadelphia dressing table, outbidding Philip Bradley, saying he heard the dressing table had a long history of ownership in Lancaster County. He paid the same price for a Chester County, Pennsylvania, spice cabinet with compass work, herringbone, and line and berry inlay on its door. A Berks County dower chest painted with lions and unicorns on a blue ground was his for $60,500 (est. $18,000/22,000), and he paid $19,800 (est. $5,000/7,000) for a carved and painted parrot attributed to Wilhelm Schimmel. A three-piece miniature Leeds tea service with a teapot, a covered sugar, and a creamer was his for $2,750. In all, he spent more than $1 million.

Many lots brought far more than estimated. A cutwork valentine sold for $38,500 (est. $6,000/8,000); a carved and painted pine rooster store display fetched $35,200 (est. $4,000/6,000); a miniature toy cradle painted with scenes and a red house realized $22,000 (est. $2,000/2,500); a swing-handled basket sold for $1,760 (est. $400/600); and a child's pitchfork went at $770 (est. $200/300).

More than 600 people were seated in the tent or standing outside it. Three phone lines accommodated bidders who did not attend, and there were some absentee bids left with the auctioneer, which generally were not successful. From time to time cell phones rang for agents in the salesroom, and the geese honked, but the auctioneer's singsong patter continued unbroken from 10:05 AM until 4:30 PM, and most people attending remained in their

Ron Pook shows off Johannes Whisler's copybook, bought as a blank volume in Carlisle in 1814. The schoolmaster and fraktur artist drew, made samples of forms he used in his scrivener's work, copied texts and lessons he used for teaching, and noted cures for common ailments in the book. It has seven full-page frakturs, two full-page folk art drawings, 14 small folk art drawings, and 164 illuminated page headings. It sold for $198,000 (est. $50,000/75,000), almost three times the $67,600 Koch paid for it in May 1988. Pook & Pook photos.

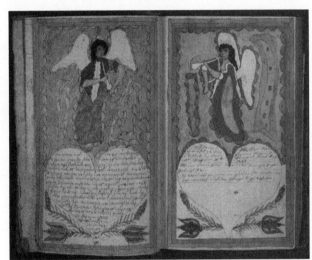

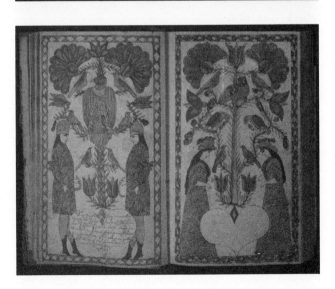

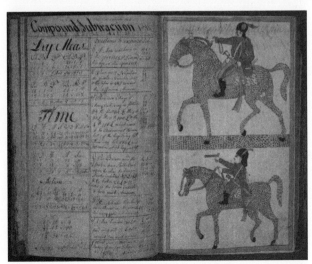

Charles C. Hofman oil painting on tin titled *My Home*, depicting the house and barns of John B. Knorr with a horse and buggy chased by a dog, signed on the lower right, "Sept. 4th 1879 from the north side, Ch. Hofman." The painting measures 16" x 24" and was not in the original frame. It was exhibited at the Abby Aldrich Rockefeller Folk Art Center in Williamsburg in 1968. Estimated at $70,000/90,000, it sold for $253,000 to Yardley, Pennsylvania, dealer Clarence Prickett. Pook & Pook photo.

seats or milled around the tent acting as if they didn't want this perfect sale to end.

The Koch family was appreciative of the response and invited everyone attending the sale to a pig and chicken roast on the front lawn immediately afterward. About half of the 600 or more that attended stayed for a final tribute to a great collector whose eye and tireless search for the best examples of Pennsylvania country set a standard.

In Pennsylvania, farm sales are a rite of passage, a final celebration of a life that the family shares with friends and neighbors. The Koch family shared their celebration of Bill Koch's life with all those who knew him or simply admired

him and heard about his legendary appetite for good country things.

Analyzing the sale afterwards, dealers wondered what would happen in the marketplace now that a Maentel brought nearly $700,000. What does this price do to the value of other Maentel portraits? If a dealer is called to appraise a Maentel of that quality, is it worth $700,000? That old adage, one price is a record, two is a trend, and three is a market, will probably prevail. The fraktur market was very strong at this sale, but prices are generally a third higher at on-site sales, and dealers probably will not be able to raise their prices much.

The Whisler copybook was expensive, but unique and of great historic and aesthetic value. The Daniel Otto fraktur with the alligator was expensive but a one-of-a-kind masterpiece, but other fraktur also seemed to bring exceptional prices, far more than similar examples now in the marketplace. That's why dealers seemed shell-shocked as they left the sale. They forgot that they had been at a local sale where local people pay a premium for local things. These people do not leave their neighborhood and spend that kind of money elsewhere. That was the purpose of holding a farm sale. That is the magic of an on-site auction.

Charles Hofman oil painting on tin titled *Hain's Church* depicting the artist Charles Hofman in the lower right as a hobo. Knorr and his wife are strolling down the lane. When he depicted himself, Hofman did not sign his works. In its original frame, it sold for $253,000 (est. $70,000/90,000) to Clarence Prickett. Pook & Pook photo.

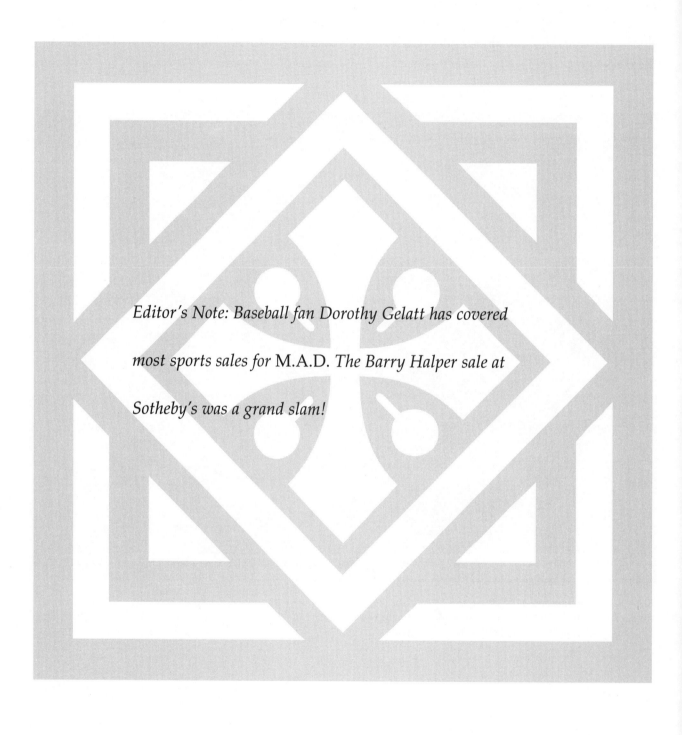

Editor's Note: Baseball fan Dorothy Gelatt has covered most sports sales for M.A.D. *The Barry Halper sale at Sotheby's was a grand slam!*

THE HALPER SALE, A GRAND SLAM

BY DOROTHY S. GELATT

If You Sell It, They Will Come

Baseball fan supreme Barry Halper has lived the ultimate collector's dream. Over a 50-year span he amassed a monumental trove of baseball memorabilia from the dawn of the game in 1839 to the dawn of the new millennium. When his private New Jersey home museum could hold no more, he sold the whole enchilada, 2481 lots in 16 sessions, at Sotheby's on September 23–29, 1999, for a cool $21,812,577!

Halper also had the sublime, powerful pleasure of watching the amazing sellout auction himself while ensconced with his nearest and dearest in one of the big comfortable skyboxes above the major new salesroom in Sotheby's enlarged New York City building. It was the best of all possible worlds—total success awash in champagne.

The $21.8 million figure doesn't begin to tell the whole story. The Baseball Hall of Fame in Cooperstown, New York, got first pick of the collection before it went on the block, yielding Mr. Halper another goodly chunk of funds, whispered to be also in the millions. The next time you're in Cooperstown you can drool over the treasures, sporting and historical, in a replica of Halper's museum created by the Hall of Fame.

But wait! That's not all. If you are a baseball fan or a 19th-century Americana collector who could kick yourself for missing the sale, you've still got another chance. Sotheby's has saved about 5,500 lower-priced lots, which are starting to appear on its new Internet auction site (www.sothebys.amazon.com). Click-click, and it's yours.

Except for the big crowded opening night of Sotheby's live Halper auctions, much of the sale might as well have been on line. Order and phone bids carried a good part of the auctions, especially in the daytime. The sales were roughly chronological, and while the big, big six-figure prices dominated the news, there were ample lots in the low and mid-thousands and even a rare sprinkling of buys in the low hundreds.

At a thrifty $287.50 (including buyer's premium) an order bidder got an empty red cardboard Reggie Jackson candy bar box inscribed by the Yankees superstar in black Sharpie ink: "My Best to Barry. The greatest collector in the world! 8/20/83 Reggie Jackson." At this low price the box did not rate a catalog photo.

Triumphant collector Barry Halper shares the excitement in his skybox with his wife Sharon (right) and her sister Marlene Rose (left) after the terrific $2,073,763 opening night sale, beating the $1.3 million high estimate.

Preview exhibitions. Left: gallery with some of the 800 baseball uniforms displayed on symbolic bleachers. Center: skybox view of a gallery laid out like a baseball diamond. A mound of turf holds old arcade baseball games. Right: walls with thousands of baseball cards displayed in sets, looking like giant patchwork quilts.

Lou Gehrig's last glove, used in his final game, April 30, 1939, went to a phone bidder at an incredible baseball glove auction record $387,500 (est. $35,000/50,000).

Ty Cobb's 1928 autographed Philadelphia Athletics jersey (est. $50,000/100,000), the only one known to exist, brought a thrilling $332,500 from dealer Dave Bushing buying for the Upper Deck trading card company. Upper Deck also bought Lou Gehrig's 1927 signed road jersey for $305,000 and will use both star items for promotion.

The opening lot, an 1868 Muller & Deacon bronze baseball figurine (est. $6,000/8,000), drew applause from the crowd, signaling the success ahead. One of the earliest and highly prized baseball statues, it went to an order bidder at a hefty $12,650.

An elegant and nostalgic 1860 full-color sheet music cover, "Live Oak Polka," sold for $25,300, its top estimate. One of the earliest and most beautiful baseball music covers, it shows players on a field swagged with the red, white, and blue American flag. The music, composed by J.H. Kalbfleisch, is "Respectfully Dedicated to the Live Oak B.B.C., Rochester, N.Y," which must have made the club proud.

Everything connected with baseball that you ever dreamed of turned up in the Halper sale: great historic balls, bats, gloves, uniforms, shoes, hats, equipment, cards, photos, player contracts, letters, autographs, games, arcade machines, toys, and every kind of ephemera, statue, pin, ring, scorecard, magazine, ad, poster, and cigar box—from every era, every team. It was all there, in depth.

The two-volume slipcased Halper catalog, an instant collectible and reference source, contains visions of the whole history of baseball, and the stunning presale exhibition of its contents was a thrill for collectors. One staggering gallery with over 800 historic uniforms in stylized bleachers boggled the collectible mind. Visitors reacted as if they were on a baseball pilgrimage throughout the elegant bi-level historic exhibit.

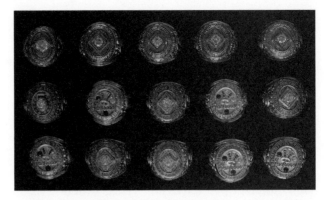

Yankees owner Del Webb's 1947-1964 World Series and American League Championship Yankees ring collection (est. $100,000/200,000). The 15 rings spanning two spectacular Yankee decades were obtained by Halper directly from Mrs. Del Webb and includes her letter of authenticity. The collection sold for $310,500. Sotheby's photo.

St. Louis Stars leather traveling case from the 1930's and 1940's, when Negro League teams barnstormed the country in beat-up old buses. Straps tied the case to the back of the bus like a spare tire. Painted with a baseball player on a gold star, the prominent team's case went at $3,162.50 (est. $1,500/2,500).

The caliber and quality of the material made all of it highly attractive to buyers, who could resist nothing. Collectors who often pass up valuable 19th-century items in favor of the more familiar 20th-century material reached for everything this time, and they paid over estimate for 85 percent of the sale. By the end of the auctions there were two major collector/dealer points of view. Some griped it was all "hype," others claimed the sale automatically repriced inventories into the stratosphere.

Barry Halper, a lifelong devout New York Yankees fan, still owns a small piece of the team itself. His collection was heavy in Yankees memorabilia, reflecting his love and admiration for his favorite club and all it has accomplished over the years.

"Live Oak Polka," one of the earliest and most beautiful pieces of baseball sheet music. The 1860 music cover, "Respectfully Dedicated to the Live Oak B.B.C., Rochester, N.Y.," shows a full-color field and players topped with an American flag. It went to a collector at $25,300, the high estimate. Sotheby's photo.

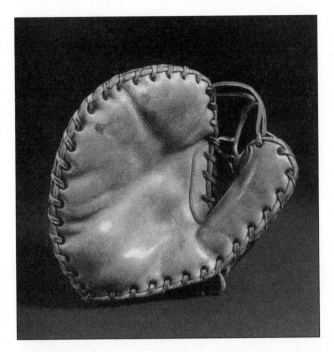

Lou Gehrig's last glove, the Spalding first baseman's mitt used by the New York Yankees legendary star in his final game, April 30, 1939. Estimated at $35,000/50,000, it sold to a phone bidder for $387,500, the sale's top lot and a monumental baseball glove auction record. Sotheby's photo.

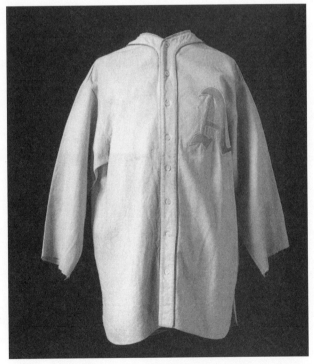

Lou Gehrig Yankees road jersey used in the 1927 and 1928 World Series, the peak of the star's career. With faded blue felt Yankees lettering on the gray flannel shirt and "Gehrig H.L." stitched in the collar next to the A.G. Spalding & Bros. label, it doubled the $150,000 high estimate, selling for $305,000 to the Upper Deck trading card company. Sotheby's photo.

Ty Cobb's 1928 final player season Philadelphia Athletics home jersey, his only signed shirt known to exist (est. $50,000/100,000). It sold for a colossal $332,500 to the Upper Deck trading card company, which will use it for promotion. Sotheby's photo.

Editor's Note: Jackson Parker has chronicled the decoy

market for M.A.D. *since 1976, explaining the fine points*

of connoisseurship and identifying all the players. The

McCleery sale was so important to collectors of decoys that

a book was published about the sale. Titled The McCleery

Auction, *it was edited by Ronald J. Gard and Robert Shaw*

and privately published in 2001 by Lake Emma Press,

Dallas, Texas. Jackson Parker's long analytical article, which

appeared in M.A.D. *in April 2000, was reproduced in full*

in the book with Parker's careful analysis of the top 50 lots.

This abbreviated version of his long review gives an idea of

the excitement of this sale and its importance.

MCCLEERY DECOYS THE BEST OF THE BEST

BY JACKSON PARKER

In the 36 years of waterfowl decoy auctions since auctioneer Richard Bourne first tested the market in 1965, there has never been a decoy auction as big as that of the considerable collection of Dr. James M. McCleery of Texas, jointly run by Sotheby's and Guyette & Schmidt in New York City on the weekend of January 22 and 23, 2000. Although the sale was conservatively estimated at $5/6 million, it made just under $11 million. For the record, 612 lots sold for $10,965,930. Subtracting 49 lots unrelated to waterfowl, which included baskets, rugs, fish decoys, traps, eel spears, etc., 563 lots sold for $10,817,746, an unbelievable average of $19,214 per decoy lot.

The McCleery auction gross is four times that of the highest decoy auction gross to date, the $2,708,825 brought by the Hillman collection in 1996, and one-and-a-half times higher than the best decoy YEAR (1986, which grossed $7,166,938.) Before the McCleery auction, the record for a decoy at auction was $335,500, paid by a folk art collector for a running curlew at a Guyette-Schmidt auction in Ogunquit, Maine, in July 1997. This record was broken by not one but by four lots at the McCleery auction, with the top lot, the Crowell preening Canada goose, selling for $684,500 (includes buyer's premium), more than double the previous record. In all the years before the McCleery auction, 16 decoy lots had sold for over $100,000 each. At the McCleery auction 16 lots sold for six figures each. There were 62 new auction records for decoy makers. In the past ten years, there have never been more than 40 in one entire year.

What made this collection so great that it caused what some called a bloodbath and others, a feeding frenzy? It was Jim McCleery's astute analysis of what made a decoy a classic and his willingness to pay top dollar to add it to his collection. At Richard Bourne's sales in Hyannis in the early 1970s, McCleery in his wheelchair followed the bidding, and, smiling, snapped up the Dilleys when most collectors didn't know what the hell they were. He understood value and took the market where no bidder had gone before. Jim was the pacemaker. Even in later years when he could no longer attend the auctions and bid by phone, his presence was felt in the auction room when the bidding would go way past the estimate, and the insiders would lip-sync "McCleery" to each other. When a decoy would enter his collection, it automatically had the McCleery seal of approval, and that's why the decoy auction market took a quantum leap upward that memorable weekend of the McCleery sale.

Contributing to the McCleery mystique were two publications, *Call to the Sky* and the Sotheby's/ Guyette & Schmidt auction catalog. *Call to the Sky: The Decoy Collection of James M.*

Canada goose by Elmer Crowell, circa 1917, sold for $684,500, a record for a decoy, topping $335,500 paid for a sickle-billed curlew by an unknown maker bought by a collector of folk sculpture at a Guyette and Schmidt decoy auction on July 25 and 26, 1997. Sotheby's and Guyette & Schmidt photo.

McCleery, M.D. covers the best of the collection, assembled for public exhibit for the first time at the Houston Museum of Natural Science from September 17, 1992, to January 10, 1993. This small book had a big impact because of the excellent photographs and the expert analysis of Bob Shaw, who wrote the introduction and catalog that put everything in perspective and whetted the collecting appetite of the reader. The auction catalog was impressive, not just for the design or having all the objects in color, but for the provenance, tracing the ownership history of the decoys. Picturing the Crowell preening Canada goose on the cover of both publications certainly helped it achieve its record price.

The auction's top lot at $684,500, more than double the previous record for any decoy, was the splendid circa 1917 preening Canada goose by

A. Elmer Crowell (1862–1952) of East Harwich on Cape Cod, Massachusetts. It turned up at Skinner's fall 1983 Americana auction where it was bought for $48,400 by auctioneer Richard Oliver and sold by him to Jim McCleery for a reputed $75,000. At the McCleery sale it was bought for a California collection by Stephen O'Brien Jr., who outbid, would you believe, Richard Oliver.

When Jim McCleery bought the ruddy turnstone by Lothrop Holmes (1824–1899) of Kingston, Massachusetts, out of the Bourne 1986 auction of the Starr collection for $67,000, it became the highest-priced shorebird at auction until it was topped by a Bowman lowhead curlew at $90,500 in 1994. At the McCleery sale once again it was in first place for a shorebird, having been sold for $470,000, the second-highest price ever paid for a decoy at auction.

When Jim McCleery bought the Bowman long-billed curlew from the Bourne auction of the Mackey collection in 1973, it shook up the market because that was the first time a decoy had sold for five figures. Old-timers moaned, "He'll never get it back!" At the McCleery sale it sold to a New Jersey collector for $464,500, the third-highest price ever paid for a decoy at auction.

Another Bowman that scored high was the nestled lesser yellowlegs that went to a Texas collector at $244,500. It is the same bird that sold at Doyle's fall 1981 auction for $25,300, the first time a decoy passed the $25,000 mark.

There was one decoy in the Mackey collection that never came to the 1973-4 auctions, and Jim

lusted after that bird. It was the ultimate Mason factory decoy, the Premier-grade wood duck that he finally bought from the Mackey family, reportedly for $350,000, shortly before he died. It sold here for $354,500, the fourth-highest price ever paid for a decoy at auction.

At the preview, two Canada geese were displayed side by side on the same pedestal—the Crowell preener and the so-called mortised goose—signifying parity in the minds of the auctioneers. Among the cognoscenti, the mortised goose was the better of the two. There are three such geese; two were offered at a Christie's auction some years ago with McCleery buying one for $13,500 and the other going to a Connecticut

This late 19th-century ruddy turnstone by Lothrop Holmes of Kingston, Massachusetts, brought $470,000, a new auction record for this maker. Sotheby's and Guyette & Schmidt photo.

This wood duck by the Mason Decoy Factory (1896-1924) of Detroit is their Premier grade, and it made $354,500, a new auction record for a Mason decoy. Sotheby's and Guyette & Schmidt photo.

collector at $11,000. When McCleery's was offered, many thought it would fetch more than the Crowell but that didn't happen. It went for $233,500 to a discerning Louisianan collector. Was it confusion about its origin? Found near the Susquehanna River, it was later determined to be a Massachusetts bird on the basis of its construction.

This auction was full of surprises. Gary Guyette admitted the first surprise was that there was that much money out there for decoys. The second was the crowd in attendance, as big as the biggest Sotheby's auctions for other popular categories. Although there were 704 registered bidders in the auction room plus 228 phone bidders and absentee bidders, there were only 145 successful bidders, but some were dealers buying for more than one client. Nancy Druckman said there were folk art collectors and collectors of Impressionist paintings bidding as well. Trouble was, they were often wiped out by the more knowledgeable decoy people. One art collector came to the preview and left absentee bids at the high estimate for a number of decoys and got nothing. Another surprise was the return to the market of the heavy hitters who had bought nothing for years. The seminar that preceded the auction was over-subscribed. The print order of 11,000 catalogs is gone.

The fear was that if collectors die or drop out and no new collectors are added, decoy values will drop, and investments will go down the drain. Well, the McCleery auction brought back collectors who had dropped out and showed every sign of making the folk art people aware and interested in decoys. Only time will tell if the decoy market holds or folds or rises again.

Found in the Susquehanna River area and thought to be by a Massachusetts carver because of its mortised neck construction, this hollow-carved Canada goose of the late 19th century sold for $233,500. A large crosspiece on the bottom of the decoy with a hole drilled in the center allowed the hunter to use the goose either as a floater or a stick up for field shooting. Sotheby's and Guyette & Schmidt photo.

The late 19th-century long-billed curlew by William Bowman of Lawrence, Long Island, New York, went at $464,500, a new auction record for this maker. Sotheby's and Guyette & Schmidt photo.

Editor's Note: When the Americana marketplace made its annual move to New Hampshire in August 2000, Ron Bourgeault's Northeast Auctions offered the private collection of Virginia Cave, a well-known collector and part-time dealer who bought wisely and well. The sale celebrated game boards and hooked rugs as graphic art. The record prices paid defined the top of the market, and this sale showed that, contrary to conventional wisdom, a dealer/collector does not have to be dead to cash in.

SUMMER SPORT: THE CAVE SALE

BY DAVID HEWETT

Once Friday, August 4, 2000, rolled around, it didn't take a genius to predict that the Northeast Auctions sale of the Americana and folk art collection of Virginia Ramsey-Pope Cave was going to be a smashing success. The Northeast crew had barely finished mounting the collection within the brick walls of the armory at the Center of New Hampshire Holiday Inn in Manchester when the early previewers descended on the place.

It was a phenomenal turnout. "We sometimes only get fifty or fewer people who come on Friday," Northeast veteran Bob Croall said. "The regular preview is on Saturday, and that's when the crowds show up, but this is just plain amazing. Everybody wants a seat. We're going to be overwhelmed."

He was right. When the sale began at 3 PM on August 5, there were over 500 people in the armory. Extra seats had to be fitted into narrowed aisles, and there still weren't enough. The standees filled the sides and lined the back walls.

What was the appeal of the Virginia Ramsey-Pope Cave collection? Was it the quality of the collection, the coincidence of demand and supply, the timing, the connection with the Museum of American Folk Art in New York, or something else? The answer is that it was all of the above.

Virginia Ramsey-Pope Cave collects with passion, she has an eye for color and form, and she could afford to indulge her passion, although she professes otherwise.

"The thing about folk art for me is its great emotional appeal," Cave said before the sale. "I never could afford to collect the great folk art

paintings, the Ammi Phillipses and John Brewsters, but I could afford the greatest rugs and boards, and that's what I bought.

"I live in New York City now, and I walk past the galleries where great pieces of modern art hang, Jackson Pollock and others, but none of it sings to me. The pieces I collected sang to me."

Cave pursued her chosen objects with determination. Another passionate collector/dealer,

The carved and painted cane was made by "Schtockschnitzler" Simmons and sold at Christie's sale of the collection of Mr. and Mrs. Paul Flack on September 16, 1997, for $12,650. Here, it brought $24,150.

The Pennsylvania fireboard is 33½" square and is a rarity. Only three Pennsylvania fireboards have been recorded. Ex-David Schorsch, it sold to a phone bidder for $255,500. The painted box in the foreground is ex-Lipman collection and brought $19,550.

Milly McGehee, spoke about one piece that Cave successfully wooed away from her. "I spotted a great early sewn rug at the Philadelphia show and bought it from Don Walters," McGehee said. "He'd bought it at the New Hampshire dealers show and had put it away for Philadelphia. It was just great, and I knew I had to have it from the first second I saw it. I was going down the aisle with it when Virginia ran after me. She asked if it was for sale, and I told her I'd have to think about it. She then asked for right of first refusal."

Virginia Cave remembered the incident well. "Oh God, yes," she said. "I sweated bullets for the next forty-five minutes until Milly decided to sell it to me."

Virginia Cave dealt from her home in Vermont for many years, beginning in the early 1970s, and she collected during all of her dealing years. She has been an active participant in the folk art scene

almost up to the present. So why sell now?

"I've sold the Vermont house. My children are too young to inherit [the collection], I didn't want to put it into storage, and I don't want to give it away. When Ron saw it, he said, 'I want it all for a one-owner sale,' and I agreed.

"Ron Bourgeault said he wanted it all, and he wasn't kidding. He said, 'No skimming. It all has to go,' and we ended up agreeing that I could keep four pieces, pieces with personal attachments, that was all. As far as my children went, Ron said they each could bid on one piece, but one piece only."

Selling the collection would also help one of Cave's favorite projects, the new library at the Museum of American Folk Art in New York City. Virginia Cave pledged 10 percent of the proceeds of the sale to that institution. (Ron Bourgeault also generously supported the museum. Two days

The painted game board with American flags is 12½" x 21" and was sold in January 1997 by Sotheby's as part of an Art Institute of Chicago consignment. It brought $25,300 then; it brought $46,000 here.

This unusual hooked rug is supposedly made from strips of old flags. It measures 54" x 50½" and was once owned by Boston dealer Stephen Score, who bought it again for a collector for $46,000. The highest previous price for a hooked rug was $74,000 for a room-size (11'7" x 11'5") example at Sotheby's in 1997. The buyer of that rug was Virginia Cave.

This chenille shirred rug, approximately 42" in diameter, was the favorite of many and sold to dealer Barbara Pollack for $25,300. She'll keep it in her collection for a while but admitted it may be for sale eventually.

after the sale he announced he'd donated $30,000 from the sale of catalogs to the library fund.)

One consideration mentioned in the days before the sale was its freshness to the market. Could the auction of a collection assembled by someone who not only was still living (it's an auction axiom that only the collections of deceased collectors do well) but who had bought some of the pieces in the collection as late as two years ago be successful?

The answer was given by the $2.45 million gross, the result of purchases made from a wide spectrum of collectors and dealers. Many of the trustees of the Museum of American Folk Art were present, as were collectors from across America.

The veteran dealers were amazed at the strength of the sale. "I think this is a turning point in the business," Barbara Pollack said. "When folk art can bring this kind of money in New England, it proves you don't have to be dead, and you don't have to sell it in New York to have a successful sale."

Dealers bought heavily, but in many cases their purchases were on behalf of collectors. Auctioneer Willis Henry, with a cell phone clamped to one ear, was a force during the early part of the sale. Henry bought several game boards, including the first lot offered, a painted Parcheesi board with drawer, for $36,800 (including buyer's premium).

Milly McGehee got several lots for clients, including another of the better Parcheesi boards for $20,700. Barbara Pollack bought a superb shirred chenille rug with a basket of flowers at the center of concentric circles for $25,300. "I've always loved that rug," Pollack said. "To me, it's a painting."

The big-bucks lots were led by a Pennsylvania fireboard painting on three panels that featured a house and landscape with trees. Pennsylvania overmantels and fireboards are rare. (Although Northeast cataloged the piece as an overmantel, dealer David Schorsch, who had owned it previously, said it was definitely a fireboard.) Only three are known.

This example, which carried a $40,000/60,000 estimate, sold to a phone bidder for $255,500.

This Goddess of Liberty weathervane is a J.W. Fiske of New York City product and is only 24" high overall. Virginia Cave had bought it from dealer David Schorsch. It brought $145,500 here. "She did very well with the pieces she bought from me," David Schorsch said after the sale.

This 16" square two-sided board with a drawer went to auctioneer Willis Henry bidding with a phone to his ear for $36,800. Northeast Auctions photo.

A green-painted Windsor side chair from Lancaster County, Pennsylvania, which had brought $32,200 at the Christie's sale of the Scott collection in 1994, went to a telephone bidder here at $96,000. A rare pair of miniature painted whirligigs, featuring male and female figures, ex-Ben Mildwoff and Barry Cohen collections, sold to David Schorsch, bidding by phone, for $90,500.

Some had predicted failure for lot 157, a rare 24" high J.W. Fiske copper weathervane of the Goddess of Liberty, which the rumor mill said Cave had bought for between $100,000 and $125,000. The naysayers said she'd be lucky to get half her investment back. They were dead wrong; it sold to a left bid of $145,500. And, to make up for the short profit spread on the weathervane, the very next lot, a Boston Federal giltwood mirror that also featured Lady Liberty, this time on an eglomisé panel, soared to $33,350. Virginia Cave paid $4,125 for it at a Northeast Auctions sale in August 1992.

Some thought that 47 game boards and an equal number of hooked rugs might be a tad too many for one auction to swallow. They were wrong too.

There is one point about the Cave sale worth considering. Its greatest appeal may have come from the fact that it was a collection. It was shown at preview displayed as a collection, with stuffed animals stacked on cabinet shelves, rabbit motif rugs mounted on panels that held five to eight other rabbit rugs, a Parcheesi game board hanging with four other Parcheesi game boards. The pieces sold individually, for the most part.

The value of a collection sometimes lies in its integration. The whole assemblage gains a personality and becomes a valued work of art in its own right. That's what Virginia Ramsey-Pope Cave created in Dorset, Vermont. That's what Ron Bourgeault re-created in the catalog and at Manchester, New Hampshire.

The Cave collection sale gave new collectors an opportunity to pick from the top in the search for material for their collections. It'll take time and huge amounts of money to equal the Cave collection, but it can be done.

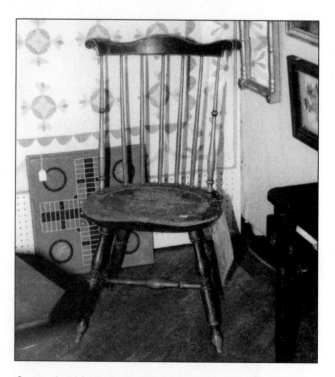

Green-painted fan-back Windsor side chair from Lancaster County, Pennsylvania. It's pretty nearly a perfect example of its type and brought $32,200 at Christie's Scott sale in Lancaster, Pennsylvania, on June 10 and 11, 1994. At least five dealers in the hall wanted it, but it went to a phone bidder for $96,000.

One's a male, one's a female, and they're only 10½" high. Miniature whirligigs are rare; a female whirligig is rare; and pairs of whirligigs are rarer still. That rarity factor added up to $90,500, paid by phone bidder dealer David Schorsch. Northeast Auctions photo.

Editor's Note: When a collection is billed as the finest in any category, M.A.D. covers it. The sales held at Doyle, New York City, to disperse the collections of Dennis Masellis—the 40-year-old payroll manager jailed for embezzling at least $7 million from Baker & McKenzie, the huge international law firm—offered the finest collection of costume jewelry ever assembled. It included Bakelite bracelets and brooches as well as costume jewelry made in France, Germany, Vienna, and the U.S. There were also purses, hats, beaded flowers, and Barbie dolls, all the best of their kind. Scholars hoped the collection would be sold to museums, but the law firm wanted its money back quickly and so it went to auction. Dealers and collectors from the U.S. and Europe competed for it with gusto. Although the prices were far less than Masellis had paid for it at retail, the sale breathed life into the costume jewelry trade, an already thriving corner of the marketplace.

THE EMBEZZLER'S BAKELITE:
THE MASELLIS SALES

BY LITA SOLIS-COHEN

On Sunday, October 29, 2000, Barbara Webb got in her van in Mentor, Ohio, drove to the Cleveland airport, picked up a friend from Chicago, then drove to Pittsburgh, picked up two more women, and went on to New Jersey and picked up one more. They all headed for New York City where they checked into a very large suite at the San Carlos Hotel and met up with three more women whose passion and obsession is Bakelite.

These eight women had not known each other very long, having met on the Internet or at a Bakelite table at the outdoor shows in Brimfield, Massachusetts. They chose a hotel near 87th Street because they needed to be at William Doyle Galleries, the auctioneers, early on Monday morning to spend the day looking over the Bakelite in a landmark sale of costume jewelry offered on November 1 and 2. After spending all day Monday previewing the sale and Tuesday figuring out who was going to bid on what, they went to the sale on Wednesday. "We've been talking about the auction since we heard about it six weeks ago," said Webb at the preview.

The collection for sale had belonged to Dennis Masellis, who, the week before the sale, was sentenced to three to nine years in prison for embezzling at least $7 million from Baker &

McKenzie, the huge law firm that has 2,700 lawyers in 61 offices around the world. Masellis, 40, was manager of the payroll unit in the firm's New York City office where he created fictitious employees and then directed their salaries be deposited directly into his bank account. According to court records, he also arranged for the computer to deduct a negative amount of money from his paycheck, a maneuver that had the effect of adding that much instead. The firm learned of his scam when it changed accounting systems last year.

Held by Barbara Webb, this group of six Bakelite dot and gumdrop bracelets of varying sizes sold for $14,950. She didn't get the lot but was the sad underbidder.

This group of red and yellow Bakelite bracelets, three with heavy carving, sold for $14,950. They might have brought more if sold separately.

Over the last decade Masellis spent his fortune on the finest costume jewelry on the market. "If Dennis wanted it, he bought it. He wanted the best and wanted it now," said a dealer who asked to remain anonymous. Masellis also bought Bes-Ben hats and pocketbooks of all sorts, including a large selection of bejeweled bags by Judith Leiber, the Faberge of couture. He also collected head vases, picture frames, beaded flowers, Barbie dolls, and Christmas ornaments.

All but the Christmas ornaments came to Doyle's for sale after Masellis was charged and confessed. There was no trial. Baker & McKenzie was the consignor. To disperse the entire collection will take two or three more sales. The law firm may get $7 million back.

Many at the sale said they had known Masellis, describing him as a fixture at the Triple Pier Shows in New York City and hard to miss. He weighed 450 pounds and dressed in brightly colored shirts, beautifully tailored with Bakelite buttons. He bought from every dealer in the business and was their favorite customer. The dealers admired his taste, and several took credit for educating him, teaching him the fine points. They offered him their best, and he bought it, aiming to buy the finest example of every designer.

The auction at Doyle's combined the Masellis collections with couture from various owners, and it brought the largest crowd ever to Doyle's semiannual sale of costumes and textiles. Collectors and dealers came from all over America and from abroad. Several bidders were bidding for museums, and a major film star was on the phone both days. The sale total came to nearly $1.9 million, the Masellis collections responsible for the majority of it.

Doyle's won't give exact figures, and in fact it would not confirm the source of the consignment, but all the dealers and many of the collectors at the preview and the sale knew the Masellis story. Dealers pointed out what they had sold him or were looking for it. Doyle's will sell the next installment on May 2 and 3, 2001, and the Barbie dolls, said to be the most complete collection known with many prototypes, will be sold in July 2001.

Some prices were stunning. The most startling were paid for American, French, and Italian designer costume jewelry, Bakelite jewelry, and a few pieces by important artists. A brass collar necklace, attributed to Alexander Calder and estimated at $800/1,200, sold for $31,050 (including buyer's premium), and a circa 1910 Wiener Werkstätte cuff bracelet attributed to Josef Hoffmann (est. $700/900) sold for $29,900. Seven of the top ten lots, and 11 of the top 20, were made of Bakelite.

A group of three Bakelite gumdrop and bow tie bracelets fetched $19,550. A lot of six Bakelite dot and gumdrop bracelets sold for $14,950; a group of four gumdrop and bow tie bracelets brought the same price. Three more gumdrop and bow tie bracelets went for $13,800, and four bow tie bracelets sold together for $8,675.

A group of four two-tone red and yellow Bakelite bracelets, three deeply carved, was considered a good buy at $14,950. A group of three hinged Bakelite bracelets, each with an insect motif, sold to a Westchester County, New York, collector for $9,200. Had the bracelets been sold individually, they might have brought more. A secondary market for them began at the back of the salesroom before the auction was over.

A single love letter Bakelite brooch, depicting a fountain pen suspending a heart and three love letters, went at $10,350. Dealer Dan Ripley of Indianapolis said Masellis paid $5,500 for it at an auction he organized for Treadway/Toomey in Chicago a couple of years ago. A group of three patriotic red, white, and blue brooches, one with the words "Win the War," sold for $9,775, and a Bakelite brooch in the form of a penguin with a rotating arm fetched $6,325.

"This is a good supply of high-quality jewelry with reserves that encourage bidders. It's a once-in-a-lifetime opportunity for collectors, and for dealers as well," said Dan Ripley, who was a major buyer at the sale.

"There was so much Bakelite, we thought we could get some great buys, but we couldn't," said

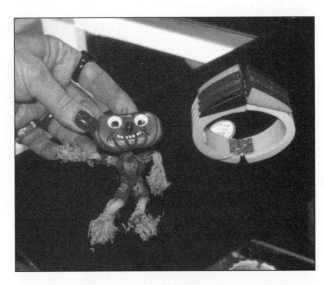

Dennis Masellis bought this Bakelite and wood googly-eye Pumpkin Man brooch for $21,000 at a 1998 Treadway/Toomey auction in Chicago. It sold at Doyle's for $8,625 to Chicago collector Sally Loeb. The so-called "Philadelphia" bracelet, a 1¾" wide Bakelite hinged five-color bracelet in cream with black, orange, green, red, and yellow raised wedges, sold for $4,312.50. Masellis reportedly paid a Philadelphia dealer $9,000 for it.

Teresa Paolucci models the unsigned brass collar attributed to Alexander Calder (est. $800/1,200). It sold for $31,050, a vote of confidence that it really was a Calder.

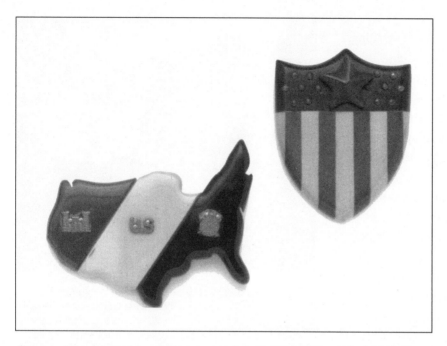

The Bakelite pin with a log suspending a tomato, carrot, potato, radish, and three leaves went at $5,175 to Illinois folk art dealer Barbara Pollack, bidding on the phone. "This is the finest vegetable pin I have ever seen. Each vegetable is twice the size of most of the others. There is great in every period," she said. "It's exciting. It's folk art of the twentieth century." Doyle photo.

This red, white, and blue lot, a shield and a map (est. $1,000/1,500) sold for $4,312.50 to Highland Park, Illinois, dealer Barbara Pollack on the phone. "I had never seen these before." she said. "I had to have them." Doyle photo.

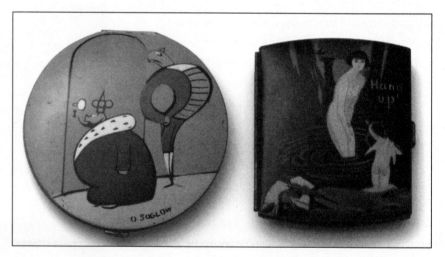

Bakelite pivoting brooch depicting a football player, $5,750 (est. $800/1,200). Doyle photo.

A comical compact and cigarette case of painted enamel were sold together as one lot for $11,500 (est. $200/225). The compact with The Little King looking through a keyhole on one side and a lady powdering her nose on the other was signed O. Soglow, the cartoonist responsible for The Little King. The cigarette case depicts a nude in a pond seen by a cupid. Doyle photo.

Barbara Webb after the sale. "We've analyzed it and discussed it, and we believe that only seven to ten percent of the total were really good buys. I watched several people spend fifty thousand dollars or more at the sale, and I got nothing."

Many complained about the size of the lots. Collectors wanted one bracelet, not four or six. Linda Donahue, who has built the couture department at Doyle's over the last 14 years, said she tried to give bidders a choice with some big lots and some individual pieces. She had just six weeks from the moment the collection was consigned to catalog it, arrange the exhibition, and bring it to auction. Each lot was pictured on Doyle's Web site, which brought forth a slew of telephone bidders. Not every piece was illustrated in the catalog.

The eight Bakelite collectors have made their hotel reservations and are saving their pennies for the next installment in May 2001. Donahue is well aware of the intensity of this market and the fact that no other collection can hold a candle to the glamour of this one. The scandal adds interest.

"Even when Dan Ripley auctioned his parents' collection of Bakelite at Treadway/Toomey in Chicago in a series of sales in 1998 and 1999, it didn't have the excitement of this one," said Barbara Webb. "It was at a Treadway/Toomey auction that Masellis paid twenty-one thousand dollars for the Pumpkin Man, still the record price for Bakelite."

At Doyle's, that Pumpkin Man was bought by Chicago collector Sally Loeb for $8,625. "I had no intention of buying it," said Loeb after the sale, "but when I didn't get anything else, I raised my hand." She said another Pumpkin Man with some damage had sold on eBay last year for $10,000, but she knows of only these two. Masellis bought that one too. It is missing an eye and may come up at a future Doyle's auction. Ripley said the underbidder at $20,000 at his sale is no longer in the market.

Ironically, among the more reasonably priced pieces of Bakelite was a convict pin. The figure with a ball and chain is dressed in yellow and black stripes and holds a hammer. It sold for $1,265, much

less than Masellis reportedly paid for it.

The buyer of the much hyped "Philadelphia" bracelet, who paid $4,312.50, said she had no thought of buying it until her husband told her to raise her hand, it was going cheap. Gael Mendelsohn, a Westchester County, New York,

Opulent 1920's English Art Deco paste necklace with a large emerald green cut stone and rhinestone bar and ring chain, in box labeled "Fortnum & Mason/ London," $6,612.50 (est. $600/700).

collector, said the "Philadelphia" bracelet is the cornerstone of every serious Bakelite collection, and all the major collectors have one. The five-color hinged bracelet with black, red, brown, green, and yellow geometric wedges attached to yellow plastic has sold for as much as $17,600 at a Treadway/Toomey auction. "Ehammer got more than six thousand dollars for one just a few weeks ago," said Mendelsohn.

The "Philadelphia" bracelet got its name in 1984 when the two from Barbara Strand's and Daniel Toepfer's Bakelite collection, offered for sale at Ben Gold's 20th Century Design Gallery in Philadelphia, sold for the then whopping high prices of $250 and $275. Barbara Strand, a New York dealer, said people fought over them. When Andrea DiNoto did a cover story for *Connoisseur* magazine a few months later, she dubbed them "Philadelphia bracelets," and the name stuck. Collectors say that article turned Bakelite from a funky avant-garde collectible to a hot ticket for the New Age.

"Bakelite is a fickle market. The fashion now is for random dots and bow ties. The market moves in waves," said Matthew Burkholz, who wrote a book on Bakelite.

If Doyle's auction is any indication, the wave for all costume jewelry is cresting. Blackamoor pins are hot items. A group of ten, some of 14k gold and including one by Hattie Carnegie, sold for $8,625. Another large lot consisting of ten Boucher pearl and enamel brooches in the form of exotic birds, a praying mantis, and plants, estimated at $250/350, sold for $8,050. A group of four Trifari crystal belly pins (known as jelly bellies), a sailfish, a snail, a peacock head, and a frog, sold for $7,475.

French costume jewelry made for name designers drew competitive bidding. A late 1950s Gripoix collarette necklace for Christian Dior, made of pavé rhinestones with blue, green, and pearl beaded flowers, marked France, sold for $4,312.50 to West Hollywood, California, dealer Maria Domont, who offered it for sale at the Modernism show a week later. A circa 1937

Chanel Star necklace of gilt metal with star chain pendants, marked "Made in France" and illustrated in *Jewels of Fantasy* (Abrams, 1992), brought $4,312.50, as did an early Chanel Gripoix dangling vine necklace of turquoise suspended from faux coral beads and rhinestone rondels.

The bejeweled small evening bags by Judith Leiber brought less than they cost new at Bergdorf and Saks. Price tags and, in one case, a Masellis sales slip, remained inside. One decorated with a 70th anniversary cover from *The New Yorker* sold for $3,450. A fantastic dragon with its $3,465 price tag inside went at $2,300, and a foo dog sold for $3,162.50. A ladybug and a penguin were purchased for $1,610 each.

Katherine Bauman bags in the shape of Cinderella, Betty Boop, and a Coke bottle brought less. Cinderella sold for $920, and the other two sold for $632.50 each. One in the shape of a baseball sold for $575, while a bejeweled *Titanic*, a limited edition of 25, went at $2,587.50.

The estimates were low and the bidders persistent, thus slowing the pace of the auction, which dragged on until nearly 7 p.m. Wednesday evening. The last seven lots, bunches of beaded flowers, ranged in price from $460 to $1,092.50.

"Everyone wants the best. Whether it is Impressionist paintings or important jewelry, the best always does far and away better than anyone expects," said an exhausted Linda Donahue after the sale. "That's what happened here. What was so powerful about this sale was that the buyers not only understood that great costume jewelry is made like fine jewelry with the finest craftsmanship, but they enjoyed its sense of humor and color. It becomes bigger than life."

The effects of the sale could be seen at the Modernism show at the Armory and at the Pier shows the following weeks. Dealers who bought at Doyle's found a ready market for their purchases at a profit, and if they had similar pieces in stock, they could cite the catalog and clinch a sale.

This lot of ten Trifari enameled figural pins (est. $600/800) sold for $3,450. Doyle photo.

Editor's Note: Covert and Gertrude Hegarty put together a peerless collection of vintage toys. The story of its dispersal at Sotheby's in a landmark sale demonstrates how children's playthings brought joy just a month after the 9/11 disasters, when dedicated toy-lovers ignored the limping stock market and national problems and pursued their passion.

THE JOYS OF TOYS: THE HEGARTY TOY SALE

BY DOROTHY S. GELATT

"I've been waiting thirty-seven years for this sale," a contented toy lover announced. And he had company. The entire opening night crowd agreed at Sotheby's handsome preview party for the legendary Covert and Gertrude Hegarty collection of antique toys.

Not scared off by the September 11 World Trade Center attack, devoted antique toy lovers all over the country got right back on airplanes and flew to New York City for Sotheby's historic toy sale on October 12, 2001.

They came to pay homage to Covert and Gertrude Hegarty, a legendary pair of pioneering American antique toy collectors, and to take home as much of the landmark collection as they could snatch from the competition.

Bidders fought over toys from all the classic makers: Ives; Kenton; Gong Bell Mfg.; Wilkins; J. & E. Stevens; Kyser & Rex; Pratt & Letchworth; Welker and Crosby; N.N. Hill Brass Co.; Althof, Bergmann & Co.; Carpenter; Weeden; Jones & Bixler; the great Hubley cast-iron toys; and many others.

Well before the American antique toy field developed its own magnificent collector books and reference works, the Hegartys scouted out early manufacturers' sales catalogs and ads to authenticate their toys. They even bought Currier & Ives 19th-century lithographs picturing the early fire equipment that toys were modeled on.

Sotheby's antique toy specialist Eric Alberta chose the Hubley cast-iron clockwork circa 1932 "Say it with Flowers" Indian three-wheel key-wound cycle van in luscious turquoise paint with gold, black, and flower trim as his absolute favorite, though when pressed he admitted to a lot of other favorites too. Estimated at $20,000/25,000, it went in a jump-bid battle to a well-known "anonymous" collector at $126,750–an auction record for a cast-iron automotive toy.

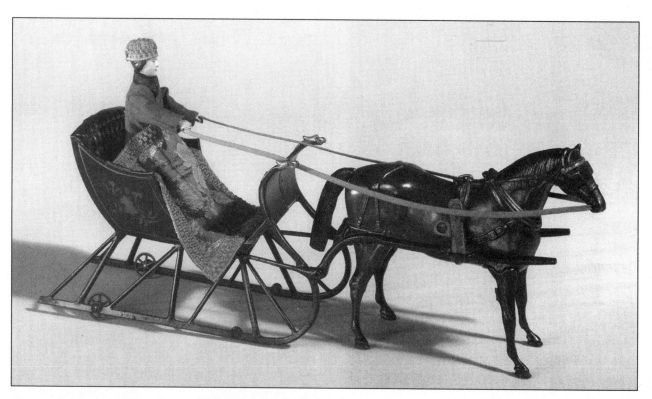

The pride of the auction was an Ives circa 1893 cast-iron cutter sleigh pulled by an articulated horse and driven by the original figure, all in magnificent condition, in rich dark paint with gold and red detail. Estimated at $20,000/30,000, it went in a four-way battle near the end of the sale to a private collector at the top-lot $159,750, with appreciative applause from the audience. Sotheby's photo.

Very rare Hubley cast-iron Penn Yan speedboat pull toy, circa 1938, in royal blue paint with gold trim and raised lettering, outboard motor with nickel trim, and three passengers in white. It has a Johnson Seahorse 10 engine decal and original Hubley decal. The toy was modeled after an actual Penn Yan boat, possibly without the company's permission. Hubley made very few, and there is no information on the toy. Estimated at $15,000/20,000, it sold for $55,375 to another "anonymous" collector in the room. Sotheby's photo.

The Pratt & Letchworth cast-iron flying artillery with caisson, circa 1895, is in dark green with red trim and soldiers in dress blue. It has four horses—a white, a tan, a black, and a brown. Estimated at $20,000/25,000, it brought $65,150 from collector Jerry Lauren, design head for his brother Ralph Lauren. "Sure, I get design ideas from everything I collect," Jerry Lauren said. Sotheby's photo.

Francis, Field and Francis hand-painted American tin omnibus, circa 1860. A favorite of Sotheby's specialist Eric Alberta, it is decorated with multicolored flowers and vines and has embossed window and roof swags. The enchanting tin omnibus has two interior bench seats, a team of two golden-mane white horses, and a driver in a red jacket atop the blue roof. Estimated at $20,000/30,000, it went to another "anonymous" collector on the floor at $43,300. Sotheby's photo.

Collectors grabbed up the paper as well as the toys listed in Sotheby's handsome catalog, which immediately joined the ranks of historic references.

Determined toy fans left Sotheby's $1 million high estimate in the dust and did not stop until they piled up a glorious $2,192,365 total. Overjoyed buyers took home all of the 300 wonderful toys but two. (Sale prices include Sotheby's buyer's premium. Estimates do not.)

It was an extraordinary auction that bucked major national problems, including a weak economy and a limping stock market, as well as the World Trade Center destruction. Most of the top lots went to private collectors who begged anonymity. They enjoyed being photographed at the preview, but they bowed out the next day when it came to dollars-and-cents public disclosure.

Privacy seems to be a personal issue with many in this uneasy season, but not for the well-known "toy twin" dealers, Steven and Leon Weiss of Gemini Antiques, Bridgehampton, New York. Waving paddles constantly, the astute Gemini dealers bought about one third of the entire catalog.

Talk about fresh to the market! Most of the toys had never been outside of the Hegartys' home since Covert Hegarty first succumbed to their charm starting in the 1940s. A special trove of cast-iron truck samples discovered by Mr. Hegarty half a century ago in a Dent factory storeroom had never been played with at all. In precious mint condition with the original Dent factory "sample" tags still attached, they were toys that tugged at the heartstrings and blew open wallets.

Sotheby's antique toy specialist Eric Alberta said the quality and beauty of the toys left him breathless. He reported that savvy collectors came to the auction house weeks early, just to get an advance look at the rarities. These days, besides dedicated toy collectors, there are also the Americana and folk art lovers, who consider early toys a part of their own historic and artistic bailiwick. Antique toys have a lot more major friends these days than when Covert and Gertrude Hegarty started collecting over half a century ago.

Concentrating especially on American cast-iron and tin toys from the 1860s to 1930s, the Hegarty collection was rich in early horse-drawn wheeled toys of every type and size, from farm wagons, delivery wagons, and early fire engines to city and country carriages, omnibuses, and sightseeing conveyances.

Imaginative painted tin and cast-iron action pull toys, push toys, and bell toys of late Victorian vintage inspired paddle holders to bid up and up for performing clowns, acrobats, elephants, dogs, horses, flowers, boats, and patriotic soldiers parading with the American flag.

Early pre-electric toy trains in brightly painted tin or cast iron lured armchair engineers. Clockwork automata, such as the rare circa 1877 Ives General Grant smoker that blows real smoke rings, a washerwoman that washes, a banjo player that plays, and a woman working her churn inspired bidders with their naive charm and their superb condition.

From the very beginning, the Hegarty collection was constantly culled and traded up, both for subject and for condition. From his collecting start in the 1940s until he died in 1968, Covert Hegarty, a Pennsylvania auto dealer, progressed from 19th-century cast-iron banks through marbles, cap pistols, early cast iron and tin, and the automata to his great cast-iron trucks of the 1930s, which were among the most coveted of the sale's top lots.

The Hegarty bank collection was sold a number of years ago, but Gertrude Hegarty, who added occasionally to the toy collection, kept the complete toy trove intact in their Pennsylvania home until she decided to move in 2001. Both she and her husband were 1966 charter members of the Antique Toy Collectors of America, and both were forever gracious hosts to interested collectors. Bob Shepard, the consultant to Sotheby's who

Althof, Bergmann & Co. patent chime with soldiers and flag bell toy, circa 1875. The windup American clockwork tin bell toy with marching soldiers, waving flag, and chiming bell was made in time for the country's 1876 centennial. Estimated at a modest $5,000/6,000, it rang up a handsome $41,000, bid by an agent for a collector on the floor. Sotheby's photo.

Pratt & Letchworth cast-iron four-seat brake, circa 1890, with two white and two caramel horses with articulated "galloping" wheels, black brake with yellow trim, and original passengers and coachman. Estimated at $9,000/12,000, it brought a runaway $43,875. Sotheby's photo.

Merriam Manufacturing American tin and cast-iron bell toy, circa 1875. The painted tin boy walks and rings the brass bell when the toy is rolled forward. The tan tin horse pulls a red- and green-painted cast-iron base with black wheels. It was estimated at $5,000/7,000. A collector bought it for well over the high estimate at a dashing $42,150. Sotheby's photo.

helped catalog the sale, first met Mrs. Hegarty in the 1970s, and he has prized memories of the toy-collecting lore she shared with him.

Although it is not widely known, Covert Hegarty traded toys with the late legendary, quirky collector of Japanese toy robots F.H. "Griff" Griffith. In fact, some of Griffith's renowned robots (see *M.A.D.*, March 2001, p. 38-C) came to him originally from the Hegartys, who scooped up some of their own toy Americana from Griff in return. Toy collectors may not yet be as formal about provenance as art collectors are, but the dedicated toy lover now makes it his business to try and find out "who had what and when," and keep the history up to date.

For those who like to shop on line, Sothebys.com also offered 182 lots of smaller Hegarty treasures such as early cap pistols and other toys from October 5 to 26. Bidders snapped up 92% of the on-line lots for $269,030.

Editor's Note: The catalog for the sale of historical letters and documents collected by the late Malcolm Forbes reads like a guide to the Forbes Museum, where items from the collection had been displayed from time to time. There was keen competition among those who realized they might never again have a chance to own a piece of history in the making, and record prices were paid even at a time when the U. S. economy was struggling.

HISTORY FOR SALE: THE FORBES SALE

BY LITA SOLIS-COHEN

When a connoisseur's collection is sold at auction, it is hard to predict how high the prices will go. The conservative $12.3 million estimate for Christie's March 27, 2002, sale was ignored when 203 letters, manuscripts, and documents from the Forbes Collection sold for $20,069,990.

"The quality of the material won the day," said Chris Coover, who cataloged the sale, pleased at having masterminded the most successful auction of American historical letters and manuscripts.

The sale set new records for 18 different presidents, including Lincoln, Truman, Jackson, Grant, Eisenhower, Teddy Roosevelt, and Jefferson Davis. Lincoln's last speech, 12 large pages in a bold hand, outlining his strategy for reconstruction, sold for $3,086,000 (including buyer's premium), the highest price ever achieved for any American historical document, almost doubling the previous record. Einstein's August 2, 1939, letter to Franklin Roosevelt, warning of the potential for the construction of extremely powerful bombs, sold for $2,096,000, a record for any letter.

Coover said the sale was a testimony to the taste of the late Malcolm Forbes, who believed that original letters and documents "make flesh and blood of key figures in our country's history."

At a time when the manuscript market was drifting downward, the Forbes sale caught people by surprise. Major collectors dug deep into their pockets. Dealers rounded up clients and encouraged high bids, old collectors came back into the

salesroom, and new people came into the field. There was a feeling in the salesroom that this was the only chance to buy what was being offered. In most cases, it was. The Forbes provenance had an intoxicating effect. Nearly everyone competing seemed to get something.

"There hasn't been a sale of this quality in a long time," said Coover. The only comparable collection was that of the late Philip Sang, dispersed in a series of sales, most of them at Sotheby Parke Bernet a quarter of a century ago.

"I think I bought the best Truman letter," said the generally reserved Joseph Rubinfine, the West Palm Beach dealer who paid $193,000 for Truman's notorious "give 'em hell" letter to Washington Post music critic Paul Hume. Truman wrote it after he read the critic's "lousy review of [his daughter] Margaret's concert" at Constitution Hall on December 5, 1950. You are "an eight ulcer man on four ulcer pay," wrote the president, in what Coover contends is "the most famous example of Presidential invective on White House stationery."

The previous lot, a letter dated February 1, 1949, from Truman to David Niles with the pen Truman used to sign the formal recognition of the State of Israel, sold for $314,000, a Truman record.

The catalog was arranged chronologically, and early material made records at the start of the sale. Rubinfine paid $270,000 for a document signed in 1761 by Button Gwinnett, whose signature is the rarest of all the signers of the Declaration of Independence. Called the finest Gwinnett in private

Seth Kaller of Kaller's America Galleries, New York City, paid $721,000 (est. $250,000/350,000) for Robert E. Lee's dramatic note to General Grant just before his surrender at Appomattox Courthouse, requesting a suspension of hostilities to discuss the terms of surrender. Forbes bought it at Sotheby's on October 26, 1988, for $220,000. Christie's photo.

hands, it is an attractive document, which Gwinnett signed in a large clear hand as a subscriber to a charity school. Gwinnett died in a duel on May 17, 1777, and only 47 of his signatures have been documented. The last time it sold at auction, in April 1978 at the first of the five Philip Sang sales at Sotheby Parke Bernet, it sold to a dealer as part of a set of signers of the Declaration of Independence for $195,000 for the entire set of 56 autographs.

A phone bidder paid $160,000 for Paul Revere's itemized expense account. Revere billed 14 pounds 2 shillings for riding from Boston to New York and back again to bring news of the Boston Tea Party, in which he was a participant. Revere charged the same for his time as he charged for the horse—4 pounds 16 shillings. Forbes paid $70,000 for it at a Sang sale at Sotheby Parke Bernet in April 1978.

The pair of opera glasses that fell from Lincoln's hands the night he was shot at Ford's Theatre sold for $424,000, a world auction record for a Lincoln artifact. Forbes paid $26,400 for them at the Crocker sale at Sotheby Parke Bernet in 1979.

Lincoln items were the most expensive of all, accounting for seven of the top ten lots. Another of the top ten was Robert E. Lee's April 9, 1865, letter to Grant requesting the suspension of hostilities. It sold for $721,000 to New York City dealer Seth Kaller of Kaller's America Galleries, a major buyer and a strong underbidder at the sale. The Kaller firm represents the Gilder Lehrman Collection, though Kaller would not say which lots he bought for that collection.

A phone bidder paid $721,000 for a Congressional copy of the Thirteenth Amendment, outlawing slavery, signed by Lincoln, members of Congress, and senators. Beverly Hills dealer Joseph Maddalena, who calls his business Profiles in History, bought four of the top Lincoln items, paying $666,000 for Lincoln's famous "wanting to work" letter, sent to Major George D. Ramsay and telling him that a woman has two sons who want to work. Lincoln writes, "Set them at it if possible.

The record for a Lincoln artifact now stands at $424,000, paid for this pair of brass opera glasses carried by President Lincoln to Ford's Theatre at the performance of *Our American Cousin*, on April 14, 1865, the night he was shot. Christie's had estimated the glasses at $40,000/60,000. Malcolm Forbes bought them at the Crocker sale at Sotheby Parke Bernet on November 28, 1979, for $26,400, at the time a record for any Lincoln artifact. Christie's photo.

Wanting to work is so rare a merit, that it should be encouraged."

Maddalena also paid $666,000 for Lincoln's letter to Grant asking for a nominal rank for his eldest son, Robert Todd Lincoln, a recent Harvard graduate. "Please read and answer this letter as though I was not President, but only a friend," it begins. It ends with Lincoln offering to pay Robert's salary. Robert Forbes, bidding for his father, had bought it at the second Philip Sang sale at Sotheby Parke Bernet in November 1978 for $32,000, a record for Lincoln at the time.

Maddalena bought an early Lincoln letter dated July 6, 1859, to Indiana Congressman Schuyler Colfax noting that "to prevent the spread and nationalization of slavery is a national concern, and must be attended to by the nation." The price was $501,000.

An autograph book with a quotation from Lincoln's second inaugural address, signed Abraham Lincoln, cost Maddalena $446,000. He also bought Mathew Brady's poignant image of Lincoln and his ten-year-old son, Thomas (Tad), taken on February 9, 1864, at Mathew Brady's Washington studio and signed A. Lincoln & Son. He paid $358,000 for it. Forbes paid $104,500 for it

Joseph Maddalena, the Beverly Hills dealer who calls his business Profiles in History, paid $666,000 (est. $250,000/350,000) for Lincoln's famous "wanting to work" letter. Lincoln answers a request from a woman, believed to be Mrs. Mary Buckley, a widow with six children who is seeking work for her two sons. Previously she had written to Lincoln seeking work for her brother, Michael Donavan, who was consequently employed at the Washington Arsenal. Having succeeded at that request, she tried again for her sons. Lincoln forwarded her request to Major Ramsay in a note dated October 17, 1861, reading, "The lady—bearer of this—says she has two sons who want to work. Set them at it if possible. Wanting to work is so rare a merit, that it should be encouraged." Christie's photo.

at the Mrs. Philip D. Sang sale at Sotheby's in March 1985.

Reached by phone after the sale, Maddalena said his favorite purchase was Grant's letter to Sherman wishing him "great good fortune" on his grand march to the sea. He paid $138,000 for it, well over its $50,000 high estimate. "Forbes bought history in the making. That is what content is all about," said Maddalena.

Collectors in this field have special interests. Albert Small, a Washington, D.C., developer, added two George Washington letters to his collection of letters and documents relating to the city of Washington. The first, a nine-page letter dated November 20, 1791, from Philadelphia, gives detailed advice to the commissioners on the construction of the new federal city and handling the troublesome designer Pierre Charles L'Enfant. It cost $138,000. The other, a Washington letter dated December 13, 1791, formally laying before Congress L'Enfant's plan of the new federal city "within the District of ten miles square," cost him $248,000. "A new museum of the city of Washington is in the works," said Small.

This sale is a "triumph of content," said Dennis Shapiro, a collector from Boston, who said he came to witness history in the making in the salesroom. A few lots brought outrageous prices. For example, one of Washington's earliest surveys, estimated at $20,000/30,000, sold for $58,750. "I sold one better for eighteen thousand. I can't get twenty thousand for an early survey," said Rubinfine, who thought Washington benefited by being sold early in the sale. "Most manuscript sale catalogs are arranged alphabetically so that Washington letters come up at the end when everyone is tired, and there are often bargains," he observed.

A few lots seemed like good buys. The log book of the *Enola Gay*, the minute-by-minute account of the historic "Little Boy" mission that dropped the world's first atomic bomb on the city of Hiroshima on August 6, 1945, in which Captain Robert A. Lewis wrote, "My God what have we

Executive Mansion,

Washington, Jan. 19   , 1865.

Lieut. General Grant:

Please read and answer this letter as though I was not President, but only a friend. My son, now in his twenty second year, having graduated at Harvard, wishes to see something of the war before it ends. I do not wish to put him in the ranks, nor yet to give him a Commission, to which those who have already served long, are better entitled, and better qualified to hold. Could he, without embarrassment to you, or detriment to the service, go into your Military family with some nominal rank, I, and not the public, furnishing his necessary means? If no, say so without the least hesitation, because I am as anxious, and as deeply interested, that you shall not be encumbered as you can be yourself.

Yours truly
A. Lincoln

Joseph Maddalena paid $666,000 (est. $70,000/100,000) for this letter signed A. Lincoln, as president, to Lt. General Ulysses S. Grant, dated January 19, 1865, seeking a "nominal rank" for his eldest son, Robert Todd Lincoln, then 22, who had graduated from Harvard. His mother, Mary Todd Lincoln, did not want to see him in the infantry, so Lincoln asked if Grant could find a position on his staff and offered to pay Robert's salary. He was appointed captain and assistant adjutant general. Forbes bought it at the Philip Sang sale at Sotheby Parke Bernet on November 8, 1978, for $32,000, then a record for a Lincoln letter. Christie's photo.

One of the finest known Congressional copies of the Thirteenth Amendment, outlawing slavery, passed by the 38th Congress and signed by Lincoln, as president, February 1, 1865, and also signed by Vice President H. Hamlin, Speaker of the House, Schuyler Colfax, secretary of the senate, J.W. Forney, and 38 senators and 114 members of the House of Representatives. It was estimated at $300,000/400,000 and sold on the phone for $721,000. An unknown number of engrossed copies submitting the resolution to the states were prepared. Thirteen copies signed by Lincoln are recorded, seven of which are in institutions. Only six are so-called Congressional copies, signed by members of the House and Senate. This is one of only two copies of the Congressional resolution signed by Lincoln to appear at auction in 25 years. The Oliver Barrett copy sold in 1952 was offered again in 1990 at Sotheby's and sold for $220,000. Malcolm Forbes bought this one at the Roy P. Crocker sale at Sotheby Parke Bernet in November 1979 for $38,500. Bidding opened at $300,000. At $480,000 New York dealer Seth Kaller began bidding, but he remained the underbidder when it was knocked down to phone bidder number 50, a major buyer at the sale. Christie's photo.

done . . . the greatest explosion man has ever witnessed," sold for $391,000. The estimate was $200,000/300,000. When Forbes bought it for $85,000 at the second Philip Sang sale at Sotheby Parke Bernet in November 1978, it was the most expensive lot in the sale. When Philip Sang bought it at Parke-Bernet in 1971, he paid $37,000 for it.

Several lots fell below expectations, but only one did not sell—an autographed quotation from John F. Kennedy's inaugural address ". . . ask not what your country can do for you, ask what you can do for your country." It had an enthusiastic $400,000/600,000 estimate because one sold privately for more. At the second Sang sale at Sotheby Parke Bernet in November 1978, Forbes had paid $17,000 for it.

The long narrow manuscript map drawn in Philadelphia between December 1767 and February 1768 by surveyors Charles Mason (1730–1787) and Jeremiah Dixon (1733–1779), shows a strip of land six miles wide along the border between Pennsylvania and Maryland, which became known as the Mason-Dixon Line. The Mason-Dixon line was later chosen as the boundary between slave states and free states, and it became the line between the North and the South during the Civil War. Estimated at $800,000/1,200,000, it sold for $556,000 to New York City dealer Donald Heald for a collector.

The reason it did not sell for more may be the fact that it was only the western part of the survey. The smaller map of the eastern boundaries is at Princeton University Library. This part was thought lost until it was rediscovered in January 1963 among the Chew family papers. It was thought at first to be an engraving, but when it was compared with the other third of the map at Princeton, it was seen to be in pencil and ink (pen and brush).

When the Forbes Collection bought the map at Christie's on April 1, 1982, it fetched $396,000, a record for a manuscript map. It was the most the Forbes Collection had paid for anything in the autograph field. "That much money would not get the best in any other category, and I think this is the best in American history," said Malcolm Forbes Jr. 20 years ago when he did the bidding. Asked then if he would lend it to Princeton, Forbes said, "I rather think I'll ask Princeton to lend the Forbes Collection the rest of the map."

This brings up the question of the future of the Forbes Museum. The Forbes Collection announced in January that it would sell parts of the collection in three sales at Christie's: historical manuscripts in March, and again on October 11, and part of the Faberge collection on April 19. In a prepared statement, Steve Forbes said, "As our interests and focuses change, obviously the nature of the collections change. One of the exciting things in life is discovering new directions and exploring new areas."

Christopher Forbes noted, "Our father, who introduced and taught us so much about what it really meant to be a collector, wrote in his book *More than I Dreamed*, 'I've often told my children, I hope that if they decide to be done with one of the collections that they will put it back on the auction block so that other people can have the same vast fun and excitement that we did in amassing it.'"

Before the sale, collectors and dealers talked about the fact that Steve Forbes had spent $60 million of his own money in his bid for the presidential nomination and that advertising revenues at *Forbes* magazine have been down substantially since September 11, intimating that a need for money is generally the reason for auctions.

Florence Grappone, a spokesman for *Forbes*, said that only part of the Forbes Collection is being sold, and the museum will remain open.

Editor's Note: During the three-year recession that followed 9/11, the market for Americana struggled, reflected in the prices and the percentage of unsold lots at the January sales in New York that act as a market barometer. Passionate collectors with deep pockets still participated. In years to come, the early part of this century may be looked on as an era of good buying opportunities. Susan Kleckner's careful analysis of Sotheby's 2003 sale records this sober time in the marketplace when dealers were not buying for stock, and some of the collectors who had pushed the market to new levels in the 1990s did not feel flush enough to participate.

THIN AIR AT THE TOP

BY SUSAN KLECKNER

In the rivalry between auction house titans, the competition to claim more sales of million-dollar lots is intense. During January 2003, in its various-owners sale of American furniture and the sale of "property from a private American collection," Sotheby's added two important notches to its belt with the sales of a rare Boston bombé chest of drawers and a Philadelphia tea table, the stars of otherwise sporadic Americana results.

"We are very pleased with the results achieved over the past several days," commented John B.A. Nye, director of Sotheby's American furniture department. "In the current economic environment,

A rare silver rococo pitcher attributed to Daniel Christian Fueter, New York, estimated at $60,000/90,000, brought $108,000 from Winterthur. Sotheby's photo.

it is more clear than ever that the market responds enthusiastically to property of outstanding quality combined with conservative estimates."

Overall, the auction house's four sales, from January 16 to 19, brought a grand total of $15,925,726, with the Americana sale of January 17 contributing $6,984,200 toward that final number (all prices include buyers' premiums). Of the 608 lots in that sale, 393 lots found interest among buyers, leaving Sotheby's with a sold percentage of 64.64% by lot and 69% by dollar.

The sale of prints, ceramics (Chinese export, English and Japanese porcelains, and English pottery), silver, furniture, and folk art was erratic at the mid-level and only slightly better at the top. For those lots deemed worthy, bidding exuberance was not irrational but measured and determined, with bidders appearing prepared to go further than in some instances they actually did. For those lots considered more decorative, even a low estimate couldn't spark interest.

Silver

Sotheby's silver sale was thinly attended, although the audience was equally representative of museum, trade, and private interests. The sale included several highly sought-after lots representing widely disparate areas of American silver production.

Mid-18th-century American silver found great interest among several buyers. A silver armorial teapot by Joseph Edwards, Jr. of Boston, made circa 1760 and engraved with the arms of the Gerrish family as well as another family, was estimated at

The Chippendale carved and blocked serpentine-front mahogany bombé chest of drawers, signed and dated by its maker, Nathan Bowen, in 1772, was among the most important lots of furniture to come to auction in the last few years. A rarely seen form, the chest of drawers sold for $1,464,000 to furniture scholar and consultant Luke Beckerdite, bidding for a collector. The price is a new record for the form. Sotheby's photo.

$30,000/50,000. Bidding on the teapot opened at $25,000 and closed when the hammer fell to Boston dealer David Firestone in the room for $72,000.

The consecutive lots following the Edwards teapot, despite one withdrawal, were all attractive to bidders. These included a two-handled cup by John Dixwell, Boston, dated 1714, that sold in the room for $24,000 (est. $20,000/30,000); a bowl made circa 1725 by Henricus Boelen, New York City, that sold for $33,600 (est. $20,000/30,000); and a circa 1765 tankard by Joseph Richardson, Sr., Philadelphia, that was captured by dealer Jonathan Trace for $57,000 (est. $25,000/35,000).

The star of Sotheby's 18th-century American silver offerings was a rare rococo pitcher attributed to Daniel Christian Fueter, circa 1769, New York City. The pitcher was estimated at $60,000/90,000 and sold in the room to Sotheby's vice president for sporting art, Andrew Rose, for $108,000. With Winterthur's Patricia Halfpenny and Donald Fennimore seated in the room, Rose announced the purchase had been made by Winterthur.

Don Fennimore, Winterthur's senior curator of metals, commented on the form after the sale. "Winterthur has a strong silver collection; however, there has long been a vexing gap—a notable example of eighteenth-century repoussé work in the rococo style. I wanted an example to illustrate that stylistic phenomenon and had long hoped something like a great Philadelphia coffeepot would come along, but it always eluded me."

As for the museum's interest in the particular example offered by Sotheby's, Fennimore said, "We decided this was the example to go after strongly for a host of reasons: its maker, its history, which, while not fully documented, is important. It is a rare form for the eighteenth century—common for the nineteenth but rare for the eighteenth. This example was better than the generic flowers, leaves, and scrolls usually seen, with mountains, waterfalls, and cattails, wonderfully graphic in iconography. The pitcher makes a strong statement compounded with the fact that it can be tied to one of the giants of the decorative arts, a master of rococo design, Juste-Aurele Meissonnier, which directly links the form to Paris, the acknowledged center of eighteenth-century decorative arts design."

Fennimore acknowledged that Winterthur's bidding strategy, having the auction house bid on their behalf, was conscious, so the museum could be a strong participant on the lot while keeping a modest profile. It was Sotheby's idea to announce the institution's successful purchase, which was acceptable to the museum.

Furniture

Sotheby's fourth session of Americana, held on Friday afternoon, January 17, focused on furniture and was standing room only. Several lots in that session were either heavily promoted by the house and thus anticipated to do well or were commonly understood to be righteous objects estimated conservatively. Of the 89 lots offered in the furniture session, four were withdrawn and 29 lots did not meet their reserve, leaving Sotheby's furniture sale with a sold-by-lot percentage of 67.4%, slightly better than the sale overall.

The most enthusiastically anticipated lot of the sale was a Boston Chippendale carved mahogany serpentine-front bombé chest of drawers, inscribed by its maker, Nathan Bowen, and dated 1772 on the inside of a backboard. A revised essay attending the lot shed new light on Bowen's apprenticeship from what was published in the auction catalog, though furniture experts appeared to appreciate the form on its own terms without these revelations. The chest was estimated at $1/1.5 million, an estimate in excess of the previous record set by Northeast Auctions in November 1995, when Ron Bourgeault sold the Ricketson serpentine-front bombé chest of drawers for $992,500. Many queried if the chest might not fetch even more than its high estimate.

Auctioneer William Stahl opened the bidding at $500,000, and after a quick rise to its estimate,

The Queen Anne carved walnut easy chair whose carving was reattributed to "school of John Welch" from Welch sold for $176,000. It was estimated at $200,000/300,000, and some experts in the field felt its overall condition was a little rough to carry such a big estimate. Nonetheless, it was one of the top sellers of Sotheby's Americana sale. Sotheby's photo.

the contest came down to Virginia-based furniture consultant and *American Furniture* journal editor Luke Beckerdite and a telephone. The chest sold to Beckerdite for $1,464,000, a new record for the form. According to Beckerdite, the chest of drawers is almost identical to an example in the Dietrich American Foundation collection, and the Sotheby's chest retained the shadows of its original chinoiserie brasses.

"The piece came out of the blue and was otherwise an unknown example of a penultimate form," recalled John Nye about the bombé chest. "Then to have it be such an important document as far as Nathan Bowen and Thomas Sherburne are concerned made it all the more interesting to handle."

Considering the condition, the finish, the importance of the form, all of that rolled together, it was a not very often in a career kind of thing."

The James and Elizabeth Bartram William and Mary turned and inlaid walnut gate-leg table made in Philadelphia, circa 1725, generated considerable interest both institutionally and privately. The table is one of very few of this early design with inlaid decoration; another is in the collection of the Chester County Historical Society. It was estimated at $250,000/350,000. Bidding opened at $100,000, and after a heated battle the table sold to Leigh Keno for $680,000, allegedly shutting out Winterthur.

The table had been extensively published and was well known to furniture scholars from its inclusion in the Philadelphia Museum of Art's 1999 catalog and exhibition, *Worldly Goods: The Arts of Early Pennsylvania, 1680-1758,* and Margaret Schiffer's *Furniture and Its Makers of Chester County, Pennsylvania,* (Schiffer, 1978).

"The Bartram table is one of the great Philadelphia William and Mary dining tables," Keno said of his purchase. "When you add the fact

The James and Elizabeth Bartram William and Mary turned, inlaid, and figured walnut gate-leg table, Philadelphia, was the subject of great presale interest, having been published in two scholarly texts and exhibited at the Philadelphia Museum of Art in 1999 in *Worldly Goods*. The table easily exceeded its estimate of $250,000/350,000 and sold to New York City dealer Leigh Keno for $680,000. Sotheby's photo.

that it is inlaid and documented, it puts the table on an even higher plane. It's an incredible survivor in terms of condition—the fact that the feet retain most of their original height and the butterfly hinges haven't been moved is incredible. The first time I saw the table was *Worldly Goods*. It was one of my favorite pieces in the exhibit, and I never dreamed the opportunity would come up to purchase it."

While Sotheby's total January successes eclipsed its shortfalls, the various-owners auction of American furniture was nonetheless seasoned with high-profile buy-ins and was more notable for its failures than its triumphs. When middle-market or attractive but problematic material sold successfully, sales were at prices reasonable for decorating but not much more. If the estimate was deemed too high by today's well-informed and belt-tightened buyers, the lot was usually returned to the owner.

Adding to Sotheby's pain was the cover lot, the Colonel Elijah St. John Chippendale carved and figured mahogany marble-top pier table made in New York circa 1775 and consigned by Stratford Hall Plantation, the Robert E. Lee Memorial Association in Virginia. The auction house announced to the salesroom that the carved pendant appliqué gracing the façade of the table was most likely replaced. The catalog's detail photograph of the skirt showed a clearly visible line above which the carved front rail was one color and below which it was another. In addition to the problematic carving on the table was an even greater question regarding the age of the marble top and its relation to the base. It was cataloged as "estimate on request," so the reserve on the table could then exist on a sliding scale, allowing the auction house to gauge best for Stratford the level of interest in the form. Bidding on the table opened at $300,000 and closed at $450,000, with the table returning south.

A rare Boston turned maple leather-back chair, estimated at $4,000/6,000, sold for $39,600 to the phone, underbid by Leigh Keno. Sotheby's photo.

Editor's Note: Look in your cupboards! Spatterware is as good as cash. Dealers and collectors want it, and most of them are men who pay big bucks for rare and unusual patterns and bright colors, especially yellow and rainbows in stripes or concentric bands.

SPATTERWARE: THE FIESTAWARE OF THE 19TH CENTURY

BY LITA SOLIS-COHEN

"For what I have in this box, I could have bought a van," said Pennsylvania collector Jim Hartenstein, holding a small carton with seven pieces of spatterware in it. "That man over there has a bigger box. He could have bought a house."

Hartenstein was pointing to a New Jersey collector who spent more than $100,000 on ten pieces of spatterware.

The men had competed for spatterware from the collection of the late Dr. Robert L. Schaeffer, consigned by Franklin & Marshall College to Downingtown, Pennsylvania, auctioneers Pook & Pook, Inc. for sale on April 26, 2003. Schaeffer loved the colorful spattered or stippled English chinaware popular in the 19th century. The spattering, sometimes in one color, sometimes in two or more colors in stripes or concentric bands, was often decorated with additional naive drawings of birds, flowers, and houses. Pieces with a rainbow of colors or with windmills, a fish, a cow, two men on a raft, a shed, or a townhouse are rare. Any yellow spatterware brings a premium.

Spatterware was sold in quantity to the Pennsylvania Germans and to people in the communities near eastern port cities from about 1820 to 1850, peaking in the 1830s. It became popular with Americana collectors in the 1920s when Henry F. du Pont and Henry Ford bought it from dealers and at Pennypacker's auctions in Reading, Pennsylvania. When the du Pont's Winterthur Museum and Ford's Greenfield Village opened to the public, other collectors wanted spatterware too.

Sam Laidaicker popularized spatterware in the 1930s and '40s in his infrequently published maga-

zine on Anglo-American china. Collectors Arlene and Paul H. Greaser published *Homespun Ceramics: A Study of Spatterware* in 1964, enlarging their first booklet for a second printing in 1965. Earl F. and Ada F. Robacker published *Spatterware and Sponge: Hardy Perennials of Ceramics* in 1978. As it became better known, prices rose steadily. In 1980 Sotheby's sold spatterware from the Garbisch and Wetzel collections, and more collectors paid higher prices.

Wolf's in Cleveland, Ohio, auctioned spatterware from the Paul Brunner collection on

Manheim, Pennsylvania, collector Harlan Miller seems to be collecting again. Even though he sold most of his collection in a series of sales at Conestoga Auction Company, he bought a green and red bull's-eye cup plate for $316.25. His red spatter handleless cup and saucer decorated with a fish still holds the record. It brought $27,500 at Conestoga on October 6, 2001. "The fish cup was one of a group of five that came out of Ohio some years back," he said. That group sold in November 1990 for $39,600 ($7,920 per cup and saucer) to Easton, Pennsylvania, dealer Bea Cohen at the Brunner sale at Wolf's in Cleveland, Ohio.

A Pennsylvania collector paid $23,000 for the vibrant green and black rainbow spatter cup and saucer painted with a red thistle (right), and to go with it he spent $16,100 for the yellow and blue rainbow spatter cup and saucer with a red thistle (left).

November 17, 1990, and set a new record for any lot of spatterware when five handleless red spatter cups and saucers decorated with fish sold as one lot for $39,600, five times the estimate. At Sotheby's Deyerle sale in May 1995, spatterware brought five-figure sums. A rainbow bowl and pitcher set sold for $11,500 and a rainbow teapot fetched $18,400!

The market spiked in 2001 with the J. Harlan Miller sale at Conestoga Auction Company in Manheim, Pennsylvania, when just one of the red spatter fish cups and saucers fetched $27,500 in October. At that same Conestoga sale, a yellow spatter tulip pattern coffeepot brought $18,700, topping the $17,050 price of a 13" yellow spatter thistle pattern platter that Miller sold at Conestoga in October 2000. In November 2001 Conestoga got $22,000 for a green and red spatter platter with a blue and red tulip, showing that the market continued to be strong.

Spatterware prices remained on that high plateau in 2003 at Pook & Pook's February and April sales of the Schaeffer collection, and prices for some forms reached higher peaks. For example,

five cups and saucers, each a different pattern, brought more than $21,000 apiece. Spatterware is considered folk art, and it brings folk art prices.

Pook & Pook sold the Schaeffer collection for the Phillips Museum of Art at Franklin & Marshall College, raising more than a million dollars for the museum's endowment fund for the maintenance of the museum's permanent collection and for acquisitions and conservation. Moreover, the museum kept a representative assortment of spatterware and Pennsylvania German folk art, textiles, ceramics, metalwork, and works on paper largely acquired in Lancaster County by Dr. Schaeffer and given to the college in 1987. A resident of Allentown, where he was professor of botany at Muhlenberg College, Schaeffer wanted his collection to go to its area of origin. He would have been pleased that most of the buyers at the sales were Pennsylvanians.

Pook & Pook offered the first portion of Schaeffer's spatterware (205 lots) in a general sale on February 22, and then by request from collectors who didn't like waiting until the end of the sale to bid on spatterware, offered the rest in a specialized sale, along with 27 lots of Gaudy Dutch ceramics, on Saturday, April 26. Some complained that it was too much spatterware at one time, but the market seemed to absorb it, and there were few bargains.

"Do you want to take a lunch break after two hundred lots?" auctioneer Ron Pook asked the group of about 75 collectors before beginning the sale at 10 AM. "Yes," they replied, but when the time came and Pook asked whether they were ready for a break, they said, "No," keep going.

"We are too excited to break," said a blonde woman on the aisle. After a morning of selling, Pook got relief from his auxiliary auctioneer, Peter Barnet, who is from Tasmania, where they have probably never heard of spatterware.

Ron Pook returned to the podium after an hour's rest, and the sale continued until after 3 PM. To the very end, the salesroom was as quiet as a church. Everyone had their catalogs open and answered responsively to the auctioneer's pleadings. There was no milling around, no conversation, and no lunch.

When the sale was over, the tally for 417 lots of chinaware came to $788,338 (including buyers' premiums). Add to that the $439,300 from the sale of 206 spatterware lots on February 22, and the total for the Schaeffer collection ceramics came to $1,227,638. Thirteen lots in all brought five-figure prices: five in February and eight in April. Estimates were ignored as passionate collectors fought for what they wanted.

"Still no record to top mine," said spatterware collector J. Harlan Miller of Manheim, Pennsylvania, who has been selling his collection at Conestoga Auction Company over the years. "A couple of years ago my fish cup and saucer sold for twenty-five thousand dollars, that is twenty-seven thousand five hundred with the ten-percent buyer's premium, and nothing in this sale or the last one made more."

No lot in the April sale topped the $25,875 paid in February for Dr. Schaeffer's five-color rainbow spatter washbowl and pitcher, bought on the phone by Martinsburg, Pennsylvania, dealer J.D. Querry for a client. No cup and saucer topped the $24,150 paid for the yellow, blue, red, and green rainbow swirl pattern cup and saucer that sold to the New Jersey collector in February.

Three bidders chased the red spatter cup and saucer painted with two men on a raft (right), and it sold for $21,850 to a New Jersey collector, who also took the red spatter cup and saucer painted with a windmill (left) for $8,625.

Green spatter cup with cow decoration, missing a 2" triangular chunk on one side and with a long crack, with no saucer, sold for $3,450.

A phone bidder paid $6,325 for a single saucer with a red and purple rainbow border and a painted hipped roof town house. That may be a record for a single spatterware saucer.

At the April sale a Pennsylvania collector paid nearly as much, $23,000, for a vibrant green and black rainbow spatter cup and saucer with a red thistle in the reserve, and the New Jersey collector paid the same amount, $23,000, for a vibrant red, blue, and green rainbow plate with a green star enclosing red half-moons, the design held in

balance by a blue inner circle and a blue border. They were the auction's top lots.

Three bidders competed for the red spatter cup and saucer decorated with two men on a raft, a very rare pattern, and the New Jersey collector got it for $21,850. Lancaster, Pennsylvania, dealer Eugene Charles paid the same price, $21,850, for an unusual 15½" long red, green, and blue rainbow platter decorated in a random crisscross pattern. "I bought it for my brother-in-law," he said. "I warned him it would cost this much."

A vibrant red, green, yellow, and blue rainbow drape cup and saucer brought $20,700 from the New Jersey collector, and a collector from Hanover, Pennsylvania, who bid often and high for pieces with striking designs, finally got a splendid four-color spatter plate with a red, yellow, green, and blue drape design for $17,250. A yellow and blue rainbow cup and saucer painted with a thistle drew much competition, and it went at $16,100 to the same Pennsylvania collector who bought the green and black cup and saucer decorated with a thistle. They make a nice pair.

The New Jersey collector paid $12,650 for a large five-color rainbow spatter mug, and when he bought the 9" tall five-color rainbow spatter pitcher for $8,050, it seemed like a bargain. Several crisper rainbow pitchers with neater rainbow stripes have been on the market for a lot more money.

When lots of multiple saucers and plates crossed the block, the major competition was between two Pennsylvania dealers, Josh Reeder, bidding for Robesonia dealer Greg Kramer, and Lampeter dealer William Kurau. Kramer bought the lion's share, but Kurau got his share too.

One active phone bidder paid $6,325 for a single saucer with a red and purple rainbow border, the center painted with a hipped roof town house. Some thought it was a record for a single spatter saucer. "It was not the rarest piece," said Lancaster County, Pennsylvania, dealer Bill Houckes. "The rarest piece was the green spatter cup with the cow painted on it."

Three bidders, J.D. Querry, a phone bidder, and a New Jersey collector, vied for this vibrant 9⅜" in diameter red, blue, and green rainbow plate. The green, in a star pattern, enclosed red half-moons, and the design was held in place by a blue interior circle and a blue border. It sold to the New Jersey collector for $23,000 (est. $3,000/4,000). It is probably the most expensive spatterware plate. Pook & Pook photo.

This 8¼" diameter four-color rainbow spatter drape pattern plate in red, green, yellow, and blue sold for $17,250 to a Hanover, Pennsylvania, collector. Pook & Pook photo.

Red, green, and blue rainbow spatter platter with a crisscross pattern, 15-½ long, sold for $21,850 to Lancaster, Pennsylvania, dealer Eugene Charles. Pook & Pook photo.

Even though the cow cup had a 2" triangular chunk out of it on one side and a long crack and no saucer, it brought $3,450!

Every lot had a printed condition report, but that didn't seem to influence prices very much. For spatterware collectors, the vibrancy of color and the rarity of design are what counts.

"There is so much stuff nobody has seen, that's why there is so much excitement," explained Easton, Pennsylvania, dealer Bea Cohen, a longtime dealer who introduced spatterware to a number of those bidding. "Some pieces may be unique."

The collection was also well documented. Each piece had a paper label with the date of purchase, which ranged from the 1940s to the 1980s, and the name of the dealer from whom it was bought. (There were no fish cups and saucers in this sale because they had not come on the market until Wolf's Brunner sale in 1990, after Dr. Schaeffer had died.)

Collectors will treasure the illustrated catalogs for the Schaeffer auctions as the record of a landmark event in the antiques marketplace. The April 26 spatterware catalog costs $25 postpaid.

Editor's Note: There were slim pickings at Americana auctions in the fall of 2003 until Skinner announced the discovery of the Robert "King" Hooper mahogany scroll-top bombé chest-on-chest, probably made in Boston circa 1765. The sixth known of this expensive form, made for the wealthiest merchants in Boston and Salem, this one has an inscription on the underside of a drawer that reads, "This piece of furniture was carried from Marblehead, Mass King Hooper House during the War of 1812 to Manchester for safekeeping was inherited in 1884 by Caroline K. Wyman, daughter of Henry N. and Priscilla Hooper. In 1916 it was purchased by Dr. James R. (Gertrude F.) from Russ Maynard. . . ." It had all the ingredients necessary for a $1.5/2 million estimate and it sold for $1.76 million to Yardley, Pennsylvania, dealer Todd Prickett, bidding for a client, who he said was prepared to go higher. It became the 31st piece of American furniture to sell for a million dollars or more, and the most expensive piece of American furniture ever sold in New England. The underbidder was Woodbury, Connecticut, dealer Wayne Pratt.

KING HOOPER'S BOMBÉ CHEST-ON-CHEST

BY JEANNE SCHINTO

The crowd of people waiting to ascend the stairs to Skinner's Boston gallery on the morning of November 1, 2003, moments before the start of the auction house's highest-grossing Americana sale in its 42-year history, resembled a rock-concert crush.

There was no stampede, but the possibility was joked about. "I thought those days were behind me," said one woman who, like many, was there to witness the selling of lot 110, the Chippendale mahogany bombé chest-on-chest that descended in the family of Robert "King" Hooper (1709–1790), loyalist, merchant, and bon vivant of Marblehead, Massachusetts.

The $1.5/2 million estimate for this iconic piece of American furniture, its maker unknown, its date also uncertain although likely pre-Revolutionary, was based on nothing but intuition, instinct, and nerve. There are only five comparable chest-on-chests known. Its closest cousin is in the collection of Colonial Williamsburg, and none of these chests have changed hands in anybody's recent or not-so-recent memory.

When the bidding was over, in a matter of 30 seconds, Todd Prickett of C.L. Prickett, Inc.,

Yardley, Pennsylvania, had paid $1,766,000 (including buyer's premium), exactly in the middle of the estimates for this elegant potbellied piece of furniture.

The sum also accounted for slightly more than 46% of Skinner's one-day record-breaking total of $3,773,000 for 466 lots of the 536 lots that were offered.

Stuart Whitehurst, one of Skinner's European furniture and decorative arts experts, was the first to see the Hooper chest, about 3½ years ago, when its owners called the auction house for an insurance appraisal. It was in their dining room, filled "in the best Yankee tradition" with items from the 1920s, said Stephen Fletcher, Skinner's executive vice president and Americana specialist. Fletcher saved the phone message from the family member who told him that while they weren't yet ready to sell the piece, Skinner would be the one to handle it when they were. "It was music to my ears," said Fletcher. "It's on my voice mail. I still have it. It was like a lovely tune that I played now and then." In the meantime, he "dared not tell a soul that I had seen this thing," nor that he had smelled its "lovely old-wood smell or whatever else that

"Every once in a while you get a special piece," said Todd Prickett, who bought the Hooper bombé chest-on-chest for $1,766,000, bidding from a rear corner of the room. "At the Ron Bourgeault sale last year, it was the David Wood shelf clock. [The one that G.W. "Bill" Samaha bought at Northeast Auctions in Manchester, New Hampshire, in November 2002 for $387,500, a Wood clock record.] That was 2002's special piece, and we were its underbidder. And this seems to be the special piece of this year." Skinner's Stephen Fletcher noted that the portrait of Robert "King" Hooper by John Singleton Copley came from the same family and is now in the collection of the Pennsylvania Academy of the Fine Arts, in Philadelphia. Skinner photo.

Stephen Fletcher and Woodbury, Connecticut, dealer Wayne Pratt (who would turn out to be the underbidder on this piece) took apart the bombé chest one more time shortly before the preview ended on the morning of the sale. "People asked me where the estimate came from," Fletcher said. "We put our heads together and guessed. You can't research that kind of thing. The only thing you can do is negotiate with the family. We did a little bit of homework. And there's some precedent of bombé pieces bringing in the area of a million dollars and a bit more. At Sotheby's in January, a bombé bureau brought one and a quarter million dollars, but this one is twice as much furniture." Peter Markham, also in this picture, wasn't a contender for the chest. He was glad to have had the opportunity to see it. Its dimensions are 84" x 46" x 23" and Fletcher, speaking of the chest's size, said the piece was "not a monster." The surface of the close-grained West Indian "island mahogany" (more expensive than "Bay mahogany" from Honduras) has an almost chocolate sheen to it. The ogee bracket feet, the 26 brasses, and the drop pendant are all original; the carved wood finials and the top one of brass are replacements. The brass one is actually a clock finial. A 1920 photo of the piece shows this finial in place, so it's been there a long time. Prickett said the old brass finial would "end up in a parts drawer" after he replaced it—or maybe as a trophy on his desk.

smell is. I don't know, but I was drunk on it for quite some time."

The chest's underbidder was Wayne Pratt of Wayne Pratt, Inc., Nantucket, Massachusetts, and Woodbury, Connecticut. In the last hour of the preview, he examined it one more time, drawer by drawer. Pratt's first look had been a week before the sale. After the sale, having arrived home with nothing more than a Nantucket basket, he said, "I was very disappointed. I thought it was a very good buy, and I congratulate the Pricketts. I would love to have bid one more time, but we just couldn't do it. I had gotten to the point where I was at the end of the line."

Prickett was elated with his win. "We were up in Boston for the Ellis Antiques Show, so we had several days to look at the piece, enjoy the piece, ponder the piece. We were astounded to purchase it at such a reasonable figure. We were prepared to go well beyond where we went. So many of the bombé forms tend to be a little heavy down in the base. This, unlike those, has perfect proportions."

There were a few other successes in the sale. A set of eight Grecian mahogany carved dining chairs, made in Boston circa 1820, brought the second-highest price of the day and there was a lot of talk about them. The chairs were consigned by a Francistown, New Hampshire, family with Boston roots. All but two of the chairs still had their original stamped velvet upholstery. They also had many inexpert (to put it kindly) repairs. One

person at the preview said they looked as if they hadn't been so much used as abused. He dropped out of the bidding soon after it exceeded the lot's typically Skinnerian—i.e., modest—estimate ($8,000/12,000). But the condition didn't deter Margaret B. "Meg" Caldwell of New York City, who bought them on the phone for $215,000. "The design is the best I've ever seen in a Boston Classical dining chair," Caldwell said later, "and to find a set of eight is extraordinary."

A Civil War memorial quilt was the third most significant lot of the day. Not only was it a stunning design, it came with a poignant story confirmed by family papers. Sewn by Mary Bell "Polly" Shawvan circa 1863, the quilt was intended to be a homecoming gift for her husband, a member of the Union Army's 1st Wisconsin Division. He was killed at Chickamauga, however, and the quilt was never used, although it was displayed at county fairs where it won ribbons. The family kept it wrapped in a pillowcase inside a battered old suitcase, and that's how they brought it to Skinner's. Fletcher said underbidder Steven Weiss of Gemini Antiques, New York City, "was very smitten with it," but it went to a private folk art collector in the room for $149,000 (est. $50,000/75,000).

One other lot brought a six-figure price, a small 7⅝" x 12" yachting picture, painted in oil on academy board and signed by James Edward Buttersworth (1817–1894), of the yacht *Columbia*

Eight mahogany carved Grecian dining chairs (three shown) with deeply and dramatically curved stiles brought $215,000. New York private dealer Meg Caldwell, who specializes in Classical and later 19th-century furniture, said they were for a client. Her underbidder was Stuart Feld of Hirschl & Adler, New York City. Skinner photo.

as it rounded the flag boat off Staten Island, New York, circa 1870. Because of its size, Fletcher dubbed it "the ultimate stocking stuffer." The many hues of blue and purple were typical of Buttersworth, said another of Skinner's Americana experts, Martha Hamilton. It sold for $138,000, making the estimate of $10,000/15,000 look like a typo.

There were a couple of notable disappointments among the most promoted lots of the sale. Only one of the two pieces attributed to John and Thomas Seymour did as well as predicted.

A mahogany and maple-veneered dressing bureau with mirror, circa 1820, brought $38,187.50 (est. $25,000/35,000), but a carved and inlaid mahogany sideboard, circa 1810, managed only $11,750 (est. $20,000/35,000). The former has an old finish. The latter was refinished and had oversized replaced brasses that "bugged" at least one prospective bidder.

After the Hooper bombé chest-on-chest was sold, the crowd, numbering easily 300 at its peak, thinned noticeably. All told, Skinner reported it had issued 156 live bidder cards, 166 absentee numbers, and took 120 bids on the phone. Ordinary pieces were left to the dealers, who took care not to overspend. The prevailing market pattern continues: the middle market remains middling and prices for unique or specialized material continue to be robust.

Meanwhile, auctioneers everywhere wait for another voice mail worthy of saving for 3½ years. An auctioneer from another Massachusetts auction house, speaking for many of his colleagues, said, "Driving around the North Shore [of Boston], we all know where the bodies are. We know there's a highboy in there, a Fitz Hugh Lane in there, a John Sloan in there, and we're all waiting for the phone call that we hope will come."

A collector bought this Civil War era memorial quilt for $149,000. The appliquéd grapes, sewn along the black silk grapevines, stood out in relief against the bright butterscotch background. At the center of the 84" x 81" quilt was a gray spread eagle whose breast was overlaid by a shield of red, white, and blue stripes. The descendants of the war widow who made it never used it.

Editor's Note: When Christie's offered six pieces of American furniture in a separate catalog on December 4, 2003, it was whispered that one or two of them might make the million-dollar list. That was not to be. A downturn in the antiques market during the three-year recession resulted in cautious bidding. A month later, in January 2004, a higher stock market and the recent discovery of two rare pieces in the families of the original owners changed the mood in the marketplace. A bureau table of unusual design made by John Townsend sold for $1,911,500 and a Boston bombé chest of drawers soared to $2,023,500, adding numbers 32 and 33 to the million-dollar furniture list.

IN 12 MINUTES CHRISTIE'S SELLS SIX PIECES FOR $2.68 MILLION

BY LITA SOLIS-COHEN

It took auctioneer John Hays just 12 minutes to sell six pieces of American furniture for $2,688,200 (including buyers' premiums) at Christie's New York on December 4, 2003. He gave bidders plenty of time to consider upping their ante before he dropped his hammer.

The furniture was consigned by the Robert E. Lee Memorial Association, which runs Stratford Hall Plantation, the birthplace of Robert E. Lee. The association is "embarking on a new interpretation" of the historic house and "its place in the lives of the four generations of Lees who lived there."

"It has been an exciting day," said a beaming Thomas C. Taylor, executive director of Stratford, as he tallied the hammer total, which came to $2.32 million. "This sale has been the result of a lot of thought and a lot of planning as we move Stratford forward and tell the story of a remarkable family of patriots who lived there for a hundred years."

Taylor, who accompanied a group of board members and volunteers to New York City for the sale, pointed out that the Lees owned furniture made in Virginia or imported from England and would not have bought the Philadelphia chairs and tea table or the New England kneehole bureau and mixing table that the late pioneer collector Caroline Clendenin Ryan Foulke had bestowed on the house over the years.

The furniture sold very close to estimates. The circa 1760 Waln-Ryerss family balloon-seat mahogany side chair with carving attributed to the Garvan carver brought $679,500 (est. $300,000/500,000). It was an auction record for a balloon-seat side chair.

"The chair dances in place. It is amazing," said the buyer, Quakertown, Pennsylvania, furniture

consultant Alan Miller. "The design is so original; it is not a knockoff of a London splat but the most fluid interpretation of a splat the carver invented seven or eight years earlier." Miller said he bought it for a private collector, not for a museum. The underbidder was a collector in the room.

The same price was paid for the Philadelphia mahogany piecrust tea table with carving also attributed to the Garvan carver (est. $600,000/900,000). On instructions from collectors in the salesroom, Christie's Dean Failey, standing

Philadelphia piecrust tea table, 1755-65, 29" high, 31⅛" in diameter, estimated at $600,000/900,000, sold for $679,500. The small size of the top allows the urn of the support to be visible when the table-top is in the vertical position. The fact that the top was not made of dramatically figured wood may have kept the price down, but it does not detract from the brilliance of its design nor its importance in the evolution of the work of the Garvan carver. Christie's photo.

at the phone desk, bid on the tea table. Two broken ankles and a refinished top made this table with its springy stance, lively carving, and classic proportions a good buy. "On another day at another time, the tea table and the Ryerss side chair could have sold for one million," said Failey after the sale.

A 1730–40 blockfront bureau with applied pilasters, its ball feet echoing its rounded blocking, was, according to a paper label attached to its door, in the household of the Right Rev. Samuel Parker, bishop of Massachusetts, at the beginning of the 19th century. Estimated at $300,000/500,000, it was knocked down for $433,100 to Virginia furniture consultant Luke Beckerdite in the salesroom, bidding for a collector.

The carved splat of the Waln-Ryerss side chair is considered a masterpiece of Philadelphia rococo carving.

The Waln-Ryerss compass-seat side chair with rococo splat carved by the Garvan high chest carver sold for $679,500. "The color is perfect, the finish untouched. It is a jewel," said furniture consultant Alan Miller, who bought it for a collector. Christie's photo.

The underbidder, dealer Roberto Freitas of Stonington, Connecticut, said his client would have bid higher if he was certain that the feet had not been replaced. Freitas, who previously worked for dealers Guy Bush and Marguerite Riordan, has been out on his own for a year and a half.

Bidding on behalf of a collector, Baltimore dealer Milly McGehee bought the sculptural Philadelphia mahogany easy chair with sweeping curves and finely carved front legs. It has a superior frame but one replaced rear leg. She paid $410,700, topping the $300,000 high estimate.

Philadelphia Museum of Art assistant curator Alexandra Kirtley let it be known that the museum wanted the circa 1770 Philadelphia side chair attributed to Benjamin Randolph that once stood in John Cadwalader's back parlor at his house on the west side of Second Street and made *en suite* with a card table in the museum's collection. Estimated at $250,000/$350,000, it sold to Kirtley in the salesroom for $365,900. There was an underbidder in the salesroom and another on the phone.

John Hays announced from the podium that the marble-top sideboard table attributed to John Goddard, Newport, Rhode Island, 1755–70, was not mahogany, as cataloged, but was made of manchineel (*Hippomane mancinella*), an exotic wood

The knee block with the leaves overlapping is a highly successful passage of naturalistic Philadelphia carving.

"We are thrilled the Cadwalader chair is going home," said Andrew Brunk, head of American furniture at Christie's. The chair, one of General John Cadwalader's so-called "second set" of hairy paw chairs from the back parlor, sold to the Philadelphia Museum of Art for $365,900. The chair will be upholstered according to evidence in original receipts and will join other hairy paw furniture, including the pair of commode card tables, the matching easy chair, and a side chair, Charles Willson Peale's portraits of the Cadwaladers, and the straight-front card table that matches this chair, all in the Powel room at the museum. Christie's photo.

imported from the West Indies and used rarely by Newport cabinetmakers, and that the marble top, cataloged as possibly a replacement, may be original, cut to fit the table when its depth was reduced by a few inches. There was little bidding for the table (est. $200,000/300,000), and it was knocked down for $119,500 to Dean Failey, who was bidding for the buyers of the piecrust tea table.

There were no additions to the million-dollar list after the December 2003 Americana sales in New York City, held to coincide with the American paintings sales in hopes of attracting some crossover clients. On the morning of December 4, Sotheby's added one more strong six-figure price to the list of expensive Philadelphia furniture.

On behalf of a client, New York City dealer Leigh Keno paid $624,000 for a circa 1760 Philadelphia mahogany marble-top pier table with original marble top and graceful cabriole legs ending in boldly carved claw-and-ball feet, the skirt and knees carved with leafage and ruffles by the same unidentified carver who embellished the Lambert family side chairs and two larger, less successful tables at Winterthur.

At the start of the new year, on January 15 and 16, 2004, Christie's added two more pieces

The Townsend family mahogany block-and-shell bureau table attributed to John Townsend, Newport, Rhode Island, circa 1790, estimated at $600,000/900,000, sold for $1,911,500 to dealer Bill Samaha, underbid on the phone. The door flush with the facade is a rare form. There is only one other example known at the Winterthur Museum in Delaware. It is one of the few surviving pieces that were owned by the Townsend family. It may have been made for the cabinetmaker's son Solomon or his daughter Mary. It became number 33 on the chronological list of pieces of American furniture that sold for $1 million or more. Christie's photo.

The record for an American clock stands at $803,200, paid for this tall-case clock with a complicated musical movement that plays eight tunes. It sold to a clock collector on the telephone, underbid by another phone bidder. The dial is inscribed "Paul Rimbault/ London," a maker of highly specialized clocks at 9 Denmark Street, St. Giles, active from about 1770 until his death in 1785. The 9'3½" tall mahogany case was made in Philadelphia. The carving on its hood has been attributed to the carvers Nicholas Bernard and Martin Jugiez, in partnership from about 1762 to 1783. The sellers, Ron and Julie Pallidino, owners of Solvang Antiques Center, Solvang, California, near Santa Barbara, were in the salesroom. They said they bought the clock 16 years ago in a small general antiques shop in Arizona and took it home for their own collection. Sotheby's photo.

of furniture to the million dollar list. Andrew Brunk, head of American furniture at Christie's, and his team made two great finds in houses within blocks of each other in Bristol, Rhode Island: a bombé chest made in Boston or Salem 1760–80 and a Newport block-and-shell bureau table made at about the same time. The Haraden-Ropes family bombé chest of drawers sold for an astonishing $2,023,500, a record for a bombé chest, to Albert Sack of Northeast Auctions, Portsmouth, New Hampshire, buying for a private collector. The underbidder was New York dealer Leigh Keno. The Townsend family block-and-shell bureau table is one of only two of the form known (the other is at Winterthur), and it sold for $1,911,500 to Bill Samaha in the salesroom; the underbidder was on the phone.

The list of American furniture that sold for a million dollars or more now stands at 33.

Records are traditionally made during the annual January sales. On January 18, 2004, Sotheby's sold a tall-case clock for $803,200, a record for an American clock at auction. It stands at 9' 3½" tall in a mahogany case made in Philadelphia, and its dial is inscribed "Paul Rimbault/ London." Its complicated English musical movement plays eight tunes. Generally English clocks in American cases do not bring a premium, but the complicated movement is a virtual jukebox of songs. The clock was probably made before the American Revolution, for among the eight melodies is "God Save the King." The towering case has boldly figured mahogany on its door, and the carving on its hood has been attributed to Nicholas Bernard and Martin Jugiez, in partnership from about 1762 to 1783. It retains most of its original finials, rosettes, cartouche, and most of its appliqués.

All the competitors were in the salesroom for this mahogany bombé chest of drawers made in Boston or Salem, 1760-80. Estimated at $600,000/900,000, it sold for $2,023,500 and became the most expensive bombé chest ever sold. The chest is closely related to ten other examples and was probably made in Boston. It descended in a Salem family, and Salem's maritime merchants supported several Boston-trained cabinetmakers working in Salem. Christie's photo.

Editor's Note: In January 2004 the tally of million-dollar lots stands at 19 for Christie's, 11 for Sotheby's, and one each for Pook & Pook, Downingtown, Pennsylvania; Ken Miller & Son, Northfield, Massachusetts; and Skinner, Boston.

AMERICAN FURNITURE THAT SOLD FOR MORE THAN $1 MILLION

(ARRANGED CHRONOLOGICALLY)

	VENUE	DATE SOLD	OBJECT	
1.	Christie's	Jan. 1986	Philadelphia mahogany tea table, 1760–70	Christie's photo
2.	Sotheby's	Oct. 1986	Philadelphia mahogany easy chair, 1760-70	Sotheby's photo
3.	Sotheby's	Jan. 1987	Philadelphia mahogany easy chair, circa 1770	Sotheby's photo
4.	Christie's	May 1987	Philadelphia mahogany chest, dressing table and two chairs (not shown), 1760-70	Christie's photo

ESTIMATE	SOLD PRICE	
$350,000/500,000	$1,045,000	The first piece of American furniture to top $1 million.
$350,000/550,000	$1,100,000	Descended in the Willing-Francis-Fisher-Cadwalader family.
$700,000/900,000	$2,750,000	Made for John Cadwalader, at the time it was a world record for any piece of furniture.
$1/1.5 million	$1,760,000	Descended in the Edwards-Harrison family, a record for a suite of furniture.

5.	Christie's	June 1989	Newport, Rhode Island, mahogany desk and bookcase, 1760-70 Christie's photo
6.	Christie's	Jan. 1990	Philadelphia mahogany pier table, 1760-70 Christie's photo
7.	Christie's	Jan. 1990	Philadelphia mahogany tea table, 1760-70 Christie's photo
8.	Sotheby's	Feb. 1991	Philadelphia mahogany card table, circa 1760 Sotheby's photo
9.	Christie's	Jan. 1995	Philadelphia mahogany tea table, 1760-70 Christie's photo
10.	Sotheby's	Jan. 1996	Newport mahogany blockfront shell-carved kneehole bureau, 1760-80 Sotheby's photo

$3/5 million	$12,100,000	Made for Nicholas Brown by John Goddard, a new world record for any piece of furniture.
$1/1.5 million	$4,620,000	Made for Richard Edwards by Thomas Tufft, the carving probably by the so-called Deshler carver, a record for any table.
$900,000/1.2 million	$1,210,000	New record for a tea table. It is one of a pair attributed to John Affleck, the carving attributed to Nicholas Bernard and Martin Jugiez.
$1/1.5 million	$1,045,000	Descended in the Willing family, the carving attributed to the Garvan carver. A record for a card table.
$800,000/1.2 million	$2,442,500	A new record for a tea table. This same table sold for $1,045,000 in Jan. 1986.
$800,000/1.2 million	$3,632,500	Made for Samuel Whitehorne, attributed to Edmund Townsend. A record for a a kneehole bureau.

11.	Sotheby's	Jan. 1996	Boston, Massachusetts, mahogany desk and bookcase, 1738-48	Sotheby's photo
12.	Christie's	Jan. 1997	Boston, Massachusetts, mahogany blocked chest-on-chest, 1770-85	Christie's photo
13.	Christie's	Jan. 1997	Providence, Rhode Island, mahogany blockfront shell-carved desk and bookcase, circa 1769	Christie's photo
14.	Christie's	Jan. 1998	Philadelphia mahogany high chest, dressing table, and chair, 1779	Christie's photos
15.	Sotheby's	Jan. 1998	Philadelphia mahogany high chest and dressing table, circa 1770	Sotheby's photos
16.	Christie's	June 1998	Newport, Rhode Island, mahogany blockfront shell-carved chest of drawers, 1792	Christie's photo

$200,000/300,000	$1,432,500	Made for Boston merchant Edward Jackson, a record for Massachusetts furniture.
$500,000/800,000	$1,212,500	Made for Jonathan Bliss, a loyalist who took it to Canada. A record for a chest-on-chest.
$500,000/800,000	$1,047,500	Made for Sarah Corlis to celebrate her marriage to William Bowen in 1769.
$1.5/2 million	$2,972,500	Made for Levi and Hannah Hollingsworth, the chair made a decade earlier. A record for a suite of furniture.
estimate on request	$1,212,500	Sold to Israel Sack, Inc., New York.
$1.5/2 million	$4,732,500	Sarah Slocum's chest with label of John Townsend, dated in script on the label November 20, 1792. It is a record for a chest of drawers.

17.	Sotheby's	Jan. 1999	Newport, Rhode Island, plum pudding mahogany desk and bookcase, 1730-50	Sotheby's photo
18.	Christie's	Jan. 1999	Philadelphia mahogany tea table	Christie's photo
19.	Christie's	Jan. 1999	Newport, Rhode Island, blockfront shell-carved chest of drawers, 1755-78	Christie's photo
20.	Pook & Pook	June 1999	Philadelphia mahogany tea table, 1760-70	Pook & Pook photo
21.	Christie's	Oct. 1999	Philadelphia walnut armchair, 1740-60	Christie's photo
22.	Christie's	Oct. 1999	Philadelphia side chair made for John Cadwalader, circa 1770	Christie's photo

$500,000/800,000	$8,252,500	Made for Nathaniel Appleton by Christopher Townsend. It was found in France. The second-highest price for American furniture.
$500,000/800,000	$1,542,500	This Eyre family tea table, possibly carved by John Pollard, sold at Christie's in 1985 for $286,000.
$800,000/1.2 million	$1,212,500	Owned by the Bartlett family, probably made by Job Townsend II.
estimate on request	$1,485,000	Made for the Philadelphia merchant Nicholas Waln.
estimate on request	$1,982,500	The Waln-Large family armchair, a record for an American armchair.
estimate on request	$1,432,500	One from a set of 20, of which seven are known. Made by Benjamin Randolph, possibly carved by John Pollard and Richard Butz. In 1982, when this chair was found in Italy and sent to Sotheby's New York for sale, it brought $275,000. A group of 5 chairs from this set turned up in Ireland in 1973 and sold at Sotheby's in November 1974 for $207,500 for the five.

23.	Sotheby's	Oct. 1999	Boston, Massachusetts, japanned high chest, 1712-25	Sotheby's photo
24.	Christie's	Jan. 2000	Massachusetts oak valuables chest	Christie's photo
25.	Christie's	Jan. 2000	Philadelphia mahogany card table	Christie's photo
26.	Christie's	Jan. 2001	Philadelphia mahogany tea table, 1760-70	Christie's photo
27.	Ken Miller & Son, Northfield, MA	June 2001	Philadelphia mahogany card table	Photo courtesy Paul Gorzocoski, Ken Miller & Son
28.	Sotheby's	Jan. 2002	Philadelphia walnut desk and bookcase	Sotheby's photo

$700,000/900,000	$1,597,500	The case marked "Park," the japanning probably by Nehemiah Partridge, Boston, 1712–25. Said to have been owned by John Adams and given to his sister-in-law Mary Smith Cranch of Quincy, Massachusetts.
$500,000/800,000 on request	$2,422,500	Made for Joseph and Bathsheba Pope in 1679. Incised with their initials "P" over "I" & "B" and the date "79." A record for a valuables chest and for Pilgrim Century furniture.
$1.5/2 million on request	$2,862,500	Made for Cornelius Stevenson, circa 1760.
estimate on request	$1,436,000	Descended through the Biddle and Cadwalader families, attributed to Benjamin Randolph.
no estimate	$1,320,000	Found in Florida, the first piece of furniture to sell for more than $1 million in New England.
$400,000/600,000	$1,105,750	The carving attributed to Samuel Harding.

29.	Sotheby's	Jan. 2003	Boston, Massachusetts, mahogany serpentine-front bombé chest of drawers, 1772	Sotheby's photo
30.	Sotheby's	Jan. 2003	Philadelphia mahogany tea table with hairy paw feet, circa 1770	Sotheby's photo
31.	Skinner	Nov. 2003	Boston, Massachusetts, mahogany bombé chest-on-chest, 1765–80	Skinner photo
32.	Christie's	Jan. 2004	Boston or Salem, Massachusetts, bombé chest of drawers, 1760–80	Christie's photo
33.	Christie's	Jan. 2004	Mahogany blockfront and shell-carved Newport, Rhode Island, bureau table, circa 1790	Christie's photo

$1/1.5 million	$1,464,000	Inscribed by its maker Nathan Bowen and dated 1772.
$800,000/1.2 million	$1,072,000	The only known tea table with hairy paw feet from colonial Philadelphia was bought at a New England auction in the summer of 1994 for less than $10,000 and sold at Christie's in January 1996 for $695,500.
$1.5/2 million	$1,766,000	Made for Robert "King" Hooper of Marblehead, Massachusetts. A new record for a chest-on-chest.
$600,000/900,000	$2,023,500	A new record for the form. It descended in the Haraden and Ropes families of Salem.
$600,000/900,000	$1,911,500	Attributed to John Townsend, possibly made for his son Solomon or his daughter Mary. A new record for the form. Only one other example is known.

AMERICAN FOLK ART THAT HAS SOLD FOR $500,000 OR MORE

(ARRANGED CHRONOLOGICALLY)

VENUE	DATE SOLD	OBJECT	

FOLK PAINTING

Christie's	Jan. 1985	Portrait of a girl in a red dress by Ammi Phillips (1788–1865)	
Sotheby's	Jan. 1988	Comfort Starr Mygatt and his daughter Lucy, circa 1799, by John Brewster (1766–1854)	
Sotheby's	Nov. 1990	*Wm. Penn's Treaty with the Indians 1681,* 1847, by Edward Hicks (1780–1849)	
Sotheby's	Oct. 1991	*Peaceable Kingdom,* circa 1833, by Edward Hicks (1780–1849)	

ESTIMATE	SOLD PRICE	
$60,000/90,000	$682,000	Record for American folk art
$750,000/1 million	$852,500	New record for American folk art
$900,000/1.2 million	$990,000	New record for American folk art
$600,000/900,000	$1,210,000	New record for American folk art

Christie's	Jan. 1993	*Peaceable Kingdom*, circa 1847, by Edward Hicks (1780–1849)	Christie's photo
Sotheby's	Jan. 1994	Mr. and Mrs. James Reynolds of West Haven, Connecticut, circa 1788, by Ruben Moulthrop (1763–1814)	Sotheby's photos
Sotheby's	Jan. 1994	Overmantel landscape from the Elisha Hurlbut House, Scotland, Connecticut, by Winthrop Chandler (1747–1790)	Sotheby's photo
Christie's	Jan. 1999	*Residence of David Twining, 1785*, painted 1845–46 by Edward Hicks (1780–1849)	
Christie's	Jan. 1999	*Peaceable Kingdom*, painted circa 1837 by Edward Hicks (1780–1849)	Christie's photo
Pook & Pook	June 1999	Portrait of Mr. and Mrs. Samuel Ensminger and their baby, 1830–35, by Jacob Maentel (1763–1863)	Pook & Pook photo

$600,000/900,000	$638,000	Sold to Berry Hill Galleries, New York City
$125,000/175,000	$745,000	Record for a pair of folk portraits
$150,000/250,000	$596,500	Record for a painted overmantel
$700,000/1 million	$1,432,500	New record for American folk art that lasted for one lot
$1.5/2 million	$4,732,500	New record for American folk art
$100,000/150,000	$687,500	Record for American folk art watercolor

| Christie's | Jan. 2000 | *Wm. Penn's Treaty 1681*, painted after 1840 by Edward Hicks (1780–1849) | 
Christie's photo |

| Sotheby's | Nov. 2001 | Mr. and Mrs. William Vaughan of Aurora, Illinois, circa 1845, by Sheldon Peck (1797–1868) | 
Sotheby's photo |

| Christie's | Jan. 2003 | Double portrait of Frances Almira Millener and her daughter Fanny Root Millener, circa 1835, by Sheldon Peck (1797–1868) | 
Christie's photo |

WEATHERVANES

| Sotheby's | Jan. 1990 | Horse and rider weathervane by J. Howard & Co, West Bridgewater, Massachusetts, circa 1860 | 
Sotheby's photo |

DECOYS

| Sotheby's and Guyette & Schmidt | Jan. 2000 | Preening Canada goose, circa 1917, by A. Elmer Crowell (1862–1952) | 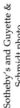 
Sotheby's and Guyette & Schmidt photo |

$500,000/800,000 on request	$635,000	Sold to a phone bidder, the fifth-highest price for a painting by Hicks
$800,000/1.2 million	$830,750	A record for the artist
$200,000/400,000	$647,500	Sold to a collector on the phone
$400,000/600,000	$770,000	A record for a weathervane
$400,000/500,00000	$684,500	A record for a decoy

| Christie's and Guyette & Schmidt | Jan. 2003 | Preening pintail, circa 1915, by A. Elmer Crowell (1862–1952) |  |

NEEDLEWORK

| Sotheby's | Jan. 1996 | Hannah Otis's canvas-work chimney piece, Boston, circa 1753, 24" x 52" |  |

| Bonhams & Butterfields, San Francisco | June 2003 | Canvas-work chimney piece, Boston, 1748–60, in its original frame, 17" x 48" |  |

$300,000/500,000	$801,500	A new record for a decoy
$300,000/500,000	$1,157,500	A record for American needlework
$20,000/30,000	$611,250	Sold to needlework dealers Stephen and Carol Huber of Old Saybrook, Connecticut

ACKNOWLEDGMENTS

It was not easy to choose a small number of stories from 30 years of a magazine that has grown to more than 250 pages each month. I apologize to those whose stories were not included.

Many people contributed to this project. The list must begin with Sam and Sally Pennington, who created *Maine Antique Digest* 30 years ago. Their integrity and responsibility in reporting facts and prices accurately have made a difference in the marketplace.

Then there are the writers for *M.A.D.* over the ensuing three decades who have made it the publication it has become. Many of them took their own photographs to accompany their stories.

Several years ago the founder of Running Press, Buz Teacher, a longtime *M.A.D.* subscriber, asked me to write a book about *Maine Antique Digest,* and he encouraged the idea of a compilation of stories as a 30-year celebration.

Sarah McCleary, *M.AD*'s business manager, embraced the idea of the book. *M.A.D.* copyeditor Sharon Adamsky oversaw the project. Sharon worked tirelessly copyediting, fact checking, and gathering together all the photographs and my edited copy. She sent it off to Running Press on time. Without her the book would not have taken shape.

Greg Jones, project editor at Running Press, saw the book through publication. Designer Alicia Freile fit in more pictures than we ever thought possible.

In the initial phases of the project several friends gave me encouragement and support.

I thank all.

Lita Solis-Cohen
Rydal, PA.

INDEX